The Dynamics of MURDER

Kill or Be Killed

The Dynamics of MURDER

Kill or Be Killed

R. Barri Flowers

CRC Press
Taylor & Francis Group
Boca Raton London New York

CRC Press is an imprint of the
Taylor & Francis Group, an **informa** business

CRC Press
Taylor & Francis Group
6000 Broken Sound Parkway NW, Suite 300
Boca Raton, FL 33487-2742

Printed in the United States of America on acid-free paper
Version Date: 2012904

International Standard Book Number: 978-1-4398-7973-3 (Hardback)

Library of Congress Cataloging-in-Publication Data

Flowers, R. Barri (Ronald Barri)
 The dynamics of murder : kill or be killed / R. Barri Flowers.
  p. cm.
 Includes bibliographical references and index.
 ISBN 978-1-4398-7973-3 (hbk. : alk. paper)
 1. Homicide--United States. 2. Homicide--United States--Prevention. 3. Violent crimes--United States. I. Title.

HV6529.F573 2013
364.1520973--dc23   2012032944

Visit the Taylor & Francis Web site at
http://www.taylorandfrancis.com

and the CRC Press Web site at
http://www.crcpress.com

To my partner in life, love, and writing, H. Loraine.

∗ ∗ ∗

*And to the memory of murder victims Sharon Tate,
Mary Beth Sowers, Marilyn Sheppard, Virginia Mochel,
Elizabeth Short, Nicole Brown Simpson, Dorothy Stratten, and the
many others whose lives were tragically cut short through homicide.*

Contents

Section I
THE DYNAMICS OF MURDER

Section II
DOMESTIC MURDER

Section III
INTERPERSONAL AND SOCIETAL MURDER

Section IV

YOUTH AND MURDER

Section V
TYPES OF KILLERS

Section VII
EXPLANATIONS FOR MURDER

List of Figures

List of Tables

Preface

Murder is the most serious crime in society for victims, offenders, and the general public. The number of murders in the United States has been on the decline as fewer people, particularly youth, are involved in lethal gun violence, which is the leading cause of criminal homicide. Notwithstanding, tens of thousands of people are involved in murder offenses as victims and as perpetrators every year in this country.

Certain types of homicides have become all too common, such as those involving intimates, family, juveniles, and youth gangs, as well as stranger homicides and drug- or alcohol-related homicides. However, in recent years, there has been a surge in school shootings, workplace homicides, hate violence, and deadly terrorist attacks in the United States. This has resulted in a greater focus on homicidal behavior, its antecedents, ways to recognize warning signs of at-risk victims and offenders, and preventive measures. It has also led to increased efforts by lawmakers to create and pass tough crime legislation, and improved federal, state, and local law enforcement response to murder and other violent crimes.

The Dynamics of Murder: Kill or Be Killed offers a comprehensive exploration of the crime of murder in American society. The book breaks new ground in homicide studies in examining issues generally ignored or neglected among researchers such as workplace homicides, bias-related homicides, terrorist perpetrated homicides, and the increasing role the Internet plays in murders. Particular attention is also given to school killings, intimate killings, intrafamilial homicides, gang homicides, sexual killers, serial murderers, mass murder, suicide, case studies, and theories on murder and violence.

The book is written as a textbook and for assigned reading for both undergraduate and graduate students in the following disciplines: criminal justice, criminology, law, police studies, corrections, violence in society, terrorism, firearms and violence, hate crimes, domestic violence, gender and crime, gender studies, racial and ethnic studies, African American studies, Hispanic studies, urban studies, substance abuse, alcohol and drugs, child abuse and neglect, juvenile delinquency, school violence, youth gangs, sociology, social science, psychology, and related disciplines.

Additionally, the timely and detailed material is appropriate for professionals in law, law enforcement, government, corrections, delinquency, family violence, intimate partner violence, substance abuse, social services, child welfare, education, race relations, medicine, psychology, sociology, psychiatry, and other occupations with an interest in homicide and its impact on individuals and society. Researchers and fellow criminologists and social scientists should also benefit from the wealth of information, findings, and references on murder and violent crime afforded them within this text.

I would like to offer thanks to CRC Press and the Taylor & Francis Group in recognizing the importance of undertaking this project in contributing to the body of work in the study of murder, murderers, and victims, as well as correlates and theories of homicidal and violent behavior.

Finally, my task would not be complete if I did not offer my profound gratitude to my wife for her tireless devotion to me and my writings, and the professionalism to which she has used her own organizational skills superbly to transform my often complicated and unkempt manuscripts into polished works of art. Thank you, H. Loraine!

Introduction

Since the September 11, 2001, terrorist hijackings of four airliners that resulted in the death of thousands of people, brought down the twin towers of the World Trade Center, and seriously damaged the Pentagon, the dynamics of murder on all scales in the United States has been given greater attention by criminologists and sociologists.

While such instances of mass murder are horrifying and deserve exploration, in reality, these types of killings (including recent deadly school shootings and workplace homicides) represent only a fraction of overall homicides in this country. Far more common are intimate partner homicides, intrafamilial murders, youth homicides, sexual homicides, single victim–single offender homicides, and those influenced by drug and alcohol abuse and related offending. As such, it is important to keep a proper perspective in the study of homicidal behavior, while at the same time seeking to understand the differences, similarities, and patterns of criminal homicide.

The Dynamics of Murder is a multifaceted probe of murder offenses, offenders, victims, and characteristics of homicide in American society. Within this context, the focus will be on examining the nature and causes of murder, the relationship between firearms and lethal violence, the criminal justice system and homicide offenders, different types of murders and murderers, antecedents and correlates to homicidal and violent behavior, and a theoretical basis for murder.

The book is divided into seven sections. Section I examines the dynamics of murder including its nature; firearms, substance abuse, and murder; and murder and the criminal justice system. Section II explores domestic murder such as intimate homicide, infanticide, parricide, and other intrafamilial homicide.

Section III discusses interpersonal and societal murder crimes including workplace homicides, bias-motivated homicides, terrorism and murder, and Internet-related homicidal violence. Section IV focuses on youth and murder including youth gangs and homicide, and school killings.

Section V examines particular categories of killers including sexual killers, serial killers, mass murderers, and self-killers. Section VI provides case studies of killers in a culture of murder. Section VII explores theories on murder.

Tables and figures accompany the text throughout the book to illustrate major points. A complete index is also provided for simple access to information and material found in the text.

The Dynamics of Murder

I

The Nature of Murder

1

Murder is considered the most serious and violent criminal offense in society. Tens of thousands of people are murdered in the United States annually. Indeed, according to official data, one murder takes place every 35.6 minutes in this country. The crime of murder is most often perpetrated by offenders using firearms, but it can also occur using numerous other things such as fists, hands, knives, poison, bombs, and bats. Murder victims and offenders come from all walks of life, but certain groups and individuals are at higher risk for involvement such as family members, intimates, youth, gang members, work associates, minorities, and those residing in high-crime areas. Recent years have seen a decline in the homicide rate, due in part to tougher gun control laws, a drop in youth gun violence, and a general decrease in overall crimes, particularly violent crime. However, a number of recent school shootings, mass killings, and deadly terrorist attacks illustrate the continual threat and concern with homicidal behavior.

What Is Murder?

In general, *murder* refers to the criminal or unlawful taking of a life. However, the term is often used interchangeably with homicide, which is defined as the killing of a person by another. Additionally, there are a number of types and subtypes of each.

The term *murder* originated sometime before the 12th century in part from "Middle English *murther* … Old English *morthor* [and] … Middle English *murdre*," to mean "the crime of unlawfully killing a person especially with malice aforethought."[1] The *World Book Encyclopedia* defines murder as "when one person intentionally kills another without legal justification or excuse."[2] *Murder* and *nonnegligent manslaughter* are combined in the Uniform Crime Reporting Program administered by the Federal Bureau of Investigation (FBI) to refer to "the willful (nonnegligent) killing of one human being by another."[3]

The term *manslaughter* originated in the 14th century and is defined as "the unlawful killing of a human being without express or implied malice."[4] *Voluntary manslaughter* is "a killing that takes place in the heat of anger and is not premeditated or committed with malice."[5] *Involuntary manslaughter* is the killing of another due to a person's negligence or "manslaughter result-ing from the failure to perform a legal duty expressly requested to safeguard human life, from the commission of an unlawful act not constituting a felony, or from the commission of a lawful act in a negligent or improper manner."[6]

Within the broad category of murder is *first degree murder*, defined as a killing that is "willful, deliberate, and premeditated," and *second degree mur-der*, a killing defined as "malicious and/or reckless without premeditation or necessarily with intent."[7]

The term *homicide* originated sometime in the 14th century from the Latin *homicida*, *homo* human being, and *idd-cide*.[8] Homicide is defined as a person who kills another or "the killing of one human being by another."[9]

There are a number of types of homicide. *Justifiable homicide* is "a killing that has legal justification," such as by a police officer in the course of duty, one that occurs in self-defense, and the killing of an individual by a private citizen in stopping a felony in progress.[10] *Excusable homicide* refers to a completely accidental or unintentional killing without blame or fault on the part of the killer, per se, though still classified as a homicide. *Vehicular homicide* is the killing of a person by another during the operation of a motor vehicle, through criminal negligence or while driving under the influence of alcohol or drugs.

Murder and nonnegligent manslaughter fall within the definition of homicide. Other subtypes of homicide refer to specific kinds of murders or killings, and include the following:

- *Familicide* is the murder of most or all of a person's family or close relatives.
- *Fratricide* is the killing of one's brother.
- *Infanticide* is the killing of an infant, usually by a parent.
- *Matricide* is the killing of one's mother.
- *Multicide* is the killing of two or more people.
- *Parricide* is the murder of one's father or mother.
- *Patricide* is the murder of one's father.
- *Sororicide* is the murder of one's sister.
- *Suicide* is the killing of oneself.
- *Uxoricide* is the murder by a man of his wife.[11]

Based on a study of homicide in Chicago from the 1960s to 1990s, Carolyn Block and Antigone Christakos argued that rather than one type of event, homicide is in fact the result of a series of events. According to the research-ers, homicide syndromes "categorize homicides according to the offender's primary motive or goal at the immediate time of the incident. Each homicide syndrome corresponds to a nonlethal sibling offense, and these lethal and nonlethal events are linked because they occupy the same position on an expressive versus instrumental continuum."[12]

In *expressive violence*, the offender's main goal "is violence itself," with other motives for the criminal behavior being of a secondary nature; whereas in *instrumental violence*, the primary goal is "not to hurt, injure or kill, but to acquire money or property."[13] Block and Christakos maintain that virtually all homicides "aside from gangland hits or contract murders correspond to a sibling offense—murder incidents in which a fatal outcome did not occur."[14] Examples of expressive fatal violence include those involving a domestic dispute, child abuse, and stranger attacks. Instrumental fatal violence may be a robbery, street gang violence, or a rape in which the sexual assault was the primary motive.

Trends in Homicides

The number of homicides in the United States has dropped significantly in the last few decades. According to the U.S. Department of Justice, since 2000, the homicide rate has dropped to levels not seen in this country since the 1960s (see Figure 1.1). From 1962 to 1979, the homicide rate more than doubled per 100,000 people in the United States from 4.6 to 9.7. The rate reached a peak in 1980 of 10.2, before falling to 7.9 in 1984 and rising in the late 1980s and early 1990s, peaking again in 1991 to 9.8. Since that time, the homicide rate has been on the decline, falling to 4.8 in 2010.

The drop in the murder rate is indicative of changing levels of gun violence, especially involving juveniles and young adults. In spite of this positive sign, experts point out that the levels of firearms-related homicides by young people were still much higher than in the early 1980s.

Other notable homicide trends and findings between 1980 and 2010 include

- Males are far more likely than females to be both homicide offenders (94 percent) and victims (77 percent).

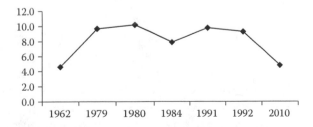

Figure 1.1 Trends in homicide rate, per 100,000 population, United States, 1962–2010. (Derived from U.S. Department of Justice, Office of Justice Programs, *Homicide Trends in the United States, 1980–2010*. Washington, D.C., Bureau of Justice Statistics, 2011, p. 2.)

- The rate of offending was nine times higher for males than for females.
- Blacks were disproportionately involved in homicides as victims and offenders, with a victimization rate six times higher than Whites and offender rate nearly eight times that of Whites.[15]
- Elderly victims have the highest percentage of murder during the commission of a felony.
- Nearly 4 in 10 murder victims age 50 and over were victimized by homicidal workplace violence.[16]
- Around 1 in 3 murder victims and nearly half of those offending were under the age of 25.
- The murder rate for victims and offenders peaked among 18- to 24-year-olds.
- The homicide victimization rate for teens and young adults peaked in 1993 at 12.0 and 24.8, respectively.
- Between 1980 and 2008, people age 18 to 24 were consistent in maintaining the highest rate of offending.[17]
- About 1 in 4 victims of gang-related homicides were under the age of 18.
- One in 5 juvenile homicide victims were murdered by family members.
- Infanticide is primarily committed by parents.
- Children had the lowest homicide victimization rate among age groups.
- Black children younger than age 5 have consistently had higher rates of homicide victimization than children of other racial groups.
- Few murders involve multiple perpetrators.
- Even fewer homicides involve multiple victims.
- Arguments tend to be the most frequent nonfelony circumstance leading to murder.[18]

Table 1.1 reflects further characteristics of homicides in the United States from 1980 to 2008, including breakdowns by victim and offender ages, murder circumstances, and multiple victims and offenders. More than 53 percent of homicide victims and over 65 percent of the offenders during the span were between the ages of 18 and 34. Around one-fifth of victims and offenders were age 35 to 49. Nearly half of the intimate murders involved victims and offenders in this age group, while roughly three-quarters of the offenders in felony, drug, and gang-related homicides were 18 to 35 years of age.

Among homicide victims under 18, around 2 in 10 murders were sex-related, 3 in 10 were drug or gang-related, with around one-fifth involving multiple victims over the span. More than one-fifth of the family-related and

Table 1.1 Homicides, by Type and Age, 1980–2008

	Victims					Offenders				
	Total (%)	Under 18 (%)	18–34 (%)	35–49 (%)	50 or older (%)	Total (%)	Under 18 (%)	18–34 (%)	35–49 (%)	50 or older (%)
All homicides	100	10.0	53.2	22.8	14.0	100	11.0	65.5	17.1	6.5
Victim–offender relationship										
Intimate	100	1.3	48.5	33.6	16.6	100	1.0	47.0	34.7	17.2
Family	100	19.3	32.8	26.0	21.9	100	6.1	50.5	27.5	15.9
Infants	100	100				100	7.4	81.2	10.2	1.1
Elders	100				100	100	9.4	47.8	20.7	22.1
Circumstances										
Felony murder	100	7.5	48.2	22.2	22.1	100	14.6	72.7	10.7	2.0
Sex related	100	18.4	45.3	18.2	18.1	100	9.7	73.1	15.2	1.9
Drug related	100	5.4	70.9	20.2	3.6	100	10.8	76.4	11.5	1.3
Gang related	100	23.7	68.8	6.2	1.3	100	28.0	70.2	1.6	0.2
Argument	100	5.7	56.2	26.3	11.8	100	7.0	60.7	23.0	9.2
Workplace	100	0.5	26.7	33.5	39.3	100	2.8	53.6	28.0	15.6
Weapon										
Gun homicide	100	8.1	59.7	22.0	10.3	100	12.2	65.9	15.1	6.9
Arson	100	27.9	26.4	20.4	25.2	100	10.6	57.0	24.9	7.5
Poison	100	28.6	20.8	16.8	33.8	100	3.5	48.8	29.8	17.8
Multiple victims or offenders										
Multiple victims	100	17.9	47.0	19.3	15.8	100	9.5	66.3	18.3	5.9
Multiple offenders	100	10.4	58.4	19.2	12.0	100	17.9	73.1	7.7	1.3

Note: Detail may not sum to total due to rounding. The percentages of victim–offender relationships are based on the 63.1% of homicides from 1980 through 2008 for which the victim–offender relationships were known. The percentages of homicides involving multiple victims or offenders were known for 69.1% of incidents.

Source: U.S. Department of Justice, Office of Justice Programs, *Homicide Trends in the United States, 1980–2010* (Washington: Bureau of Justice Statistics, 2011) p. 5.

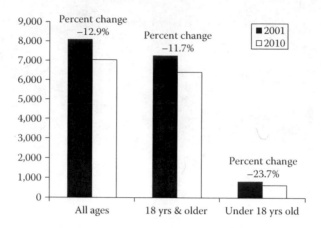

Figure 1.2 Ten-year arrest trends for people arrested for murder and nonnegligent manslaughter, by age, 2001–2010. (Derived from U.S. Department of Justice, Federal Bureau of Investigation, *Crime in the United States: Uniform Crime Reports 2010*, Ten Year Arrest Trends, Totals, 2001–2010, http://www.fbi.gov/aboutus/cjis/ucr/crime-in-the-u.s/2010/crime-in-the-u.s.-2010/tables/10tbl32.xls, March 14, 2012.)

felony homicide victims were age 50 and over, whereas most homicide offenders in this age group tended to murder in the workplace or due to an argument.

Where it pertained to weapons during the period, guns were used to kill nearly 60 percent of the victims 18 to 34, with two-thirds of the perpetrators of homicides using guns in this age range. Multiple victims and offenders were predominantly in the 18 to 34 age range.

Recent arrest trends continue to illustrate an overall decline in homicides. According to the FBI's Uniform Crime Reports, between 2001 and 2010, the number of people arrested in the United States for murder and nonnegligent manslaughter fell nearly 13 percent, as shown in Figure 1.2. For arrestees under the age of 18, total arrests dropped nearly 24 percent, compared with an almost 12 percent decrease in arrests of people age 18 and older.

During the 10-year arrest trend, the number of female arrests for murder and nonnegligent manslaughter dropped 29.2 percent, nearly three times the decline of male arrests at 10.5 percent.[19] However, arrests of males under the age of 18 for these offenses fell 24 percent, compared with a decline of just over 21 percent for female arrestees under age 18.

The one year to the next arrest data for murder and nonnegligent manslaughter also indicates the downward trend, albeit at a lower rate of decline.[20] Between 2009 and 2010, total arrests for these offenses fell 8.3 percent. However, when broken down by sex and age of arrestees, arrests of males under age 18 fell 9.2 percent while arrests of females under age 18 for murder and nonnegligent manslaughter actually increased 15.4 percent during the 2-year trend. This increase represented only 10 more arrests of underage females for these crimes, or a total of 75 arrests in 2010. Overall, males of all ages are far more likely to be arrested for and charged with murder than their female counterparts.[21]

The Dynamics of Murder

According to the FBI, there were an estimated 14,748 victims of murder in the United States in 2010.[22] Nearly 8 in 10 of the murder victims were male. An estimated 15,094 people committed murder during the year, of which more than 90 percent were male if gender was reported.

Regionally, the South recorded the highest number of murders, constituting 44 percent of all murders, followed by the West, Midwest, and Northeast, accounting for 20.6 percent, 19.9 percent, and 15.6 percent, respectively.

Tables 1.2 and 1.3 reflect the FBI's expanded homicide data on murder offenders and victims in the United States by age, sex, and race in 2010. Males constituted the vast majority of murderers. Of the 15,094 murder offenders recorded, 9,972, or two in three, were male. Just over 7 percent, or 1,075, were female, with the gender of offenders unknown for around one-quarter of the murder offenders.

Blacks were disproportionately represented as murder offenders, accounting for more than 38 percent at 5,770, while Whites accounted for about one-third of the murder offenders at 4,849. The race was unknown for 28 percent of the murderers, and fewer than 2 percent were of other races.

Murder offenders were nearly 12 times more likely to be over 18 years of age as under age 18. Around one in five murderers were under the age of 22.

Table 1.2   Murder Offenders, by Age, Sex, and Race, 2010

Age	Total	Sex			Race			
		Male	Female	Unknown	White	Black	Other	Unknown
Total	15,094	9,972	1,075	4,047	4,849	5,770	251	4,224
Percent distribution[a]	100.0	66.1	7.1	26.8	32.1	38.2	1.7	28.0
Under 18[b]	802	726	76	0	272	497	22	11
Under 22[b]	3,239	2,981	257	1	1,104	2,035	65	35
18 and over[b]	9,445	8,442	990	13	4,477	4,643	225	100

[a] Because of rounding, the percentages may not add to 100.0%.

[b] Does not include unknown ages.

Source: Derived from U.S. Department of Justice, Federal Bureau of Investigation, *Crime in the United States: Uniform Crime Reports 2010*, Expanded Homicide Data Table 3, Murder Offenders by Age, Sex, and Race, 2010, http://www.fbi.gov/about-us/cjis/ucr/crime-in-the-u.s/2010/crime-in-the-u.s.-2010/tables/10shrtbl03.xls (March 16, 2012).

Table 1.3   Murder Victims, by Age, Sex, and Race, 2010

Age	Total	Sex			Race			
		Male	Female	Unknown	White	Black	Other	Unknown
Total	12,996	10,058	2,918	20	6,043	6,470	331	152
Percent distribution[a]	100.0	77.4	22.5	0.2	46.5	49.8	2.5	1.2
Under 18[b]	1,277	890	386	1	599	622	37	19
Under 22[b]	3,172	2,540	631	1	1,278	1,800	65	29
18 and over[b]	11,566	9,069	2,493	4	5,385	5,797	291	93

[a] Because of rounding, the percentages may not add to 100.0%.
[b] Does not include unknown ages.
Source: Derived from U.S. Department of Justice, Federal Bureau of Investigation, *Crime in the United States: Uniform Crime Reports 2010*, Expanded Homicide Data Table 3, Murder Victims by Age, Sex, and Race, 2010, http://www.fbi.gov/about-us/cjis/ucr/crime-in-the-u.s/2010/crime-in-the-u.s.-2010/tables/10shrtbl02.xls (March 16, 2012).

Among murder victims, more than 77 percent, or 10,058, were male, with females constituting nearly 23 percent of victims with 2,918. Almost half of the murder victims were Black, with nearly 47 percent White. Other races and unknown races accounted for less than 4 percent of the murder victims.

Murder victims were more than nine time as likely to be age 18 and over as under the age of 18. More than one in four murder victims were under the age of 22.

Circumstances of Murder

The majority of murders committed in the United States in 2010 were nonfelony homicides as the result of firearms, as shown in Table 1.4. Of the 12,996 murders for which expanded information was provided by law enforcement agencies, 6,351 victims were killed by other than felony-type circumstances, representing nearly 49 percent of all murder victims. These included such circumstances as a romantic triangle, brawls due to alcohol or narcotics influence, juvenile gang killings, and other arguments.

There were 1,923 murders of a felony type, constituting nearly 15 percent of total murders that involved such circumstances as rape, robbery, burglary, arson, narcotics law violations, and sex offenses. Around 3 in 10 murders had circumstances that were unknown.

Firearms killed more than two-thirds of murder victims in 2010. Of these, around 69 percent were the victims of handguns. A number of studies support the strong relationship between lethal violence and firearms, particularly handguns.[23] About 72 percent of the felony-type murders and 62 percent of the nonfelony murders were perpetrated with firearms in 2010.

Table 1.4   Murder Circumstances, by Offense and Firearm, 2010

Circumstances	Total Murder Victims	Total Firearms	Handguns	Rifles	Shotguns	Other Guns or Type Not Stated
Total	12,996	8,775	6,009	358	373	2,035
Felony-type total	1,923	1,391	976	53	60	302
Rape	41	0	0	0	0	0
Robbery	780	603	463	16	19	105
Burglary	80	49	29	3	3	14
Larceny-theft	20	11	7	0	1	3
Motor vehicle theft	37	15	9	0	0	6
Arson	35	7	3	0	0	4
Prostitution & commercialized vice	5	1	0	0	0	1
Other sex offenses	14	3	3	0	0	0
Narcotic drug offenses	463	391	264	7	12	108
Gambling	7	6	5	0	1	0
Other—not specified	441	305	193	27	24	61
Suspected felony-type	66	44	31	2	2	9
Other than felony-type total	6,351	3,960	2,842	187	204	727
Romantic triangle	90	59	43	4	4	8
Child killed by babysitter	36	1	1	0	0	0
Brawl due to influence of alcohol	121	55	38	4	8	5
Brawl due to influence of narcotics	58	29	24	1	1	3
Argument over money or property	181	112	79	11	10	12
Other arguments	3,215	1,937	1,346	91	120	380
Gangland killings	176	160	102	4	3	51
Juvenile gang killings	673	624	529	10	7	78
Institutional killings	17	0	0	0	0	0
Sniper attack	3	3	0	3	0	0
Other—not specified	1,781	980	680	59	51	190
Unknown	4,656	3,380	2,160	116	107	997

Source: Derived from U.S. Department of Justice, Federal Bureau of Investigation, *Crime in the United States: Uniform Crime Reports 2010*, Expanded Homicide Data Table 11, Murder Circumstances by Weapon, 2010, http://www.fbi.gov/about-us/cjis/ucr/crime-in-the-u.s/2010/crime-in-the-u.s.-2010/tables/10shrtbl11.xls (March 17, 2012).

Table 1.5   Murder Victims, by Type of Weapon Used, 2008–2010

Weapons	2008	2009	2010
Total	14,224	13,752	12,996
Total firearms	9,528	9,199	8,775
Handguns	6,800	6,501	6,009
Rifles	380	351	358
Shotguns	442	423	373
Other guns	81	96	96
Firearms, type not stated	1,825	1,828	1,939
Knives or cutting instruments	1,888	1,836	1,704
Blunt objects (clubs, hammers, etc.)	603	623	540
Personal weapons (hands, fists, feet, etc.)[a]	875	817	745
Poison	9	7	11
Explosives	11	2	4
Fire	85	98	74
Narcotics	34	52	39
Drowning	16	8	10
Strangulation	89	122	122
Asphyxiation	87	84	98
Other weapons or weapons not stated	999	904	874

[a] Pushed is included in personal weapons.

Source: Derived from U.S. Department of Justice, Federal Bureau of Investigation, *Crime in the United States: Uniform Crime Reports 2010*, Expanded Homicide Data Table 8, Murder Victims by Weapon, 2006–2010, http://www.fbi.gov/about-us/cjis/ucr/crime-in-the-u.s/2010/crime-in-the-u.s.-2010/tables/10shrtbl08.xls (March 17, 2012).

Table 1.5 describes the type of weapons used on murder victims in this country from 2008 to 2010. While the overall number of victims and weapons used against them declined each year, along with the use of handguns, firearms were by far still responsible for most murder victimizations. Handguns were the most likely weapon used to kill victims in 2010, followed by unspecified types of firearms, knives or cutting instruments, other or unstated weapons, personal weapons such as fists or feet, and blunt objects (see also Chapter 2).

Use of some weapons to kill actually rose in 2010 from the prior year, such as rifles, unspecified firearms, poison, and asphyxiation.

Characterizing the Murder Offender–Victim Relationship

More than 4 in 10 murders committed in the United States in 2010 involved an unknown relationship between the victim and offender (see Figure 1.3).

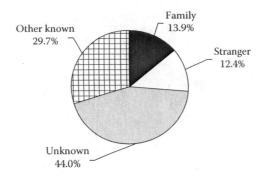

Figure 1.3 Murder victim–offender relationship, 2010. (Derived from U.S. Department of Justice, Federal Bureau of Investigation, *Crime in the United States: Uniform Crime Reports 2010*, Expanded Homicide Data Figures, Murder by Relationship, 2010, http://www.fbi.gov/about-us/cjis/ucr/crime-in-theu.s/2010/crime-in-the-u.s.-2010/offenses-known-to-law-enforcement/expanded/expandedhomicide-data-figure, March 14, 2012.)

Around 1 in 3 of the murder victims knew their offender or offenders apart from family members, such as boyfriend or girlfriend, acquaintance, friend, neighbor, or co-worker. Nearly 14 percent of murders were intrafamilial in nature, whereas just over 12 percent involved strangers to the victims.

Most murders involve a single offender and single victim, as illustrated in Figure 1.4. Almost half of the murders perpetrated in this country in 2010 consisted of a single victim and offender. In around 3 in 10 homicides, there was a single victim and unknown number of offenders. Nearly 13 percent of murders involved a single victim with multiple offenders, with around 6

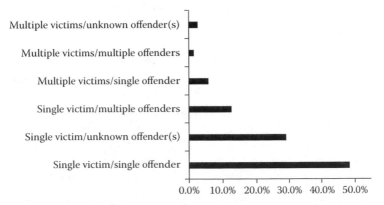

Figure 1.4 Single and multiple murder victims and offenders, 2010. (Derived from U.S. Department of Justice, Federal Bureau of Investigation, *Crime in the United States: Uniform Crime Reports 2010*, Expanded Homicide Data Table 4, Murder by Victim/Offender Situations, 2010, http://www.fbi.gov/about-us/cjis/ucr/crime-in-the-u.s/2010/crime-in-the-u.s.-2010/tables/10shrtbl04.xls, March 17, 2012.)

Table 1.6   Victim–Offender Relationship, by Age, 2010

	Single Victim–Single Offender			
		Age of Offender		
Age of Victim	Total	Under 18	18 and Over	Unknown
Total	6,284	293	5,614	377
Under 18	665	93	556	16
18 and over	5,558	198	5,006	354
Unknown	61	2	52	7

Source: Derived from U.S. Department of Justice, Federal Bureau of Investigation, *Crime in the United States: Uniform Crime Reports 2010*, Expanded Homicide Data Table 5, Murder, Age of Victim by Age of Offender, 2010, http://www.fbi.gov/about-us/cjis/ucr/crime-in-the-u.s/2010/crime-in-the-u.s.-2010/tables/10shrtbl05.xls (March 17, 2012).

percent multiple victims and a single offender. Less than 5 percent of murders included multiple murder victims and an unknown number of killers.

Table 1.6 demonstrates the murder victim–offender relationship for single victim–offender homicides, by age, in 2010. Of 6,284 total murders, the vast majority of murder offenders (5,614) and murder victims (5,558) were age 18 and over. Juveniles were more likely to be victims of murder than per-petrators, with 665 known victims under the age of 18 compared with 556 known offenders younger than 18. The age of the offender was unknown in 377 homicides.

The relationship between victims and offenders nationally in single victim–single offender homicides by sex and race in 2010 can be seen in Table 1.7. Males are predominantly more likely than females to be the victims and offenders in homicides. In 7 out of 10 murders where gender was known, the victim was male, whereas in more than 9 in 10 of the homicides where the offender was identified by gender, the perpetrator was male. Females were nearly three times more likely to murder males than females.

With respect to race and murder, the victim and offender relationship is largely intraracial. More than 9 out of 10 Black homicide victims in this country were murdered by Black offenders in 2010, while more than 8 of every 10 White homicide victims were killed by White perpetrators. More than half of the murder victims of other races were slain by killers of other races, representing more offenders than White, Black, and unknown offenders combined. Murder victims of unknown race were most likely to be killed by offenders of unknown races and White offenders.

The overrepresentation of Blacks as murder offenders and victims has been noted and examined by a number of researchers,[24] relating it to such variables as the high rate of crime in inner cities, access to and arming with

Table 1.7   Victim–Offender Relationship, by Sex and Race, 2010

Single Victim–Single Offender

		Sex of Offender			Race of Offender			
	Total	Male	Female	Unknown	White	Black	Other	Unknown
Race of Victim								
White	3,327	2,975	289	63	2,777	447	40	63
Black	2,720	2,439	245	36	218	2,459	7	36
Other race	179	156	19	4	47	30	98	4
Unknown race	58	31	5	22	20	14	2	22
Sex of Victim								
Male	4,362	3,872	405	85	2,777	447	40	63
Female	1,864	1,698	148	18	218	2,459	7	36
Unknown sex	58	31	5	22	47	30	98	4

Source: Derived from U.S. Department of Justice, Federal Bureau of Investigation, *Crime in the United States: Uniform Crime Reports 2010*, Expanded Homicide Data Table 6, Murder, Race and Sex by Age and Sex of Offender, 2010, http://www.fbi.gov/about-us/cjis/ucr/crime-in-the-u.s/2010/crime-in-the-u.s.-2010/tables/10shrtbl06.xls (March 17, 2012).

illegal weapons, youth gangs, drug dealing, and even discrimination within the criminal justice system in arrests and incarceration.[25]

Although ethnicity is often excluded from official data on murder, people of Hispanic origin have been found to be disproportionately likely to be murder offenders and victims—linking this to culture, drug offending, youth gangs, territorial disputes, and gun possession and accessibility.[26]

The Risk of Murder Victimization

What are the risks over a lifetime of becoming a murder victim? Data on the lifetime victimization rate of murder based on the Uniform Crime Reports' Supplemental Homicide Report, the National Center for Health Statistics' U.S. Life Tables, and U.S. population estimates from the U.S. Bureau of the Census can be seen in Table 1.8.

Over the course of a lifetime, males are much more likely to be murdered than females; Blacks have a far greater chance than Whites or other races to become murder victims, with Black males being more likely to be murdered than any other group when combining race and sex.

The figures indicate that in 1997, 1 out of every 240 people per 100,000 in the U.S. population would become a murder victim. The probability of a male being murdered was 1 in 155, or more than 3 times that of a female, at 1 in 553. Blacks had a victimization rate of 1 out of 68, which meant they were

Table 1.8 Lifetime Victimization Rate of Murder (5 Year)[a]

Age	U.S. Total	Male	Female	White	White Male	White Female	Black	Black Male	Black Female	Other	Other Male	Other Female
0	240	155	553	410	280	794	68	40	199	407	288	709
5	248	158	595	426	288	848	69	41	213	424	296	764
10	250	159	603	429	289	859	70	41	216	429	298	787
15	252	160	614	433	291	874	70	41	219	436	302	799
20	291	186	674	488	330	957	81	48	239	523	370	909
25	381	250	789	600	413	1,106	110	66	282	623	457	992
30	487	328	921	730	513	1,263	145	89	337	742	568	1,095
35	620	422	1,133	895	632	1,520	191	117	427	853	678	1,184
40	786	536	1,418	1,092	769	1,843	251	154	558	1,014	823	1,373
45	998	684	1,751	1,336	951	2,177	332	202	741	1,169	931	1,647
50	1,287	889	2,177	1,670	1,197	2,646	440	268	959	1,524	1,315	1,964
55	1,610	1,125	2,610	2,079	1,513	3,150	554	313	1,158	1,805	1,572	2,345
60	2,033	1,434	3,162	2,610	1,927	3,782	679	411	1,397	2,242	2,079	2,782
65	2,556	1,857	3,661	3,138	2,410	4,175	898	538	1,801	2,846	3,235	3,064
70	3,117	2,335	4,157	3,734	3,025	4,522	1,106	631	2,335	3,118	3,755	3,461
75	3,918	3,043	4,836	4,639	3,874	5,322	1,362	800	2,436	3,829	6,595	3,938
80	4,653	3,603	5,567	5,333	4,380	6,068	1,697	993	2,756	5,814	N/A	5,511

[a] Table shows only 80 years of age because the low number of U.S. citizens and murders occurring in age groups over the age of 80 may improperly inflate odd ratios and murder rates and may not reflect the true nature of murder in these groups. Based on 1997 murder rates, which may not remain constant over time. There were no reported murders for other males aged 80 and older in 1997.

Source: U.S. Department of Justice, Federal Bureau of Investigation, *Crime in the United States: Uniform Crime Reports 1999* (Washington: Government Printing Office, 2000), p. 281.

around 6 times as likely to be murdered as Whites were, at 1 in 410, or those of other races, at 1 in 407.

Black males had a likelihood of 1 in 40 of being murdered over a life span, with Black females second most likely at 1 in 199. Compared with other groups, when broken down by race and sex, Black males were 7 times more likely to be victims of murder than White males or other males. Black males had nearly a 20 times greater probability to be murdered than White females, who had the lowest victimization rate at 1 in 794, followed by females of other races at 1 in 709.

The risk of murder victimization decreased with age for all groups. Although Blacks continued to be more likely to be murdered at any age than people of other races, at age 30 the Black murder rate was significantly lower than at birth. Males age 30 were about half as likely and females age 30 were one-third less likely to be murder victims as at age 15.

As indicated earlier, murder rates have dropped steadily in recent years, reducing the likelihood of victimization for most people in every age, racial, and gender group.

Murder and the Law

Murder is primarily controlled in society through laws prohibiting it and serious consequences for those perpetrating the act of murder. Murder is a felony crime or criminal homicide in every state, with penalties for offenders usually ranging from long prison terms to capital punishment, depending on the degree of murder, nature of the crime, and the state where it was committed.

A representative murder statute is Michigan's Criminal Code on first and second degree murder, which reads:

> A person who commits any of the following is guilty of *first degree* murder and shall be punished by imprisonment for life: (1) murder perpetrated by means of poison, lying in wait, or any other willful, deliberate, and premeditated killing; (2) murder committed in the perpetration of, or attempt to perpetrate, arson, criminal sexual conduct in the first or third degree, child abuse in the first degree, a major controlled substance offense, robbery, breaking and entering of a dwelling, larceny of any kind, extortion, or kidnapping; (3) a murder of a peace officer or a corrections officer committed while the [person] is lawfully engaged in the performance of any of his or her duties as a peace officer or corrections officer, with knowledge that the [person] is ... engaged in the performance of his or her duty.[27]
>
> All other kinds of murder shall be murder of the *second degree*, and shall be punished by imprisonment in the state prison for life, or any term of years, in the discretion of the court trying the same.[28]

Furthermore, the Michigan Criminal Code on manslaughter states: "Any person who shall commit the crime of *manslaughter* shall be guilty of a felony punishable by imprisonment in the state prison, not more than fifteen years or by fine of not more than $7,500, or both, at the discretion of the court."[29]

On the federal level, the crime of murder and other violent offenses, particularly those committed when using lethal weapons, recently led to the most sweeping crime bill in U.S. history. The Violent Crime Control and Law Enforcement Act (Federal Crime Bill) was signed into law in 1994.[30] The act provided for 100,000 new police officers to fight violent crime, almost $10 billion for prison construction, more than $16 billion for crime prevention programs, and $2.6 billion for new federal law enforcement personnel. Penalties were also stiffened for many types of offenses including federal crimes, violent crimes, gang-involved crimes, sex offenses, and white-collar crimes.

Highlights of the act's provision include the following:

- The ban of manufacturing 19 military assault weapons and weapons with certain combat features
- Expansion of the death penalty to include about 60 offenses, such as homicides associated with terrorism, the murder of a federal law officer, carjackings, and drive-by shootings resulting in death, and large-scale drug trafficking operations
- New and stiffer penalties for gang crimes of violence and drug trafficking
- Strengthened federal licensing requirements for dealers of firearms
- Prohibiting the sale of firearms to or possession of firearms by individuals with domestic violence restraining orders against them
- Requirement of sexually violent criminals to register with state law enforcement agencies
- Doubling the penalties for repeat sex criminals convicted of federal sex crimes
- A mandatory sentence of life in prison with no possibility of parole for federal offenders with three or more convictions for serious violent felonies or drug trafficking offenses
- The authorization of prosecuting in adult criminal court persons 13 years of age and older charged with certain types of serious violent crimes
- The creation of new crimes or increasing penalties for such offenses as the use of semiautomatic weapons, interstate trafficking of firearms, hate crimes, drive-by shootings, sex crimes, crimes against the elderly, and interstate domestic violence

Additionally, recent federal laws enacted to respond to criminal homicide and other violent crimes include hate crime statutes and antiterrorism legislation (see Chapters 9 and 10).

Endnotes

1. YourDictionary.com, http://yourdictionary.com/.
2. World Book Encyclopedia, http://search.cssvc.worldbook.compuserve.com/wbol/wbsearch/na/se/co?st1 = murder.
3. U.S. Department of Justice, Federal Bureau of Investigation, *Crime in the United States: Uniform Crime Reports 1999* (Washington: Government Printing Office, 2000), p. 13.
4. YourDictionary.com.
5. D. Lester, *Serial Killers: The Insatiable Passion* (Philadelphia: Charles Press, 1995), p. 10.
6. YourDictionary.com.
7. Lester, *Serial Killers*, p. 10. See also Maureen Harrison and Steve Gilbert, *The Murder Reference: Everything You Never Wanted to Know About Murder in America* (San Diego: Excellent Books, 1996), pp. 34, 48, 57–58, 72.
8. YourDictionary.com.
9. *Ibid.*
10. C. F. Welford, Homicide, *World Book Online Americas Edition*, http://www.cssvc.worldbook.compuserve.com/wbol/wbpage/na/ar/co/260800, November 25, 2001.
11. See R. B. Flowers & H. L. Flowers, *Murders in the United States: Crimes, Killers and Victims of the Twentieth Century* (Jefferson: McFarland, 2001); C. P. Ewing, *Fatal Families: The Dynamics of Intrafamilial Homicide* (Thousand Oaks: Sage, 1997).
12. C. R. Block & A. Christakos, Chicago Homicide From the Sixties to the Nineties: Major Trends in Lethal Violence, in U.S. Department of Justice, *Trends, Risks, and Interventions in Lethal Violence: Proceedings of the Third Annual Spring Symposium of the Homicide Research Working Group* (Washington: National Institute of Justice, 1995), p. 28.
13. *Ibid. See also* L. Berkowitz, Some Varieties of Human Aggression: Criminal Violence as Coercion, Rule-Following, Impression Management and Impulsive Behavior, in A. Campbell & J. J. Gibbs, Eds., *Violent Transactions: The Limits of Personality* (Oxford: Basil Blackwell, 1986), pp. 87–103.
14. Block and Christakos, Chicago Homicide From the Sixties to the Nineties, p. 29.
15. U.S. Department of Justice, Office of Justice Programs, *Homicide Trends in the United States, 1980–2010* (Washington: Bureau of Justice Statistics, 2011), p. 3.
16. *Ibid.*, p. 5.
17. *Ibid.*, p. 4.
18. U.S. Department of Justice, Federal Bureau of Investigation, *Crime in the United States: Uniform Crime Reports 2010*, Expanded Homicide Data Table 10, Murder Circumstances by Relationship, 2010, http://www.fbi.gov/about-us/cjis/ucr/crime-in-the-u.s/2010/crime-in-the-u.s.-2010/tables/10shrtbl10.xls (March 16, 2012).

19. *Crime in the United States 2010*, Table 33, Ten-Year Arrest Trends, by Sex, 2001–2010.

20. *Ibid.*, Table 37, Current Year Over Previous Year Arrest Trends, by Sex, 2009–2010.

21. *Ibid.* See also R. B. Flowers, *Male Crime and Deviance: Exploring Its Causes, Dynamics and Nature* (Springfield: Charles C Thomas, 2003).

22. *Crime in the United States 2010.*

23. See, for example, P. J. Cook & M. H. Moore, Guns, Gun Control, and Homicide, in M. D. Smith & M. A. Zahn, Eds., *Studying and Preventing Homicide: Issues and Challenges* (Thousand Oaks: Sage, 1999), pp. 246–71; G. Kleck, *Point Blank: Guns and Violence in America* (New York: Aldine de Gruyter, 1991); J. D. Wright, J. F. Sheley, & M. D. Smith, Kids, Guns, and Killing Fields, *Society* 30, 1 (1992): 84–89.

24. See, for example, R. B. Flowers, *Minorities and Criminality* (Westport: Greenwood, 1988), pp. 83–94; E. Green, Race, Social Status, and Criminal Arrest, *American Sociological Review* 35 (1970): 476–90; D. F. Hawkins, African Americans and Homicide, in M. Dwayne Smith & Margaret A. Zahn, eds., *Studying and Preventing Homicide: Issues and Challenges* (Thousand Oaks: Sage, 1999), pp. 143–56; H. M. Rose & P. D. McClain, *Race, Place, and Risk: Black Homicide in Urban America* (Albany: State University of New York Press, 1990).

25. Flowers, *Minorities and Criminality*, pp. 83–94, 121–2; Hawkins, African Americans and Homicide, pp. 143–56; K. Harries, *Serious Violence: Patterns of Homicide and Assault in America* (Springfield: Charles C Thomas, 1990).

26. Flowers, *Minorities and Criminality*, pp. 95–104; J. W. Moore, *Homeboys: Gangs, Drugs and Prison in the Barrios of Los Angeles* (Philadelphia: Temple University Press, 1978), pp. 100–6; L. M. Romero & L. G. Stelzner, Hispanics and the Criminal Justice System, in P. Cafferty & W. C. McCready, Eds., *Hispanics in the United States: A New Social Agenda* (New Brunswick: Transaction Books, 1985); R. Martinez, Jr., Latinos and Lethal Violence: The Impact of Poverty and Inequality, *Social Problems* 43 (1996): 131–46; R. Martinez, Jr., & M. T. Lee, Latinos and Homicide, in M. D. Smith & M. A. Zahn, Eds., *Studying and Preventing Homicide: Issues and Challenges* (Thousand Oaks: Sage, 1999), pp. 159–72.

27. Michigan Criminal Code 750.316. *See also* Harrison and Gilbert, *The Murder Reference*, pp. 65–66.

28. Michigan Criminal Code 750.317.

29. Harrison & Gilbert, *The Murder Reference*, pp. 65–66; Michigan Criminal Code 750.321/.329.

30. P. L. 103-322 (1994).

Firearms, Substance Abuse, and Murder

2

The most common correlates of murder are use of firearms and the influence of drugs or alcohol in the perpetrator's commission of the crime. Around two in every three murders in the United States are committed with firearms. Handguns are the weapons of choice for most murderers. Homicides involving guns are especially associated with intimate murders, gang homicides, drug-related murders, mass murders, youth homicides, and school killings. Recent gun-control legislation has helped reduce firearm-related lethal violence in society; however, weapons possession and use continue to have the strongest cause-and-effect relationship to murder.

Much of the research on homicide shows a strong association between deadly violence and substance abuse, as well as drug and alcohol use and other violent offenses, and serious drug offenses such as drug dealing. Prisoner data reveal that nearly half the violent inmates had used drugs in the month prior to committing the crimes, while more than one in five violent prisoners had been under the influence of alcohol when perpetrating the offense. Many incarcerated violent offenders admit to using drugs and alcohol while committing the violent crime.

Arrest trends indicate that fewer people are being arrested for murder and weapons offenses, as well as alcohol-related crimes. However, arrests for drug abuse violations have shown an increase, suggesting that the tripartite relationship between murder, firearms, and substance abuse may vary according to the type of substance abuse, with the negative connotations nevertheless potentially lethal.

Firearms and Murder

Firearms are closely related to murder, according to experts. Guns are believed to be responsible for tens of thousands of murders and at least three times as many nonfatal injuries sustained by victims, and are also used to threaten hundreds of thousands of others each year.[1] The FBI estimated firearms were used in more than two-thirds of the 12,996 murders committed in the United States in 2010.[2] The National Crime Victimization Survey reported that in 2010, there were 337,960 violent victimizations in this country, such as aggravated assault, rape, and robbery, where the perpetrator(s)

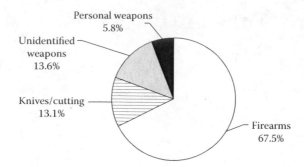

Figure 2.1 Murders in the United States, by type of weapon used, 2010. (Derived from U.S. Department of Justice, Federal Bureau of Investigation, *Crime in the United States: Uniform Crime Reports 2010*, Expanded Homicide Data Table 7, Murder, Types of Weapons Used, http://www.fbi.gov/about-us/cjis/ucr/crime-in-theu.s/2010/crime-in-the-u.s.-2010/tables/10shrtbl07.xls, March 15, 2012.)

possessed a firearm.[3] A weapon of some sort is present in more than one in every five crimes of violence.[4]

Firearms are used to commit murder more than any other type of weapon. As shown in Figure 2.1, in 2010, 67.5 percent of all murders in the United States involved the use of a firearm; 13.1 percent are committed with a knife or cutting device; 13.6 percent involve an unidentified or other dangerous weapon; and 5.8 percent are perpetrated by use of fists, hands, or other personal weapons. Among firearms-related homicides, victims were far more likely to be killed by handguns than any other type of firearm, followed by unstated types of firearms, shotguns, rifles, and other guns.[5]

The circumstances of murder involving firearms in 2010 can be seen in Table 2.1. According to the national data provided by law enforcement agencies, of the 12,996 murder victims, 8,775 were killed by firearms. Of this group, 6,009 victimizations involved the use of a handgun, and 2,035 murders were perpetrated with other guns or unknown types. Nearly half of all murders committed with firearms were other than felony types, including murders involving romantic triangles, brawls due to alcohol or narcotics influence, other arguments, and gang-related killings. Felony circumstances accounted for 1,391 of the victims murdered by firearms, involving such crimes as rape, robbery, burglary, and narcotic drug offenses.

Trends in Firearm-Related Injuries and Fatalities

Violent crimes involving firearms have been on the decline in the United States. FBI figures indicate that between 2001 and 2010, arrests for murder and nonnegligent manslaughter decreased by nearly 13 percent. During the same period, arrests for weapons violations dropped nearly 2 percent (see Figure 2.2).

Table 2.1 Murder Circumstances Involving Firearms, by Offense, 2010

Circumstances	Total Murder Victims	Total Firearms	Handguns	Other Guns
Total[a]	12,996	8,775	6,009	2,035
Felony-type total	1,923	1,391	976	302
Rape	41	0	0	0
Robbery	780	603	463	105
Burglary	80	49	29	14
Larceny-theft	20	11	7	3
Motor vehicle theft	37	15	9	6
Arson	35	7	3	4
Prostitution & commercialized vice	5	1	0	1
Other sex offenses	14	3	3	0
Narcotic drug offenses	463	391	264	108
Gambling	7	6	5	0
Other—not specified	441	305	193	61
Suspected felony-type	66	44	31	9
Other than felony-type total	6,351	3,960	2,842	727
Romantic triangle	90	59	43	8
Child killed by babysitter	36	1	1	0
Brawl due to influence of alcohol	121	55	38	5
Brawl due to influence of narcotics	58	29	24	3
Argument over money or property	181	112	79	12
Other arguments	3,215	1,937	1,346	380
Gangland killings	176	160	102	51
Juvenile gang killings	673	624	529	78
Institutional killings	17	0	0	0
Sniper attack	3	3	0	0
Other—not specified	1,781	980	680	190
Unknown	4,656	3,380	2,160	997

[a] Total firearms include rifles and shotguns.

Source: Derived from U.S. Department of Justice, Federal Bureau of Investigation, *Crime in the United States: Uniform Crime Reports 2010*, Expanded Homicide Data Table 11, Murder Circumstances by Weapon, 2010, http://www.fbi.gov/about-us/cjis/ucr/crime-in-the-u.s/2010/crime-in-the-u.s.-2010/tables/10shrtbl11.xls (March 16, 2012).

The interrelationship of homicides and weapons—particularly firearms—is believed to account for much of the rise and fall in the murder rate.

According to the most recent Bureau of Justice Statistics, between 1993 and 1997, homicides perpetrated with a firearm dropped 27 percent, while the number of nonfatal gunshot injuries due to assaults decreased 39 percent (see Figure 2.3). About 30 percent of nonfatal violent crimes were perpetrated with a firearm, while 44 percent of all fatalities resulting from a firearm were

Figure 2.2 Ten-year arrest trends for murder (includes nonnegligent manslaughter) and weapons offenses (includes carrying and possessing weapons), 2001–2010. (Derived from U.S. Department of Justice, Federal Bureau of Investigation, *Crime in the United States: Uniform Crime Reports 2010*, Table 32, Ten-Year Arrest Trends, http://www.fbi.gov/about-us/cjis/ucr/crimein-the-u.s/2010/crime-in-the-u.s.-2010/tables/10tbl32.xls, March 16, 2012.)

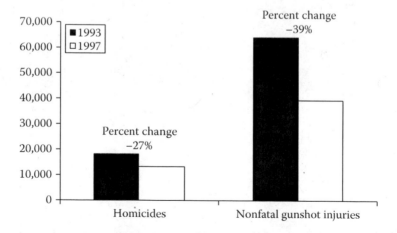

Figure 2.3 Firearm-related homicides and nonfatal injuries from assaults, 1993–1997. (Derived from U.S. Department of Justice, Bureau of Justice Statistics Selected Findings, *Firearm Injury and Death from Crime, 1993–97*, Washington, D.C.: Office of Justice Programs, 2000, p. 7.)

homicides during the period.[6] Data from 1998 indicate a further decline in firearm-related homicides and nonfatal injuries nationally.[7]

Information from the *Morbidity and Mortality Weekly Report* reveals that from 1993 to 1998, victims of assault or legal intervention fatal and non-fatal gunshot injuries were predominantly male, Black non-Hispanic, White non-Hispanic, and ages 20 to 34 years.[8]

Other trends in firearm-related fatalities over the span include the following:

- Males were more than five times as likely as females to sustain fire-arm-related fatal injuries due to an assault.
- Hispanics were five times more likely than non-Hispanic Whites to receive fatal injuries from firearms as a result of an assault.
- Black non-Hispanics were more than twice as likely as Hispanics to experience fatal injuries from firearms caused by an assault.
- Victims ages 14 to 19 had the second highest rate of fatal and nonfatal firearm-related injuries resulting from an assault.
- Suicide attempts using firearms were more likely to result in fatalities than other types of gunshot injuries.[9]

Gun Ownership, Availability, and Lethality

The relationship between gun laws, gun ownership, availability, and lethality as a consequence is strongly supported in studies.[10] According to the National Opinion Research Center's General Social Survey, more than 4 in every 10 households in the United States have one or more firearms.[11] Around 3 in 10 people of adult age claim gun ownership.[12] In a recent survey of private gun ownership, it was estimated that there were an average of 4.4 guns in households owning firearms.[13] It is estimated that there may be as many as 200 million guns currently in circulation.[14]

The handgun has proven particularly popular among gun owners and is used primarily for self-defense, suicide, or to commit a crime.[15] Approximately 30,000 people die from homicide, suicide, and accidental death due to gunfire each year in the United States.[16]

Firearms-related homicide victims and offenders are greatly overrepresented among males, youth, and African Americans.[17] The latter group is particularly disproportionately involved in lethal gun violence and criminality involving handguns and more sophisticated firearms,[18] as are people of Hispanic origin or Latinos.[19]

Supply and demand is believed to be a key factor in gun violence and fatalities. Relatively easy access to both legal and illegal guns increases the risk that these guns will be used to kill. Arthur Kellerman and colleagues found that homicide was more likely to occur in the home when a firearm was present.[20] A high percentage of teenagers, students, and youth gang members have reported having easy access to guns and other weapons.[21] Studies show that criminals often circumvent the licensed gun dealers and legal requirements for gun ownership in favor of obtaining illegal guns from family, associates, theft, street connections, and other sources.[22] Furthermore, increased possession of legal guns in public by citizens and potential victims as a self-protective device in troubled times merely increases the risk for personal victimization and general gun violence in society, often with deadly results.[23]

Alcohol, Drugs, and Murder

Alcohol and drug use have been commonly associated with violent crimes, particularly the crime of murder.[24] According to the Uniform Crime Reports, in 2010, there were 642 murders committed in the United States that were directly attributed to circumstances involving narcotic drug laws and brawls due to the influence of drugs or alcohol.[25] However, many criminologists believe there is a much greater cause-and-effect correlation between alcohol, drugs, and murder.

In a study of criminal homicide, Marvin Wolfgang and R. B. Strohm found alcohol to be a factor in more than 60 percent of the cases.[26] Wolfgang further found that criminal homicides involving alcohol tended to be the most violent.[27] A study by Harwin Voss and John Hepburn reached similar conclusions. They found that alcohol was a factor in more than half of the 370 cases examined.[28] Herbert Block and Gilbert Geis linked alcohol to homicide, aggravated assault, and sexual crimes[29]; whereas R. N. Parker and L. Rebhun focused on the relationship between alcohol, selective disinhibition, and homicide.[30]

Other research has associated drug use with homicide and other violent crimes.[31] The National Institute of Justice recently found that more than half of the people arrested in Washington, D.C., and New York City for violent crimes had been using one or more illicit drugs when the crime was perpetrated.[32] Another study found that anywhere from one-half to three-quarters of violent crime arrestees in 12 large cities tested positive for illegal drug use.[33]

Such drugs as cocaine, crack cocaine, and marijuana and their use have been related to homicide offenders in studies by B. Spunt and colleagues,[34] and P. Goldstein and associates.[35] Researchers have found that offenders and victims in drug-involved homicides were far more likely than those in homicides not related to drugs to be known to law enforcement as drug users or traffickers in drugs.[36] A number of studies have shown that drug use has a positive correlation to drug dealing and violent crime, including murder.[37]

Table 2.2   Ten-Year Arrest Trends for Drug Abuse
Violations and Alcohol-Related Offenses, 2001–2010

Offense	2001	2010	Percent Change
Drug abuse violations	961,056	1,014,383	+5.5
Driving under the influence	860,398	836,018	−2.8
Liquor laws	403,068	321,255	−20.3
Drunkenness	399,835	373,886	−6.5

Source: U.S. Department of Justice, Federal Bureau of Investigation,
Crime in the United States: Uniform Crime Reports 2010, Table
32, Ten-Year Arrest Trends, 2001–2010, http://www.fbi.gov/
about-us/cjis/ucr/crime-in-the-u.s/2010/crime-in-the-u.s.-
2010/tables/10tbl32.xls (March 16, 2012).

In a study of murder cases in the 75 largest counties in the country, illegal drugs related to use, buying, dealing, and manufacturing were found to be involved in 16 percent of the murders and 18 percent of the defendants.[38] Violence associated with drug use and illegal drug networks has been referred to as "systemic" or the "traditionally aggressive patterns of interaction within the system of drug distribution and use."[39]

Arrest trends indicate that arrests for drug abuse offenses are on the rise, while alcohol-related offenses are declining overall. As seen in Table 2.2, from 2001 to 2010, total arrests for drug abuse violations increased 5.5 percent. Among arrestees for alcohol-related crimes, arrests for liquor law violations decreased the most at more than 20 percent, with arrests for drunkenness and driving under the influence dropping 6.5 percent and 2.8 percent, respectively, during the period.

In spite of the drop in homicide rates, the significant correlation between substance abuse and homicide or other violent crimes is clearly evident in self-report prisoner surveys. According to the Bureau of Justice Statistics (BJS), more than half of jail inmates convicted of violent crimes had been drinking alcohol before committing the crime.[40] Almost 7 in 10 people convicted of manslaughter had used alcohol prior to the incident. More than 4 in 10 violent prison inmates had used illegal drugs in the month preceding the offense, while nearly half of all male and female prisoners were under the influence of drugs or alcohol at the time of the crime.

Domestic Partner Homicide and Substance Abuse

Domestic homicides involving intimate partners has been strongly linked to substance abuse by the perpetrator and/or victim.[41] Abusive and homicidal male partners have been especially associated with alcohol and drug abuse,[42] including use of psychoactive drugs and a combination of alcohol and drug use.[43]

Studies on intimates, drugs, and homicide have found that battered women who murdered their batterers were more likely than abused women who did not kill their partners to use alcohol and other types of drugs.[44] Furthermore, male homicide victims of battered women have been shown to be almost twice as likely to have used alcohol on a daily basis than male partners of women nonkillers.[45]

Minorities, Substance Abuse, and Homicide

It appears that race and ethnicity does play a role with respect to substance abuse and homicide. A number of studies have found a disproportionate involvement of people in minority racial and ethnic groups in alcohol- or drug-related homicides.[46] In particular, African Americans, Native Americans, and Hispanics tend to have a significantly higher rate of homicide offending associated with alcohol or drugs than do other groups.[47] Researchers have further shown a strong relationship between minorities, gang involvement, drug crimes, the inner city, and murder.[48] (See also Chapter 1.) However, some studies have found a lower rate of alcohol or drug involvement among some minority homicide offenders, such as African Americans.[49]

Juveniles, Substance Abuse, and Murder

A significant correlation exists between juveniles who kill and substance abuse.[50] According to Kathleen Heide, the majority of the juveniles she evaluated who committed felony homicides used drugs and/or alcohol.[51] Other researchers have linked youth substance abuse to possession of firearms, bullying, gangs, and violent behavior, including murder.[52] Recent acts of school killings and juvenile parricide have predominantly involved substance abuse.[53] Drug and alcohol use by teenagers appears to predispose them to a number of violent behaviors such as murder and suicide.

Endnotes

1. U.S. Department of Justice, Bureau of Justice Statistics Selected Findings, *Firearm Injury and Death From Crime, 1993–97* (Washington: Office of Justice Programs, 2000), pp. 1–7; Philip J. Cook & Mark H. Moore, Guns, Gun Control, and Homicide, in M. Dwayne Smith & Margaret A. Zahn, Eds., *Studying and Preventing Homicide: Issues and Challenges* (Thousand Oaks: Sage, 1999), pp. 246–50.
2. U.S. Department of Justice, Federal Bureau of Investigation, *Crime in the United States: Uniform Crime Reports 2010*, http://www.fbi.gov/about-us/cjis/ucr/crime-in-the-u.s/2010/crime-in-the-u.s.-2010/tables/10shrtbl11.xls (March 14, 2012).

3. U.S. Department of Justice, National Crime Victimization Survey, Criminal Victimization, 2010 (Washington: Office of Justice Programs, 2011), p. 8, http://bjs.ojp.usdoj.gov/content/pub/pdf/cv10.pdf.

4. *Ibid.*

5. *Crime in the United States*, Expanded Homicide Data Table 8, Murder Victims, by Weapon, 2006–2010, http://www.fbi.gov/about-us/cjis/ucr/crime-in-the-u.s/2010/crime-in-the-u.s.-2010/tables/10shrtbl08.xls (March 14, 2012).

6. *Firearm Injury and Death From Crime, 1993–97*, p. 1.

7. Cited in U.S. Department of Justice, Bureau of Justice Statistics, *Sourcebook of Criminal Justice Statistics,* Table 3.127, http://www.albany.edu/sourcebook/index.html (March 11, 2012).

8. *Ibid.*, Table 3.128.

9. *Ibid.*; V. Beaman, J. L. Annest, J. A. Mercy, M. Kresnow, & D. A. Pollock, Lethality of Firearm-Related Injuries in the United States Population, *Annals of Emergency Medicine* 35 (2000): 258–66.

10. See, for example, R. S. Jung & L. A. Jason, Firearm Violence and the Effects of Gun Control Legislation, *American Journal of Community Psychology* 16 (1988): 515–24; P. J. Cook, The Effect of Gun Availability on Violent Crime Patterns, *Annals of the American Academy of Political and Social Sciences* 455 (1981): 63–79; S. H. Decker, S. Pennell, & A. Caldwell, *Illegal Firearms: Access and Use by Arrestees* (Washington: National Institute of Justice, 1997).

11. Cited in Cook & Moore, Guns, Gun Control, and Homicide, p. 247.

12. *Ibid.*

13. P. J. Cook & J. Ludwig, *Guns in America: Results of a Comprehensive National Survey on Firearms Ownership and Use* (Washington: Police Foundation, 1996).

14. *Ibid.*

15. Cook & Moore, Guns, Gun Control, and Homicide, p. 248; *Firearm Injury and Death From Crime, 1993–97*, pp. 1–5.

16. Cook & Moore, Guns, Gun Control, and Homicide, p. 248.

17. *Ibid.*, p. 249; A. Blumstein, Youth Violence, Guns, and the Illicit-Drug Industry, *Journal of Criminal Law and Criminology* 86 (1995): 10–36; K. M. Heide, Why Kids Keep Killing: The Correlates, Causes, and Challenges of Juvenile Homicide, *Stanford Law and Policy Review* 71 (1996): 43–49; H. M. Rose & P. D. McClain, *Race, Place, and Risk: Black Homicide in Urban America* (Albany: State University of New York Press, 1990).

18. *Firearm Injury and Death from Crime, 1993–97*, p. 2; *Crime in the United States*, pp. 14–16; D. F. Hawkins, Explaining the Black Homicide Rate, *Journal of Interpersonal Violence* 5 (1990): 151–63; R. B. Flowers, *Minorities and Criminality* (Westport: Greenwood, 1988).

19. Flowers, *Minorities and Criminality*, pp. 95–104; R. W. Beasley & G. Antunes, The Etiology of Urban Crime: An Ecological Analysis, *Criminology* 22 (1974): 531–50; Carolyn R. Block, Race/Ethnicity and Patterns of Chicago Homicide, 1965–1981, *Crime and Delinquency* 31 (1985): 104–16; R. Martinez, Latinos and Lethal Violence: The Impact of Poverty and Inequality, *Social Problems* 43 (1996): 131–46.

20. A. L. Kellerman, F. P. Rivara, N. B. Rushforth, J. G. Banton, D. T. Reay, J. T. Francisco, A. B. Locci, J. P. Prodzinski, B. B. Hackman, & G. Somes, Gun

Ownership as a Risk Factor for Homicide in the Home, *New England Journal of Medicine* 329 (1993): 1084–91.

21. Blumstein, Youth Violence, Guns, and the Illicit-Drug Industry, pp. 10–36; J. F. Sheley & J. D. Wright, *In the Line of Fire: Youth, Guns, and Violence in America* (New York: Aldine de Gruyter, 1995); R. Barri Flowers, *Kids Who Commit Adult Crimes: A Study of Serious Juvenile Criminality and Delinquency* (Binghamton: Haworth, 2002).

22. Cook & Moore, Guns, Gun Control, and Homicide, p. 256; Decker, Pennell, & Caldwell, *Illegal Firearms*; M. D. Smith, Sources of Firearm Acquisition Among a Sample of Inner City Youths: Research Results and Policy Implications, *Journal of Criminal Justice* 24 (1996): 361–67.

23. Cook & Moore, Guns, Gun Control, and Homicide, pp. 256–65; D. McDowall, C. Loftin, & B. Wiersema, Easing Concealed Firearms Laws: Effects on Homicide in Three States, *Journal of Criminal Law and Criminology* 86 (1995): 193–206; F. E. Zimring & G. J. Hawkins, *Crime Is Not the Problem: Lethal Violence in America* (New York: Oxford University Press, 1997).

24. See, for example, W. Wieczorek, J. Welte, & E. Abel, Alcohol, Drugs, and Murder: A Study of Convicted Homicide Offenders, *Journal of Criminal Justice* 18 (1990): 217–27; K. Auerhahn & R. N. Parker, Drugs, Alcohol, and Homicide, in M. D. Smith & M. A. Zahn, Eds., *Studying and Preventing Homicide: Issues and Challenges* (Thousand Oaks: Sage, 1999), pp. 97–114; P. Lindquist, Homicides Committed by Abusers of Alcohol and Illicit Drugs, *British Journal of Addiction* 86 (1991): 321–26.

25. *Crime in the United States*, Expanded Homicide Data Table 8, Murder Circumstances by Relationship, 2010, http://www.fbi.gov/about-us/cjis/ucr/crime-in-the-u.s/2010/crime-in-the-u.s.-2010/tables/10shrtbl10.xls (March 15, 2012).

26. M. E. Wolfgang & R. B. Strohm, The Relationship Between Alcohol and Criminal Homicide, *Quarterly Journal of Studies on Alcoholism* 17 (1956): 411–26.

27. M. E. Wolfgang, *Patterns in Criminal Homicide* (Philadelphia: University of Pennsylvania Press, 1958).

28. H. L. Voss & J. R. Hepburn, Patterns in Criminal Homicide in Chicago, *Journal of Criminal Law, Criminology, and Political Science* 59 (1968): 499–508.

29. H. A. Block & G. Geis, *Man, Crime, and Society* (New York: Random House, 1962).

30. R. N. Parker & L. Rebhun, *Alcohol and Homicide: A Deadly Combination of Two American Traditions* (Albany: State University of New York Press, 1995).

31. R. B. Flowers, *Drugs, Alcohol and Criminality in American Society* (Jefferson: McFarland, 1999), pp. 40–43, 148–50.

32. Cited in *Ibid.*, p. 42.

33. *Ibid.*

34. B. Spunt, H. Brownstein, P. Goldstein, M. Fendrich, & H. J. Liberty, Drug Use by Homicide Offenders, *Journal of Psychoactive Drugs* 27 (1995): 125–34.

35. P. Goldstein, H. H. Brownstein, P. J. Ryan, & P. A. Bellucci, Crack and Homicide in New York City, 1988: A Conceptually Based Event Analysis, *Contemporary Drug Problems* 16 (1989): 651–87.

36. H. H. Brownstein, H. Baxi, P. Goldstein, & P. Ryan, The Relationship of Drugs, Drug Trafficking, and Drug Traffickers to Homicide, *Journal of Crime and Justice* 15 (1992): 25–44.
37. Flowers, *Drugs, Alcohol, and Criminality in American Society*, pp. 42–43, 148–50.
38. U.S. Department of Justice, Bureau of Justice Statistics, *Murder in Large Urban Counties, 1988* (Washington: Government Printing Office, 1993), p. 5.
39. U.S. Department of Justice, Bureau of Justice Statistics, *Drugs, Crime, and the Justice System* (Washington: Government Printing Office, 1992), p. 5.
40. Flowers, *Drugs, Alcohol, and Criminality in American Society*, pp. 40–42, 170–72; U.S. Department of Justice, Bureau of Justice Statistics, *Survey of State Prison Inmates, 1991* (Washington: Government Printing Office, 1993), p. 23.
41. R. B. Flowers, *Domestic Crimes, Family Violence, and Child Abuse: A Study of Contemporary American Society* (Jefferson: McFarland, 2000), pp. 61–64; J. C. Campbell, *Assessing Dangerousness: Violence by Sexual Offenders, Batterers, and Child Abusers* (Thousand Oaks: Sage, 1995); N. C. Jurik & R. Winn, Gender and Homicide: A Comparison of Men and Women Who Kill, *Violence and Victims* 5, 4 (1990): 227–42; G. K. Kantor & M. A. Straus, Substance Abuse as a Precipitant of Wife Abuse Victimization, *American Journal of Drug and Alcohol Abuse* 15 (1989): 173–89.
42. G. K. Kantor & J. L. Jasinski, Dynamics and Risk Factors in Partner Violence, in J. L. Jasinski & L. M. Williams, Eds., *Partner Violence: A Comprehensive Review of 20 Years of Research* (Thousand Oaks: Sage, 1998), pp. 20–23; R. J. Gelles, *The Violent Home: A Study of Physical Aggression Between Husbands and Wives* (Thousand Oaks: Sage, 1972); J. Fagan, *Set and Setting Revisited: Influences of Alcohol and Illicit Drugs on the Social Context of Violent Events* (Rockville: National Institution on Alcohol Abuse and Alcoholism Research, 1993), pp. 161–91.
43. J. Fagan, Intoxication and Aggression, in M. Tonry & J. Q. Wilson, Eds., *Drugs and Crime* (Chicago: University of Chicago Press, 1990), pp. 241–320; P. J. Goldstein, P. A. Bellucci, B. J. Spunt, & T. Miller, *Frequency of Cocaine Use and Violence: A Comparison Between Women and Men* (New York: Narcotic and Drug Research, 1989).
44. W. R. Blount, I. J. Silverman, C. S. Sellers, & R. A. Seese, Alcohol and Drug Use Among Abused Women Who Kill, Abused Women Who Don't, and Their Abusers, *Journal of Drug Issues* 24 (1994): 165–77.
45. *Ibid.* See also J. W. Welte & E. L. Abel, Homicide: Drinking by the Victim, *Journal of Studies on Alcohol* 50 (1989): 197–201.
46. Flowers, *Minorities and Criminality*, pp. 83–130; D. Huizinga, R. Loeber, & T. P. Thornberry, *Urban Delinquency and Substance Abuse* (Washington: Office of Justice Programs, 1994); G. LaFree, Race and Crime Trends in the United States, 1946–1990, in D. F. Hawkins, Ed., *Ethnicity, Race and Crime: Perspectives Across Time and Place* (Albany: State University of New York Press, 1995), pp. 169–93.
47. Flowers, *Minorities and Criminality*, pp. 39–55, 83–130; R. T. Schaefer, *Racial and Ethnic Groups*, 5th ed. (New York: Harper Collins, 1993); M. B. Harris, Aggression, Gender, and Ethnicity, *Aggression and Violent Behavior* 1, 2 (1996): 123–46; A. Valdez, Persistent Poverty, Crime, and Drugs: U.S.–Mexican Border Region, in J. Moore & R. Pinderhughes, Eds., *In the Barrios: Latinos and the*

Underclass Debate (New York: Russell Sage, 1993), pp. 195–210; R. Bachman, *Death and Violence on the Reservation: Homicide, Family Violence, and Suicide in American Indian Populations* (Westport: Auburn House, 1992).

48. J. Fagan, The Social Organization of Drug Use and Drug Dealing Among Urban Gangs, *Criminology* 27 (1989): 633–69; P. J. Meehan & P. W. O'Carroll, Gangs, Drugs, and Homicide in Los Angeles, *American Journal of Disease Control* 146 (1992): 683–87; H. J. Brumm & D. O. Cloninger, The Drug War and the Homicide Rate: A Direct Correlation? *Cato Journal* 14 (1995): 509–17; J. Kasarda, Inner-City Concentrated Poverty and Neighborhood Distress: 1970–1990, *Housing Policy Debate* 4, 3 (1993): 253–302.

49. See, for example, Wieczorek, Welte, and Abel, Alcohol, Drugs, and Murder, pp. 217–27.

50. A. Blumstein, Youth Violence, Guns, and the Illicit-Drug Industry, pp. 10–36; M. Fendrich, M. E. Mackesy-Amiti, P. Goldstein, B. Spunt, & H. Brownstein, Substance Involvement Among Juvenile Murderers: Comparisons With Older Offenders Based on Interviews with Prison Inmates, *International Journal of the Addictions* 30 (1995): 1363–82.

51. K. M. Heide, Youth Homicide, in M. D. Smith & M. A. Zahn, Eds., *Studying and Preventing Homicide: Issues and Challenges* (Thousand Oaks: Sage, 1999), p. 188.

52. Flowers, *Kids Who Commit Adult Crimes*; Heide, Youth Homicide, p. 188; D. W. Osgood, *Drugs, Alcohol, and Violence* (Boulder: University of Colorado, Institute of Behavioral Science, 1995); R. M. Lerner, *America's Youth in Crisis* (Thousand Oaks: Sage, 1994).

53. Flowers, *Kids Who Commit Adult Crimes*; R. B. Flowers & H. L. Flowers, *Murders in the United States: Crimes, Killers, and Victims of the Twentieth Century* (Jefferson: McFarland, 2001), pp. 147–52, 183–87.

Murder and the Criminal Justice System

3

Violent crimes have been on the decline in recent years in the United States, with murder and nonnegligent manslaughter in particular showing the greatest reduction. This is attributed to a combination of factors including a decrease in gun violence by young people, law enforcement crackdowns on violent crime, and new laws imposing stiffer penalties and longer periods of incarceration for violent offenders. As a result, fewer people are being arrested for murder and going through the criminal justice process. However, the felonious killing of law enforcement has been on the rise, causing concern among those responsible for bringing violent and homicidal offenders to justice. Moreover, thousands of homicides continue to be committed each year in this country, affecting individuals from every walk of life. Blacks and Hispanics tend to be disproportionately involved in arrests and incarceration for murder, but Whites and offenders from other racial and ethnic groups are represented as well in homicide offender statistics. The crime of murder remains the top priority of law enforcement on the whole, and convicted murderers represent the most serious offenders among the nation's inmate population, including virtually all death row inmates.

Arrests and Murder

Official arrest data is collected through the Federal Bureau of Investigation's Uniform Crime Reporting (UCR) Program, which is a "nationwide cooperative statistical effort of over 17,000 city, county, and state law enforcement agencies voluntarily reporting data on crimes brought to their attention."[1] According to the UCR, in 2010 there were an estimated 14,748 arrests for murder and nonnegligent manslaughter in the United States, defined as "the willful (nonnegligent) killing of one human being by another. The classification of this offense ... is based solely on police investigation as opposed to the determination of a court, medical examiner, coroner, jury, or other judicial body."[2] The figure excludes "deaths caused by negligence, suicide, or accident; justifiable homicides; and attempts to murder or assaults to murder, which are scored as aggravated assaults."[3]

Murder Clearances

A crime is cleared or solved by a law enforcement agency "when at least one person is arrested, charged with the commission of an offense, and turned over to the court for prosecution … Just as the arrest of one individual may clear multiple crimes, the arrest of many persons may clear only one offense. Furthermore, clearances recorded for a specific year … may include offenses that occurred in previous years."[4] Exceptional clearances may occur when circumstances prevent formally charging an offender, such as the person's death due to suicide or justifiable homicide, or inability to extradite the offender.

In 2010, almost 65 percent of murders in the United States were cleared by law enforcement agencies, giving it the highest clearance rate among violent offenses, defined by the UCR as crimes involving force or the threat thereof. The percent of homicides cleared as the result of an arrest or exceptional means in cities, counties, and suburban areas in 2010 can be seen in Figure 3.1. In cities, 63.9 percent of the murder and nonnegligent manslaughter offenses were cleared by arrest or exceptional means, with metropolitan counties at 64.7 percent, nonmetropolitan counties at 75 percent, and suburban areas at 65.5 percent.

As shown in Figure 3.2, among the geographical regions in the country, the highest percentage of murders and nonnegligent manslaughters cleared by arrest or exceptional means in 2010 was in the South at 70.1 percent, followed by the West at 66.3 percent. The clearances were lowest in the Northeast and Midwest, where the percentages were 58.8 percent and 52 percent, respectively.

Murder clearances predominantly link homicides to adult offenders and victims. Whereas proportionately, the rate of juvenile involvement in murder clearances is typically lower than for any other serious offense.

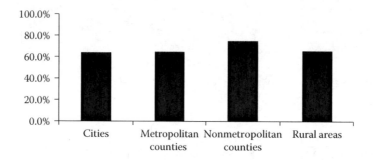

Figure 3.1 Percent of murder offenses[a] cleared by arrest or exceptional means, by population group, 2010. [a]Includes nonnegligent manslaughter. (Derived from U.S. Department of Justice, Federal Bureau of Investigation, *Crime in the United States: Uniform Crime Reports 2010*, Table 25, Percent of Offenses Cleared by Arrests or Exceptional means, by Population Group, 2010, http://www.fbi.gov/about-us/cjis/ucr/crime-in-the-u.s/2010/crime-in-the-u.s.-2010/tables/10tbl25.xls, March 17, 2012.

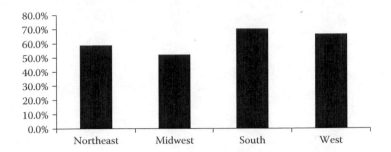

Figure 3.2 Percent of murder offenses (includes nonnegligent manslaughter) cleared by arrest or exceptional means, by geographical region, 2010. (Derived from U.S. Department of Justice, Federal Bureau of Investigation, *Crime in the United States: Uniform Crime Reports 2010*, Table 26, Percent of Offenses Cleared by Arrests or Exceptional Means, by Region and Geographic Division, 2010, http://www.fbi.gov/about-us/cjis/ucr/crime-in-the-u.s/2010/crime-in-the-u.s.-2010/tables/10tbl26.xls, March 17, 2012.)

Age of Arrestees for Murder

The vast majority of people arrested for murder and nonnegligent manslaughter are age 18 and older (see Figure 3.3). Ninety-one percent of the arrestees in the United States in 2010 were of adult age, with 9 percent juveniles, or younger than 18 years of age. More than 47 percent of those arrested for murder and nonnegligent manslaughter were under the age of 25, with 28 percent under 21 years of age. The highest number of arrestees of any age group for murder and nonnegligent manslaughter were those between the

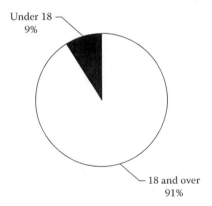

Figure 3.3 Persons arrested for murder and nonnegligent manslaughter, by age, 2010. (Derived from U.S. Department of Justice, Federal Bureau of Investigation, *Crime in the United States: Uniform Crime Reports 2010*, Table 41, Arrests, Persons Under Age 15, 18, 21, and 25 Years of Age, 2010, http://www.fbi.gov/aboutus/cjis/ucr/crime-in-the-u.s/2010/crime-in-the-u.s.-2010/tables/10tbl41.xls, March 19, 2012.)

ages of 18 and 21. Among juveniles, around 76 percent of arrestees for these offenses were ages 16 and 17.[5]

Sex of Arrestees for Murder

Murder is largely a male crime. In 2010, males constituted just over 89 percent of the total number of people arrested for murder and nonnegligent manslaughter in the United States, with females representing just under 11 percent of the arrestees (see Figure 3.4). With respect to sex and age, a proportionately higher number of adult females than adult males were arrested for murder and nonnegligent manslaughter, with about 92 percent of female arrestees age 18 and older, compared with around 91 percent of male arrestees.[6]

Race of Arrestees for Murder

Blacks are overrepresented in homicide arrests relative to their population figures. In 2010, Blacks constituted nearly half of all people arrested in the United States for murder and nonnegligent manslaughter (see Figure 3.5). Official data reveals that 48.7 percent of the arrestees were Black. However, Whites had the highest overall percentage of arrests for murder and nonnegligent manslaughter, with nearly 49.3 percent, and American Indian or Alaska Native and Asian or Pacific Islanders accounting for 2 percent of the total arrests.

A higher proportion of juvenile arrestees for murder were Black, while the proportion from other races was lower. Blacks accounted for 56.2 percent of those under the age of 18 arrested for murder and nonnegligent

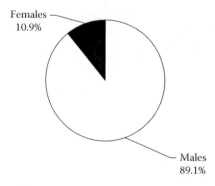

Figure 3.4 Persons arrested for murder and nonnegligent manslaughter, by sex, 2010. (Derived from U.S. Department of Justice, Federal Bureau of Investigation, *Crime in the United States: Uniform Crime Reports 2010*, Table 42, Arrests by Sex, 2010, http://www.fbi.gov/about-us/cjis/ucr/crime-in-the-u.s/2010/crime-in-the-u.s.-2010/tables/10tbl42.xls, March 19, 2012.)

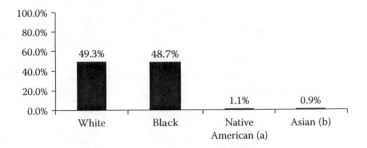

Figure 3.5 Persons arrested for murder and nonnegligent manslaughter, by race, 2010. (a) Includes American Indians and Alaskan Natives; (b) includes Pacific Islanders. (Derived from U.S. Department of Justice, Federal Bureau of Investigation, *Crime in the United States: Uniform Crime Reports 2010*, Table 43, Arrests by Race, 2010, http://www.fbi.gov/about-us/cjis/ucr/crime-in-the-u.s/2010/crime-in-the-u.s.-2010/tables/table-43, March 20, 2012.)

manslaughter, with Whites comprising 42.5 percent of the arrestees, and other racial minorities making up just over 1 percent of the total.[7]

Young Blacks in particular face the highest risk for involvement in homicidal behavior as arrestees, offenders, and victims.[8] Various studies have supported this conclusion, relating it to such correlates as a higher concentration of Blacks in high-crime-rate inner cities, possession of illegal weapons, youth gangs, and drug dealing.[9]

Although the UCR does not record ethnic differences among arrestees, many studies have found that Hispanics have a disproportionately high rate of involvement in homicides as arrestees and offenders.[10] Hispanic murder offenders tend to have some of the same characteristics as African American murder offenders with regard to inner-city dynamics and gang and drug involvement,[11] though some cultural differences exist in the commission and nature of homicides.[12]

Arrest Trends for Murder

UCR data indicates that fewer people are being arrested for murder. Ten-year arrest trends show that between 2001 and 2010, total arrests for murder and nonnegligent manslaughter in the United States dropped nearly 13 percent. The decline was even more dramatic among arrestees under the age of 18, decreasing by almost 24 percent, compared with nearly 12 percent for arrestees age 18 and older (see also Chapter 1).

Significant reductions in homicide arrests were also recorded by sex (see Figure 3.6). Between 2001 and 2010, male arrests for murder and nonnegligent manslaughter fell by almost 11 percent, while female arrests dropped by more than 29 percent.

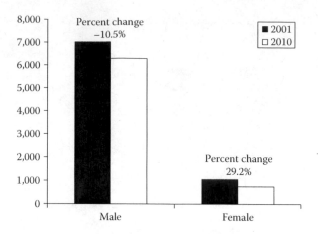

Figure 3.6 Ten-year arrest trends for murder and nonnegligent manslaughter, by sex, 2001–2010. (Derived from U.S. Department of Justice, Federal Bureau of Investigation, *Crime in the United States: Uniform Crime Reports 2010*, Table 33, Ten-Year Arrest Trends, by Sex, 2010, http://www.fbi.gov/aboutus/cjis/ucr/ crime-in-the-u.s/2010/crime-in-the-u.s.-2010/tables/10tbl33.xls, March 20, 2012.)

The decline was even steeper for male and female arrests under 18 for murder and nonnegligent manslaughter, decreasing 24 percent and just over 21 percent during the span, respectively.[13]

Limitations of the Uniform Crime Reports

Though the UCR program is currently the most important measurement of homicide and other serious and violent offenses, including arrest and offender characteristics, there are shortcomings that hamper the program's effectiveness. The most important with respect to homicide data may be the "unknown relationship between the number of crimes actually committed, the number of those reported to the police, and the number of those so reported, actually recorded and reported by the police."[14]

Each year there are hundreds, perhaps even thousands, of people reported (or not reported) missing in the United States and never heard from again. Many of these people could be the victims of foul play, but cannot be ascertained as such. In other instances where law enforcement may be aware of a homicide, more than 3 in 10 such cases are never cleared or solved to appear in UCR arrest data.

Other common criticisms against the UCR program include

- Official data reflect only those crimes that law enforcement agencies are aware of.
- Law enforcement agencies may be politically motivated or have other motives in underreporting or inflating arrest statistics.

- There is an over-reliance on percent changes in the total volume of violent and property offenses.
- There is an overlap in defining what constitutes a crime—such as arrest, charge, conviction, and/or incarceration.[15]

Some of the shortcomings of the UCR program are being addressed through its redesigned National Incidence-Based Reporting System (NIBRS) that "collects data on each single incident and arrest within 22 offense categories made up of 46 specific crimes called Group A offenses."[16] Included among these offenses are the homicide offenses of murder and nonnegligent manslaughter, negligent manslaughter, and justifiable homicide.

According to the FBI, "The goals of NIBRS are to enhance the quantity, quality, and timeliness of crime data collected by law enforcement and to improve the methodology used for compiling, analyzing, auditing, and publishing the collected crime data."[17] As such, the NIBRS is believed to be able to "provide law enforcement with … more detailed, accurate, and meaningful data than produced by the traditional summary UCR Program."[18]

In spite of the promise of the NIBRS, a study of its effects on UCR crime statistics with respect to homicide data found that "when comparing data from the same year for the jurisdictions in this study … murder rates are the same," for the UCR program and NIBRS.[19]

In 2007, 31 state UCR programs were certified for participation in the NIBRS, with more than 6,400 law enforcement agencies supplying NIBRS information to the UCR program.[20]

Law Enforcement Officers Killed

As the front line in the war on violent crimes and homicide, police are vulnerable when attempting to make arrests or investigating crimes. According to the FBI, in 2010 there were 56 law enforcement officers "feloniously killed" in the line of duty in the United States—8 more than were killed while on duty in 2009 and 15 more than the officers murdered in 2008.[21]

Firearms were the weapon used most often to kill police officers, with 55 dying by firearms, including 38 as the result of a handgun. Thirty-eight officers died in spite of wearing body armor during the fatal encounter, and 21 were murdered with firearms while being 5 feet or less from the shooter.[22]

Regionally, the vast majority of police officers were killed in the South (see Figure 3.7). Twenty-two officers were killed in the line of duty in southern states, 18 in western states, and 10 in midwestern states, with 3 officers of the law murdered in northeast states and 3 in the U.S. territory of Puerto Rico.

There were 69 known assailants alleged to have been involved in the 56 murders of law enforcement officers. All except 2 were identified as male,

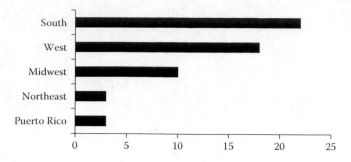

Figure 3.7 Law enforcement officers killed while on duty, by geographic region, 2010. (Derived from U.S. Department of Justice, Federal Bureau of Investigation, *Crime in the United States: Uniform Crime Reports 2010*, Law Enforcement Officers Killed and Assaulted, Officers Feloniously Killed, http://www.fbi.gov/about-us/cjis/ucr/leoka/leoka-2010/officersfeloniously-killed, March 21, 2012.)

with 83 percent of the alleged assailants having previously been arrested for criminal activity.

Murder and Prison Inmates

According to the Bureau of Justice Statistics, about 14.3 percent of sentenced state prisoners in the United States were convicted of murder or nonnegligent manslaughter.[23] The vast majority of homicide offenders behind bars are male, representing nearly 94 percent of such inmates. Overall, males constitute more than 9 in 10 state and federal prisoners, and people age 18 and over represent more than 99 percent of all those under state and federal correctional authority.[24]

The characteristics of state prison inmates convicted of murder by sex, race, and Hispanic origin in 2009 can be seen in Table 3.1. An estimated 195,900

Table 3.1 Estimated Number of Sentenced Prisoners Under State Jurisdiction for Homicide Offenses, by Gender, Race, and Hispanic Origin, 2009

Offense	All Inmates	Male	Female	White[a]	Black[a]	Hispanic
Total	1,365,800	1,272,200	93,600	532,000	582,100	212,100
Violent offenses	726,100	692,600	33,600	265,600	319,700	117,800
Murder[b]	179,000	168,800	10,200	55,700	84,000	32,300
Manslaughter	16,900	14,800	2,200	8,200	6,400	1,900

[a] Excludes Hispanics and persons identifying as two or more races.
[b] Includes nonnegligent manslaughter.
Source: Adapted from U.S. Department of Justice, Bureau of Justice Statistics, *Prisoners in 2010* (Washington: Office of Justice Programs, 2011), p. 28.

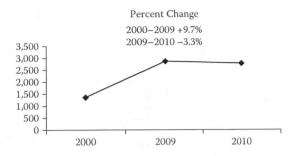

Figure 3.8 Sentenced federal prisoners convicted of homicide, 2000–2010 (includes murder, nonnegligent manslaughter, and negligent manslaughter). (Derived from U.S. Department of Justice, Bureau of Justice Statistics, *Prisoners in 2010*, Washington, D.C.: Office of Justice Programs, 2011, p. 30.)

sentenced prisoners were under state jurisdiction for murder and nonnegligent manslaughter. Of these, 183,600—or more than 9 out of every 10—were male inmates, with females constituting only around 6 percent of inmates.

With respect to race, an estimated 90,400 Blacks were incarcerated for murder and nonnegligent manslaughter, compared with 63,900 Whites. Blacks are overrepresented as sentenced prisoners for murder, accounting for nearly half the inmates.[25]

Hispanics are also disproportionately represented as prison inmates sentenced for murder. In 2009, there were approximately 34,200 state prisoners of Hispanic origin incarcerated for murder and nonnegligent manslaughter.

Nearly 17,000 inmates were imprisoned in state facilities for manslaughter in 2009, defined as "the unlawful killing of one human being by another without express or implied intent to do injury."[26] Whites constituted more than 48 percent of the prisoners sentenced for manslaughter.

Among sentenced federal prisoners in 2009, there were 2,863 inmates convicted of homicide offenses. This represented nearly a 10 percent increase from 2000 (see Figure 3.8). However, between 2009 and 2010, the number of sentenced inmates in federal prisons for murder, nonnegligent manslaughter, and negligent manslaughter fell by more than 3 percent.

Surveys of inmates show that a high percentage of homicide offenders were either victims of abuse or abused drugs or alcohol prior to being admitted to state prison.[27] Studies on homicide have found that killers often have histories of child physical or sexual abuse and substance abuse, both seen as antecedents to homicidal behavior.[28]

Capital Punishment

In 2010, there were 3,158 prisoners on death row for various murder offenses in the United States, including 58 with the Federal Bureau of Prisons,

Table 3.2 Prisoners Under Sentence of Death Who Were Executed or Received Other Dispositions, by Race and Hispanic Origin, 1977–2010

Race/Hispanic Origin	Total Under Sentence of Death, 1977–2010[b]	Prisoners Executed		Prisoners Who Received Other Dispositions[a]	
		Number	Percent of Total	Number	Percent of Total
Total	7,879	1,234	15.7%	3,487	44.3%
White[c]	3,816	700	18.3%	1,710	44.8%
Black[c]	3,225	424	13.1%	1,497	46.4%
Hispanic	715	96	13.4%	231	32.3%
All other races[c,d]	123	14	11.4%	49	39.8%

[a] Includes people removed from a sentence of death because of statutes struck down on appeal, sentences or convictions vacated, commutations, or death other than execution.

[b] Includes 5 people sentenced to death prior to 1977 who were still under sentence of death on 12/31/10; 374 people sentenced to death prior to 1977 whose death sentence was removed between 1977 and 12/31/10; and 7,500 people sentenced to death between 1977 and 2010.

[c] Excludes people of Hispanic/Latino origin.

[d] Includes American Indians, Alaska Natives, Asians, Native Hawaiians, and other Pacific Islanders.

Source: U.S. Department of Justice, Bureau of Justice Statistics, *Capital Punishment 2010–Statistical Tables* (Washington: Office of Justice Programs, 2011), p. 17.

according to the Justice Department.[29] Of these, 98 percent were men and 2 percent were women. More than half of the inmates with death sentences were White (55 percent), with 42 percent disproportionately Black. Hispanics constituted 14 percent of death row inmates. There were 15 fewer inmates sentenced to death in 2010 than in 2009.

Forty-six people were executed in the United States in 2010 (6 fewer than in 2009), while 20 death row inmates died through other means, and 53 were taken off death row due to their sentences being overturned or commuted.

Between 1977 and 2010, a total of 7,879 people were under a sentence of death in the United States (see Table 3.2). Among those on death row, less than 10 percent were executed, with more than 1 in 3 receiving dispositions other than execution.

The vast majority of inmates under a sentence of death are White or Black. More than 18 percent of the Whites on death row during the period were executed, while nearly 45 percent were given other dispositions. Just over 13 percent of Blacks and Hispanics under sentence of death were executed, while more than 46 percent of Blacks and over 32 percent of Hispanics received other dispositions. Death row inmates belonging to other racial groups were the least likely to be executed, at just over 11 percent, with around 4 in 10 given other dispositions.

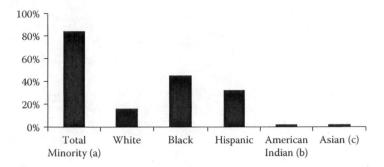

Figure 3.9 Juveniles in residential placement for criminal homicide, by race and ethnicity, 2010. (a) Includes persons categorized as "other race"; (b) includes Alaskan Natives; (c) includes Pacific Islanders. (Derived from U.S. Department of Justice, Office of Juvenile Justice and Delinquency Prevention, Statistical Briefing Book, Juveniles in Corrections, Race/Ethnicity Profile of Juveniles in Residential Placement, 2010, http://www.ojjdp.gov/ojstatbb/corrections/qa08205. asp?qaDate=2010, March 26, 2012.)

Juvenile Killers in Detention

Although an increasing number of juvenile murderers are being tried as adults, less than 1 percent of people in state and federal adult correctional facilities are 17 years of age and younger.[30] Most juveniles convicted of murder are held in juvenile residential placement facilities as opposed to private facilities. According to the Office of Juvenile Justice and Delinquency Prevention, in 2010, around 1 percent of juveniles in residential placement were there as the result of criminal homicide.[31]

Minorities are disproportionately likely to be in juvenile residential placement for murder. As shown in Figure 3.9, 84 percent of juveniles being held for criminal homicide in 2010 were minorities and 16 percent were White. Among minorities in detention, 45 percent were Black and 32 percent were Hispanic. Native American and Asian youths held for criminal homicide represented 2 percent each of the minority detainees.

Endnotes

1. U.S. Department of Justice, Federal Bureau of Investigation, *Crime in the United States: Uniform Crime Reports 1999* (Washington: Government Printing Office, 2000), p. 1.
2. *Ibid.*, pp. 13, 212.
3. *Ibid.*, p. 13.
4. *Ibid.*, p. 201.
5. U.S. Department of Justice, Federal Bureau of Investigation, *Crime in the United States: Uniform Crime Reports 2010*, http://www.fbi.gov/about-us/cjis/ucr/crime-in-the-u.s/2010/crime-in-the-u.s.-2010/index-page (March 19, 2012).

6. *Ibid.*

7. *Ibid.*

8. R. Barri Flowers, *Minorities and Criminality* (Westport: Greenwood, 1988), pp. 83–88, 131–39; L. A. Fingerhut & J. C. Kleinman, International and Interstate Comparisons of Homicide Among Young Males, *Journal of the American Medical Association* 263 (1990): 292–95; W. Bonger, *Race and Crime* (New York: Columbia University Press, 1943); H. M. Rose & P. D. McClain, *Race, Place, and Risk: Black Homicide in Urban America* (Albany: State University of New York Press, 1990).

9. See, for example, D. F. Hawkins, Explaining the Black Homicide Rate, *Journal of Interpersonal Violence* 5 (1990): 151–63; Y. Shin, D. Jedlicka, & E. S. Lee, Homicide Among Blacks, *Phylon* 39 (1977): 399–406; A. Blumstein, Youth Violence, Guns, and the Illicit-Drug Industry, *Journal of Criminal Law and Criminology* 86 (1995): 10–36.

10. Flowers, *Minorities and Criminality*, pp. 95–104; R. Martinez, Jr., & M. T. Lee, Latinos and Homicide, in M. D. Smith & M. A. Zahn, Eds., *Studying and Preventing Homicide: Issues and Challenges* (Thousand Oaks: Sage, 1999), pp. 159–74; F. Bean & M. Tienda, *The Hispanic Population of the United States* (New York: Russell Sage, 1987).

11. Flowers, *Minorities and Criminality*, pp. 83–104, 131–38; Martinez, Jr., & Lee, Latinos and Homicide, pp. 159–72; R. N. Parker, Poverty, Subculture of Violence, and Type of Homicide, *Social Forces* 67 (1989): 983–1007.

12. R. T. Shaefer, *Racial and Ethnic Groups*, 5th ed. (New York: Harper Collins, 1993); R. Martinez, Homicide Among Miami's Ethnic Groups: Anglos, Blacks, and Latinos in the 1990s, *Homicide Studies* 1 (1997): 17–34; R. D. Alba, J. R. Logan, & P. Bellair, Living With Crime: The Implications of Racial/Ethnic Differences in Suburban Location, *Social Forces* 73 (1994): 395–434.

13. *Crime in the United States 2010*, Table 33, Ten-Year Arrest Trends, by Sex, 2001–2010, http://www.fbi.gov/about-us/cjis/ucr/crime-in-the-u.s/2010/crime-in-the-u.s.-2010/tables/10tbl33.xls (March 20, 2012).

14. Charles H. Shireman & Frederic G. Reamer, *Rehabilitating Juvenile Justice* (New York: Columbia University Press, 1986), p. 20.

15. R. B. Flowers, *Female Crime, Criminals and Cellmates: An Exploration of Female Criminality and Delinquency* (Jefferson: McFarland, 1995), p. 20; E. W. Sutherland & D. R. Cressey, *Criminology*, 10th ed. (Philadelphia: J. B. Lippincott, 1978), p. 29.

16. FBI National Incidence-Based Reporting System, http://www.fbi.gov/ucr/faqs.htm.

17. FBI, http://www/fbi.gov/hq/cjisd/ucr.htm.

18. FBI National Incidence-Based Reporting System.

19. U.S. Department of Justice, Bureau of Justice Statistics Special Report, *Effects of NIBRS on Crime Statistics* (Washington: Office of Justice Programs, 2000), p. 1.

20. *Crime in the United States 2010*, NIBRS General FAQs, http://www.fbi.gov/about-us/cjis/ucr/frequently-asked-questions/nibrs_faqs.

21. *Ibid.*, Table 1, Law Enforcement Officers Feloniously Killed, 2000–2009, http://www2.fbi.gov/ucr/killed/2009/data/table 01.html.

22. *Ibid.*, Law Enforcement Officers Killed and Assaulted, Officers Feloniously Killed, 2010, http://www.fbi.gov/about-us/cjis/ucr/leoka/leoka-2010/officers-feloniously-killed.

23. U.S. Department of Justice, Bureau of Justice Statistics, *Prisoners in 2010* (Washington: Office of Justice Programs, 2011), p. 26.

24. *Ibid.*; U.S. Department of Justice, Bureau of Justice Statistics, *Correctional Populations in the United States, 1997* (Washington: Department of Justice, 2000).

25. U.S. Department of Justice, Bureau of Justice Statistics Bulletin, *Prisoners in 1999* (Washington: Office of Justice Programs, 2000), p. 10.

26. *American Heritage Dictionary* (New York: Dell, 1994), p. 506.

27. U.S. Department of Justice, Bureau of Justice Statistics, *Prior Abuse Reported by Inmates and Probationers* (Washington: Office of Justice Programs, 1999), p. 3; R. B. Flowers, *Drugs, Alcohol and Criminality in American Society* (Jefferson: McFarland, 1999), pp. 171–73.

28. Flowers, *Drugs, Alcohol and Criminality in American Society*, pp. 163–73; R. B. Flowers, *Domestic Crimes, Family Violence and Child Abuse: A Study of Contemporary American Society* (Jefferson: McFarland, 2000), pp. 197–202, 217.

29. U.S. Department of Justice, Bureau of Justice Statistics, *Capital Punishment 2010—Statistical Tables* (Washington: Office of Justice Programs, 2011), p. 1.

30. *Correctional Populations in the United States, 1997.*

31. U.S. Department of Justice, Office of Juvenile Justice and Delinquency Prevention, Statistical Briefing Book, *Juveniles in Corrections*, Offense Profile of Juveniles in Residential Placement by Sex, 2010, http://www.ojjdp.gov/ojstatbb/corrections/qa08304.asp?qaDate = 2010 (March 26, 2012).

Domestic Murder

II

Intimate Homicide 4

Domestic homicides are most likely to involve intimates. Each year in the United States, thousands of people are killed by husbands, wives, ex-spouses, boyfriends, girlfriends, and other ex-intimates. These homicides are typically a symptom of overall violence between intimates and often correlate with substance abuse, possession of firearms, sexual jealousy, separation, and related factors. Women are especially likely to be victims of intimate homicide, usually after a pattern of spousal or domestic violence. On the other hand, women are most likely to kill male intimates in self-defense from male violence or the threat of violence. Intimate homicides have been on the decline in recent years, but still pose a serious threat among intimates and often reflect other intrafamilial violent and homicidal behavior.

The Extent of Intimate Partner Homicide

How significant is the problem of homicide involving intimates? According to the U.S. Department of Justice, 1,336 people were murdered by an intimate—defined as a current or former spouse, or boyfriend or girlfriend—in the United States in 2010.[1] Intimate partner murders represented just over 10 percent of all homicides.

Women are far more likely to be victims of intimate homicide than men (see Figure 4.1). In 2010, 82 percent of those murdered by an intimate partner were female, compared with 18 percent male. Females in every age category are more likely to be victims of intimate partner homicide than males, with female and male victims in the 35- to 45-year-old age group murdered at a higher rate than intimates who are slain in other age categories.[2]

Women are more likely to be murdered by a male intimate than any other type of killer.[3] Studies show that more than twice as many women are murdered by an intimate partner than by a stranger.[4] Seven in 10 female victims of homicide were killed by a husband, ex-husband, boyfriend, or ex-boyfriend.[5] Separated or divorced women are especially at risk for being murdered by an ex-intimate. In one study, approximately half of the intimate homicides of women were committed after the victim separated from the male murderer.[6] Another study found that 1 in 4 women slain by intimate partners were killed while trying to separate.[7]

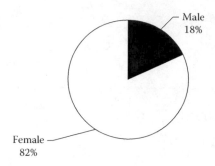

Figure 4.1 Victims of intimate partner homicides, by gender, 2010. (From U.S. Department of Justice, Federal Bureau of Investigation, *Crime in the United States: Uniform Crime Reports 2010*, Expanded Homicide Data Table 10, Murder Circumstances by Relationship, 2010, http://www.fbi.gov/about-us/cjis/ucr/crime-in-the-u.s/2010/crime-in-the-u.s.-2010/tables/10shrtbl10.xls, March 27, 2012.)

In spite of the general one-sided nature of intimate partner homicides, both men and women have shown themselves to be capable of committing intimate murder, as the following cases indicate:

- In December 2010, 42-year-old Jennifer Trayers stabbed her 41-year-old Navy doctor husband, Frederick Trayers, to death in San Diego, California, after he got home from night duty at Balboa Naval Medical Center. She was despondent upon learning that he was having an affair. On February 12, 2012, a jury convicted her of second degree murder.
- On September 11, 2009, 56-year-old Steve Nunn shot to death his ex-fiancée Amanda Ross in the parking lot of her apartment in Lexington, Kentucky. Six months earlier, Ross had gotten a protective order against Nunn, son of former Kentucky Governor Louie Nunn, for domestic violence. Steve Nunn, once a member of the Kentucky House of Representatives and Commonwealth of Kentucky Deputy Secretary of Health and Human Services, was motivated by revenge after losing his job. On June 28, 2011, Nunn avoided a possible death sentence by pleading guilty to the murder of Ross and was given a life sentence.
- On July 4, 2009, 20-year-old Sahel Kazemi shot to death her 36-year-old married lover, Steve McNair, in a condominium in downtown Nashville, Tennessee, before fatally shooting herself. McNair, a retired NFL football player, had been dating Kazemi, whose murder-suicide was apparently motivated by financial problems and a belief that McNair was seeing another woman outside his marriage.

- On January 24, 2009, 44-year-old Derek Lamont Wilson beat to death his 33-year-old girlfriend, Leanet McGee, at the couple's home in Dayton, Ohio, out of jealousy. On March 21, 2011, Wilson was convicted on counts that included murder, felonious assault, and evidence tampering.
- On November 16, 2007, 64-year-old James Wease stabbed to death his 43-year-old wife, Dana Wease, inside their home in Anchorage, Alaska, after the two got into a fight. Wease, who had previously been convicted of second degree murder in 1978 for killing a man, later tossed his wife's remains along a ravine. On March 20, 2012, a jury found Wease guilty of second degree murder and tampering with evidence.
- On July 5, 2002, 42-year-old Dana Chandler shot to death her 47-year-old ex-husband, Mike Sisco, and his fiancée, Karen Harkness, at Harkness's home in Topeka, Kansas. Enraged that Sisco had planned to remarry, Chandler drove from Denver to Topeka to carry out the execution. On March 22, 2012, a jury convicted Chandler on two counts of premeditated first degree murder.
- On May 28, 1998, 40-year-old Brynn Hartman shot to death her 49-year-old actor husband, Phil Hartman, before killing herself in their home in Encino, California. Brynn Hartman, a one-time model, had a history of substance abuse, temper tantrums, and jealousy.
- On January 16, 1997, Scott Falater stabbed his wife, Yarmila, to death at the couple's home in Phoenix, Arizona. The 42-year-old engineer had a history of sleepwalking and was under tremendous work stress when he killed his wife. A jury found him guilty of first degree murder and sentenced him to life in prison with no chance of parole.
- On October 23, 1989, 30-year-old Charles Stuart shot to death his pregnant wife, Carol, in their car in Boston, Massachusetts. The couple's infant child, delivered by cesarean section, died 17 days later. Stuart, who was having an affair, stood to gain financially by collecting his wife's life insurance. In January 1990, he committed suicide as authorities closed in on him.
- On March 4, 1985, 76-year-old Roswell Gilbert shot to death his 73-year-old wife, Emily, in the couple's condominium in Ft. Lauderdale, Florida. The victim suffered from Alzheimer's disease. Gilbert, a retired engineer, was found guilty of first degree murder and sentenced to life in prison with no chance for parole. On August 2, 1990, the 81-year-old intimate killer was granted clemency by Florida's governor and released from prison.
- In the 1980s, Betty Lou Beets murdered two husbands and attempted to murder a third in Texas. The black widow murderess was motivated

by monetary gain in collecting on life insurance and a pension. Beets was charged with capital murder in the shooting deaths of Doyle Barker and James Beets, found guilty, and sentenced to death. She was executed in February 2000.

- On March 10, 1980, 56-year-old Jean Harris shot and killed her 69-year-old lover Herman Tarnower in his home in Purchase, New York. The murder of the author of *The Scarsdale Diet* book came following a 14-year tumultuous relationship between the two. Harris was convicted and sentenced to 15 years to life in prison. In January 1993, she was released after the governor commuted her sentence.[8]

Trends in Intimate Partner Homicides

Homicide long-term trends indicate an overall decrease in the number of intimate-related murders. According to the Bureau of Justice Statistics' *Homicide Trends in the U.S.*, an estimated 64,529 women and men were killed by an intimate partner in the United States between 1976 and 2005 (see Table 4.1). Since 1983, the number of male victims of intimate homicide was below a thousand each year, while female victims of intimate murder has remained above a thousand every year since 1976.

As shown in Figure 4.2, the number of males murdered by an intimate fell by nearly 75 percent from 1976 to 2005, while females killed by an intimate dropped almost 26 percent over the period. However, from 2004 to 2005, the number of females murdered by an intimate rose by more than 2 percent, with the number of male victims of intimate homicide decreasing by just over 4 percent during the span.

Since 2000, around one in three female homicide victims were killed by an intimate partner, compared with about 3 percent of male homicide victims being murdered by an intimate.[9] The proportion of female victims of murder in which the killer was an intimate has been on the rise, whereas the proportion of male murder victims killed by a romantic partner or ex-partner has been on the decline. In a study of gender-specific differences in homicide rates between 1976 and 1987 involving victims and offenders age 16 and older, A. L. Kellermann and J. A. Mercy found that more than twice the number of women were shot and killed by their spouses or other intimate partners than were slain by strangers with firearms, with knives, or by other methods.[10]

Most victims of intimate partner homicide are killed by a husband or wife (see Figure 4.3). Between 2000 and 2005, 4,651 intimate homicide victims in the United States were murdered by a spouse, with 4,185 victims killed by a boyfriend or girlfriend. The lowest numbers of intimate homicides during the period were those involving ex-spouses as victims and perpetrators, at 331.

Table 4.1 Intimate Partner Homicide, by Gender, 1976–2005

	Number of Victims of Intimate Partner Homicide				
Year	Male	Female	Year	Male	Female
1976	1,304	1,587	1991	734	1,492
1977	1,248	1,421	1992	662	1,436
1978	1,159	1,473	1993	638	1,563
1979	1,229	1,498	1994	654	1,401
1980	1,169	1,543	1995	521	1,311
1981	1,232	1,558	1996	476	1,299
1982	1,093	1,477	1997	413	1,202
1983	1,067	1,456	1998	460	1,302
1984	947	1,432	1999	381	1,195
1985	927	1,542	2000	382	1,232
1986	946	1,581	2001	344	1,187
1987	891	1,482	2002	339	1,182
1988	816	1,568	2003	330	1,156
1989	862	1,410	2004	344	1,155
1990	820	1,485	2005	329	1,181

Note: Information on the relationship between the victim and the offender was not reported for 35.2% of all homicides from 1976 to 2005. These data are not included in the above table.

Source: Office of Justice Programs, Bureau of Justice Statistics, *Homicide Trends in the U.S.*, http://bjs.ojp.usdoj.gov/content/homicide/intimates.cfm#intimates (March 27, 2012).

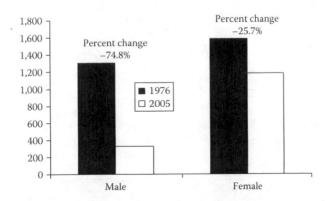

Figure 4.2 Intimate partner homicides, by gender, 1976–2005. (Derived from Office of Justice Programs, Bureau of Justice Statistics, *Homicide Trends in the U.S.*, http://bjs.ojp.usdoj.gov/content/homicide/intimates.cfm#intimates, March 27, 2012.)

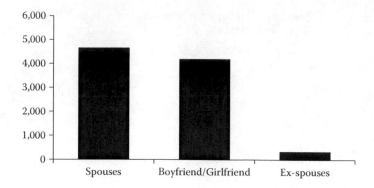

Figure 4.3 Intimate partner homicide victims, by relationship to killer, 2000–2005. (Derived from Office of Justice Programs, Bureau of Justice Statistics, Homicide Trends in the U.S., Intimate Homicide Victims by Relationship, http://bjs.ojp.usdoj.gov/content/homicide/intimates.cfm#intimates, March 28, 2012.)

A breakdown of intimate homicide victims in 2010, by relationship to the killer, can be seen in Figure 4.4. There were a total of 1,336 victims of intimate homicide where the victim was a wife, husband, girlfriend, or boyfriend. Victims were far more likely to be wives or girlfriends than husbands or boyfriends. Female victims of intimate homicide constituted 82 percent of total victims during the year.

With respect to race and gender, intimate homicide rates of victimization for Blacks and White males have generally declined among spouses and unmarried significant others between 1976 and 2005, according to the Bureau of Justice Statistics.[11] However, for White female girlfriends in particular, the

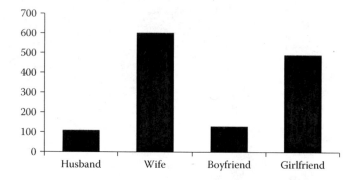

Figure 4.4 Intimate homicide victims, by relationship to perpetrator, 2010. (From U.S. Department of Justice, Federal Bureau of Investigation, *Crime in the United States: Uniform Crime Reports 2010* , Expanded Homicide Data Table 10, Murder Circumstances by Relationship, 2010, http://www.fbi.gov/about-us/cjis/ucr/crime-in-the-u.s/2010/crime-in-the-u.s.-2010/tables/10shrtbl10.xls, March 28, 2012.)

2005 rate of victimization was higher than in 1976 and rose from 2004, as was the case for victimization among White spouses or ex-spouses.

The rate of victimization also grew for Black female spouses and ex-spouses and girlfriends from 2004 to 2005. Black girlfriends had the highest intimate homicide rate of any group in 2005, in spite of a 66 percent decrease since 1976. The victimization rate for Black male spouses or ex-spouses was 20 times higher in 1976 than the 2005 rate.

The Dynamics of Domestic Violence

The strong relationship between domestic violence and intimate homicide has been clearly documented in studies.[12] According to the National Crime Victimization Survey (NCVS), roughly 509,230 crimes of violence were perpetrated against people by husbands, wives, former spouses, and boyfriends and girlfriends in the United States in 2010.[13] Of these, 407,700—or around 80 percent—of the intimate partner victimizations were against women. Among violent victimizations, females were about four times as likely as males to be victims of intimate violence. Around 4 in 10 female victims of domestic violence live in households with children younger than 12 years of age, and half of the victims sustained physical injuries as a result of the intimate partner violence.

Other researchers have put the number of intimate partners involved in domestic violence into the millions. The American Medical Association reported that 4 million spouses are beaten in the United States every year;[14] the Family Violence Prevention Fund estimated that 3.9 million women married or living with someone were victims of intimate violence annually.[15]

Some studies show that males are also being battered, if not to the same degree and duration as females. Robert Langley and Richard Levy estimated that 12 million men have been physically abused by their spouses at some time during their marriage.[16] Suzanne Steinmetz estimated that 280,000 men are battered by their partners every year in this country.[17] Another study estimated that 2 million husbands and 1.8 million wives have been victims of severe marital violence.[18] Murray Straus approximated that 65 percent of all married couples were involved in spousal abuse, with 25 percent of the incidences were of a serious nature.[19]

Gender studies in domestic violence indicate that the typical pattern of abuse has the male as the aggressor and the female as the victim. According to the NCVS, the rate of female victimization in intimate violence was five times greater than the rate of male victimization.[20] Police reports of complaints of intimate violence perpetrated by males outnumber reports of domestic violence committed by females about 12 to 1.[21] Richard Gelles found that 47 percent of the husbands sampled had ever battered a spouse, compared to 32 percent of wives.[22]

Studies show that in intimate homicides, men are significantly less likely than women to have been physically assaulted by the victim before committing the murder.[23] However, men are far more likely than women to kill an intimate somewhere other than a shared residence, as well as commit multiple murders in the process of killing a female intimate and take their own lives after perpetrating the intimate partner homicide.[24]

Researchers have further found the following characteristics and nature of intimate violence:

- One-third of women and men have been witnesses to an act of domestic violence.
- Three in 10 women admitted to a hospital emergency department sustained injuries identified as due to battering.
- Four in 10 severely injured battered women in hospital emergency departments required prior medical treatment due to intimate violence.
- Females age 16 to 24 have the highest victimization rate of nonlethal intimate violence.
- Black women have a higher rate of victimization due to intimate violence than White women do.
- Seven out of 10 female victims of domestic violence were physically assaulted.
- Women in low-income households have a higher rate of nonlethal intimate violence than women in high-income households.
- Three-fourths of nonlethal intimate violence occurs at or near the victim's home.[25]

Intimate Violence Among Nonmarital and Estranged Couples

While much of the research on domestic violence has focused on married couples, studies show that the incidence of intimate violence among non-married or divorced intimates may be as high or higher, and is also a factor in intimate partner homicides. A disproportionate number of cohabiting couples have been found to be involved in intimate violence.[26] Kersti Yllo and Murray Straus found that cohabiting couples reported more incidents of domestic violence than did married couples.[27]

According to the BJS, separated or divorced women are 14 times more likely than married women to report having been battered by a spouse or ex-spouse.[28] Although separated or divorced women constitute only 10 percent of all women, they reported 75 percent of all violence between intimates.[29] Experts on intimate homicide have found that women who leave or threaten to leave their abusive spouse have a greater likelihood of being killed by their partner than women who stay in the marriage.[30]

Dating couples also face the risk of intimate violence and homicide. One study found that 60 percent of young women were currently in an abusive relationship.[31] Surveys reveal that about one in three females will be victimized by intimate violence before turning eighteen.[32] Dating violence has been shown to mirror marital violence in many respects. "Victims dating their batterers experience the same patterns of power and control as their counterparts in abusive marriages or cohabitators, and clearly dating violence can be just as lethal."[33]

Why Men Murder Intimates

Men typically commit uxoricide or murder a nonmartial intimate in relation to such factors as a history of abusing the partner, arguments, sexual jealousy, separation or divorce, child custody issues, substance abuse, problems on the job, suicidal behavior, and mental illness.[34] Studies further show that homicidal men are at a significantly higher risk of murdering an intimate if such men were victims of or witnesses to domestic violence during childhood,[35] have a history of involvement with the criminal justice stystem,[36] or had protective or restraining orders issued against them.[37]

Most experts agree that male loss of control over an intimate mate is one of the most important correlates of domestic homicide. According to Charles Ewing, "Batterers have an obsessive if not a pathological need to control the lives of the women with whom they share intimate relationships."[38] Ronald Holmes and Stephen Holmes have suggested that for many male perpetrators of intimate murder killing may be viewed as "an act of control," in response to an inability to control a female mate's desire for independence or self-direction.[39]

Researchers have noted a correlation between uxoricidal men and their victim wives and abandonment, separation, rejection, and divorce. In George Barnard and colleagues' study of spouse homicide, nearly 60 percent of the male offenders were separated from their wives when they murdered them.[40] Similarly, more than half of the women murdered by intimates in J. Campbell's study were estranged from their spouses at the time of the homicide.[41] Angela Browne and associates found in their study of intimate partner homicides that the risk for women to become victims of spouse murder after a separation or divorce could last for years.[42]

Many men kill their intimates as a result of intense rage or an act of revenge. Such men are more likely to be especially brutal in intimate partner homicides. Studies have found a high percentage of overkill or violent murders (involving multiple types of acts perpetrated against or injuries sustained by the victim) among male-perpetrated intimate killings.[43]

In exploring the differences between male and female intimate partner homicides, Rebecca Dobash and colleagues note that

> men often kill wives after lengthy period of prolonged physical violence ... the roles in such cases are seldom if ever reversed.... Men commonly hunt down and kill wives who have left them; women hardly ever behave similarly. Men kill wives as part of planned murder-suicides; analogous acts by women are almost unheard of. Men kill in response to revelations of wife infidelity; women almost never respond similarly.... A large proportion of the spouse-killing perpetrated by wives, but almost none ... perpetrated by husbands, are acts of self-defense.[44]

Why Women Murder Intimates

Most women who kill their intimate male partners do so in self-defense or to protect others from harm. Studies show that women perpetrators of spouse murder tend to more often kill as a self-defense mechanism when being battered, threatened as such, or feel that they or their children face the serious risk of bodily harm or death.[45]

The correlation between the battering of women and lethal violence perpetrated by or against their abusive mates has been clearly documented in the literature.[46] According to the book *Domestic Crimes, Family Violence and Child Abuse*, a woman is battered by her husband every nine seconds in the United States; and 1 in 5 abused women have reported being the victim of at least three assaults by a husband or ex-husband within the past six months.[47] It has been estimated that up to two million women are the victims of severe intimate partner violence every year in this country.[48] Diana Russell reported that more than 2 out of every 10 women who had ever been married were the victims of domestic spousal violence during some time in their lives.[49]

Research has shown that intimate violence accounts for roughly one-fifth of all violent crimes against women.[50] As many as 7 in 10 female homicide victims are killed by a spouse, ex-spouse, or boyfriend.[51] About two-thirds of the victims are battered women.[52]

For many women, within this dangerous, violent, and potentially deadly atmosphere, striking back with lethal force may seem the only option for survival. A study of female perpetrated spouse killings in Kansas City found that in 90 percent of the cases, the police had responded to domestic disturbance calls at least once in the two years prior to the homicide; and in half of the cases the police had gone to the house of the offender and victim on at least five occasions.[53] In a study of 30 female state prisoners in California who had murdered their husbands, 28 percent were identified as victims of wife battering.[54]

A psychosocial study of homicidal women by J. Totman found that key factors in intimate partner homicides committed by women were male intimate physical aggression and the perception that there were no other viable choices to escape the abusive environment.[55] A similar finding was made by Browne in the study of why battered women kill their mates.[56]

According to Lenore Walker, "most women who killed their batterers have little memory of any cognitive processes other than an intense focus on their own survival."[57] Eilssa Benedek described the typical pattern of a battered woman driven to murder her male intimate partner:

> Such a woman often comes from a home where she has observed and experienced ... violence and sees ... as a norm in social interaction and as a solution for conflict. Marriage is frequently seen as an escape route, but her choice of husband is not intelligently determined. Thus, the potential offender often chooses a mate with a high penchant for violence. She has been beaten repeatedly and brutally for a period of years by a spouse or lover who may be drunk, sober, tired, depressed, elated, mentally ill, or just angry. Lacking educational and financial resources, she describes a feeling of being trapped. This feeling increases proportionately with the number of young children she has.... The battered wife has turned to social agencies, police, prosecutors, friends, ministers, and family, but they have not offered meaningful support or advice.... Abused women who have murdered their spouses reveal that they feel that homicide was the only alternative left to them.[58]

Although most female killers of intimates reflect the battered women's syndrome as the primary motivation, some women kill their mates for other reasons, such as financial motives. History is replete with examples of women, known as *black widows*, who kill a mate or successive mates to collect insurance payments or other financial or material gain.[59] In fact, the evidence suggests that historically, more females may have killed intimates for profit than males.[60]

Women have also been known to murder husbands or lovers due to jealousy, control issues, adultery one way or the other, substance abuse, stress, and mental illness.[61] Some studies suggest that biological factors such as depression and premenstrual syndrome may play a role in partner homicide and other crimes of violence committed by women.[62]

Endnotes

1. U.S. Department of Justice, Federal Bureau of Investigation, *Crime in the United States: Uniform Crime Reports 2010*, Expanded Homicide Data Table 10, Murder Circumstances by Relationship, 2010, http://www.fbi.gov/about-us/cjis/ucr/crime-in-the-u.s/2010/crime-in-the-u.s.-2010/tables/10shrtbl10.xls (March 27, 2012).

2. *Ibid.*; Office of Justice Programs, Bureau of Justice Statistics, *Homicide Trends in the U.S.*, http://bjs.ojp.usdoj.gov/content/homicide/intimates.cfm#intimates (March 27, 2012).

3. A. Browne & K. R. Williams, Exploring the Effect of Resource Availability and the Likelihood of Female-Perpetrated Homicides, *Law and Society Review* 23 (1989): 75–94; A. L. Kellermann & J. A. Mercy, Men, Women, and Murder: Gender-Specific Differences in Rates of Fatal Violence and Victimization, *Journal of Trauma* 33 (1992): 1–5; M. A. Zahn, Homicide in the Twentieth Century: Trends, Types and Causes, in T. R. Gurr, ed., *Violence in America; Vol. 1. The History of Violence* (Thousand Oaks: Sage, 1989), pp. 216–34.

4. Kellermann & Mercy, Men, Women, and Murder, pp. 1–5.

5. J. Campbell, "Prediction of Homicide of and by Battered Women," in J. Campbell & J. Milner, Eds., *Assessing Dangerousness: Potential for Further Violence of Sexual Offenders, Batterers, and Child Abusers* (Thousand Oaks: Sage: 1995).

6. U.S. Department of Justice, Bureau of Justice Statistics, *Female Victims of Violent Crime* (Washington: Office of Justice Programs, 1991), p. 5.

7. *Ibid.*; L. Saltzman & J. Mercy, Assaults Between Intimates: The Range of Relationships Involved, in A. Wilson, ed., *Homicide: The Victim/Offender Connection* (Cincinnati: Anderson, 1993).

8. R. B. Flowers & H. L. Flowers, *Murders in the United States: Crimes, Killers and Victims of the Twentieth Century* (Jefferson: McFarland, 2001), pp. 77–78, 110, 118, 140; Woman Convicted in 2002 Murders of Ex-Husband, His Fiancée, *Kansas City Star*, http://www.kansascity.com/2012/03/22/3507641/woman-convicted-in-2002-murders.html (March 26, 2012); Lou Grieco, "Man Convicted of Killing His Girlfriend," *Dayton Daily News* (March 21, 2011), http://www.daytondailynews.com/blogs/content/shared-gen/blogs/dayton/daytoncourts/entries/2011/03/21/man_convicted_of_killing_his_g.html; Wikipedia, the Free Encyclopedia, Steve Nunn, http://en.wikipedia.org/wiki/Steve_Nunn (March 27, 2012); Casey Grove, Anchorage Man Convicted of Killing His Wife in 2007, *Anchorage Daily News* (March 21, 2012), http://www.adn.com/2012/03/20/2381977/anchorage-man-convicted-of-killing.html.

9. *Homicide Trends in the U.S.* See also R. B. Flowers, *Domestic Crimes, Family Violence and Child Abuse: A Study of Contemporary American Society* (Jefferson: McFarland, 2000), p. 62.

10. Kellermann & Mercy, Men, Women, and Murder, pp. 1–5.

11. *Homicide Trends in the U.S.*; U.S. Department of Justice, Bureau of Justice Statistics Special Report, *Intimate Partner Violence* (Washington: Office of Justice Programs, 2000), p. 3.

12. Flowers, *Domestic Crimes, Family Violence and Child Abuse*, pp. 17, 62–64; Campbell, Prediction of Homicide of and by Battered Women; Neil Websdale, *Understanding Domestic Homicide* (Boston: Northeastern University Press, 1999), pp. 19–23; P. W. Easteal, *Killing the Beloved: Homicide Between Adult Sexual Intimates* (Canberra: Australian Institute of Criminology, 1993).

13. *Intimate Partner Violence*, p. 1; U.S. Department of Justice, Bureau of Justice Statistics, National Crime Victimization Survey, Criminal Victimization, 2010 (Washington: Office of Justice Programs, 2011), pp. 9–10.

14. Cited in Flowers, *Domestic Crimes, Family Violence and Child Abuse*, p. 16.

15. The Commonwealth Fund, First Comprehensive National Health Survey of American Women Finds Them at Significant Risk, news release, New York, July 14, 1993.
16. R. Langley & R. C. Levy, *Wife Beating: The Silent Crisis* (New York: Dutton, 1977).
17. S. K. Steinmetz, The Battered Husband Syndrome, *Victimology* 2 (1978): 507.
18. R. J. Gelles, The Myth of Battered Husbands, *Ms* (October 1979): 65–66, 71–72.
19. Cited in Flowers, *Domestic Crimes, Family Violence and Child Abuse*, p. 30.
20. U.S. Department of Justice, Bureau of Justice Statistics Factbook, *Violence by Intimates* (Washington: Office of Justice Programs, 1998), p. 3.
21. R. B. Flowers, *Demographics and Criminality: The Characteristics of Crime in America* (Westport: Greenwood, 1989), p. 154.
22. R. J. Gelles, *The Violent Home: A Study of Physical Aggression Between Husbands and Wives* (Thousand Oaks: Sage, 1972), pp. 50–52.
23. A. Browne, K. R. Williams, & D. G. Dutton, Homicide Between Intimate Partners, in M. D. Smith & M. A. Zahn, eds., *Studying and Preventing Homicide: Issues and Challenges* (Thousand Oaks, Sage, 1999), p. 68.
24. *Ibid.*; P. M. Marzuk, K. Tardiff, & C. S. Hirsh, The Epidemiology of Murder-Suicide, *Journal of the American Medical Association* 267 (1992): 3179–83.
25. Flowers, *Domestic Crimes, Family Violence and Child Abuse*, pp. 17–18, 45.
26. B. E. Carlson, Battered Women and Their Assailants, *Social Work* 22, 6 (1977): 456; J. J. Gayford, Wife Battering: A Preliminary Survey of 100 Cases, *British Medical Journal* 1 (1975): 194–197.
27. K. Yllo and M. A. Straus, Interpersonal Violence Among Married and Cohabiting Couples, paper presented at the annual meeting of the National Council on Family Relationships, Philadelphia, 1978.
28. *Female Victims of Violent Crime*, p. 5.
29. *Ibid.*
30. Campbell, Prediction of Homicide of and by Battered Women.
31. R. Bettin, Young Women's Resource Center, testimony at Iowa House of Representatives Public Hearing on Dating Violence, March 31, 1992.
32. S. Kuehl, Legal Remedies for Teen Dating Violence, in B. Levy, ed., *Dating Violence: Young Women in Danger* (Seattle: Seal Press, 1998), p. 73.
33. Flowers, *Domestic Crimes, Family Violence and Child Abuse*, p. 78.
34. *Ibid.*, pp. 82–91; Websdale, *Understanding Domestic Homicide*, p. 19; M. Wilson & M. Daly, Spousal Homicide Risk and Estrangement, *Violence and Victims* 8, 1 (1993): 3–16; J. Buteau, A. Lesage, & M. Kiely, Homicide Followed by Suicide: A Quebec Case Series, 1988–1990, *Canadian Journal of Psychiatry* 38 (1993): 552–56.
35. J. Fagan, D. Stewart, & K. Hanson, Violent Men or Violent Husbands: Background Factors and Situational Correlates of Domestic and Extra-Domestic Violence, in D. Finkelhor, R. Gelles, G. Hotaling, & M. Straus, Eds., *The Dark Side of Families* (Thousand Oaks: Sage, 1983); D. S. Kalmuss, The Intergenerational Transmission of Marital Aggression, *Journal of Marriage and the Family* 46 (1984): 16–19.
36. A. Browne, *When Battered Women Kill* (New York: Free Press, 1987).
37. Websdale, *Understanding Domestic Homicide*, p. 19.

38. C. P. Ewing, *Fatal Families: The Dynamics of Intrafamilial Homicide* (Thousand Oaks: Sage, 1997), p. 22.

39. R. M. Holmes & S. T. Holmes, *Murder in America* (Thousand Oaks: Sage, 1994), p. 27.

40. G. W. Barnard, H. Vera, M. Vera, & G. Newman, 'Till Death Do Us Part?' A Study of Spouse Murder, *Bulletin of the American Academy of Psychiatry and Law* 10 (1982): 271–80.

41. J. Campbell, 'If I Can't Have You, No One Can': Power and Control in Homicide of Female Partners, in J. Radford & D. E. Russell, Eds., *Femicide: The Politics of Woman Killing* (New York: Twayne, 1992), pp. 99–113.

42. Browne, Williams, & Dutton, Homicide Between Intimate Partners, p. 71.

43. *Ibid.*, pp. 72–73; Campbell, 'If I Can't Have You, No One Can,' pp. 99–113; M. A. Straus, Domestic Violence and Homicide Antecedents, *Bulletin of the New York Academy of Medicine* 62 (1976): 446–65.

44. R. E. Dobash, R. P. Dobash, M. Wilson, & M. Daly, The Myth of Sexual Symmetry in Marital Violence, *Social Problems* 39, 1 (1992): 81.

45. Ewing, *Fatal Families*, pp. 26–36; Websdale, *Understanding Domestic Homicide*, pp. 19–21; R. B. Flowers, *Female Crime, Criminals and Cellmates: An Exploration of Female Criminality and Delinquency* (Jefferson: McFarland, 1995), pp. 86–89.

46. Flowers, *Domestic Crimes, Family Violence and Child Abuse*, pp. 25–26, 61–64; Flowers, *Female Crime, Criminals and Cellmates*, pp. 86–89; Browne, Williams, & Dutton, Homicide Between Intimate Partners, pp. 55–78.

47. Flowers, *Domestic Crimes, Family Violence and Child Abuse*, p. 15.

48. *Ibid.*

49. D. E. Russell, *Rape in Marriage* (New York: Macmillan, 1982).

50. Flowers, *Domestic Crimes, Family Violence and Child Abuse*, p. 18.

51. *Ibid.*, p. 62; Campbell, "Prediction of Homicide of and by Battered Women."

52. Flowers, *Domestic Crimes, Family Violence and Child Abuse*, p. 62; *Violence by Intimates*, pp. 5–6.

53. Cited in Flowers, *Female Crime, Criminals and Cellmates*, p. 86.

54. *Ibid.*

55. J. Totman, *The Murderesses: A Psychosocial Study of Criminal Homicide* (San Francisco: R & E Associates, 1978).

56. Browne, *When Battered Women Kill*, pp. 130–135.

57. L. E. Walker, *The Battered Woman Syndrome* (New York: Springer, 1984), p. 40.

58. E. P. Benedek, "Women and Homicide," in B. L. Danto, J. Bruhns, & A. H. Kutscher, Eds., *The Human Side of Homicide* (New York: Columbia University Press, 1982), p. 155.

59. Flowers & Flowers, *Murders in the United States*, pp. 109–16.

60. *Ibid.*

61. *Ibid.*, pp. 123–40; Websdale, *Understanding Domestic Homicide*, p. 20; K. Polk & D. Ransom, The Role of Gender in Intimate Homicide, *Australian and New Zealand Journal of Criminology* 24 (1991): 20.

62. Flowers, *Female Crime, Criminals and Cellmates*, pp. 88–89; J. Horney, Menstrual Cycles and Criminal Responsibility, *Law and Human Behavior* 2, 1 (1978): 25–36; S. Shah & L. Roth, Biological and Psychological Factors in Criminality, in D. Glaser, Ed., *Handbook of Criminology* (Chicago: Rand McNally, 1974), p. 145.

Infanticide

5

Every year hundreds of infants are victims of intrafamilial homicide in the United States. Young mothers are predominantly responsible for these deaths, referred to as infanticide, which typically involves suffocating, drowning, dumping in garbage, and poisoning. Experts on child murder or *maternal filicide* attribute infanticide as a form of homicide to various causes including mental illness, depression, jealousy, child abuse and/or neglect, unwanted children, financial problems, and a history of violent behavior. Several recent high-profile cases of mothers murdering their children have placed greater focus on this disturbing problem as a reflection of the overall issue of violence in the family.

Infanticide Historically

Infanticide—or the killing of infants, usually by parents, family, or with the consent of the community—is believed to be the single greatest cause of child deaths in history, with the possible exception of the bubonic plague.[1] The practice of infanticide has taken place in virtually every nation since the beginning of recorded time, resulting in the murder of untold numbers of children.

The literature is filled with references of infanticide. The Old Testament describes the killing of countless children in Jericho by Joshua and his nomadic warriors,[2] while the New Testament tells of the "slaughter of the innocents," from which Jesus was saved.[3] King Nimrod killed every first-born child in his kingdom after being told by his astrologer that a boy would be born in Mesopotamia who would declare war upon the king.[4] An estimated 70,000 children were slain.

Young children were burned at the stake during the reign of Queen Mary,[5] and "in rural areas of Ireland 'changeling babies' were sometimes roasted alive over fires, even in the twentieth century."[6] The killing of female infants was once such a common practice that in many societies the male population was four to five times greater than the female population.[7]

Up until the 19th century, dead or abandoned infants were almost commonplace in the United States. Historically, infanticide has been characterized by the "silent acceptance or active participation by elements in the society in which it flourished."[8] Its existence has been attributed to individual and collective acts of faith, proof of worthiness, religious appeasement, response to prophecies of doom, Darwinian survival, Malthusian population control, illegitimate births, and medical reasons.

Women and Infanticide

Infanticide is defined today as the killing of an infant, usually shortly after birth. This form of homicide is almost always perpetrated by women. Infanticide has traditionally been viewed as a sex-specific offense, which "actually excludes the members of one sex by legal definition."[9] Under the English legal system, it has been observed that "infanticide does not apply to the British principle of equal applicability because it is an offense in which only women are considered the perpetrators."[10]

Infanticide is predominantly committed by a parent of the victim. Although some fathers do kill their young offspring, mothers are most responsible for the killing of infants. According to D. T. Lunde, mothers who commit infanticide are usually "severely disturbed, suffer from extreme bouts of depression and many experience delusions. Before a woman kills her offspring, she is likely to go through a preliminary period when she thinks about how to commit the crime, visualizes the dead child, and considers suicide."[11] A study on infanticide reported that young, unmarried, undereducated mothers were more likely to kill their infant children.[12] Poverty, depression, and women experiencing feelings of anomie have also been linked to infanticide.

Recent cases of infanticide are listed below:

- On November 22, 2004, 35-year-old Dena Schlosser amputated the arms of her 11-month-old daughter at their apartment in Plano, Texas. The daughter died the next day, and Schlosser, who suffered from postpartum psychosis, was charged with capital murder. After the jury deadlocked in her first trial, on April 6, 2006, in a retrial, the judge found Schlosser not guilty by reason of insanity. She was committed to a state mental facility.[13]
- On June 20, 2001, 37-year-old Andrea Yates drowned her five young children in the bathtub of the family's residence in Clear Lake, Texas. With a history of depression, Yates pleaded not guilty by reason of insanity. In March 2002, the insanity defense was rejected and she was found guilty of capital murder and sentenced to life imprisonment. The conviction was overturned on appeal. On July 26, 2006, a second jury found Yates not guilty by reason of insanity. She was committed to a high-security mental hospital and later placed in a low-security state mental health facility.[14]

- In July 1996, 27-year-old Kimberlee Snyder killed her 5-month-old daughter in Findlay, Ohio. Using postpartum depression as her defense, she pleaded guilty to involuntary manslaughter and child endangerment and was sentenced to 15 years behind bars.[15]
- On October 19, 1994, Susan Smith murdered her two young children by drowning them in a lake in Union, South Carolina. With a history of mental illness and as a victim of sexual abuse, the 23-year-old Smith was found competent to stand trial. She was convicted of two counts of first degree murder and sentenced to life in prison.
- Between 1986 and 1989, Paula Marie Sims murdered her two infant children. Loralei Sims's skeletal remains were discovered on June 20, 1986, just 15 days after her birth, in a wooded area in Brighton, Illinois. Her sister Heather's corpse was discovered in a garbage can in St. Charles County, Missouri, on May 3, 1989, less than 2 months after she was born. Unable to be found guilty in the first death, Sims was convicted of murder in the death of her second daughter and sentenced to life in prison with no possibility of parole.
- Between 1972 and 1985, New Yorker Marybeth Tinning was suspected of murdering her eight young children by suffocation. Initially most of the deaths had been attributed to sudden infant death syndrome (SIDS), including that of her 3-month-old daughter, Tami Lynne, who died on December 20, 1985. After an investigation, Tinning confessed to suffocating three of her children by smothering them with a pillow. She was convicted of second degree murder in the death of Tami and given a sentence of 20 years to life in prison.[16]

The Extent of Infanticide

How big is the problem of infanticide? No one knows for sure, given the problem of misdiagnosis and other difficulties in determining the cause of child deaths. The U.S. Department of Justice estimated that there are 600 cases of maternal filicide—mothers killing their children—annually.[17] In a study of child fatalities committed by parents, Phillip Resnick found that most deaths occurred during the first year of life.[18]

In the early 1990s, an estimated 9 per 100,000 newborn infants were killed by parents in the United States.[19] Many such deaths were attributed to unintentional fatal injuries, child abuse, or neglect. Recent data suggests that the number of cases of infanticide involving children age 1 and under is on the decline.[20] However, overall rates of infanticide have remained relatively stable between 1976 and 2011.

The frightening specter of infanticide was described by Maria Piers:

A doctoral candidate in the social sciences at one of the large Midwestern universities, who was teaching courses in the social sciences to employees of a large city sewer system, learned from these employees that during the previous year, four corpses of newborns had been found in the sewer screen. The newborns had been thrown directly after birth into the sewers, a preferred place for children's corpses for millennia. No identification or investigation was attempted in these cases of infant death.[21]

Types of Infanticidal Mothers

Researchers have developed typologies of mothers who kill their infants or other progeny. Robert Butterworth, a psychologist, identified eight types of infanticidal mothers as follows:

- *Mentally ill mothers.* Women suffering from serious psychological problems often initiated during childhood or from biological transference. May be acutely psychotic and have difficulty controlling aggression.
- *Retaliating mothers.* Women who are jealous or envious of their newborns because of the attention given by others, which the mother may have lacked herself during childhood.
- *Angry mothers.* Vengeful women whose anger is taken out on their babies, particularly male infants, who may bear the brunt of anger felt toward the father.
- *Depressed mothers.* Studies show that more than one-third of mothers who kill their young children suffer from depression or are suicidal.
- *Unwanted or unexpected mothers.* Mothers with unwanted or unexpected children are at greater risk to kill or abandon their newborns.
- *Merciful mothers.* These women kill their children to protect them from the pain and suffering that life presents or will bring.
- *Batterer mothers.* Women who beat their child to death, often in a fit of rage of in response to the child's nonstop wailing.[22]

According to Cheryl Meyer, there are five categories of mothers who murder their offspring:

- Mothers who kill as a result of neglect
- Mothers who kill as a result of abuse
- Mothers who perpetrate neonaticide
- Mothers who have assistance or are coerced in the killing of their child
- Mothers who intentionally murder their child[23]

Neonaticide is the killing of a child within 24 hours of birth. Research indicates that an estimated one out of three cases of infanticide is neonaticide.[24] The psyche of the neonaticidal woman is described by Steven Pitt and Erin Bale:

> Women who commit neonaticide generally have no plans for the birth or care of their child. They often conceal the pregnancy from both family and friends. Massive denial of the gravid state is a prominent feature ... [that] can be so powerful that it affects not only the mother's own perception but those of their family, friends, teachers, employers and even physicians.[25]

What Causes Mothers to Commit Infanticide?

Why do mothers murder their infants and young children? Like most murderers, there may be a variety of reasons for committing such a crime, ranging from mental illness to economics to suicidal or violent tendencies to desperation to shame. However, experts on infanticide have concentrated on some antecedents in particular that appear to reflect a high proportion of infanticidal women such as postpartum depression, Munchausen by proxy, and a sense of desperation and helplessness that leads to murder.

Postpartum Depression

Postpartum depression, or the "baby blues," is a common occurrence among women after giving birth. Studies show that between 50 and 80 percent of all women suffer from some form of depression following childbirth, such as sadness and psychosis.[26] Most of these symptoms are of short duration. Approximately 1 in 5 women experience serious symptoms of depression including insomnia, severe mood swings, suicidal ideation, and anorexia.[27] Only 2 women in every 1,000 become psychotic because of postpartum depression.[28]

The correlation between infanticide and postpartum depression is noted in the American Psychiatric Association's *Diagnostic and Statistical Manual of Mental Disorders* (*DSM-IV*): "Infanticide is most often associated with postpartum psychotic episodes that are characterized by command hallucinations to kill the infant or delusions that the infant is possessed, but it can also occur in severe postpartum mood episodes without such specific delusions or hallucinations."[29]

According to the *DSM-IV*, a woman's risk of psychosis resulting from postpartum depression is increased significantly if she has previously experienced psychotic episodes. Researchers have estimated that the odds of recurrence of postpartum depression, whether or not psychosis is present, are anywhere between 30 and 84 in 100.[30]

Postpartum depression has been linked to such biological correlates as hormonal levels during pregnancy, while some experts relate postpartum depression to the environment, or an interaction of environmental variables and hormonal influences.[31]

Munchausen Syndrome by Proxy

Some women who kill their infants and young children suffer from Munchausen syndrome by proxy (MBP), a rare mental disorder first brought to light in the 1970s.[32] Victims of MBP often manufacture or fake physical illness in their children, bringing them to doctors or hospitals to be treated. Munchausen parents are almost always mothers who appear to be loving and caring of their children and greatly involved with the medical practitioner in treatment options. Few such mothers give the appearance of being psychotic or otherwise suffering from any serious psychopathology.

According to the *DSM-IV*, in cases of MBP, "Typically, the victim is a young child and the perpetrator is the child's mother. The motivation for the perpetrator's behavior is presumed to be a psychological need to assume the sick role by proxy."[33] The MBP offender induces or feigns the child victim's disease or illness, then "presents the victim for medical care while disclaiming any knowledge about the actual etiology of the problem."[34]

In cases of MBP, common factors include

- The child's illness continues with inconsistent and often confusing symptoms, confounding medical practitioners.
- There is a recurrence in the child victim's medical treatment.
- The mother typically has some training in a medical field, such as a nurse, or medical knowledge.
- The mother is especially attentive to the child's welfare while under medical care.
- The mother is particularly helpful and cooperative with medical personnel.
- A symbiotic relationship exists between mother and child.[35]

The extent of MBP-related child homicides is unclear, but it appears to be on the rise. Around half of all confirmed MBP cases concern illnesses of the central nervous system such as breathing and sleep-related disorders.[36] Cases of MBP are commonly misdiagnosed as SIDS.

Women who suffer from MBP are generally characterized as having low self-esteem and feeling lonely, inadequate, and incompetent—beyond the façade of caring, loving mother. For most, at least part of the motivation is the attention and sense of importance derived from the MBP.

In spite of the seriousness of MBP, surveys reveal that most medical practitioners are not even aware of the disorder, compounding the problem and
potential for fatal consequences.[37]

Desperation

Many women who kill their infants do so out of desperation in being confronted with an unplanned, undesirable situation and feeling they have no
other viable alternative. Studies indicate that most mothers who fall into this
category of child killer tend to be very young, White, single, and with little to
no financial resources or family support.[38] Many of them are also likely to be
victims of child abuse and neglect and are increasingly substance abusers.[39]

Often the desperate mother or mother-to-be is motivated by fear, hopelessness, and shame in deciding to murder her newborn. Secrecy is also a
common factor in the scheme of things. Many manage to keep their pregnancy unknown to even family and close friends.

Desperation and despair often lead such mothers to dump their newborns in garbage cans or dumpsters or otherwise abandon them on the
streets. The result is usually the same: separation of mother and child, often
permanently and, in many cases, fatally.

Other Reasons

Women who commit maternal filicide are also often motivated by other
factors in perpetrating their crimes. According to researchers, among the
primary causes are altruistic filicide, where a mother with misguided love
believes she is acting in the best interests of her child in sparing them from a
world with too many problems.[40] Suicidal mothers are also prone to killing
their children, particularly young ones, so they can leave the world together
while ending the mother's suffering.

For some mothers who kill their children, fatal maltreatment filicide is the
outcome of child abuse, neglect, or mistreatment that occurs over time and
was not necessarily intended. Though relatively rare, some mothers murder
their offspring as revenge filicide against a spouse or the child's father, to inflict
mental anguish.[41] This is typically motivated by the spouse or father leaving
the relationship, the mother being the victim of domestic violence, or other
circumstances that prompt the mother to do the unthinkable as retribution.

Endnotes

1. Theo Solomon, History and Demography of Child Abuse, *Pediatrics 51*, 4
   (1973): 773–76.

2. *The Holy Bible*, Book of Joshua, 6:17–21.
3. R. B. Flowers, *Female Crime, Criminals and Cellmates: An Exploration of Female Criminality and Delinquency* (Jefferson: McFarland, 1995), p. 84.
4. Solomon, History and Demography of Child Abuse, p. 773.
5. C. Morris, *The Tudors* (London: Fontana, 1967).
6. J. E. Oliver, The Epidemiology of Child Abuse, in S. M. Smith, Ed., *The Maltreatment of Children* (Baltimore: University Park Press, 1978), p. 95.
7. S. O'Brien, *Child Abuse: Commission and Omission* (Provo: Brigham Young University Press, 1980), p. 5.
8. R. B. Flowers, *Children and Criminality: The Child as Victim and Perpetrator* (Westport: Greenwood, 1986), p. 4.
9. C. Smart, *Women, Crime and Criminology: A Feminist Critique* (Boston: Routledge and Kegan Paul, 1977), p. 6.
10. *Ibid.* See also Flowers, *Female Crime, Criminals and Cellmates*, pp. 84–86.
11. D. T. Lunde, Hot Blood's Record Month: Our Murder Boom, *Psychology Today* 9 (1975): 35–42.
12. Cited in L. S. Wissow, Infanticide, *New England Journal of Medicine* 339, 17 (1998): 1239; R. M. Holmes & S. T. Holmes, *Murder in America* (Thousand Oaks: Sage, 1994), pp. 48–49.
13. Mother Confesses to Severing Baby's Arms, *Crime & Courts on MSNBC.com* (November 23, 2004), http://www.msnbc.msn.com/id/6561617; Woman Tried for Severing Baby's Arms Found Not Guilty by Insanity, *FoxNews.com* (April 7, 2006), http://www.foxnews.com/story/0%2C2933%2C190955%2C00.html.
14. Wikipedia, the Free Encyclopedia, Andrea Yates, http://en.wikipedia.org/wiki/Andrea_Yates (March 28, 2012); Timothy Roche, Andrea Yates: More to the Story, *Time U.S.* (March 18, 2002), http://www.time.com/time/nation/article/0,8599,218445,00.html.
15. Cited in M. Tolson, Criminal Punishment Widely Disparate in Maternal Filicide Cases Such as Yates, http://www.chron.com/cs/CDA/story.hts/special/drownings/1041253; J. S. Dillon, Judge Routson: No Early Release for Kimberlee Snyder, *TheCourier.com* (August 11, 2009), http://www.thecourier.com/Issues/2009/Aug/11/ar_news_081109_story2.asp?d = 081109_story2,2009,Aug,11&c = n.
16. R. B. Flowers & H. L. Flowers, *Murders in the United States: Crimes, Killers and Victims of the Twentieth Century* (Jefferson: McFarland, 2001), pp. 123–39.
17. Cited in R. B. Flowers, *Domestic Crimes, Family Violence and Child Abuse: A Study of Contemporary American Society* (Jefferson: McFarland, 2000), p. 25.
18. P. J. Resnick, Child Murder by Parents: A Psychiatric Review of Filicide, *American Journal of Psychiatry* 126, 3 (1969): 325–34.
19. Wissow, Infanticide, p. 1239.
20. FBI, Supplementary Homicide Reports, http://www.ojp.usdoj.gov/bjs/homicide/children.htm.
21. M. W. Piers, *Infanticide* (New York: W. W. Norton, 1978), p. 14.
22. Cited in D. Moore, Infanticide, http://www.drdonnica.com/display.asp?article = 3506.
23. C. L. Meyer, Mothers Who Kill Often Give Warnings, http://www.womensenews.org/article.cfm/dyn/aid/595/context/archive.
24. *Ibid.*

25. Quoted in C. P. Ewing, *Fatal Families: The Dynamics of Intrafamilial Homicide* (Thousand Oaks: Sage, 1997), p. 87. *See also* S. E. Pitt & E. M. Bale, Neonaticide, Infanticide, and Filicide: A Review of the Literature, *Bulletin of the American Academy of Psychiatry and Law 23* (1995): 379.

26. A. Toufexis, Why Mothers Kill Their Babies, *Time* (June 20, 1998), p. 81.

27. When Do New Mom's 'Baby Blues' Become More Serious Illness? *Chicago Tribune* (November 27, 1988), p. 3.

28. *Ibid.*

29. American Psychiatric Association, *Diagnostic and Statistical Manual of Mental Disorders*, 4th ed. (Washington: American Psychiatric Association, 1994), p. 386.

30. E. Lichtblau, A Long Road for Massip: Postpartum Psychosis: Recovery Is Torturous, *Los Angeles Times* (February 3, 1989), p. 1.

31. Ewing, *Fatal Families*, pp. 62–63; Marianne Yen, High-Risk Mothers; Postpartum Depression, in Rare Cases, May Cause an Infant's Death, *Washington Post* (August 23, 1988), p. 18.

32. Ewing, *Fatal Families*, pp. 37–55; Flowers and Flowers, *Murders in the United States*, p. 121.

33. *Diagnostic and Statistical Manual of Mental Disorders*, p. 725.

34. *Ibid.*

35. Ewing, *Fatal Families*, p. 48.

36. *Ibid.*, pp. 53–54.

37. Cited in *Ibid.*, p. 54.

38. T. Terrace, A Gift Abandoned, *St. Petersburg Times* (April 14, 1991), p. 5.

39. Flowers, *Female Crime, Criminals and Cellmates*, pp. 87–89.

40. S. H. Friedman & P. J. Resnick, Child Murder by Mothers: Patterns and Prevention, *World Psychiatry 6*, 3 (2007): 137–41, http://www.ncbi.nlm.nih.gov/pmc/articles/PMC2174580/(March 29, 2012).

41. *Ibid.*

Parricide

6

One of the least-studied areas of intrafamilial homicide is parricide, the murdering of one's mother, father, or like relative. Although parricide is a relatively rare occurrence in modern society, a number of highly publicized cases of parricidal behavior in recent years have placed greater attention on its dynamics, nature, at-risk perpetrators and victims, and ways to prevent it. Parricide is much more likely to be perpetrated by adult offenders, often as a murder-suicide or a reflection of homicidal behavior directed as well at people outside the family. The parricidal adult often has a history of mental illness. Juvenile parricide, while less common, is often more shocking and devastating because of the age of the offender and characteristics of the offense. Most juveniles who kill their parents are the victims of child abuse, abuse drugs or alcohol, or are described as dangerously antisocial. Parricide itself is often indicative of other family violence, dysfunction, and troubles.

The Nature of Parricide

Parricide is defined as the killing of a parent by a son or daughter. Though historically this form of murder has been taboo in most cultures, it is not a new phenomenon. Episodes of parricide, filicide, fratricide, and multiple suicides spanning three generations in one family are chronicled in the Greek myth of Oedipus.[1] Today, parricide is seen as another example of family violence and homicidal behavior that often results from a history of intrafamilial abuses and dysfunction[2] as well as interrelated variables outside the family.[3] Experts have found that differences exist between adult and juvenile parricide[4] and completed and attempted parricide.[5] Substance abuse is often a factor in parricidal behavior,[6] as is a history of violent behavior and psychiatric troubles,[7] and the use and availability of firearms.[8]

Studies show that killers of parents or stepparents are predominantly over the age of 18.[9] The adult parricide offender is typically found to suffer from severe mental illness or psychopathy.[10]

Though some juvenile parricide offenders also have a history of mental illness, the typical child murderer of a mother or father is more often a victim of severe child abuse or is considered seriously antisocial.[11] In many instances of juvenile parricide, siblings conspire to murder their mother, father, or both.

Recent cases of parricide illustrate this disturbing and far-too-common form of intrafamilial homicide in American society:

- On October 17, 2010, Rebecca Olenchock, age 24, bludgeoned and burned her mother, Kimberly Venose, in the hut where they lived in Bucks County, Pennsylvania. Venose died of her injuries and Olenchock was charged with first degree murder and arson. She was found guilty but mentally ill, entitling her to mental health treatment during a life sentence.

- On July 2, 2009, Jerry D. Snider, Jr., 29, attacked his father, Jerry Snider, Sr., with a hatchet in his Rangely, Colorado, home, killing him. The elder Snider's wallet, credit cards, and truck were stolen after the murder. After turning himself in, Snider Jr. was charged with first degree murder and aggravated robbery. On June 14, 2011, he was convicted of murdering his father and sentenced to spend the rest of his life in prison without any chance for parole, along with 48 years for the aggravated robbery.

- On July 5, 2004, 14-year-old Cody Posey shot and killed his 34-year-old father, 43-year-old stepmother, and 13-year-old stepsister in Hondo, New Mexico. He hid their bodies in a pile of manure. Posey's defense was that it was a reaction to years of psychological and physical abuse. He was convicted of murder for killing his stepmother and stepsister, and voluntary manslaughter for the death of his father and sentenced as a juvenile. Posey was released in October 2010.

- In April 2003, 17-year-old Frances Choy set her family's home on fire in Brockton, Massachusetts, killing her parents, Jimmy Choy and Anne Trinh-Choy, in hopes of receiving a payout on their life insurance. On May 16, 2011, a jury found Choy guilty of two counts of first degree murder as well as arson. She was sentenced to life imprisonment without the possibility of parole.

- On February 27, 1995, Bryan Freeman, 17, and David Freeman, 15, bludgeoned and stabbed to death their parents in the family's home in Pennsylvania. The brothers had neo-Nazi affiliations and violent histories. Both pleaded guilty to murder and were given life sentences with no chance for parole.

- On July 12, 1993, Herman Dutton, 15, and James Dutton, 12, used a deer rifle to shoot to death their father, Lonnie Dutton, while he slept in the family home in Rush Springs, Oklahoma. Both boys claimed their father had physically and sexually abused them for years. The Dutton's pleaded no contest to the charge of manslaughter and were placed in foster homes.

- On August 20, 1989, Lyle Menendez, 22, and Erik Menendez, 19, shot to death their wealthy parents, José and Mary Menendez, in the family's Beverly Hills, California, home. Both killers claimed they acted in self-defense following years of physical, sexual, and emotional abuse. The Menendez brothers were convicted of first degree murder and sentenced to life in prison.
- On January 1, 1987, following an argument, 16-year-old Sean Stevenson shot and killed his parents, then raped and murdered his 18-year-old sister at their home in Washington. He was found guilty of first degree murder and aggravated murder and given a life sentence without the possibility of parole.
- On February 17, 1986, Matthew Gasparovich, Jr., 15, and his 12-year-old sister, Heidi, shot to death their father as he slept in his home in Iowa. The troubled (or obstinate) youth tried to flee to California after the murder. Tried as juveniles, the Gasparovich's were found guilty of patricide and placed in juvenile detention until the age of 18.
- On September 8, 1984, 15-year-old Patrick DeGelleke set ablaze the house of his adoptive parents in Rochester, New York, as they slept, killing them. DeGelleke had a history of violence and an uncontrollable temper. He was convicted of murder.
- On November 16, 1982, 16-year-old Richard Jahnke, Jr., shot and killed his father in the driveway of the family home in Wyoming. Charged as an accomplice in the murder was his 17-year-old sister, Deborah Jahnke. Both claimed the father had been physically, psychologically, and sexually abusive. Richard Jahnke, Jr., was convicted of manslaughter and sentenced to 5 to 15 years in prison. Deborah Jahnke received a 3- to 8-year sentence for aiding and abetting.[12]

How Often Does Parricide Occur?

According to FBI figures, there were 242 murders in 2010 in which the victim was identified as a father or mother in relationship to the offender.[13] Studies estimate that 300 parents are killed by their progeny annually in the United States.[14]

Despite these numbers and the publicity often generated in cases of parricide, this type of intrafamilial homicide is quite rare. Official data indicate that in 2010, parricide constituted less than 2 percent of total homicides committed in this country.[15] In a review of FBI parricide statistics, Kathleen Heide found that the rate of patricides (the killing of one's father) ranged from 0.7 percent to 1.1 percent of all homicides, while the rate of matricides (the killing of one's mother) was between 0.6 percent and 0.8 percent of total murders.[16] California parricide data corresponds with that on the national level, accounting for between 0.9 percent and 1.1 percent of the state's homicides.[17]

While the percentage of juvenile cases of parricide is relatively small, juveniles are much more likely to kill their parents than to commit murder in general. Around 10 percent of murders in the United States annually are perpetrated by offenders younger than 18 years of age.[18] However, according to Heide, 34 percent of stepfathers, 30 percent of stepmothers, 25 percent of fathers, and 15 percent of mothers in the study were victims of parricide committed by sons and daughters under the age of 18.[19]

Characteristics of Parricide Offenders and Victims

Most people who kill their parents are of adult age. It is estimated that more than three-quarters of parricide perpetrators are people over the age of 18.[20] The typical parricidal offender tends to have a history of serious psychiatric problems while exhibiting little indication of a background of violence against their parents.[21] Studies show that male parricide offenders are more likely to kill their mothers than fathers, with female parricide offenders most often murdering their mothers.[22] The killing of both parents has been shown to be committed almost wholly by sons.[23]

Researchers have identified other characteristics of parricide offenders as follows:

- Most are White males.
- Most are non-Hispanics.
- More than 7 in 10 killers of fathers, stepfathers, or stepmothers are under the age of 30.
- Almost 7 out of 10 killers of mothers are between the ages of 20 and 50.
- Most adolescent offenders are between 16 and 18 years of age and come from middle- and upper-middle-class backgrounds.
- Around 1 in 4 parricide victims are murdered by a son or daughter younger than 18.[24]

Victims of parricide come from all racial, ethnic, and economic backgrounds and include parents of juvenile and adult parricide offenders. Fathers are more likely to be murdered by offspring than mothers.[25] Parricide experts have found that the typical parent or stepparent victim of parricide is White, non-Hispanic, and usually in their 40s and 50s.[26] Stepparent victims tend to be younger than parent victims.

Types of Adult Parricide Perpetrators

Most killers of mothers and fathers are adult perpetrators. Adult parricide offenders are most often described in the literature as seriously mentally ill or psychopathic.[27] Researchers have characterized the adult who kills a parent as a paranoid schizophrenic "who is embroiled in a hostile-dependent relationship with the victim."[28] According to psychiatrists, this type of parricide is termed *catathymic homicide*, in reference to

> chronic emotional tension caused by traumatic experiences, projection of responsibility for the internal tension state onto the external situation, and the perception of violence as the only way out of the situation. The criminal act is perpetrated in a sudden rush of emotional tensions, with little premeditation or deliberation, and thus often leads to judicial verdict of insanity, involuntary manslaughter or simple assault.[29]

The second most common type of adult parricide perpetrator is one who kills a mother or father for sociopathic purposes, such as having a history of violence or receiving insurance payments upon the death. In some instances, the victim may have previously been subjected to parent abuse or elderly exploitation due to dependency.

Parricidal adults often also direct homicidal violence against their family members such as a spouse or children, or people outside the family, and are frequently suicidal as well.[30]

Types of Juvenile Parricide Perpetrators

Researchers have identified three primary types of juveniles who kill their parents: (1) the severely abused child, (2) the severely mentally ill child, and (3) the dangerously antisocial child.[31] The characteristics of each are described as follows:

- *Severely abused child.* The most common type of adolescent parricide perpetrator who has been the victim of or witness to brutal, chronic abuse in the family and kills in response to this, in self-defense, or to protect others from the abuser.
- *Severely mentally ill child.* This type of parricidal child is considered psychotic or seriously mentally ill. Such parricide offenders typically have a history of psychiatric problems, which leads to the murder of a parent.

- *Dangerously antisocial child.* This type of parricide offender kills a mother or father for selfish or deviant reasons. Such parent killers are described in psychiatry as possessing conduct disorders or antisocial personalities, depending on the offender's age and other criteria. The dangerously antisocial child is not considered psychotic.

According to Heide, severely abused adolescent parricide perpetrators are typically diagnosed following the parental murder as suffering from depression or posttraumatic stress disorder (PTSD).[32] Such offenders often experience feelings of sadness, hopelessness, fatigue, difficulties in concentrating, and suicidal ideation.

The dangerously antisocial child who is diagnosed as a conduct-disordered youth motivated to commit parricide for self-serving purposes may often have a history of violent behavior, substance abuse, and involvement with antisocial groups.[33]

What Causes a Person to Commit Parricide?

Studies show that the causes of or important factors in parricidal behavior include a history of mental illness, child physical or sexual abuse, violent or antisocial conduct, and substance abuse.[34] Greed or profit as a motive has also been shown to motivate some parricide offenders to kill their parents. A good example is that of the Menendez brothers, two young adults who murdered their wealthy parents. In spite of their allegations that they suffered years of abuse from their father and mother, a jury convicted them primarily on the basis of murder for financial gain.

Adult parricide offenders tend to kill in relation to serious psychiatric problems or profit motive, whereas youthful parricide offenders are more likely to kill after being subjected to a pattern of severe parental abusive treatment. More often than not, juvenile parricide involving a sibling conspiracy involves physical, sexual, and/or psychological abuse perpetrated by the murdered parent.

In some cases, child parricide offenders may kill one parent as the unwitting "lethal agent" of the other parent "who unconsciously incites [the child] to kill in order that the [parent] can vicariously enjoy the benefits of the act."[35] L. Bender and F. J. Curran posited that the most common factor in child-perpetrated homicide or attempted murder is "the child's tendency to identify himself with aggressive parents, and pattern after their behavior."[36]

Some researchers have found that parricide and other homicide may be related to pent-up emotions that explode in homicidal violence before they can be rechanneled. According to Bruno Cormier and colleagues: "Amongst those adolescents who kill within the nuclear group, there is an inability to displace those problems encountered with the parents on to a broader group, such as their peers, where the problem can be defused and new gratifications experienced."[37]

Endnotes

1. R. Graves, *Greek Myths* (New York: Penguin, 1962).
2. N. Websdale, *Understanding Domestic Homicide* (Boston: Northeastern University Press, 1999), pp. 12–13; K. M. Heide, *Why Kids Kill Parents: Child Abuse and Adolescent Homicide* (Thousand Oaks: Sage, 1995).
3. R. B. Flowers, *Domestic Crimes, Family Violence and Child Abuse: A Study of Contemporary American Society* (Jefferson: McFarland, 2000), pp. 68–70.
4. Heide, *Why Kids Kill Parents*; T. J. Chamberlain, The Dynamics of Parricide, *American Journal of Forensic Psychiatry* 7 (1986): 11–23; K. M. Heide, Parents Who Get Killed and the Children Who Kill Them, *Journal of Interpersonal Violence* 8, 4 (1993): 531–44.
5. A. M. Weisman & K. K. Skarma, Parricide and Attempted Parricide, in U.S. Department of Justice, *The Nature of Homicide: Trends and Changes—Proceedings of the 1996 Meeting of the Homicide Research Working Group* (Washington: National Institute of Justice, 1997), pp. 234–44.
6. Heide, *Why Kids Kill Parents*, pp. 37, 42–43; M. Maloney, Children Who Kill Their Parents, *Prosecutor's Brief: California District Attorney's Association Journal* 20 (1994): 20–22.
7. Heide, *Why Kids Kill Parents*; Charles P. Ewing, *Fatal Families: The Dynamics of Intrafamilial Homicide* (Thousand Oaks: Sage, 1997), pp. 104–14.
8. R. B. Flowers, *Kids Who Commit Adult Crimes: A Study of Serious Juvenile Criminality and Delinquency* (Binghamton: Haworth, 2002); T. J. Young, Parricide Rates and Criminal Street Violence in the United States: Is There a Correlation? *Adolescence* 28, 109 (1993): 171–72.
9. Heide, *Why Kids Kill Parents*; Weisman and Skarma, Parricide and Attempted Parricide, p. 234.
10. K. M. Heide, Dangerously Antisocial Kids Who Kill Their Parents: Toward a Better Understanding of the Phenomenon, in U.S. Department of Justice, *The Nature of Homicide: Trends and Changes—Proceedings of the 1996 Meeting of the Homicide Research Working Group* (Washington: National Institute of Justice, 1997), p. 229.
11. *Ibid.*, pp. 228–30.
12. R. B. Flowers & H. L. Flowers, *Murders in the United States: Crimes, Killers and Victims of the Twentieth Century* (Jefferson: McFarland, 2001), pp. 76, 147–51; Larry King, Bucks Woman Who Clubbed, Burned Mother Gets Life, *The Inquirer*, (October 12, 2011), http://articles.philly.com/2011-10-12/news/30271297_1_murder-conviction-first degree-murder-life-sentence; B. Karas, Teen Who Killed Family on Donaldson Ranch Goes Free, *CNN Justice* (October 8, 2010), http://www.cnn.com/2010/CRIME/10/08/new.mexico.posey.release/index.html; Brockton Woman Convicted of Killing Parents in Fire, *BostonHearald.com* (May 16, 2011), http://bostonherald.com/news/regional/

view/20110516brockton_woman_convicted_of_killing_parents_in_fire; Bobby Gutierrez, Snider Sentenced to Life Without Parole, *Herald Times* (November 11, 2011), http://www.theheraldtimes.com/snider-sentenced-to-life-without-parole/rangely.

13. U.S. Department of Justice, Federal Bureau of Investigation, *Crime in the United States: Uniform Crime Reports 2010*, Expanded Homicide Data Table 10, Murder Circumstances by Relationship, 2010, http://www.fbi.gov/about-us/cjis/ucr/crime-in-the-u.s/2010/crime-in-the-u.s.-2010/tables/10shrtbl10.xls (March 31, 2012).

14. Heide, Dangerously Antisocial Kids Who Kill Their Parents, p. 229; Ewing, *Fatal Families*, p. 103.

15. *Crime in the United States 2010*; Weisman & Skarma, Parricide and Attempted Parricide, p. 234.

16. Heide, "Parents Who Get Killed and the Children Who Kill Them," pp. 531–44.

17. Cited in Weisman & Skarma, Parricide and Attempted Parricide, p. 234.

18. U.S. Department of Justice, Federal Bureau of Investigation, *Crime in the United States: Uniform Crime Reports 1999* (Washington: Government Printing Office, 2000), p. 14.

19. Heide, *Why Kids Kill Parents*, p. 3.

20. Heide, Parents Who Get Killed and the Children Who Kill Them, pp. 531–532.

21. Weisman & Skarma, Parricide and Attempted Parricide, p. 234.

22. C. E. Newhill, Parricide, *Journal of Family Violence* 64 (1991): 375–94; J. R. Meloy, *Violent Attachments* (Northvale: Aronson, 1992).

23. Weisman and Skarma, Parricide and Attempted Parricide, p. 235.

24. Ewing, *Fatal Families*, pp. 103–04; Heide, Why Kids Kill Parents, p. 3; P. A. Mones, *When A Child Kills: Abused Children Who Kill Their Parents* (New York: Pocket Books, 1991).

25. *Crime in the United States 1999*, p. 19.

26. Ewing, *Fatal Families*, p. 103.

27. Heide, Dangerously Antisocial Kids Who Kill Their Parents, p. 229.

28. Weisman & Skarma, Parricide and Attempted Parricide, p. 235.

29. *Ibid.*, pp. 235–36; Meloy, *Violent Attachments*; L. S. Tucker & T. P. Cornwall, Mother-Son Folie a Duex: A Case of Attempted Parricide, *American Journal of Psychiatry 134*, 10 (1977): 1146–47.

30. Flowers & Flowers, *Murders in the United States*, pp. 76, 136.

31. Heide, Dangerously Antisocial Kids Who Kill Their Parents, pp. 228–33; *American Psychiatric Association, Diagnostic and Statistical Manual of Mental Disorders*, 4th ed. (Washington: American Psychiatric Association, 1994); L. Walker, *Sudden Fury* (New York: St. Martin's Press, 1989); D. Kleiman, *A Deadly Silence* (New York: Atlantic Monthly Press, 1988).

32. Heide, Dangerously Antisocial Kids Who Kill Their Parents, p. 228.

33. *Ibid.*, p. 230.

34. *Ibid.*, pp. 228–30; Ewing, *Fatal Families*, pp. 103–11; D. E. Russell, A Study of Juvenile Murderers of Family Members, *International Journal of Offender Therapy and Comparative Criminology 28* (1984): 177–92.

35. R. B. Flowers, *Children and Criminality: The Child as Victim and Perpetrator* (Westport: Greenwood, 1986), p. 59. *See also* D. Sargeant, Children Who Kill: A Family Conspiracy? in J. Howells, Ed., *Theory and Practice of Family Psychiatry* (New York: Brunner-Mazel, 1971).
36. L. Bender & F. J. Curran, Children and Adolescents Who Kill, *Journal of Criminal Psychopathology 1*, 4 (1940): 297.
37. Cited in Flowers, *Children and Criminality*, p. 59.

Other Intrafamilial Homicide

7

Every year in the United States, there are thousands of intrafamilial homicides, or murders involving parents, children, siblings, and entire families. Many of these are the result of child abuse, domestic violence, self-defense, murder-suicide, substance abuse, mental illness, jealousy, rivalry, greed, and other family dysfunction and difficulties. Murderers within the family have been described as "passive and submissive, preferring to avoid open conflict when possible, especially if playing a masochistic role leads to gaining their affection."[1] The suicidal nature of domestic homicide has been noted in the literature in which some victims are believed to "so aggressively provoke violence toward themselves by a family member that they can be viewed as suicides."[2] The complex dynamics of family life can often act as precursors to murder among family members.

The very real threat of bodily harm and lethal intrafamilial victimization led one expert on domestic violence to observe: "The home is a very dangerous place and we have more to fear from close members of our family than total strangers."[3] These sentiments were echoed in an article on family violence in which the authors asserted:

> With the exception of the police and the military, the family is perhaps the most violent social group, and the home the most violent social setting in our society. A person is more likely to be hit or killed in his or her own home by another family member than anywhere else or by anyone else.[4]

Unfortunately, this is all too true when it comes to murder.

Domestic Murder of Children

Filicide—the killing of one's child—is perhaps the saddest form of intrafamilial homicide. According to the Justice Department, in 2010 there were 453 murders in which the victims were identified as sons or daughters of the perpetrator in the United States.[5] Most experts believe that many more children are the victims of murder committed by parents annually, and that the majority of these are caused by or involve child abuse of some type. Every year more than a million children are the victims of substantiated child abuse and neglect in this country.[6] More than 3 million reports of child maltreatment are investigated by child protective services agencies annually.[7]

Pediatric News reported that one child dies every day from child abuse.[8] Vincent Fontana estimated that 700 children are killed by parents in the United States each year.[9] The National Incidence Study reported that approximately 1,000 children die annually as a result of child abuse or neglect.[10] Sandra Arbetter estimated that there are 600 cases of women alone who murder their children every year.[11]

According to Alex Morales, 3,000 children will die from abuse every year in the United States, with half the victims under the age of 1 year and 90 percent younger than age 4.[12] Ray Helfer warned that unless steps were taken to halt the abuse of children, more than 5,000 child deaths per year could result.[13]

The National Child Abuse and Neglect Data System (NCANDS) estimated 1,262 child fatalities nationwide in 2010, in which the vast majority were attributed to child abuse or neglect.[14] As shown in Table 7.1, among single maltreatment types, 700 child fatalities out of 747 were caused by physical abuse or neglect, with medical neglect, psychological or sexual abuse, and other types of maltreatment responsible for the other deaths from individual

Table 7.1   Child Deaths, by Maltreatment Type, 2010

Maltreatment Type	Unique Child Fatalities	
	Number	Percent
Single Maltreatment Type		
Medical Neglect	9	1.5
Neglect	411	32.6
Other	21	1.7
Physical Abuse	289	22.9
Psychological Abuse	4	0.3
Sexual Abuse	3	0.2
Unknown	0	0.0
Multiple Maltreatment Types		
Two or more maltreatment types	515	40.8
Total	1,262	
Percent		100.0

Note: Table is based on data from 44 states.

Source: U.S. Department of Health and Human Services, Administration of Children and Families, Children's Bureau, *Child Maltreatment 2010*, p. 71, http://www.acf.hhs.gov/programs/cb/pubs/cm10/index.htm (March 31, 2012).

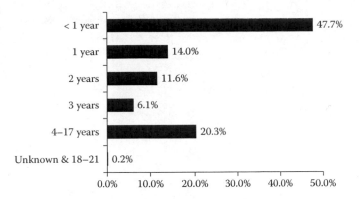

Figure 7.1 Child deaths from maltreatment, by age, 2010. (Derived from U.S. Department of Health and Human Services, Administration of Children and Families, Children's Bureau, *Child Maltreatment 2010*, p. 59, http://www.acf. hhs.gov/programs/cb/pubs/cm10/index.htm, April 1, 2012.)

causes. For more than 4 in 10 child deaths from maltreatment, the fatality came as a result of two or more kinds of maltreatment.

Young children are the most susceptible to death due to child abuse and neglect (see Figure 7.1). Nearly 80 percent of maltreatment-related child fatalities in the United States in 2010 were under 4 years of age. Almost half the victims were younger than 1 year old, dying at a rate of 17.89 per 100,000. More than 1 in 4 child fatalities were between the ages of 1 and 2 years old, while around 1 in 5 child fatalities were ages 4 to 17. Less than 1 percent of the victims of child abuse and neglect were age 18 to 21 or unknown.

With regard to race and child deaths caused by child abuse and neglect, more than 4 in 10 victims were White, with African American victims constituting almost 3 in 10 child fatalities, and Hispanics nearly 17 percent of the total for the year (see Figure 7.2). Native American and Asian children accounted for fewer than 2 percent of the fatalities attributable to child maltreatment. Less than 5 percent of the victims were of mixed races or ethnicity.

Recent cases of filicide can be seen below:

- On December 26, 2008, Carlese Hall, 31, stabbed her 7-year-old daughter to death and then set their home on fire in Washington, D.C. Hall, who was under the influence of PCP at the time of the crime, was convicted of felony murder, arson, and additional charges on April 29, 2011. She was sentenced to 55 years behind bars.
- On October 6, 2006, Said Biyad, 42, stabbed to death his four young children and raped and attempted to kill his estranged wife after an argument in her Louisville, Kentucky, apartment. Biyad, a Somali immigrant, was found guilty in April 2011 of the mass murder and

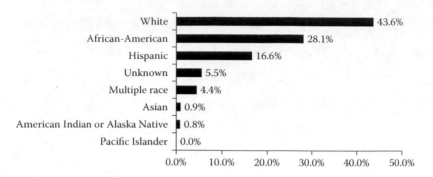

Figure 7.2 Child deaths from maltreatment, by race and ethnicity, 2010. (Derived from U.S. Department of Health and Human Services, Administration of Children and Families, Children's Bureau, *Child Maltreatment 2010*, p. 59, http://www.acf.hhs.gov/programs/cb/pubs/cm10/index.htm, April 1, 2012.)

attacking his wife, and was sentenced to life imprisonment without the possibility of parole.

- On June 20, 2001, Andrea Yates, 37, drowned her five young children in the bathtub of their home in Clear Lake, Texas. With a history of severe mental illness, she pleaded not guilty by reason of insanity. In March 2002, Yates was found guilty of the murders and given a life sentence. In July 2006, a second jury found her not guilty by reason of insanity. She was sent to a mental health facility.
- On December 4, 1999, Kao Xiong used a high-powered rifle and shotgun to murder five of his seven children before killing himself in the family's apartment in Del Paso Heights, California. The Laos native had argued with his wife prior to the mass filicide-suicide.
- On October 26, 1997, Susan Eubanks, 35, shot to death her four young sons in the family home in San Marcos, California. The unemployed nursing assistant had a history of substance abuse and bad relationships. She was convicted of all four murders and sentenced to death.
- On May 19, 1983, Elizabeth Downs, 28, murdered her 7-year-old daughter and tried to kill her two other children in Springfield, Oregon, reportedly because they hindered her love life. She was convicted of murder and two counts of attempted murder and sentenced to life in prison plus 50 years.[15]

Characterizing Filicide Perpetrators

According to NCANDS, parents were responsible for child fatalities in nearly 8 out of 10 cases across the nation in 2010. As seen in Figure 7.3, mothers are more likely to be the perpetrators of filicide than fathers. Mothers accounted for over 29 percent of the child deaths from maltreatment caused by a single

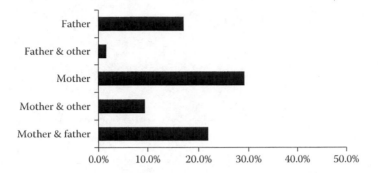

Figure 7.3 Child deaths from maltreatment, by perpetrator, 2010. (Derived from U.S. Department of Health and Human Services, Administration of Children and Families, Children's Bureau, *Child Maltreatment 2010*, p. 60, http://www. acf.hhs.gov/programs/cb/pubs/cm10/index.htm, April 1, 2012.)

parent, compared with around 17 percent of the fathers. More than 1 in 5 child fatalities were perpetrated by the mother and father. Almost six times as many child deaths were committed by a mother and another person as a father and someone else.

In spite of these figures, much of the research indicates that males tend to commit the vast majority of child maltreatment-related homicides.[16] Most of these come as the result of physical child abuse.[17] One study found that 80 percent of child deaths due to trauma of the head and body were perpetrated by male offenders.[18]

While mothers who kill their children are believed to suffer from severe mental illness or serious depression, such as the aforementioned case of Andrea Yates, according to D. T. Lunde:

> Fathers rarely kill their young children, but when they do, they also build up to the crime, and often have a history of child abuse. Fathers who murder are more likely to kill their teenage sons. These men are marginally adequate husbands and fathers who feel inferior and frustrated by life. Guns and alcohol play significant roles in their lives. Their criminal records, if any, usually involve drinking, drunk driving, and disorderly conduct. They rarely have a history of psychiatric illness. They simply are explosive individuals who kill impulsively.[19]

In a 12-year study of filicidal men, J. F. Campion, J. M. Cravens, and F. Covan characterized the offenders as having a stressful history, including experiencing domestic violence, child abuse, and broken homes.[20] Three-quarters of the men were found to have had mental or neurological disorders during childhood, while many had been put out of the house due to antisocial behavior or parental mistreatment.

Studies show that the majority of parents who murder their children are in their 20s,[21] with less than 7 percent younger than 18 years of age.[22] Most filicide offenders kill their victims as the result of injuries inflicted to the head. In a study of child abuse fatalities, Patricia Schloesser and colleagues found that nearly 60 percent of the deaths were caused by head injuries.[23] Similarly, in Richard Krugman's analysis of child maltreatment deaths, 71 percent were due to injuries to the head.[24]

Filicide by shooting is also becoming more common as more offenders gain access to firearms. In Neil Websdale's study of domestic homicide, 1 in 4 perpetrators of filicide used a gun to kill their victim.[25]

Sibling Homicide

Every year, more than 100 people are murdered by a sibling in the United States. According to the Uniform Crime Reports, in 2010, there were 107 sibling homicides in this country. Males are much more likely to be victims and perpetrators of sibling homicide than females. Eighty-eight of the homicides, or just over 82 percent, were fratricides (the killing of one's brother), and 19, or around 18 percent, were sororicides (the killing of one's sister).[26]

In a recent Department of Justice survey of homicides in urban counties, 1.5 percent were sibling-perpetrated homicides.[27] More than 80 percent of the offenders and victims were adults, while approximately 85 percent of the sibling killers and 73 percent of the victims were male. In nearly 70 percent of cases, the perpetrator and victim were the same sex; and in 65 percent of the sibling homicides, the offender and victim were Black. Firearms were used in less than 40 percent of the murders.

Recent cases of sibling homicide can be seen as follows:

- On January 14, 2010, John Kalisz, 55, killed his sister Kathryn Donovan and another woman, and wounded two others at a home in Brooksville, Florida. Later that day, Kalisz murdered a deputy sheriff as part of a shooting spree, for which he pled guilty, receiving a life sentence. In January 2012, he was convicted on two counts of first degree murder, two other counts of attempted murder, and armed burglary, receiving the death penalty.
- On July 25, 2005, Ronald Eric Salazar, age 14, raped, strangled, and slit the throat of his 11-year-old sister at their home in Miami, Florida. After he killed her, he covered her body in a Winnie the Pooh comforter. After rejecting an insanity defense, in October 2009 a jury found Salazar guilty of murder in the first degree and sexual battery. He was sentenced to two life terms of imprisonment.
- On January 3, 1996, Tom Grentz, 87, used a .25 caliber gun to shoot to death his 85-year-old sister and then himself in the house they shared in Baltimore, Maryland. Both had been seriously ill in recent years.

- On October 26, 1995, Dana Jokela, 18, beat to death his 20-year-old brother Cary with a baseball bat at the family's home in Ohio following an argument. There had been a history of violence between the siblings. Jokela pleaded guilty to manslaughter.
- On July 9, 1985, Steven Benson, 34, planted two pipe bombs beneath the family's van outside their Naples, Florida, home. The explosion killed his brother and mother and seriously injured his sister. The heir to a tobacco fortune killed out of greed. He was convicted on a number of counts, including two murders, and given two consecutive life sentences.
- On July 3, 1995, Richard Gibson, 38, shot to death his 41-year-old brother Allen following an argument at the house they shared with their father in Detroit, Michigan. The younger Gibson then turned the gun on himself, committing suicide.[28]
- In April 1985, Britt Kellum, age 9, got into a fight with his 11-year-old brother before shooting him to death with a 16-gauge shotgun at the family's home near Flint, Michigan. On October 30, 1989, after 4 years of psychotherapy, Kellum used his father's .38 caliber handgun to kill his 6-year-old brother while playing Russian roulette.[29]

Sibling homicide is often a reflection of sibling violence and other family violence and instability. According to the Bureau of Justice Statistics, in 2008, there were roughly 83,934 single-offender crimes of violence committed against brothers and sisters.[30] In a study of family violence, Murray Straus and colleagues estimated that based on an "ever happened" premise, some 8.3 million children in the United States have been "beaten up" by a sibling, while 2.3 million have at some point used a gun or knife on a sister or brother.[31]

Reasons Why Siblings Kill Siblings

People commit fratricide and sororicide for various reasons, including a history of bad blood between them, sibling rivalry or abuse, substance abuse, domestic violence, unemployment, relationship problems, and mental illness. The *American Journal of Psychiatry* found that intrafamilial homicidal behavior by children is often associated with extremely violent parents (especially the father), a history of psychomotor seizures and suicidal behavior, and prior psychiatric treatment by the mother.[32] Bruno Cormier and colleagues attributed murder by children within the family as an inability to transfer parental-related problems to the outside world where they might be defused.[33]

The unresolved conflicts and stresses between siblings, often lasting into adulthood, can trigger a homicidal reaction. This may be particularly true when adult siblings live close by or in the same house, as Charles Ewing notes:

Where adult siblings end up living together and/or under the same roof as their parents, competition among them may continue if not intensify. Even though few adult siblings kill one another, it should come as no surprise that many who do ... were living with their sibling-victims at the time of the killings.[34]

The relationship between sibling homicide and mental illness has been demonstrated in studies. According to a Department of Justice study, nearly one in five cases of sibling murder involved an offender whose history was characterized by mental illness.[35] Similarly, substance abuse often plays a strong role in homicide between siblings. The study found that over half the offenders and almost 35 percent of the victims had been drinking at the time the murder occurred.[36]

Studies reveal that some cases of sibling homicide are motivated by a history of violent behavior by the perpetrator and other antisocial behavior.[37] Some instances of children killing siblings are classified as accidental killings but are often a reflection of antecedents such as behavioral problems, mental illness, child neglect, or mental illness.[38]

Familicide

Familicide, or the killing of most or all of one's family, is relatively rare compared with other domestic homicides. There are no national statistics on familicide; however, the killing of family in American history has been documented.[39] Websdale points out that "analysis of modern-day familicides emphasize the manner in which socioeconomic pressures and perpetrators' concerns about their social standing compound or supersede psychiatric problems as the primary cause of these tragedies."[40] Notable cases of familicide can be seen below:

- On December 21, 2011, 53-year-old Penelope Luddy grabbed a 12-gauge shotgun and murdered her 79-year-old father and 10-year-old daughter, before committing suicide in their home in Perinton, New York. Luddy, who had been described as very distraught, had sent her husband to visit an ill relative before committing familicide.
- On July 16, 2011, 17-year-old Tyler Hadley is alleged to have used a hammer to beat to death his parents, Blake and Mary Jo Hadley, at their home in Port St. Lucie, Florida. He then reportedly covered their bodies and posted a message on Facebook, inviting friends over to drink beer. The suspect had apparently threatened to kill his parents previously and was believed to have had a drug abuse problem. On September 14, 2011, Hadley was indicted by a grand jury on two counts of first degree murder.

- On March 10, 2009, 28-year-old Michael McLendon, heavily armed, went on a shooting spree in Alabama, murdering 10 people in Geneva and Coffee Counties. The victims included his mother, grandmother, uncle, and other family members. McLendon, who left behind a hit list, then killed himself.
- On March 19, 1990, Roxanne Jones used a .22 caliber rifle to shoot to death her two teenage sons and young daughter while they slept in their Los Angeles, California, home, before killing herself. Troubled following two stormy marriages, she left several suicide notes.
- On December 28, 1987, Ronald Simmons went on a deadly shooting spree, including the murder of 14 family members in Russellville, Arkansas. He was found guilty of 16 counts of murder and put to death by lethal injection.
- On August 3, 1978, Rachal David pushed or forced seven of her children off an 11th-story balcony of a Salt Lake City, Utah, hotel and then jumped, killing six of the children and herself. Two days earlier, her husband, wanted by the authorities for fraudulent crimes, had committed suicide.
- On March 30, 1975, James Ruppert, 40, gunned down 11 members of his family (including his mother) during an Easter Sunday dinner in Hamilton, Ohio. He was convicted of the crimes and received a life sentence.
- On November 13, 1974, Ronald DeFeo, Jr., 23, used a .35 caliber rifle to murder his parents and four siblings at their home in Amityville, New York. Inspiring the movie *The Amityville Horror*, DeFeo claimed to have been possessed by Satan when he committed the mass murder. He was convicted of the murders and sentenced to six consecutive life terms.
- On February 17, 1970, Jeffrey MacDonald, a 26-year-old army doctor, bludgeoned and stabbed to death his wife and two young children in their Fort Bragg home in Wilmington, North Carolina. In spite of claiming innocence, MacDonald was found guilty of the murders and given three life sentences behind bars.[41]

Characterizing the Familicide Offender

Familicide is committed primarily by adult males, and often ends up with suicide by the perpetrator. According to Ewing, the typical familicide offender is a "white male in his thirties or forties who reacts to extreme stress by killing his wife and child(ren) and then himself. Usually the killings are committed with a firearm that belongs to the perpetrator and has been present in the home for some time."[42]

Researchers have characterized the perpetrator of familicide as often suffering from depression or paranoia and is usually intoxicated.[43] He tends to kill the entire family if he can, including extended family members and even pets. Most familicidal men are unable to handle extreme stress or disruptions in family or outside life. The "dependent-protective" motivation to commit familicide has been identified by some experts on domestic homicide.[44] Peter Marzuk and associates asserted that the perpetrator of familicide-suicide typically likes to control his family and take care of their needs. When his domination is weakened or otherwise undermined, his frustration results in rage that turns homicidal and suicidal.[45] The familicide offender commonly erupts from not only a disintegrating family situation, but loss of control over every aspect of his life and times, which reaches an often deadly breaking point.

Although it is rare that females will murder most of or the entire family, as noted earlier, it does occur. Such familicide offenders are usually despondent over a lost intimate relationship or a hopeless situation. Most are depressed or suffer from severe mental illness.[46]

Juvenile familicide offenders are predominantly male. As with adult murderers of the family, most juvenile perpetrators commit suicide as part of the mass domestic homicide and are often reacting to extreme stress. Such family killers typically suffer from chronic psychiatric problems and have been victimized by child abuse or other domestic violence.[47]

Endnotes

1. R. B. Flowers, *Children and Criminality: The Child as Victim and Perpetrator* (Westport: Greenwood, 1986), p. 58. See also M. Houts, *They Asked for Death* (New York: Cowles, 1970), p. 241; L. Schultz, The Victim-Offender Relationship, *Crime and Delinquency* 14, 2 (1968): 135–41.
2. R. B. Flowers, *Domestic Crimes, Family Violence and Child Abuse: A Study of Contemporary American Society* (Jefferson: McFarland, 2000), p. 62. See also M. Wolfgang, Who Kills Whom, *Psychology Today* 3, 5 (1969): 54–56.
3. M. A. Freeman, *Violence in the Home* (Farnborough: Saxon House, 1979), p. 6.
4. R. J. Gelles & M. A. Straus, Violence in the American Family, *Journal of Social Issues* 35, 2 (1979): 15–39.
5. U.S. Department of Justice, Federal Bureau of Investigation, *Crime in the United States: Uniform Crime Reports 2010*, Expanded Homicide Data Table 10, Murder Circumstances by Relationship, 2010, http://www.fbi.gov/about-us/cjis/ucr/crime-in-the-u.s/2010/crime-in-the-u.s.-2010/tables/10shrtbl10.xls (March 31, 2012).
6. Flowers, *Domestic Crimes, Family Violence and Child Abuse*, p. 112.
7. *Ibid.*; J. M. Leventhal, The Challenges of Recognizing Child Abuse: Seeing Is Believing, *Journal of the American Medical Association* 281, 7 (1999): 657.
8. One Child Dies Daily From Abuse: Parent Probably Was Abuser, *Pediatric News* 9 (1975): 3.

9. V. J. Fontana, *Somewhere a Child Is Crying* (New York: Macmillan, 1973).
10. Cited in P. D. Mayhall & K. Norgard, *Child Abuse and Neglect: Sharing Responsibility* (Toronto: John Wiley & Sons, 1983), p. 98.
11. S. Arbetter, Family Violence: When We Hurt the Ones We Love, *Current Health* 22, 3 (1995): 6.
12. A. Morales, Seeking a Cure for Child Abuse, *USA Today 127*, 2640 (1998): 34.
13. Cited in Flowers, *Children and Criminality*, p. 58.
14. U.S. Department of Health and Human Services, Administration of Children and Families, Children's Bureau, *Child Maltreatment 2010*, pp. 66–67, http://www.acf.hhs.gov/programs/cb/pubs/cm10/index.htm (March 31, 2012).
15. R. B. Flowers & H. L. Flowers, *Murders in the United States: Crimes, Killers and Victims of the Twentieth Century* (Jefferson: McFarland, 2001), pp. 76–77, 128–29, 137; M. Pettus, Mom Gets 55 Years in Prison for Killing Daughter, *WUSA9.com* (April 29, 2011), http://www.wusa9.com/news/article/148815/373/Mom-Gets-55-Years-In-Prison-For-Killing-Daughter; D. Kemp, Father Sentenced to Life Without Parole in Quadruple Slaying, *WLKY.com* (June 9, 2011), http://www.wlky.com/news/28182980/detail.html.
16. M. Levine, J. Freeman, & C. Compaan, Maltreatment-Related Fatalities: Issues of Policy and Prevention, *Law and Policy 16*, 449 (1994): 458.
17. *Ibid.*; Flowers, *Domestic Crimes, Family Violence and Child Abuse.*
18. Cited in Levine, Freeman, & Compaan, Maltreatment-Related Fatalities.
19. D. T. Lunde, Hot Blood's Record Month: Our Murder Boom, *Psychology Today* 9 (1975): 35–42.
20. J. F. Campion, J. M. Cravens, & F. Covan, A Study of Filicidal Men, *American Journal of Psychiatry 145* (1988): 1141.
21. Levine, Freeman, & Compaan, Maltreatment-Related Fatalities, p. 458.
22. *Ibid.*
23. P. Schloesser, J. Pierpont, & J. Poertner, Active Surveillance of Child Abuse Fatalities, *Child Abuse and Neglect 16* (1992): 3–10.
24. R. D. Krugman, Fatal Child Abuse: An Analysis of 20 Cases, *Pediatrics 12* (1983–1985): 68–72.
25. N. Websdale, *Understanding Domestic Homicide* (Boston: Northeastern University Press, 1999), pp. 170–71.
26. U.S. Department of Justice, Federal Bureau of Investigation, *Crime in the United States: Uniform Crime Reports 1999* (Washington: Government Printing Office, 2000), p. 19.
27. U.S. Department of Justice, *Murder in Families* (Washington: Bureau of Justice Statistics, 1994).
28. C. P. Ewing, *Fatal Families: The Dynamics of Intrafamilial Homicide* (Thousand Oaks: Sage, 1997), p. 116.
29. Flowers & Flowers, *Murders in the United States*, pp. 75, 150; D. Ovalle, Miami Teen Who Raped, Killed Sister, to Use Insanity Defense, *Palm Beach Post News* (October 15, 2009), http://www.wsvn.com/news/articles/local/MI134548; J. W. Cox, John Kalisz Sentenced to Death for the Murder of Two Hernando County Women, *Tampa Bay Times* (March 7, 2012), http://www.tampabay.com/news/courts/criminal/john-kalisz-sentenced-to-death-for-murder-of-two-hernando-county-women/1218566.

30. U.S. Department of Justice, Bureau of Justice Statistics, Office of Justice Programs, *Criminal Victimization in the United States—Statistical Tables Index*, Victim-Offender Relationship, http://www.bjs.gov/content/pub/html/cvus/victim_offender_relationship.cfm (April 2, 2012).
31. M. A. Straus, R. J. Gelles, & S. K. Steinmetz, *Behind Closed Doors: Violence in the American Family* (Garden City: Doubleday/Anchor, 1980).
32. Cited in Flowers, *Domestic Crimes, Family Violence and Child Abuse*, pp. 69–70.
33. *Ibid.*, p. 70.
34. Ewing, *Fatal Families*, p. 118.
35. *Murder in Families.*
36. *Ibid.*
37. Ewing, *Fatal Families*, pp. 120–24.
38. *Ibid.*, pp. 124–25.
39. D. A. Cohen, Homicidal Compulsion and the Conditions of Freedom: The Social and Psychological Origins of Familicide in America's Early Republic, *Journal of Social History*, Summer (1995): 725–64.
40. Websdale, *Understanding Domestic Homicide*, p. 18.
41. Flowers & Flowers, *Murders in the United States*, pp. 74–77; Grand Jury Indicts Teen Accused of Killing Parents, Having Party, *CNN Justice* (September 15, 2011), http://www.cnn.com/2011/CRIME/09/15/florida.parents.killed/index.html?iref = allsearch; NY Mom Sends Husband on Errand, Then Kills Family, *CBS News* (December 21, 2011), http://www.cbsnews.com/8301-501363_162-57346734/ny-mom-sends.
42. Ewing, *Fatal Families*, p. 134.
43. *Ibid.*; P. Marzuk, K. Tardiff, & C. Hirsch, The Epidemiology of Murder-Suicide, *Journal of the American Medical Association 267* (1992): 3181.
44. Ewing, Fatal Families, p. 135; A. L. Berman, Dyadic Death: Murder-Suicide, *Suicidal and Life Threatening Behavior 9* (1979): 15.
45. Marjuk, Tardiff, & Hirsch, The Epidemiology of Murder-Suicide, p. 3181.
46. Flowers, *Domestic Crimes, Family Violence and Child Abuse*, p. 68.
47. Ewing, *Fatal Families*, pp. 138–39.

Interpersonal and Societal Murder III

Workplace Homicide

8

The focus on violence in the workplace has increased in recent years as seemingly more work-related stresses and other factors have manifested themselves into violent behavior on the job. Particularly disturbing have been the high-profile cases of lethal workplace violence in the United States in recent times. Most of these have been perpetrated by strangers, with many involving former or current workers holding a grudge against an employer or co-worker, a vengeful stalker, or someone otherwise venting their frustrations against those in a familiar work setting. Homicidal violence in the workplace has taken on a somewhat new and ominous dimension since 2001, with international terrorist attacks of the Pentagon and World Trade Center and biological terrorism in the form of anthrax aimed at news organizations, government offices, and the U.S. Postal Service. In spite of these examples, workplace violence is a relatively low occurrence in comparison to overall violence in society and continues to be largely of a domestic nature. Identifying at-risk victims and offenders and preventive measures continues to be an important undertaking for researchers and policymakers.

In the Context of Workplace Violence

The National Crime Victimization Survey (NCVS) defines workplace violence as "violent acts against a person at work or on duty, including physical assaults (rape and sexual assault and aggravated and simple assault) and robbery. Attempts are included with completed victimizations."[1]

How big is the problem of violence in the workplace? According to U.S. Department of Justice, workplace violence constituted around 24 percent of all nonfatal violent crimes perpetrated against workers 16 years of age and older in the United States in 2009, while accounting for about 15 percent of total nonfatal crimes of violence against individuals age 16 and older.[2]

According to data from the NCVS, in 2009 there were about 572,000 nonfatal crimes of violence committed against people age 16 or older in the workplace or on duty. This represented four nonfatal crimes of violence per 1,000 individuals age 16 years and older who were employed.

In terms of fatalities in the workplace resulting from acts of violence, these constitute only around 4 percent of total homicides in the United States each year. In 2009, for example, there were 521 victims age 16 and older of homicides in the workplace.[3]

During much of the 1990s, there were more than 2 million workplace violent victimizations in this country each year, with an average of nearly 1.5 million simple assault victimizations annually, accounting for the vast majority of workplace violence.[4] Homicides accounted for less than 1 percent of the workplace violent victimizations, averaging just over 1,023 murders per year.[5]

Other studies supported these findings on the magnitude of workplace violence. For instance, a Northwestern National Life survey of physical assaults occurring in the workplace between 1992 and 1993, estimated that there were 2.2 million such assaults.[6]

Some researchers have examined workplace violence in terms of risk factors for victimization,[7] injuries incurred,[8] the frequency of occurrence and circumstances of nonfatal violence in various work settings, and differences between nonfatal and fatal workplace violence.[9]

In the 2000s, workplace violence has been on the decline, according to the Bureau of Justice Statistics (BJS). Between 2002 and 2009, nonfatal violence in the workplace dropped 35 percent.[10] From 2005 to 2009, the average rate of workplace violence annually was about one-third the rate of violence outside the workplace.

Though workplace violence is not as big a problem as violence occurring away from the work environment, it is clearly serious and affects millions with implications that go well beyond the work setting. These include medical, financial, familial, and the reality that many acts of workplace violence begin elsewhere.

Characteristics of Workplace Violence

Who are the people who perpetrate and are victimized by workplace violence? Where is workplace violence most likely to occur? Studies show that perpetrators of violence in the workplace are overwhelmingly male, White, and over the age of 30. In a Justice Department report, males constituted nearly 83 percent of the lone offenders of workplace violence, while females made up just over 14 percent of single offenders of violence in the workplace in the United States.[11]

Nearly 6 in 10 offenders of workplace violence were White, while almost 3 in 10 were Black, in disproportion to their population figures. Other races comprised less than 10 percent of the perpetrators.

Workplace violence was most likely to be committed by people age 21 and over. Nearly half the offenders were age 30 and over, while almost 30 percent fell between the ages of 21 to 29.

Table 8.1   Victims of Workplace Violence and Relationship to Offenders, by Sex, 2005–2009

Victim/Offender Relationship	Workplace Violence	
	Male (%)	Female (%)
Total[a]	100.0	100.0
Intimate partners[b]	0.8	1.7
Other relatives[b]	0.6	0.7
Well-known/casual acquaintances	11.7	18.9
Work relationships	25.5	31.7
Customer/client	3.9	6.5
Patient	1.5	6.0
Current or former:		
Supervisor	1.2	3.3
Employee	2.6	1.7
Co-worker	16.3	14.3
Do not know relationship	8.5	6.1
Stranger	52.9	40.9

[a] Numbers may not add to total because of rounding.
[b] Based on 10 or fewer sample cases.
Source: U.S. Department of Justice, Bureau of Justice Statistics Special Report, *Workplace Violence, 1993–2009* (Washington: Office of Justice Programs, 2011), p. 6.

Studies show that more than two-thirds of violence in the workplace is perpetrated by strangers, though much of the attention is given to violence involving nonstrangers.[12] According to the Office of Justice Programs, between 2005 and 2009, strangers were responsible for nearly 53 percent of workplace violence perpetrated against males and almost 41 percent of the violence against women in the workplace across the country (see Table 8.1). The offender and victim had a work relationship of some sort in about 1 in 4 cases where the victim was a male and in around 1 in 3 instances where the victim was a female. The relationship tended to be largely that of co-workers for male and female victims and their offenders. In nearly 1 in 5 cases of workplace violence involving a female victim, the perpetrator was a well-known or casual acquaintance.

Researchers have characterized the typical workplace violence offender as follows:

- Has a prior history of violence, especially toward women, children, and animals
- Is a loner, often withdrawn, and fears change
- Has emotional problems such as depression and low self-esteem
- Has a substance abuse problem

- Has occupation frustrations including losing job or unsteady employment history
- Has an adversarial association with other people
- Often obsessed with weapons, violence, a person, job, or zealotry[13]

Perpetrators of workplace violence are more likely to commit the acts of violence without use of weapons than with a weapon. As seen in Table 8.2, which compares use of weapons in workplace and nonworkplace violence between 2005 and 2009, more than three-quarters of workplace violence did not involve use of weapons, compared with less than two-thirds of violence outside the workplace.

Just over 18 percent of workplace violence involved weapons such as firearms and knives, while nearly 27 percent of nonworkplace violence included using one or more weapons, with more than 1 in 10 such episodes involving the use of a firearm.

Victims of workplace violence are predominantly male, White, married, under 50 years of age, and making $50,000 or more in household income annually, according to a government report on workplace violence (see Table 8.3). From 2005 to 2009, males were the victims in more than 6 out of 10 cases of workplace violence, compared with females being the victims in less than 4 in 10 workplace victimizations. For nonworkplace violence, the percentage of victimization for males was less than for workplace violence at around 57 percent, and higher for females at just over 43 percent.

Where it concerns race and ethnicity and workplace victimization, more than three-quarters of victims were White between 2005 and 2009, which was more than 12 percent higher than for White victims of violence outside

Table 8.2   Use of Weapons in Workplace and Nonworkplace Violence, 2005–2009

| | Nonfatal Violent Victimizations in | |
Weapon Type	Workplace (%)	Nonworkplace (%)
Total[a]	100.0	100.0
No weapon	77.5	65.4
Weapon	18.3	26.6
Firearm	5.2	10.4
Knife	5.2	6.8
Other weapon	7.0	7.8
Unknown weapon type	1.0	1.6
Do not know if offender had weapon	4.2	8.0

[a] Numbers may not add to total because of rounding.

Source: U.S. Department of Justice, Bureau of Justice Statistics Special Report, *Workplace Violence, 1993–2009* (Washington: Office of Justice Programs, 2011), p. 7.

Table 8.3   Characteristics of Workplace Violence Victims, 2005–2009

Victim Characteristic	Workplace (%)	Nonworkplace (%)	Employed People Age 16 or Older (%)
Total[a]	100.0	100.0	100.0
Sex			
Male	62.9	56.7	54.1
Female	37.1	43.3	45.9
Race/origin			
White[b]	77.9	65.5	70.0
Black/African American[b]	8.7	13.4	10.8
Hispanic/Latino[c]	7.8	14.8	13.5
American Indian[c]	1.3	1.0	0.5
Asian/Pacific Islander[b]	3.1	2.2	4.4
Two or more races[b]	1.3	3.0	0.8
Age			
16–19 years old	3.0	13.7	4.8
20–24	13.7	22.1	10.1
25–34	29.3	25.8	21.7
35–49	34.0	26.8	35.4
50–64	18.8	10.9	24.3
65 or older	1.3	0.7	3.8
Marital status			
Never married	35.0	51.7	29.0
Married	47.2	24.8	56.4
Widowed	1.8	0.9	1.9
Divorced or separated	16.0	22.6	12.7
Annual household income			
Less than $7,500	1.0	6.2	1.8
$7,500 to $14,999	4.4	7.5	3.1
$15,000 to $24,999	7.8	10.2	6.4
$25,000 to $34,999	8.2	11.4	8.1
$35,000 to $49,999	12.2	13.4	12.5
$50,000 to $74,999	22.4	11.5	16.3
$75,000 or more	23.5	16.4	27.5
Unknown	20.6	23.4	24.3

[a] Numbers may not add to total because of rounding.
[b] Excludes people of Hispanic or Latino origin.
[c] Includes all racial groups.
Source: U.S. Department of Justice, Bureau of Justice Statistics Special Report, *Workplace Violence, 1993–2009* (Washington: Office of Justice Programs, 2011), p. 6.

the workplace. African Americans and Hispanics had the second and third highest percentage of victimization in the workplace, at around 9 percent and 8 percent, respectively. Less likely to be victims of workplace violence and nonworkplace violence were Native Americans, Asians, and people of mixed race.

More than 6 in 10 victims of workplace violence fell between the ages of 25 and 49 during the 2005–2009 time span, while nearly 1 in 5 victims were 50 to 64 years of age. Fewer than 1 in 5 victims of violence in the workplace were age 24 and under.[14]

Murder in the Workplace

Although murder in the workplace represents only a fraction of total homicides in the United States, workplace homicide is one of the country's fastest growing types of murder. Furthermore, homicide is the leading cause of women's death on the job, and the second leading cause of men's workplace deaths. Overall, homicide is the second leading cause of death due to injury occurring at work, according to the Bureau of Labor Statistics.[15]

Lethal violence in the workplace has increasingly become mass murder in recent years by disgruntled employees, vengeful current or ex-intimates, and others with an ax to grind. Recent cases of workplace violence in the United States illustrate this ongoing problem:

- On February 10, 2011, Alexander Figueroa, 38, walked into a pharmacy in Astoria, New York, where his estranged wife and mother of his two children, Guimmia Villa, 32, worked. He handed her flowers before shooting her fatally in the face. Figueroa, an ex-con and former tow-truck driver who was unemployed and bitter about an impending divorce and child custody issues, left the scene of the crime before committing suicide.
- On September 9, 2010, Yvonne Hiller, a 43-year-old suspended employee, walked into a Kraft Foods plant in Philadelphia, Pennsylvania, armed with a .357 magnum and opened fire in a break room, killing two co-workers and critically injuring a third. Having just been escorted from the building following an argument, Hiller returned moments later to carry out the attack. She was arrested and charged with two counts of murder, one count of attempted murder, and additional charges.
- On February 12, 2010, Amy Bishop, a 44-year-old biology professor armed with a 9 mm handgun, went on a shooting spree at the University of Alabama in Huntsville in Huntsville, Alabama, killing three members of the faculty and wounding three others. The

previous year, the university had denied Bishop tenure. In 1994, Bishop and her husband were questioned regarding a pipe bomb plot aimed at a Harvard doctor who was her lab supervisor at the time. She has been charged with capital murder and three counts of attempted murder in the university shootings, and also charged with killing her 18-year-old brother Seth Bishop in 1986.

- On November 5, 2009, Nidal Malik Hasan, a 39-year-old U.S. Army psychiatrist, entered the Soldier Readiness Processing Center at Fort Hood, Texas, with a semi-automatic pistol and opened fire, killing 13 and wounding 29 in the worst case of mass casualties to occur at a U.S. military base. Hasan, an American Muslim, was shot and left paralyzed. In a military court, he was charged with 13 counts of premeditated murder and another 32 counts of attempted murder. His trial is set for October 2012.

- On September 11, 2001, hijacked airliners were crashed into the World Trade Center in New York City and the Pentagon in Washington, D.C., by terrorists. Thousands of people were killed.

- On December 26, 2000, Michael McDermott, a 42-year-old computer software technician who was angry over a tax dispute with the Internal Revenue Service and his employer, Edgewater Technology, Inc., went on a deadly shooting rampage at the company in Wakefield, Massachusetts. Armed with an AK-47, shotgun, and semiautomatic pistol, McDermott fatally wounded seven co-workers before he was subdued. He was found guilty of seven counts of first degree murder and sentenced to seven consecutive life sentences without the possibility of parole.

- On July 29, 1999, Mark Orrin, a 44-year-old day trader entered two Atlanta, Georgia, brokerage firms and shot to death 9 people and wounded 12 others. He later committed suicide after being surrounded by police. Orrin was reportedly upset after having incurred heavy losses in the stock market.

- On June 18, 1990, James Pough, a 42-year-old laborer who was angry about having his car repossessed, entered a General Motors Acceptance Corporation office in Jacksonville, Florida, where he opened fire with a .30 caliber rifle. He killed nine and wounded two others before killing himself.

- On September 14, 1989, Joseph Westbecker, a 47-year-old mentally ill employee on disability from Standard Gravure, a Louisville, Kentucky, printing plant, entered the place heavily armed with an AK-47, a SIG Sauer 9mm pistol, several other firearms, and a bayonet. He opened fire, killing 8 and injuring 12, before shooting himself to death.

- On February 16, 1988, Richard Farley, a 39-year-old software developer obsessed with a co-worker, went to a Silicon Valley defense plant's offices in Sunnyvale, California. There, he opened fire, killing seven and wounding four. He was apprehended, convicted, and sentenced to death in the gas chamber.

- On August 21, 1986, Patrick Sherrill, a 44-year-old part-time postal worker, entered an Edmond, Oklahoma, post office heavily armed. He shot to death 14 co-workers and wounded 6 more before killing himself. He was reportedly about to be fired.
- On August 20, 1982, Carl Brown, a 51-year-old history teacher, entered a Miami, Florida, welding machine shop, apparently upset over a bill for work he had had done. He unloaded a 12-gauge shotgun, killing eight employees. Brown was killed when a car ran him over.[16]

The Scope and Nature of Workplace Homicide

Though most workplace violence does not involve deadly use of weapons, lethal workplace violence commands the most attention and occurs often enough to be of concern to workers and law enforcement. According to data from the National Traumatic Occupational Fatalities (NTOF) Surveillance System, between 1980 and 1989, nearly 7,600 workers were homicide victims in the United States. Other findings included

- Eighty percent of victims were male.
- The homicide rate was three times greater for male workers than female workers.
- Homicide was the leading cause of occupational deaths of women, representing four times as many such deaths as among men.
- Almost half the victims of workplace homicide were between the ages of 25 and 44.
- The highest rate of occupational homicide was for workers age 65 and older.
- Three-quarters of all workplace homicide victims were White.
- Nearly 20 percent of victims of occupational homicide were Black.
- Firearms were used in 3 out of every 4 workplace homicides.
- Weapons such as knives and other cutting instruments were responsible for less than 15 percent of occupational homicides.[17]

In a BJS report on workplace violence between 1992 and 1996, an estimate of more than 1,000 homicides occurred in the workplace every year, accounting for around 1 out of every 6 occupational fatalities.[18]

More recently, there has been a decline in workplace homicides in the United States. The Bureau of Labor Statistics' Census of Fatal Occupational Injuries reported that between 1993 and 2009, the number of workplace homicide victims age 16 and older fell around 51 percent from 1,068 to

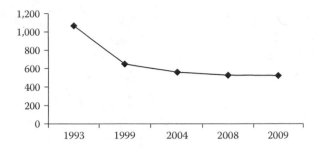

Figure 8.1 Trends in workplace homicides, 1993–2009. (From U.S. Department of Justice, Bureau of Justice Statistics Special Report, *Workplace Violence, 1993– 2009,* Washington, D.C.: Office of Justice Programs, 2011, p. 9.)

521 (see Figure 8.1). The 2009 figure was five fewer than the 526 homicides recorded in the workplace in 2008.

Firearms are by far the most likely weapon used to commit murder in the workplace. As shown in Figure 8.2, between 2005 and 2009, 80 percent of the workplace violence fatalities in the country came as a result of a shooting. Stabbing accounted for around 8 percent of the workplace homicides, followed by assaulting with personal weapons such as hitting and kicking. The type of weapon was unknown in about 6 percent of homicides in the workplace.

Workplace homicides are most likely to occur in sales occupations, according to the BJS and shown in Figure 8.3. Between 2005 and 2009, sales workers were homicide victims in around one-third of the cases of murder in the work setting. Service workers had the second highest percentage of victimization, comprising about 30 percent of the workplace fatalities, followed by production and transportation employees at almost 16 percent. Workers

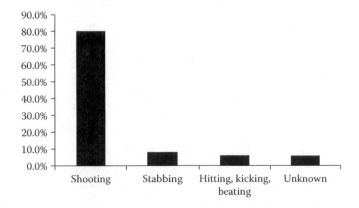

Figure 8.2 Workplace homicides (percentage of workplace homicide victims 16 years of age or older), by type of incident, 2005–2009. (Derived from U.S. Department of Justice, Bureau of Justice Statistics Special Report, *Workplace Violence, 1993–2009,* Washington, D.C.: Office of Justice Programs, 2011, p. 11.)

Figure 8.3 Workplace homicides (percentage of workplace homicide victims 16 years of age or older), by victim's occupation, 2005–2009. (Derived from U.S. Department of Justice, Bureau of Justice Statistics Special Report, *Workplace Violence, 1993–2009*, Washington, D.C.: Office of Justice Programs, 2011, p. 10.)

in other occupations accounted for around one-fifth of the workplace homicide victims.

Studies of occupational homicide have found the highest risk groups for murder include law enforcement personnel; hotel, motel, and gas station employees; and workers in stores, bars, and restaurants.[19]

Characteristics of Workplace Homicide Victims and Offenders

Victims of workplace violence can be men, women, and children of all racial and ethnic persuasions and socioeconomic backgrounds, as evidenced by the Oklahoma City bombing. However, in general, homicide victims in the workplace tend to be overwhelmingly male, White, and people in their mid-20s to mid-50s. Table 8.4 shows workplace homicides in the United States, by characteristics of victims age 16 and over, from 2005 to 2009. Victims were male in almost 82 percent of the murders in the workplace, while fewer than 1 in 5 were female.

Nearly 7 in 10 victims of workplace homicide during the period fell between the ages of 25 and 54, with about one-quarter of all homicide victims in the 35 to 44 age range. Victims under the age of 25 accounted for fewer than 10 percent of workplace homicide victims.

In almost half of the workplace homicides, the victims were White, with more than 2 in 10 African American. More than 16 percent of the victims were Hispanic and around 11 percent were Asian. Native Americans, other races, and those of more than one race accounted for fewer than 2 percent of the victims of workplace homicide.

Perpetrators of workplace homicides are most often robbers, other assailants, or work associates. As seen in Table 8.5, which provides data on workplace homicides by offender between 2005 and 2009, robbers and other assailants accounted for more than 7 in 10 offenders. Nearly 4 in 10 of these

Table 8.4   Workplace Homicides, by Victim Characteristics, 2005–2009

Victim Characteristic	Workplace Homicide Victims Age 16 or Older (%)
Total[a]	100.0
Sex	
Male	81.6
Female	18.4
Age	
16–19 years old	2.2
20–24	7.4
25–34	21.0
35–44	25.4
45–54	22.6
55–64	14.8
65 or older	6.3
Race/origin	
White[b]	48.9
Black/African American[b]	21.7
Hispanic/Latino[c]	16.2
American Indian[b]	0.4
Asian/Pacific Islander[b]	11.2
Two or more races[b]	0.1
Other or race not reported	1.3

[a] Includes 2009 preliminary data. Numbers may not add to total because of rounding.
[b] Excludes people of Hispanic or Latino origin.
[c] Includes all racial groups.
Source: U.S. Department of Justice, Bureau of Justice Statistics Special Report, *Workplace Violence, 1993–2009* (Washington: Office of Justice Programs, 2011), p. 10.

were robbers, with other kinds of assailants making up about one-third of the total.

Work associates were responsible for around one-fifth of the workplace homicides, with co-workers and former co-workers slightly more likely to perpetrate such homicides than customers or clients. Relatives and other personal acquaintances constituted fewer than 1 out of every 10 perpetrators of workplace homicide.

Causes of Workplace Homicide

Workplace homicides are typically caused by stranger robberies and other crimes, vengeful current or former employees, spouses, ex-spouses, other

Table 8.5   Workplace Homicides, by Type of Offender, 2005–2009

Offender Type	Workplace Homicide Victims Age 16 or Older (%)
Total	100.0
Robbers and other assailants	70.3
Robbers	38.3
Other assailants	32.0
Work associates	21.4
Co-worker, former co-worker	11.4
Customer, client	10.0
Relatives	4.0
Spouse	2.9
Other relatives	0.8
Other personal acquaintances	4.3
Current or former boyfriend or girlfriend	2.0
Other acquaintances	2.3

Note: Excludes strangers or assailants who were unknown. Includes 2009 preliminary data. Numbers may not add to total because of rounding.
Source: U.S. Department of Justice, Bureau of Justice Statistics Special Report, *Workplace Violence, 1993–2009* (Washington: Office of Justice Programs, 2011), p. 11.

intimates, and obsessed or stalker killers. However, as we have seen in recent years, the workplace is also a murder target of terrorists, extremists, and others with a personal or political agenda.

Researchers have identified a number of risk factors that may cause or contribute to workplace homicides:

- Job stresses such as termination, demotion, or promotion
- Personal problems such as divorce, financial losses, or child custody issues
- Work involving extensive contact or the exchange of money with the public
- Working alone or with few others around
- Late night or early morning work
- Employment in high-crime areas
- Working in government or military occupations
- Work in high-security occupations
- Work in general public contact professions such as law enforcement or taxicab drivers[20]

According to the National Institute for Occupational Safety and Health:

Differences between fatal and nonfatal workplace assaults may arise from different distributions of instrumental and expressive violence. It may be that instrumental violence in the workplace (robbery) is more likely to result in a fatal outcome than expressive violence (anger displayed by frustrated customers or clients, or coworkers). The premeditated use of a firearm to facilitate robbery may contribute to more fatal outcomes.[21]

Studies show that occupational homicides can be reduced through adopting various behavioral and environmental standards in high-risk work settings, including

- Making such high-risk areas more visible
- The installation of better outside lighting, surveillance cameras, and silent alarms
- Having more people on duty
- Keeping only small amounts of cash on hand
- Nonresistance when encountering a robber
- Training workers in conflict resolution and responding to issues in a nonviolent manner
- Routine law enforcement observation of workplace establishments[22]

Endnotes

1. U.S. Department of Justice, Bureau of Justice Statistics Special Report, *Workplace Violence, 1992–96* (Washington: Office of Justice Programs, 1998), p. 1.
2. U.S. Department of Justice, Bureau of Justice Statistics Special Report, *Workplace Violence, 1993–2009* (Washington: Office of Justice Programs, 2011), p. 1.
3. *Ibid.*; D. N. Castillo & E. L. Jenkins, Industries and Occupations at High Risk for Work-Related Homicide, *Journal of Occupational Medicine* 36 (1994): 125–32.
4. *Workplace Violence, 1992–96,* p.2.
5. *Ibid.*
6. Northwest National Life, *Fear and Violence in the Workplace: A Survey Documenting the Experience of American Workers* (Minneapolis: Northwest National Life, 1993).
7. C. A. Bell, Female Homicides in United States Workplaces, 1980–1985, *American Journal of Public Health* 81 (1991): 729–32; G. M. Liss & C. A. Craig, Homicide in the Workplace in Ontario: Occupations at Risk and Limitations of Existing Data Sources, *Canadian Journal of Public Health* 81 (1990): 10–15.
8. H. P. Davis, A. Honchar, & L. Suarez, Fatal Occupational Injuries of Women, Texas 1975–1984, *American Journal of Public Health* 77 (1987): 1524–27; J. L. Thomas, Occupational Violent Crime: Research on an Emerging Issue, *Journal of Safety Research* 23 (1992): 55–62.

9. See, for example, J. A. Liscomb & C. C. Love, Violence Toward Health Care Workers: An Emerging Occupational Hazard, *American Association of Occupational Health Nurses Journal* 40 (1992): 219–28; R. Erickson, Convenience Store Homicide and Rape, in U.S. Department of Justice, *Convenience Store Security: Report and Recommendations* (Alexandria: U.S. Department of Justice, 1991), pp. 16–18; D. N. Castillo, Nonfatal Violence in the Work Place: Directions for Future Research, in U.S. Department of Justice, *Trends, Risks and Interventions in Lethal Violence: Proceedings of the Third Annual Spring Symposium of the Homicide Research Working Group* (Washington: National Institute of Justice, 1995), pp. 225–35.

10. *Workplace Violence, 1993–2009*, pp. 1–3.

11. *Workplace Violence, 1992–96*, p. 5; National Institute for Occupational Safety and Health, Preventing Homicide in the Workplace, http://www.cdc.gov/niosh/homicide.html.

12. Cited by U.S. Department of Justice, 1998, http://www.workplace-violence-hq.com/.

13. *Ibid.*

14. *Ibid.*; *Workplace Violence, 1993–2009*, p. 6.

15. Cited in *Workplace Violence, 1992–96*, p. 6.

16. R. B. Flowers & H. L. Flowers, *Murders in the United States: Crimes, Killers and Victims of the Twentieth Century* (Jefferson: McFarland, 2001), pp. 78–83; S. Dewan, S. Saul, & K. Zezima, For Professor, Fury Just Beneath the Surface, *New York Times* (February 20, 2010), http://www.nytimes.com/2010/02/21/us/21bishop.html?pagewanted = 1&_r = 1; Trial Delayed for Professor in Ala. Shooting Spree, *BostonGlobe.com* (March 12, 2012), http://www.boston.com/news/local/massachusetts/articles/2012/03/12/trial_delayed_for_professor_in_ala_shooting_spree/; J. Goudreau, Female Employee Yvonne Hiller Kills Two in Kraft Shooting, *Forbes* (September 10, 2010), http://www.forbes.com/sites/jennagoudreau/2010/09/10/female-shooter-yvonne-hiller-kills-two-at-kraft-shooting; L. Celona & K. Conley, Man Brings Flowers to Ex, Then Shoots Her in the Face, *New York Post* (February 10, 2011), http://www.nypost.com/p/news/local/queens/man_kills_ex_wife_in_astoria_pharmacy_wPcii5rwVNJAC0pbv6v8TO.

17. Preventing Homicide in the Workplace.

18. *Workplace Violence, 1992–96*, p. 6.

19. Castillo, Nonfatal Violence in the Work Place, p. 229; T. Hales, P. Seligman, C. Newman, & C. L. Timbrook, Occupational Injuries Due to Violence, *Journal of Occupational Medicine* 30 (1988): 483–87.

20. U.S. Department of Justice, 1998; J. F. Kraus, Homicides While at Work: Persons, Industries, and Occupations at High Risk, *American Journal of Public Health* 77, 10 (1987): 1285–89.

21. Castillo, Nonfatal Violence in the Work Place, pp. 229–30.

22. See, for example, S. G. Chapman, *Cops, Killers and Staying Alive: The Murder of Police Officers in America* (Springfield: Charles C Thomas, 1986); W. J. Crow & R. Erickson, *The Store Safety Issue: Facts for the Future* (Alexandria: National Association of Convenience Stores, 1989).

Bias-Motivated Homicide

9

One of the most disturbing areas of homicide in the United States concerns bias-motivated murders. These killings occur primarily due to prejudice by the offender against specific groups in society such as a race, ethnicity, sexual orientation, or religion. Recent years have seen a number of highly publicized, tragic cases of bias-related homicides. Perpetrators of these crimes are predominantly male, usually young, and often belong to extremist or hate groups or otherwise have strong feelings of intolerance or resentment against those targeted.

Bias or hate crimes have long existed in this country, fueled by bigotry and intolerance, along with advances in civil rights. However, only since the early 1990s have a series of laws been passed to address the national concern over serious and violent criminal behavior motivated by hatred. In spite of this, hate crimes continue to manifest themselves in homicidal violence, including the recent terrorist attacks of hatred directed toward the entire U.S. population.

What Are Hate Crimes?

According to the Department of Justice, a hate crime, also called a bias crime, is "a criminal offense committed against a person, property, or society which is motivated, in whole or in part, by the offender's bias against a race, religion, disability, sexual orientation, or ethnicity/national origin."[1]

An expert on hate crimes defines them as "message crimes. They are different from other crimes in that the offender is sending a message to members of a certain group that they are unwelcome."[2]

The definition of a hate crime can vary from state to state. In a study of hate crimes and state definitions, Eve Garber found that "twenty-one states include mental and physical disability ... twenty-two states include sexual orientation. Three states and the District of Columbia impose tougher penalties for crimes based on political affiliation."[3]

Hate crimes may include any offense motivated by a person's bias such as murder and nonnegligent manslaughter, forcible rape, aggravated assault, simple assault, and intimidation, along with robbery, burglary, larceny-theft, motor vehicle theft, arson, and property destruction, damage, or vandalism.

Bias-motivated crime offenders come from every racial and ethnic group, nationality, and socioeconomic and educational background. What they share in common is the willingness to commit criminal acts that are often violent, borne out of and sustained by hatred and related factors aimed at vulnerable victims who conform to the offender's biases.

Homicidal hate crimes are often perpetrated by multiple offenders who share a particular bias toward someone or something a potential victim symbolizes. For instance, in 1998, Aaron McKinney and Russell Henderson beat to death gay college student Matthew Shepard in Laramie, Wyoming. The brutal nature of the attack led to increased efforts to strengthen anti–hate crime legislation.[4]

In September 2001, 19 men of Middle Eastern descent expressed their hatred against American society and its policies by hijacking four airliners, crashing two of them into the World Trade Center and another into the Pentagon, causing the death of thousands of people (see also Chapter 16).

The vast majority of hate crimes are single-bias incidents or motivated by a single circumstance or cause. Multiple-bias incidents involving more than one reason for the offense have also occurred.

The Magnitude of Hate Crimes

How large is the scope of hate offenses? Prior to 1990, there was no official national tracking of hate crimes in the United States. Public pressure led Congress to enact the Hate Crimes Statistics Act (HCSA), signed into law in 1990. This act required the federal government to collect statistics "about crimes that manifest evidence of prejudice based on race, religion, sexual orientation, or ethnicity."[5] In 1994, it was amended by the Violent Crime Control and Law Enforcement Act to include physical and mental disabilities as possible bias motivations.[6] Data collection on disability-related bias started in 1997.

According to the Uniform Crime Reports, in 2010 there were 6,628 hate crime incidents in the United States reported to the FBI (see Table 9.1). These entailed 7,699 offenses. The vast majority of the cases were single bias, with 6,624 incidents that included 7,690 offenses, 8,199 victims, and 6,001 known offenders. There were four multiple-bias incidents that included 9 offenses, 7 offenders, and 9 victims.

Race was the most likely single-bias factor, accounting for 3,135 incidents and 3,725 offenses involving 3,949 victims and 2,934 known offenders. Anti-Black hate crime incidents occurred far more often than any other racial bias, with 2,201 such incidents and 2,600 offenses with 2,765 victims and 1,974 offenders. Anti-White incidents occurred second most often for single-bias crimes, followed by hate crimes targeting persons from multiple races, Asians, and Native Americans.

Table 9.1   Hate Crime Incidents, Offenses, Victims, and Known Offenders, by Bias Motivation, 2010

Bias Motivation	Incidents	Offenses	Victims[a]	Known Offenders[b]
Total	6,628	7,699	8,208	6,008
Single-bias incidents	6,624	7,690	8,199	6,001
Race	3,135	3,725	3,949	2,934
Anti-White	575	679	697	649
Anti-Black	2,201	2,600	2,765	1,974
Anti–American Indian/Alaskan Native	44	45	47	43
Anti-Asian/Pacific Islander	150	190	203	156
Anti–multiple races, group	165	211	237	112
Religion	1,322	1,409	1,552	606
Anti-Jewish	887	922	1,040	346
Anti-Catholic	58	61	65	22
Anti-Protestant	41	46	47	6
Anti-Islamic	160	186	197	125
Anti–other religion	123	134	141	72
Anti–multiple religions, group	48	53	55	30
Anti-atheism/agnosticism/etc.	5	7	7	5
Sexual orientation	1,277	1,470	1,528	1,516
Anti-male homosexual	739	851	876	904
Anti-female homosexual	144	167	181	152
Anti-homosexual	347	403	420	412
Anti-heterosexual	21	21	22	21
Anti-bisexual	26	28	29	27
Ethnicity/national origin	847	1,040	1,122	887
Anti-Hispanic	534	681	747	593
Anti–other ethnicity/national origin	313	359	375	294
Disability	43	46	48	58
Anti-physical	19	22	24	28
Anti-mental	24	24	24	30
Multiple-bias incidents[c]	4	9	9	7

[a] The term *victim* may refer to a person, business, institution, or society as a whole.

[b] The term *known offender* does not imply that the identity of the suspect is known, but only that an attribute of the suspect has been identified, which distinguishes him/her from an unknown offender.

[c] In a multiple-bias incident, two conditions must be met: (1) more than one offense type must occur in the incident and (2) at least two offense types must be motivated by different biases.

Source: U.S. Department of Justice, Federal Bureau of Investigation, *Crime in the United States: Uniform Crime Reports 2010,* Hate Crime Statistics, Table 1, Incidents, Offenses, Victims, and Known Offenders by Bias Motivation, 2010, http://www.fbi. gov/about-us/cjis/ucr/hate-crime/2010/tables/table-1-incidents-offenses-victims- and-known-offenders-by-bias-motivation-2010.xls (April 6, 2012).

Religious bias made up the second most likely single-bias factor, with 1,322 incidents and 1,407 offenses; followed closely by sexual orientation bias with 1,277 incidents and 1,470 offenses. However, there were more known offenders in sexual orientation offenses than religious motivated offenses, outnumbering them by more than 2.5 to 1.

Ethnicity/national origin bias had the fourth most single-bias incidents during the year with 847, and the third most known offenders by category; with disability bias accounting for the fewest single-bias incidents, offenses, offenders, and victims.

Table 9.2 reflects bias motivation by victim type and incident in 2010. The vast majority of incidents were aimed at the individual in all categories, with race and sexual orientation drawing the most single-bias incidents.

Unknown or multiple victim types were the second most likely to be victimized by bias offenders; followed by business and financial institutions, government, and religious organizations. In a Gallup Poll, more than 8 in 10 racial, ethnic, and religious minorities and more than 3 in 4 homosexuals were afraid of becoming the victim of a hate crime.[7]

As shown in Table 9.3, the majority of hate crime incidents and offenses committed in the United States in 2010 were crimes against people, with 3,978 incidents and 4,824 offenses. These included such crimes as murder and nonnegligent manslaughter, forcible rape, aggravated and simple assault, and intimidation. Most crimes involved intimidation, followed by assaultive crimes. There were 6 incidents and 7 offenses involving murder and nonnegligent manslaughter with 7 victims and 9 offenders.

Crimes against property represented most other offenses reported to law enforcement agencies during the year as bias motivated, with 2,861 such incidents and the same number of offenses involving 3,370 victims and 1,419 offenders. The crimes consisted largely of destruction of property and vandalism, with other offenses including larceny-theft, robbery, and burglary.

The fewest hate crimes recorded in all categories in 2010 were crimes against society, with 14 incidents and 14 offenses, along with 14 victims and 18 offenders.

Murder Caused by Hate

In 2010, there were 6 bias-motivated incidents and 7 offenses involving murder and nonnegligent manslaughter in the United States. These included 7 victims and 9 known offenders.[8] Nine years earlier, in 2001, the victims of hate crimes rose considerably with the terrorist attacks and bioterrorist anthrax attacks resulting in the death of thousands in America.[9] Other homicides in recent years may have been bias-related but were misidentified or have not been solved.

Table 9.2 Bias-Motivation Incidents, by Victim Type, 2010

Bias Motivation	Total Incidents	Victim Type					
		Individual	Business/Financial Institution	Government	Religious Organization	Society/Public[a]	Other/Unknown/Multiple
Total	6,628	5,236	331	267	188	9	597
Single-bias incidents	6,624	5,232	331	267	188	9	597
Race	3,135	2,574	167	162	20	7	205
Religion	1,322	678	112	74	163	0	295
Sexual orientation	1,277	1,177	30	18	1	0	51
Ethnicity/national origin	847	764	21	13	4	1	44
Disability	43	39	1	0	0	1	2
Multiple-bias incidents[b]	4	4	0	0	0	0	0

[a] The victim type *society/public* is collected only in the National Incident-Based Reporting System.

[b] In a multiple-bias incident, two conditions must be met: (1) more than one offense type must occur in the incident and (2) at least two offense types must be motivated by different biases.

Source: U.S. Department of Justice, Federal Bureau of Investigation, *Crime in the United States: Uniform Crime Reports 2010*, Hate Crime Statistics, Table 8, Incidents, Victim Type, by Bias Motivation, 2010, http://www.fbi.gov/about-us/cjis/ucr/hate-crime/2010/tables/table 8-incidents-victim-type-by-bias-motivation-2010.xls (April 6, 2012).

Table 9.3   Hate Crime Dynamics, by Type of Offense, 2010

Bias Motivation	Incidents[a]	Offenses	Victims[b]	Known Offenders[c]
Total	6,628	7,699	8,208	6,008
Crimes against persons:	3,978	4,824	4,824	4,873
Murder and nonnegligent manslaughter	6	7	7	9
Forcible rape	4	4	4	7
Aggravated assault	695	888	888	1,144
Simple assault	1,472	1,681	1,681	1,972
Intimidation	1,790	2,231	2,231	1,726
Other[d]	11	13	13	15
Crimes against property:	2,861	2,861	3,370	1,419
Robbery	146	146	168	290
Burglary	125	125	163	88
Larceny-theft	175	175	195	141
Motor vehicle theft	16	16	16	8
Arson	43	43	45	30
Destruction/damage/vandalism	2,321	2,321	2,747	831
Other[d]	35	35	36	31
Crimes against society[d]	14	14	14	18

[a] The actual number of incidents is 6,628. However, the column figures will not add to the total because incidents may include more than one offense type, and these are counted in each appropriate offense type category.

[b] The term *victim* may refer to a person, business, institution, or society as a whole.

[c] The term *known offender* does not imply that the identity of the suspect is known, but only that an attribute of the suspect has been identified, which distinguishes him/her from an unknown offender. The actual number of known offenders is 6,008. However, the column figures will not add to the total because some offenders are responsible for more than one offense type; and they are, therefore, counted more than once in this table.

[d] Includes additional offenses collected in the National Incident-Based Reporting System.

Source: U.S. Department of Justice, Federal Bureau of Investigation, *Crime in the United States: Uniform Crime Reports 2010*, Hate Crime Statistics, Table 2, Incidents, Offenses, Victims, and Known Offenders, by Offense Type, 2010, http://www.fbi.gov/about-us/cjis/ucr/hate-crime/2010/tables/table 2-incidents-offenses-victims-and-known-offenders-by-offense-type-2010.xls (April 6, 2012).

Between 2005 and 2010, there were 19 incidents and 40 offenses pertaining to murder and nonnegligent manslaughter in this country, involving 40 victims and 99 known offenders (see Figure 9.1). The number of hate-crime-related homicide victims was highest in 2007 with 9 victims, and lowest in 2006 with 3 victims. The number of offenders with a bias motivation to commit murder was highest in 2009 with 47 known offenders, and lowest in 2006 with 4 known offenders.

Most bias-motivated homicides in this country are not the work of foreign terrorists or hate groups but are committed by domestic groups or

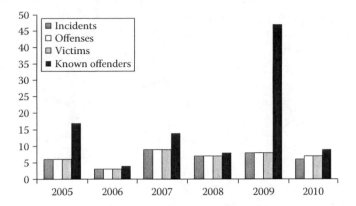

Figure 9.1 Murder-related hate crimes, by incidents, offenses, victims, and offenders, 2005–2010. Figures include nonnegligent manslaughter. (Derived from U.S. Department of Justice, Federal Bureau of Investigation, *Crime in the United States: Uniform Crime Reports 2010*, Hate Crime Statistics, Incidents, Offenses, Victims, and Known Offenders by Offense Type, 2005–2010, http://www.fbi.gov/about-us/cjis/ucr/hate-crime/2010/index, April 8, 2012.)

individuals. Notable cases of murder and mass murder perpetrated largely by hatred of the victims, government, or what they represented include the following:

- On June 26, 2011, James Anderson, an African American, was murdered in Jackson, Mississippi, in a racially motivated attack that involved the victim being hit with a pickup truck. Federal hate-crime charges were filed against the White perpetrators, Deryl Dedmon, 19; John Rice, 18; and Dylan Butler, 20—all of whom pled guilty to the charges. Dedmon, who owned and drove the truck that killed Anderson, pled guilty on state charges to murder and was given two life sentences in prison.
- On December 7, 2008, Jose Sucuzhanay, an Ecuadoran immigrant, was beaten to death with a bat in Brooklyn, New York. Arrested and charged with the murder as a hate crime was Keith Phoenix, 28. Phoenix and Hakim Scott, 26, mistook Sucuzhanay and his brother Romel Sucuzhanay for a gay couple in the attack. In June 2010, Phoenix was convicted of the hate crime, receiving a sentence of 37 years to life behind bars. Scott was found guilty of manslaughter.
- In October and November 2001, bioterrorism consisting of inhalation anthrax killed five people in the United States. Dozens of people were infected by inhaled or cutaneous anthrax nationwide, believed to have originated from contaminated mail at U.S. postal facilities. In spite of a number of suspects, no one was actually brought to justice in connection with the crimes.

- On September 11, 2001, four American airliners were hijacked by 19 terrorists, all identified as having Middle Eastern roots. Two planes crashed into the Twin Towers of the World Trade Center in New York, causing both towers to collapse; another plane crashed into the Pentagon; and the fourth plane went down in Pennsylvania. Thousands of people lost their lives, including the hijacker-terrorists, while thousands of others developed health problems related to the attacks. This terrorist attack, the deadliest in U.S. history, was blamed on the Al Qaeda terrorist organization, led by its leader, Osama bin Laden.
- On November 8, 1998, two Mexican laborers were shot to death in a California border town. Arrested for the crime were teenagers Kenneth Kovzelove and Dennis Bencivenga. Kovzelove pleaded guilty to two counts of first degree murder and received a sentence of 50 years to life. Bencivenga pleaded guilty to two counts of manslaughter and was sentenced to 14 years in prison.
- On October 12, 1998, Matthew Shepard, a gay college student, was viciously attacked in Laramie, Wyoming. He died a few days later. Aaron McKinney and Russell Henderson were arrested and charged with the crime. Both were convicted and given two consecutive life sentences behind bars.
- In June 1998, James Byrd, Jr., an African American, was beaten and dragged to his death in Jasper, Texas. Arrested and convicted for the murder were White supremacists Shawn Berry, John King, and Lawrence Brewer. King and Brewer received death sentences, and Berry was given 40 years to life behind bars.
- On April 22, 1970, Rainey Pool, an African American sharecropper, was the victim of a fatal mob attack near the town of Louise, Mississippi. Nearly 30 years later, White racists James Caston, Charles Caston, and Hal Crimm were found guilty of manslaughter in Pool's death.
- On April 4, 1968, civil rights leader Martin Luther King, Jr., was assassinated in Memphis, Tennessee. Arrested and convicted for the murder was James Earl Ray. He was sentenced to 99 years in prison, though he later recanted his guilty plea.
- On January 10, 1966, civil rights activist Vernon Dahmer was the victim of a firebombing in Mississippi. After five trials for the murder, former Ku Klux Klan leader Samuel Bowers was convicted in 1998 and sentenced to life in prison. Bowers had previously served time for his role in the 1964 murders of three other civil rights workers.
- On June 12, 1963, NAACP activist Medgar Evars was gunned down in front of his home in Jackson, Mississippi. More than three decades later, Byron De La Beckwith, a White supremacist, was convicted of the murder.[10]

Who Are the Perpetrators of Bias Crimes?

The vast majority of hate crimes are committed by young White males.[11] Most are considered "lone wolves" who act in small cells, pairs, or alone.[12] FBI data on known bias-motivated offenders in 2010 shows that more than 41 percent were White and nearly 12 percent were Black (see Figure 9.2). Just over 3 percent of known offenders were of multiple races, while less than 2 percent were Native American or Asian. More than 42 percent of the hate crime offenders were of an unknown race or unknown offenders.

Many offenders are either directly or indirectly affiliated with or influenced by hate organizations such as Ku Klux Klan and neo-Nazi groups. According to the Southern Poverty Law Center, more than 500 hate groups were in existence in the United States in 1998.[13] The Los Angeles–based Simon Wiesenthal Center monitors reportedly more than 2,100 hate sites operating on the Internet.[14]

Some researchers contend that most perpetrators of hate crimes are not considered "skinheads" or otherwise belonging to a neo-Nazi organization. In a study of 1,459 hate crimes perpetrated in Los Angeles from 1994 to 1995, fewer than 5 percent of the perpetrators were found to belong to hate organizations.[15]

Young offenders account for a high proportion of the hate crimes committed in the United States. More than half of all bias-motivated murders are committed by people under the age of 21.[16] Many of these are described as thrill seekers rather than hardcore hate offenders. In a Northeastern University study of bias crimes, 60 percent of the perpetrators committed their offenses for the thrill of it.[17]

According to forensic psychologist Karen Franklin, the most widespread and socially acceptable type of hate crime among youthful offenders are

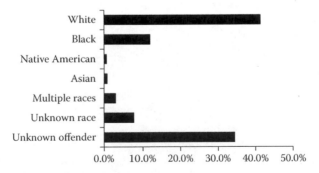

Figure 9.2 Total known offenders of bias crimes, by race, 2010. (Derived from: U.S. Department of Justice, Federal Bureau of Investigation, *Crime in the United States: Uniform Crime Reports 2010*, Hate Crime Statistics, Table 5, Offenses, Known Offender's Race, by Bias Motivation, 2010, http://www.fbi.gov/about-us/cjis/ucr/hatecrime/2010/tables/table-5-offenses-known-offenders-race-by-bias-motivation-2010.xls, April 8, 2012.)

those motivated by a sexual orientation bias. She breaks down these offenders into four categories:

- *Ideology assailants* base their bias crimes on negative beliefs and feelings they believe are shared by others in the community or an extremist group they may belong to.
- *Thrill seekers* tend to be adolescent offenders who perpetrate their hate crimes to relieve boredom, for fun and excitement, and as a means to feel power.
- *Peer dynamics* hate crime offenders are often youthful and perpetrate their offense as a part of peer group toughness and acceptance.
- *Self-defense assailants* perceive their actions as in defense of unwanted advances or positions taken such as by homosexuals.[18]

What Causes Hate Crimes?

Hate crimes are caused by various conditions, ideologies, and bigotries. Researchers have found that most bias-motivated offenses are committed by "otherwise law-abiding [citizens] who see little wrong with their actions."[19] Although alcohol and drugs often play a role in hate crime participation, most experts believe that the primary cause of bias offending is individual prejudice, which "colors people's judgment, blinding the aggressors to the immorality of what they are doing. Such prejudice is most likely rooted in an environment that disdains someone who is 'different' or sees that difference as threatening."[20]

The most extreme bias-motivated crimes—such as those involving particularly brutal homicides or other assaultive behavior—tend to be perpetrated by offenders with a history of serious and violent offending or other aggressive behavior.

Some social scientists have related hate crimes to downturns in the economy. Others believe that hate crimes are "sporadic, isolated, uncoordinated, and not tied to economic fluctuation."[21] According to Donald Green, Jack Glaser, and Andrew Rich, who co-authored a study on hate crime: "Rather than economic downturns, neighborhood influxes of ethnically diverse people were most likely to spur bigoted violence. The only time economic hardship relates to hate crime is when established political leaders convince the public that specific groups are to blame."[22] An example of this may be the recent terrorist attack in America in which people of Middle Eastern origin or Islamic religion became the victims of hate offenders after the terrorists were identified as extremists from the Middle East.

Studies have found that bias-motivated crimes "are not necessarily random, uncontrollable, or inevitable occurrences."[23] On the contrary, most

evidence indicates that society and policymakers can create effective strate-
gies for reducing or preventing the occurrence of hate crimes and other types
of violence.[24]

Hate Crime Legislation

A number of laws have been enacted in recent years designed to combat hate
crimes. These include the Hate Crimes Prevention Act, the Church Arson
Prevention Act, and the Hate Crime Sentencing Enhancement Act.

Hate Crimes Prevention Act

The Hate Crimes Prevention Act of 1999 made it a crime to interfere with
a person's federal right by way of violence or the threat of as a result of the
individual's race, ethnicity, gender, religion, national origin, or sexual orientation.[25] The act provides federal prosecutors greater authority to investigate
hate crimes and prosecute offenders.

Church Arson Prevention Act

The Church Arson Prevention Act of 1996 mandated that the collection of
hate crime data become a permanent aspect of the FBI's Uniform Crime
Reporting Program.[26] The act created the National Church Arson Task Force,
whose purpose is to oversee the investigation and prosecution of arson perpetrated at houses of worship across the United States. It also allowed for greater
federal jurisdiction for such criminality and a rebuilding recovery fund.

Hate Crime Sentencing Enhancement Act

The Hate Crime Sentencing Enhancement Act is part of the Violent Crime
Control and Law Enforcement Act of 1994.[27] The act allows for longer sentences for hate crime offenses or those motivated by a victim's race, ethnicity,
color, gender, sexual orientation, or disability.

Endnotes

1. U.S. Department of Justice, Federal Bureau of Investigation, *Crime in the United
   States: Uniform Crime Reports 1999* (Washington: Government Printing Office,
   2000), p. 58.
2. Quoted in R. V. Siasoco, Defining Hate Crimes: No Longer a Black and White
   Issue, http://www.infoplease.com/spot/hatecrirmes.html.
3. *Ibid.*

4. R. B. Flowers & H. L. Flowers, *Murders in the United States: Crimes, Killers and Victims of the Twentieth Century* (Jefferson: McFarland, 2001), p. 181.
5. 28 U.S.C. 534 (1990).
6. *Crime in the United States*, p. 59.
7. G. Gallup, Jr. & A. Gallup, *The Gallup Poll Monthly*, No. 401 (Princeton: The Gallup Poll, 1999), pp. 28–29.
8. U.S. Department of Justice, Federal Bureau of Investigation, *Crime in the United States: Uniform Crime Reports 2010,* Hate Crime Statistics, Table 2, Incidents, Offenses, Victims, and Known Offenders, by Offense Type, 2010, http://www.fbi.gov/about-us/cjis/ucr/hate-crime/2010/tables/table-2-incidents-offenses-victims-and-known-offenders-by-offense-type-2010.xls (April 8, 2012).
9. Wikipedia, the Free Encyclopedia, September 11 Attacks, http://en.wikipedia.org/wiki/September_11_attacks (April 8, 2012); National Commission on Terrorist Attacks, *The 9/11 Commission Report: Final Report of the National Commission on Terrorist Attacks Upon the United States* (New York: W.W. Norton, 2004); P. L. Bergen, *Holy War, Inc.: Inside the Secret World of Osama Bin Laden* (New York: Free Press, 2001).
10. Flowers & Flowers, *Murders in the United States*, pp. 178–82; Pair Sentenced in Brooklyn Hate Crime Murder, ABCNews.com (April 5, 2010), http://abclocal.go.com/wabc/story?section=news/local&id=7594314; K. Severson, Three Plead Guilty to Hate Crimes in Killing of Black Man in Mississippi, *New York Times* (March 22, 2012), http://www.nytimes.com/2012/03/23/us/three-plead-guilty-to-hate-crimes-in-killing-of-black-man-in-mississippi.html?scp=1&sq=three%20plead%20guilty%20to%20hate%20crime&st=cse.
11. See http://www.civilrights/publications/cause_for_concern/p.10.html; http://www.teemings.com/issue05/hatecrimes.html.
12. Siasoco, Defining Hate Crimes.
13. *Ibid.*
14. *Ibid.*
15. Cited in American Psychological Association, Hate Crimes Today: An Age-Old Foe in Modern Dress, http://www.apa.org/pubinfo/hate/#top.
16. W. Lin, Perpetrators of Hate, *Yale Political Quarterly* 19, 2 (1997): 12.
17. Cited in http://www.civilrights.org/publications/cause_for_concern/p.10.html.
18. Cited in American Psychological Association, Hate Crimes Today.
19. *Ibid.*
20. *Ibid.*
21. American Psychological Association, "Study Finds No Evidence That Economic Downturn Spur Hate Crimes, 1998, http://www.apa.org/.
22. *Ibid.*
23. American Psychological Association, Hate Crimes Today.
24. *Ibid.*
25. 18 U.S.C. 245; as amended by H.R. 1082 (1999).
26. 18 U.S.C. 247 (1996).
27. P.L. 103-322, Sec. 280003 (1994).

Terrorism and Murder   10

On September 11, 2001, terrorism and mass murder struck America like never before in its history. That fateful day, 19 determined foreign terrorists hijacked four United States airliners, crashing two into the Twin Towers of the World Trade Center and another into the Pentagon, causing the death of thousands of innocent victims. This came just over six years after the Oklahoma City bombing, which had been the nation's worst terrorist attack. Both have led to increased antiterrorism measures as well as a general sense of vulnerability to this disturbing and persistent form of violent and homicidal behavior. Though other acts of terrorism since then on U.S. soil have been thwarted or responded to by the Department of Homeland Security and ever-diligent law enforcement across the country, terrorist experts and criminologists continue to put forth renewed efforts in identifying terrorists and terrorist organizations, causes of terrorism, the correlation between terrorism and homicide, and ways to avert disaster before it strikes.

What Is Terrorism?

Terrorism is a term used to denote acts of terror that instill fear and intimidation, and are often violent and of a political nature. Specifically, the dictionary defines terrorism as "(1) the political use of violence or intimidation and (2) the systematic use of terror especially as a means of coercion."[1] The word *terrorism* originated during the French Revolution in the late 1700s to reflect what was known as the Reign of Terror, in which some revolutionists seized and maintained power through violence.[2]

Over the years, terrorism has been defined by various international organizations, governments, scholars, and experts on terrorism and terrorists. In 1937, the League of Nations Convention defined terrorism as "all criminal acts directed against a State and intended or calculated to create a state of terror in the minds of particular persons or a group of persons or the general public."[3] According to the *World Book*, terrorism is "the use or threat of violence to create fear and alarm. Terrorists murder and kidnap people, set off bombs, hijack airplanes, set fires, and commit other serious crimes. But the goals of terrorists differ from those of ordinary criminals who (generally) want money or some other form of personal gain. But most terrorists commit crimes to support political causes."[4]

Under Title 22 of the U.S. Code, the term *terrorism* is defined as "premeditated, politically-motivated violence perpetrated against noncombatant targets by subnational groups or clandestine agents, usually intended to influence an audience. 'International terrorism' is terrorism involving the territory or the citizens of more than one country," while the term *terrorist group* refers to "any group that practices, or has significant subgroups that practice, international terrorism."[5]

In a 1999 United Nations Resolution, terrorism was defined as "criminal acts intended or calculated to provoke a state of terror in the general public, a group of persons, or particular persons for political purposes," while being strongly condemned as "criminal and unjustifiable, whatever the considerations of a political, philosophical, ideological, racial, ethnic, religious or other nature that may be invoked to justify them."[6]

Among academics, terrorism has been defined as

> an anxiety-inspiring method of repeated violent action, employed by (semi) clandestine individual, group or state actors, for idiosyncratic, criminal or political reasons, whereby—in contrast to assassination—the direct targets of violence are not the main targets. The immediate human victims of violence are generally chosen randomly ... or selectively ... from a target population, and serve as message generators. Threat- and violence-based communication processes between terrorist (organization), (imperiled) victims, and main targets are used to manipulate the main target (audience(s)), turning it into a target of terror, a target of demands, or a target of attention, depending on whether intimidation, coercion, or propaganda is primarily sought.[7]

Others have been terse but effective in defining terrorism. For example, David Lester and H. A. Cooper note that terrorism "generates a high level of fear in society, has a coercive purpose, and requires a human audience."[8] Whereas Benjamin Wolman's definition of terrorism is "a grave sociopolitical and psychological problem that requires a thorough and responsible analysis."[9]

Perhaps Walter Laquer's broad interpretation of terrorism puts it in a proper definitional context with today's wide ranging, multi-causal, and motivational terrorism:

> Terrorism ... has been waged by national and religious groups, by the left and by the right, by nationalist as well as international movements, and it has been state-sponsored ... Terrorist movements have frequently consisted of members of the educated middle classes, but there has also been agrarian terrorism, terror by the uprooted and the rejected, and trade union and working-class terror.... Terror has been directed against autocratic regimes as well as democracies; sometimes there has been an obvious link with social

dislocation and economic crisis, at other times there has been no such connection. Movements of national liberation and social revolution (or reaction)
have turned to terrorism after political action has failed. But elsewhere, and
at other times, terrorism has not been the consequence of political failure, but
has been chosen by militant groups even before other options were tried.[10]

Deadly Terrorist Attacks Against the United States and Americans

The incidence of international and domestic terrorist-related deadly attacks
against the United States, its citizens, or interests has risen dramatically in
the 1990s and early 2000s. This is primarily due to recent terrorist-perpe-
trated mass murders at the Oklahoma City Federal Building, New York's
World Trade Center, and the Pentagon in Washington, D.C. Other terrorist
attacks have also contributed to this alarming trend. Recent acts of deadly
terrorism involving Americans and America include the following:

- On December 12, 2008, a homemade bomb detonated at a West
  Coast Bank in Woodburn, Oregon, killed an Oregon state trooper
  bomb squad technician and a captain with the Woodburn Police
  Department, and seriously injured the Woodburn police chief.
  Charged with the crime were Bruce Turnidge, 57, and his son Joshua
  Turnidge, 32, who had reportedly fantasized about robbing banks,
  making bombs, and organizing a militia as well as idolized domestic terrorist Timothy McVeigh. On December 8, 2010, the Turnidges
  were both found guilty on 18 counts, including aggravated murder,
  attempted aggravated murder, and additional assault charges. A jury
  sentenced the pair to death.
- In October and November 2001, bioterrorism in the form of inhalation anthrax killed five people in the United States. Dozens of people
  were infected by inhaled or cutaneous anthrax nationwide, believed
  to have originated from contaminated mail at U.S. postal facilities.
  Though the FBI targeted several individuals as suspects, no one has
  ever been formally charged with the crimes to date.
- On September 11, 2001, four American airliners were hijacked by 19
  terrorists, all identified as having Middle Eastern roots. Two planes
  were crashed into the Twin Towers of the World Trade Center in
  New York, causing both to collapse; another plane was crashed into
  the Pentagon, and the fourth plane went down in Pennsylvania. In
  all, thousands of people lost their lives, including the hijacker-terrorists. The deadliest terrorist attack in U.S. history was blamed on the
  Al Qaeda terrorist organization, led by its leader, Osama bin Laden.

- On October 12, 2000, terrorists in a boat detonated a bomb outside the *U.S.S. Cole* in the harbor at Aden, Yemen, killing 17 sailors and injuring more than 30 others. Those responsible have yet to be brought to justice.
- On August 7, 1998, terrorist bombs exploded at the U.S. Embassies in Nairobi, Kenya, and Dar es Salaam, Tanzania, killing 224 people, including 12 Americans, and wounding more than 1,000. The attack was blamed on Osama bin Laden and members or associates of his Al Qaeda network. On November 4, 1998, a federal grand jury indicted bin Laden on charges in connection with the bombing.
- On June 25, 1996, a fuel truck loaded with explosives detonated outside the Khobar Towers apartment complex in Dhahran, Saudi Arabia, killing 19 American military personnel and wounding 372 others. On June 21, 2001, 14 terrorists were indicted for the attack, including 13 Saudis and 1 Lebanese.
- On April 19, 1995, a powerful bomb inside a Ryder rental truck exploded outside the Alfred P. Murrah Federal Building in Oklahoma City, Oklahoma. The explosion killed 168 people and injured hundreds of others. Timothy McVeigh, a 29-year-old Gulf War veteran, and Terry Nichols, 40, were charged with what was at the time the country's deadliest act of domestic terrorism. Both men were convicted. McVeigh, sentenced to death, was executed in June 2001. Nichols was sentenced to life in prison.
- Between 1978 and 1995, Theodore Kaczynski, known as the Unabomber, raged a campaign of domestic terror as he mailed homemade bombs to professors, corporations, and computer companies, killing 3 and injuring 23. The former math professor avoided the death penalty under a plea agreement. He received four consecutive life sentences without the possibility of parole, along with 30 years.
- On February 26, 1993, a truck bomb exploded in the underground parking garage of the World Trade Center in New York, killing 6 people and wounding more than 1,000. Convicted and imprisoned for the deadly crime were six Islamic extremists, including mastermind Ramzi Yousef, a 29-year-old Kuwati, and his fellow conspirator, Eyad Ismoil, age 26.
- On December 21, 1988, a bomb exploded on Pan Am Flight 103 over Lockerbie, Scotland, killing all 259 on board and 11 on the ground. The jetliner was en route to the United States. Two Libyans were charged with the terrorist attack and were tried in May 2000. One was convicted.
- On October 23, 1983, a truck bomb exploded outside the U.S. Marine headquarters in Beirut, killing 243 American members of a peacekeeping force. No one was ever brought to justice for the mass murder.

- On April 18, 1983, a 2,000-pound bomb in a van exploded at the U.S. Embassy in Beirut, killing 63 people inside, including 17 Americans, and the bomber. Those responsible were never captured.[11]

The vast majority of terrorist-related fatal attacks against Americans are perpetrated by international terrorists. As seen in Table 10.1, between 1981 and 1999, there were 651 Americans killed and 2,226 wounded as a result

Table 10.1   Casualties Resulting from International Terrorism Involving U.S. Citizens, by Type of Casualty, 1981–1999

Year	Total	U.S. Citizens	
		Killed	Wounded
Total	2,877	651	2,226
1981	47	7	40
1982	19	8	11
1983	386	271	115
1984	42	11	31
1985	195	38	157
1986	112	12	100
1987	54	7	47
1988	231	192	39
1989	34	16	18
1990	43	9	34
1991	23	7	16
1992	3	2	1
1993	1,011[a]	7	1,004
1994	11	6	5
1995	70	10	60
1996	535[b]	25	510
1997	27	6	21
1998	23	12	11
1999	11	5	6

[a] Includes the bombing of the World Trade Center in New York City on Feb. 26, 1983.

[b] Includes the bombing of the Khobar U.S. military housing complex near Dhahran, Saudi Arabia, on June 25, 1996.

Source: Adapted from U.S. Department of Justice, Bureau of Justice Statistics, *Sourcebook of Criminal Justice Statistics 1999* (Washington: Government Printing Office, 2000), p. 334.

of international terrorism. However, more people were killed in the 1996 Oklahoma City act of domestic terrorism than in all but two individual years of international terrorism between 1981 and 1999.

From 1995 to 2000, 77 Americans were victims of deadly attacks by international terrorists, for an average of 13 casualties per year.[12] Over the same time span, 651 Americans were wounded as a result of international terrorism, for an average of 109 per year. Between 1995 and 2000, North America had the lowest concentration of international terrorist perpetrated attacks, with 15. However, one coordinated effort in September 2001 by international terrorists led to a higher number of casualties than any previous group terrorist attack, with nearly 3,000 people losing their lives, including 125 people working at the Pentagon.

The vast majority of terrorist attacks against the United States come in the form of bomb attacks (see Table 10.2). Between 1982 and 1997, 81 percent of terrorist incidents targeted against the United States were bombing attacks. Kidnappings, assaults, and assassinations were the second most likely form of terrorist attacks. Commercial establishments were the most likely to be

Table 10.2   Terrorist Incidents, by Type of Incident and Target, United States, 1982–1997

Incident/Target	Number
Total	183
Type of incident	
Bombing attacks[a]	147
Malicious destruction of property	4
Acts of sabotage	2
Hostile takeover	4
Arson	8
Kidnapping, assaults, alleged assassinations, assassinations	11
Robbery, attempted robbery	6
Hijacking	1
Type of target	
Private residence/vehicle	18
Military personnel/establishments	33
Educational establishments	6
Commercial establishments	76
State and United States government buildings/property	33
Diplomatic establishments	17

[a] Includes detonated and undetonated devices, tear gas, pipe bombs, letter bombs, and firebombs.

Source: Adapted from U.S. Department of Justice, Bureau of Justice Statistics, *Sourcebook of Criminal Justice Statistics 1999* (Washington: Government Printing Office, 2000), p. 334.

targeted by terrorists and more than twice as likely as military targets and state and federal government buildings.

Terrorist Organizations

Although some terrorist attacks are perpetrated by individuals with no particular affiliation to a terrorist group—such as in the case of Timothy McVeigh and Terry Nichols—most terrorists act as part of a terrorist organization. The CIA recently estimated that there are a minimum of 140 current terrorist organizations worldwide.[13] Table 10.3 lists some of the most well-known terrorist groups.

Long believed to be the largest and most deadly terrorist organization is Al Qaeda. Led by Saudi militant Osama bin Laden until he was killed by U.S. Navy SEALs in Pakistan on May 2, 2011, Al Qaeda has an international network of Muslim extremists.[14] The terrorist organization's primary objective "is the overthrow of what it sees as the corrupt and heretical governments of Muslim states, and their replacement with the rule of *Sharia* (Islamic law). Al Qaeda is intensely anti-Western and views the United States in particular as the prime enemy of Islam."[15]

In 1996, Osama bin Laden issued a *fatwa*, or religious ruling, against the United States, calling upon Muslims to kill Americans. Bin Laden and his Al Qaeda network are believed to be behind the September 2001 terrorist attacks on the United States, as well as the deadly bombings of the *U.S.S. Cole* ship and the U.S. Embassies in Africa.

While most terrorism directed against the United States and its citizens is perpetrated by international terrorist organizations, domestic terrorist groups also exist and pose a serious threat. Extremist and hate groups such as the Ku Klux Klan have long orchestrated terrorist attacks on African Americans and other minority groups. Researchers have found that domestic terrorists and antigovernment militias such as the Covenant and the Minnesota Patriots Council have shown an interest in using unconventional weapons such as biological or chemical agents to wage their war on America.[16] Recent deadly anthrax attacks in this country illustrate the potential threats of domestic and international terrorism.

The Roots of Terrorism

The modern roots of terrorism can be traced to the dictatorships of Germany's Adolf Hitler, Italy's Benito Mussolini, and the former Soviet Union's Joseph Stalin in the 1930s and 1940s, in which terrorism was used against those who opposed their rule.[17] According to one expert on the justification of such

Table 10.3   Known Terrorist Organizations

Name of Organization	Location
Al Qaeda	Afghanistan
Armata Corsa	France
Armed Islamic Group (GIA)	Algeria
Aum Shinrikyo	Japan
Basque Fatherland and Liberty (ETA)	Spain
Democratic Front for the Liberation of Palestine (DFLP)	Palestinian
Fatah-Revolutionary Council (Abu Nidal Organization)	Lebanon
Gama'a al-Islamiyya (the Islamic Group, 1G)	Egypt
Hamas (Islamic Resistance Movement)	Palestinian
Harakat al-Mujahedin (HUM)	Pakistan
Hizballah (Party of God)	Lebanon
Irish Republican Army (IRA)	Northern Ireland
Japanese Red Army (JRA)	Japan
Jihad Group	Egypt
Kach and Kahane Chai	Israel
Kurdistan Workers' Party (PKK)	Turkey
Liberation Tigers of Tamil Eelan (LTTE)	Sri Lanka
Manuel Rodriguez Patriotic Front (FPMR)	Chile
Mujahedin-e Khalq Organization (MKO)	Iran
National Liberation Army (ELN)	Colombia
New People's Army (NPA)	Philippines
Palestine Liberation Front (PLF)	Iraq
Palestine Islamic Jihad (PIJ)	Palestinian
Popular Struggle Front (PSF)	Syria
Red Army Faction (RAF)	Germany
Revolutionary Armed Forces of Colombia (FARC)	Colombia
Revolutionary Organization 17 November (17 November)	Greece
Revolutionary People's Liberation Party/Front (DHCP/F)	Turkey
Sendero Luminoso (Shining Path)	Peru
Tupac Armaru Revolutionary Movement (MRTA)	Peru

Source: Terrorist Organizations, http://www.ict.org.il/inter/org.cfm; Crime
        and Punishment, http://member.compuserve.com/crime/terror.jsp.

terrorism: "Dictatorial systems believe that the end justifies the means, and
they have the right to impose their will on the rest of humankind ... They
believe they ... have the right to kidnap, torture, and murder."[18]

Terrorist acts of violence have been used in Northern Ireland by Roman
Catholic and Protestant extremist groups "to push for, respectively, the
end of or the continuation of, British rule."[19] Since the 1960s, such terrorist
groups as the Red Brigades and Red Army Faction formed to destroy their
homeland's political and economic systems and establish new ones; while

the Palestinian terrorist organizations such a Hezbollah and Hamas have raged terror campaigns against Israel in hopes of establishing an independent Palestinian state.

More recent terrorist groups such as the Al Qaeda network have proven to be even more deadly, violent, and organized in their hatred and political and religious objectives, as evidenced by the September 2001 attack on America.

Characterizing Terrorists

Most terrorists are young, usually poor men who are easily influenced by radical extremists and their message of hatred toward and violence against groups, governments, and individuals. These terrorists are often willing to die for their cause, whether national or not, making them even more dangerous to innocent people. According to one researcher, "the receptivity of young men to terror's radical message is enormously increased by [the] legacy of conflict, dislocation, and ... poverty."[20] This is particularly true in the Middle East and South Asia.

However, people from wealthy Western nations can also be sold on the same message. "These people can still powerfully identify with communities elsewhere that they believe have been exploited, victimized, reduced to crushing poverty, or otherwise treated with disrespect."[21]

The perception of victimization and disrespect against a vulnerable group was apparently what motivated Timothy McVeigh to blow up the federal building in Oklahoma City. The terrorist attack came 2 years after the government's siege against a religious cult in Waco, Texas, ended with a fatal fire, killing 58 members of the cult. "In the case of radical Islamic terrorists, such grievances are often expressed as anger over American policy toward Israel and Iraq and American support for 'un-Islamic' Middle Eastern governments."[22]

Most terrorists' actions or reactions often reflect mental instability and the desire to make their mark in a violent and effective way, such as with mail bomber Theodore Kaczynski.[23]

Murder-Suicide Terrorists

Many terrorists kill themselves in the process of killing or attempting to kill others, as in the case of the 19 men who hijacked four airplanes and committed suicide along with murdering nearly 3,000 others on September 11, 2001. Although suicide bombers are perhaps most identified with terrorist attacks, experts indicate that the majority of terrorists, "while willing to risk their lives, do not undertake actions that require their deaths in order to succeed. They wish to live after the terrorist act in order to benefit from their accomplishments."[24]

Suicide terrorists, however, have somewhat different motivations in perpetrating suicidal terrorism. Most do not regard their deaths as suicide per se, but rather see themselves as martyrs for the cause. Those who run terrorist organizations are seen as "cold and rational, rather than suicidal. For them, suicide terrorism has inherent tactical advantages over 'conventional' terrorism."[25] According to terrorism experts, such advantages include the following:

- Keeps the operation simple and low-cost, without need for escape routes or rescue operations
- Ensures mass casualties and considerable damage, as the suicide bomber need not be concerned with his welfare and safety
- No concern about captured terrorists being interrogated and revealing information about the network, since the probability of death is high
- Has a strong effect on the public and government due to the shared grief and feelings of helplessness

In a survey of terrorist groups that have employed suicide terrorist activities since 1983, it was found that some organizations "that resort to suicide terrorism do so rarely and unsympathetically, while others adopt it as a strategy. It has also been dropped as a tactic when the leaders of terrorist organizations perceive it is counterproductive—either because of massive retaliation or the loss of public sympathy for a cause."[26]

Combating Terrorism in America

In general, governments combat terrorism by not giving in to terrorist demands, enacting tough antiterrorism laws, tightening security at vulnerable targets of terrorists, and going after the terrorists themselves. With respect to the September 11, 2001, terrorist attacks in this country, the federal government has responded through various policy initiatives, heightened security provisions, offering rewards for information leading to the capture of suspected terrorists, and attacking and seeking to bring to justice those believed to be responsible.

Specifically, the following actions have been taken in the war on terrorism to protect America and its citizens:

- Antiterrorism and Effective Death Penalty Act was enacted into law in 1996.[27] The act includes habeas corpus reform, victim restitution, and provisions for stopping the financing of terrorists and barring or deporting alien terrorists.

- U.S.A. Patriot Act was signed into law in October 2001.[28] The act expands the FBI's authority for wiretapping and electronic surveillance, increases penalties for the harboring or financing of terrorists, and increases the number of offenses defined as terrorist acts while imposing stiffer penalties against terrorists. The bill also allows law enforcement new, broad antiterrorism powers, including the ability to search the homes and businesses of people suspected of terrorism and eavesdrop on phone conversations and computer messages.
- Emergency Supplemental Appropriations Act for Recovery From and Response to Terrorist Attacks on the United States was enacted in September 2001.[29] The act provided for emergency supplemental appropriations for the fiscal year for further disaster assistance, antiterrorism initiatives, and assistance in recovering from the terrorist attack of September 11, 2001.
- Aviation Security Bill was signed into law on November 19, 2001.[30] The legislation allows for federal oversight of airport passenger and baggage screeners and will eventually make all such workers federal employees. Other provisions include more inspection of checked baggage, fortifying cockpit doors on airliners, and increasing the number of federal marshals on flights.
- Biological and chemical weapons legislation has received bipartisan support in the Senate as of November 15, 2001, in response to the threat of biological and chemical terrorist attacks. Important provisions of the bill include $1.1 billion to increase the stockpiles of vaccines in the United States for such diseases as anthrax and smallpox, $1 billion in improving the public health system's ability to respond to chemical or biological attacks, and $1.1 billion to improve detecting procedures of food-borne terrorist attacks.[31]
- Military tribunals became a new weapon in the war on terrorism on November 13, 2001, after President George Bush gave emergency approval for the use of a special military court. The framework of the tribunal would allow the option of trying accused terrorists more quickly and in greater secrecy than in regular criminal courts. Such tribunals could be held abroad, with less evidence needed to convict. American citizens would be excluded from being brought before a military court.[32]

Endnotes

1. *American Heritage Dictionary* (New York: Dell, 1994), p. 835; http://www.your-dictionary.com.
2. M. C. Bassiouni, Terrorism, World Book Online Americas Edition, 2001, http://www.cssve.worldbook.compuserve.com/wbol/wbpage/na/ar/co/551940.

3. UN Office for Drug Control and Crime Prevention, Proposed Definitions of Terrorism, http://www.undep.org/terrorism_definitions.html.
4. Bassiouni, Terrorism.
5. U.S. Code, Title 22, Sec. 2656 (f); http://jurist.law.pitt.edu/terrorism1.htm.
6. Proposed Definitions of Terrorism.
7. *Ibid.*
8. D. Lester, *Serial Killers: The Insatiable Passion* (Philadelphia: Charles Press, 1995), p. 141; H. A. Cooper, Terroristic Fads and Fashions, in B. L. Danto & A. H. Kutscher, Eds., *The Human Side of Homicide* (New York: Columbia University Press, 1982).
9. B. B. Wolman, *Antisocial Behavior: Personality Disorders From Hostility to Homicide* (Amherst: Prometheus Books, 1999), p. 18.
10. S. Bakhash, The Riddle of Terrorism, http://www.nybooks.com/artiches/4662; Walter Laquer, *The Age of Terrorism* (New York: Little Brown, 1987).
11. R. B. Flowers & H. L. Flowers, *Murders in the United States: Crimes, Killers and Victims of the Twentieth Century* (Jefferson: McFarland, 2001), pp. 53–57, 81; Terrorist Attacks on U.S., http://member.compuserve.com/crime/terrorism.jsp; Daily Mail Reporter, Sentenced to Death: The Father and Son Who Bombed Oregon Bank ... Then Blamed Each Other, *Mail Online* (December 23, 2010), http://www.dailymail.co.uk/news/article-1341030/Oregon-bank-bombers-Bruce-Joshua-Turnidge-sentenced-death.html; B. Leibowitz, Bruce and Joshua Turnidge, Father-Son Bank Bombers, Convicted of Murdering Two Ore. Cops in '08, *CBS News* (December 8, 2010), http://www.cbsnews.com/8301-504083_162-20025053-504083.html?tag=contentMain;contentBody; Aimee Green, Two Officers Confirmed Dead in Woodburn Bank Bombing, *OregonLive.com* (December 13, 2008), http://www.oregonlive.com/news/index.ssf/2008/12/police_identify_colleagues_kil.html.
12. The Heritage Foundation, Facts and Figures About Terrorism, http://www.heritage.org/shorts/20010914terror.htm.
13. Cited in Wolman, *Antisocial Behavior*, p. 143.
14. P. L. Bergen, *Holy War, Inc.: Inside the Secret World of Osama Bin Laden* (New York: Free Press, 2001); Y. Alexander & M. S. Swetman, *Usama bin Laden's al-Quada: Profile of a Terrorist Network* (Ardsley: Transnational Publishers, 2001).
15. Terrorist Organizations, Al-Qu'ada the Base, http://www.ict.org.il/inter_ter/org.cfm. *See also* Gabriel Weimann & Conrad Winn, *The Theater of Terror: Mass Media and International Terrorists* (New York: Longman, 1994).
16. G. Ackerman & C. Loeb, Watch Out for America's Own Extremists, http://cns.miis.edu/pubs/other/watchout.htm.
17. Bassiouni, Terrorism; Wolman, *Antisocial Behavior*, p. 141.
18. Wolman, *Antisocial Behavior*, p. 18.
19. Bassiouni, Terrorism.
20. T. H. Dixon, Why Root Causes Are Important, http://www.pugwash.org/September11/letter-homerdixon.htm.
21. *Ibid.*
22. *Ibid.*
23. Kaczynski Gets Life, Says Government Lied, (May 4, 1998), http://www7.cnn.com/US/9805/04/kaczynski.sentencing/index.html.

24. National Center for Policy Analysis, Suicide Terrorists, http://www.ncpa.org/pi/congress/pd091201e.html.
25. *Ibid.*
26. *Ibid.*
27. P. L. 104-132 (1996).
28. Bush Signs Antiterrorism Bill Into Law, http://www.cnn.com/2001/US/10/26/gen.attack.on.terror/index.html.
29. P. L. 107-38 (2001).
30. Associated Press, Lawmakers Reach Aviation Security Deal, http://www.cnn.com/2001/TRAVEL/NEWS/11/15/rec.aviation.security2ap/index.html.
31. M. Garrett, The Bush White House Will Endorse a $3.25 Billion Senate Bill, http://www.cnn.com/2001/ALLPOLITICS/11/15/bush.bioterror/index.html.
32. Anne Gearan, Terrorists Could Face Military Trial, http://member.compuserve.com/news/story.jsp?floczff-PLS-PLS&id=60816662&dt=2001111480300&w+APO&coview=

Internet and Murder

11

Cyber crime has become as prevalent in today's society as legal use of cyber-space or the Internet. Though most of the news surrounding computer crime or criminality involving the World Wide Web tends to focus largely on sex crimes and exploitation against children, cyber-generated terrorism, cyber-stalking, fraudulent schemes, identity theft, and other intellectual property crimes, Internet-related murders have also become part of the landscape in the 21st century. Many killers have targeted their unsuspecting and gullible victims over the Internet, often gaining their trust through dating ads or services, or otherwise using opportunities afforded homicidal persons to find victims to kill. Such victims often take risks they might not normally take in meetings and communications offline. They provide personal information and/or agree to meet at less-than-secure locations, with the results proving deadly. Cyber murder has joined other cyber crimes in getting the attention of law enforcement to combat and bring perpetrators to justice.

Cyber Crime

Criminality has moved to the Internet in all forms, affecting many citizens and businesses across the country. Indeed, cyber crime is a global problem, with many types of Internet criminal activity originating overseas. Cyber crimes include cyber attacks such as hacking and computer viruses; cyber theft such as identify theft, fraud, and other property crimes; online sexual predators, prostitution, sextortion, and child pornography; cyberbullying; terrorism; and crimes of violence such as sexual assaults and murder.[1] In the latter instances, these offenses originate online through communication between the victim and offender, before the crime and victimization occur outside the world of virtual reality in real time and at real places.

The FBI and many state and local law enforcement agencies have made it a priority to investigate cyber crimes and criminals as well as educate potential victims and assist current or previous ones. For instance, the FBI has "cyber action teams," or CATS, who "travel the world to catch cyber criminals."[2] The FBI and the Department of Defense Cyber Crime Center have also partnered with other government agencies and international alliances in a National Cyber Investigative Joint Task Force (NCIJTF) in investigating domestic cyber criminality.[3] Computer Crime Task Forces have also been established in the country, such as in Connecticut, as part of the "the front lines of one state's war on all crimes cyber."[4]

In spite of these and other efforts to fight cyber crime, it remains an uphill battle as cyber criminals adapt to changing technology and become more heterogeneous and widespread while making it difficult to track down and contain cyber threats.

The Internet and Homicide

The relationship between the Internet and homicide typically involves cases of murder in which the victim and offender met online through e-mails, chat rooms, instant messaging, bulletin boards, social networking sites such as Facebook and Twitter, dating or friendship services, advertising sites, and other means of digital communication. The lethal relationship or encounter has often been referred to as *Internet homicide, Internet murder, cyber murder,* and even *Internet suicide* or *self-murder,* as well as *consensual suicide,* where there is a murder and suicide pact involved in the cyber deaths. The dynamics of murder in most of these instances tend to reflect more the offline characteristics and circumstances than online habits and activities. Yet, because of the cyberspace connection, it adds a new classification to homicidal crimes that show a cause and effect, directly or otherwise, to the Internet and its role in facilitating meetings in person.

Some serial killers are also believed to use the Internet to search for potential victims, due to its broad cyber landscape and lower rate of detection. In one such example, during the 1990s, serial killer John Edward Robinson used the name "Slavemaster" in social networking sites in luring women to play the role of submissive partner in sexual relations. Referred to by some as the "first Internet serial killer," Robinson was convicted in the murder of three of these women in Kansas and sentenced to death, while being suspected of murdering other women as well.[5]

There are also times when the Internet plays an indirect role in murders, in which a killer or would-be killer may communicate with family or friends online, leaving messages, photographs, or other information about crimes already committed or planned by the person. Perpetrators of recent school shootings, for instance, have often bragged about their intentions or actions online in seeking an audience to encourage them, applaud them, or vent with.

There are no hard statistics on the number of people who are murdered or commit murders in the United States after becoming acquainted through the Internet, with much of what we know based on high-profile cases of Internet-related homicide. Neither the FBI's Uniform Crime Reports nor the Bureau of Justice Statistics Crime Victimization in the United States' series specifically tracks cyber-related homicides or crimes of violence. However, in the book *Final Exits: The Illustrated Encyclopedia of How We Die,* author Michael Largo estimates that since 1995 more than 400 homicides have occurred after the perpetrator and victim first met on the Internet.[6] Murders have also been linked to cyberspace involving intimates, friends, and acquaintances who met outside the Internet.[7]

The number of such murders pales in comparison to homicides that do not originate online. Or, for that matter, to many other crimes in cyberspace, such as identity theft, confidence schemes, computer hacking, online crimes, and child sexual exploitation.

Nevertheless, with the finality and violence often associated with Internet murder cases, this makes it an important aspect of the overall focus on cyber crime and its implications for society at large, in spite of the relatively low number of homicides that occur in association with the Internet annually.

Internet Murders

A number of high-profile and unnerving Internet murders have occurred over the years to put faces and places to this type of homicide and victimization. The following examples illustrate the frightening nature of such crimes; the predatory, deceptive, and opportunistic dimensions of perpetrators; and also the vulnerability of victims who in many cases tend to let down their guard on the Internet rather than use more commonsense safeguards often employed when meeting people outside of cyberspace.

- Between December 2010 and April 2011, the remains of 10 women in the sex trade industry were discovered by authorities along the Ocean Parkway, a 15.59-mile stretch on Long Island, New York. The women were all victims of foul play, believed to be the work of a single serial killer, dubbed the "Long Island serial killer." At least 4 of the women were missing prostitutes who had advertised on Craigslist. The killer remains at large as of August 2012.[8]
- On June 5, 2009, 27-year-old Korena Roberts bludgeoned to death 21-year old Heather Snively, using a collapsible police baton, after luring the pregnant woman to her Beaverton, Oregon, home. The two had met on the online classified service Craigslist, where Snively had been searching for baby clothes after having recently relocated from Maryland to be with her fiancé. Fixated on having a child, Roberts cut the baby boy from Snively's abdomen and tried to pass him off as her own. She stuffed Snively's body in a crawlspace. The child died,

and Roberts was charged with aggravated murder and first degree robbery. In October 2010, Roberts pleaded guilty to one count of aggravated murder, for which she was sentenced to life imprisonment with no chance for parole.[9]

- On April 14, 2009, 24-year-old Phillip Markoff was alleged to have committed an armed robbery before murdering Julissa Brisman in a Marriott hotel in Boston, Massachusetts. Markoff, a medical student, was charged with these crimes as well as two other armed robberies of a paid escort and an exotic dancer. He was referred to as the "Craigslist killer" because Markoff was alleged to have met Brisman and the other women through online advertisements they placed on Craigslist for erotic services. On August 5, 2010, while in custody and awaiting trial, Markoff committed suicide.[10]

- On March 20, 2009, 16-year-old John Katehis murdered 47-year-old radio reporter George Weber in the victim's apartment in Brooklyn, New York. The two had met online through a Craigslist personal advertisement placed by Weber. He was stabbed more than 50 times by the killer. Katehis, who was charged as an adult for the crime, was convicted in November 2011 of second degree murder and sentenced to 25 years to life in prison.[11]

- On October 25, 2007, 19-year-old Michael Anderson used a .357 magnum revolver to shoot to death Katherine Ann Olson, 24, in his home in Savage, Minnesota, after luring her there through a phony online advertisement on Craigslist for a nanny. In March 2009, Anderson, also dubbed a Craigslist killer, was found guilty of premeditated murder and additional charges and sentenced to life behind bars with no chance for parole.[12]

- On September 15, 2006, 47-year-old Thomas Montgomery used a military .30 caliber rifle to shoot to death 22-year-old Brian Barrett in the parking lot of his employer, Dynabrade Inc., in Clarence, New York. It was the deadly culmination of an Internet love triangle involving two middle-aged people posing as teenagers, including ex-Marine Montgomery, and his co-worker Barrett, both of whom were involved in an online relationship with the same woman, pretending to be an 18-year-old. Montgomery, who was married with a family, murdered Barrett in a jealous rage. He pleaded guilty to the crime and was sentenced to 20 years behind bars.[13]

- On December 17, 2004, Lisa Montgomery, 36, strangled to death 23-year-old, Bobbie Jo Stinnett, who was 8 months pregnant. The victim was murdered in her home in Skidmore, Missouri. The two women had met in an online chat room and further communicated by e-mail. After strangling Stinnett, Montgomery cut the baby from her womb and pretended to be the mother. The child survived and

Montgomery was arrested. On October 22, 2007, she was found guilty of kidnapping resulting in the death of Stinnett, a capital offense, in a U.S. District Court and sentenced to death.[14]

- On October 16, 1996, 45-year-old Robert Glass strangled to death Sharon Lopatka, 35, in his mobile home in Collettsville, North Carolina, in what was believed to be a case of consensual homicide. Lopatka, who advertised pornography on the Internet as part of her sexual fetishes, apparently looked for someone to torture and kill her. She had established an e-mail connection with Glass before they met. He killed Lopatka with a nylon cord after torturing her for days. In January 2000, Glass pleaded guilty to voluntary manslaughter and other charges related to child pornography on his computer. He was given a sentence for the manslaughter of 36 to 53 months behind bars. On February 20, 2002, he died of a heart attack while still incarcerated.[15]

The relationship between the Internet and murder continues to evolve as more and more people become comfortable doing everything online from dating to banking to advertising and more, unwittingly exposing themselves to dangerous predators who are equally drawn to the Internet for the accessibility and anonymity it affords them to potential victims. In the book *Killers on the Web: True Stories of Internet Cannibals, Murderers and Sex Criminals*, authors Christopher Berry-Dee and Steve Morris refer to the "darkest recesses of the World Wide Web," reporting on cases that range from "cannibals ordering a human meal by email to mail-order brides whose quest for better lives end in grisly murder."[16]

Though the vast majority of homicides in the United States continue to occur in the typical ways described throughout the book with cyberspace not a factor, the propensity for online-related murders and victimization can only grow in the future as the Internet's powerful reach expands in society, creating legitimate and illegitimate opportunities for communication and real-life contact and interaction.

Endnotes

1. *American Heritage Dictionary* (New York: Dell, 1994), p. 835; http://www.yourdictionary.com.
2. U.S. Department of Justice, Federal Bureau of Investigation, FBI Cyber Action Teams: Traveling the World to Catch Cyber Criminals, http://www.fbi.gov/news/stories/2006/march/cats030606 (April 25, 2012).
3. *Ibid.*; U.S. Department of Justice, Federal Bureau of Investigation, National Cyber Investigative Joint Task Force, http://www.fbi.gov/about-us/investigate/cyber/ncijtf (April 25, 2012).

4. *Ibid*; U.S. Department of Justice, Federal Bureau of Investigation, Netting Cyber Criminals: Inside the Connecticut Computer Crimes Task Force, http://www.fbi.gov/news/stories/2006/january/ccctf012506 (April 25, 2012). See also U.S. Department of Justice, "Computer Crime and Intellectual Property Section," http://www.justice.gov/criminal/cybercrime/(April 26, 2012).

5. Wikipedia, the Free Encyclopedia, John Edward Robinson, http://en.wikipedia.org/wiki/John_Edward_Robinson_(serial_killer) (April 24, 2012).

6. Cited in *Ibid.*, Internet Homicide, http://en.wikipedia.org/wiki/Internet_homicide (April 25, 2012). See also M. Largo, *Final Exits: The Illustrated Encyclopedia of How We Die* (New York: William Morrow, 2006).

7. For instance, on November 17, 1995, James Pritchert, 60, murdered his wife of nearly 3 decades, Lila Pritchert, 52, in their home in Pebble Beach, California, for spending too much time online. He confessed to the murder and in March 1996 was sentenced to 11 years in prison. See also American Murderers, http://www.shortopedia.com/A/M/American_murderers__page4 (April 25, 2012); Murderpedia, James D. Pritchert, http://www.murderpedia.org/male.P/p/pritchert-james.htm (April 26, 2012).

8. *Ibid.*; Long Island Serial Killer, http://en.wikipedia.org/wiki/Long_island_killer (April 25, 2012); M. Lyshak, Police Suspect Murder Victims Found on Long Island's Gilgo Beach Were Murdered by Single Serial Killer, *NYDailyNews.com* (November 29, 2011), http://www.nydailynews.com/new-york/police-suspect-murder-victims-found-long-island-gilgo-beach-murdered-single-serial-killer-article-1.984318; C. Pelisek, Terror on Long Island, *The Daily Beast* (April 17, 2011), http://www.thedailybeast.com/newsweek/2011/04/17/terror-on-long-island.html.

9. E. E. Smith, Korena Roberts Pleads Guilty; Sentenced to Life in Prison, *OregonLive.com* (October 6, 2010), http://www.oregonlive.com/washington-county/index.ssf/2010/10/korena_roberts_pleads.html.

10. Alleged Craigslist Killer Commits Suicide, *ABC News Videos* (August 15, 2010), http://abcnews.go.com/WNT/video/alleged-craigslist-killer-commits-suicide-11407124; The Craigslist Killer: Seven Days of Rage, *48 Hours Mystery* (August 20, 2010), http://www.cbsnews.com/2100-18559_162-6791591.html.

11. D. Tsakas, John Katehis, 18, Given Maximum Sentence for Brutal Slaying, *National Herald* (April 25, 2012), http://www.thenationalherald.com/article/52974; Teen Convicted of Fatally Stabbing Brooklyn Radio Reporter, NY1.com (November 15, 2011), http://brooklyn.ny1.com/content/top_stories/150835/teen-convicted-of-fatally-stabbing-brooklyn-radio-reporter/.

12. 'Craigslist Killer' Michael John Anderson gets life in murder of Katherine Olson, *NYDailyNews.com* (April 3, 2009), http://www.nydailynews.com/news/world/craigslist-killer-michael-john-anderson-life-murder-katherine-olson-article-1.361506; S. Michels, Craigslist Killer Lured Victim With Baby Sitter Ad, *ABC News* (April 1, 2009), http://abcnews.go.com/Technology/story?id=7227285&page=1; C. Havens & J. Walsh, Online Nanny Ad Ends in Slaying, *Star Tribune* (October 8, 2007), http://www.startribune.com/local/south/11545261.html?page=1&c=y.

13. J. Avila, G. Martz, & J. Napolitano, Online Love Triangle, Deception, End in Murder, *ABC 20/20* (August 27, 2011), http://abcnews.go.com/US/online-love-triangle-deception-end-murder/story?id=14371076; 22-Year-Old New York Man Murdered After Being Drawn Into Internet Love Triangle, *FoxNews.com* (January 21, 2007), http://www.foxnews.com/story/0,2933,245222,00.html.
14. Wikipedia, the Free Encyclopedia, Lisa M. Montgomery, http://en.wikipedia.org/wiki/Lisa_M._Montgomery (April 25, 2012); B. Mears, Woman Gets Death Sentence in Fetus-Snatching Murder, *CNN Justice* (April 4, 2008), http://articles.cnn.com/2008-04-04/justice/pregnant.slaying_1_lisa-montgomery-bobbie-jo-stinnett-death-sentence?_s=PM:CRIME.
15. Internet Lures Sexual Predators, Experts Say, The Free Library, http://www.thefreelibrary.com/INTERNET + LURES + SEXUAL + PREDATORS%2c + EXPERTS + SAY.-a084001234 (April 25, 2012); Rachael Bell, "Internet Assisted Suicide-The Story of Sharon Lopatka," *TruTV*, http://www.trutv.com/library/crime/notorious_murders/classics/sharon_lopatka/1.html (April 25, 2012).
16. Internet Homicide; C. Berry-Dee, & S. Morris, *Killers on the Web: True Stories of Internet Cannibals, Murderers and Sex Criminals* (London: John Blake, 2006).

Youth and Murder IV

Youth Gangs and Homicide

12

Youth street gangs have long been associated with a disproportionate involvement in homicides and other violent crimes. This is particularly true for racial and ethnic minority gangs. The easy availability and possession of modern, sophisticated weapons by gang members is believed to play a major role in youth gang-related homicides, including drive-by shootings and those related to drug dealing and school violence. In spite of the recent migration of gangs to different cities and states across the country and gang rivalries leading to violence, youth gang homicides have declined in general since the 1990s. Yet the number of violent and deadly youth gangs continues to be a problem for law enforcement as well as a barometer for the study of youth violence and homicidal behavior.

Defining the Youth Gang

What is a youth gang? Definitions of youth gangs have varied over the years, often relating to the nature and pattern of the gang's activities, particularly with respect to antisocial and violent behavior. Sociologist Frederic Thrasher was one of the first to define the adolescent gang in the 1920s as

> an interstitial group originally formed spontaneously and then integrated through conflict. It is characterized by ... meeting face to face, milling, movement through space as a unit, conflict, and planning. The result of this collective behavior is the development of tradition, unreflective internal structure, espirit de corps, solidarity, morale, group awareness, and attachment to local territory.[1]

In the 1970s, Walter Miller, an expert on youth gangs, defined the juvenile delinquent gang as "a group of recurrently associating individuals with identifiable leadership and internal organization, identifying with or claiming control over territory in the community, and engaging either individually or collectively in violent or other forms of illegal behavior."[2]

More recently in the book *The Adolescent Criminal*, the delinquent youth gang was defined as

> a loosely organized or disorganized group of juveniles distinguished by colors, race and ethnicity, neighborhood, and principles; and whose delinquent

and criminal activities relate to status, respect, revenge, celebrity, satisfaction, and profit, and include murder, gang wars, and drug dealing.[3]

Although youth gangs are typically composed of juvenile members, many may also contain young adults and be affiliated with adult and prison gangs. Most youth gangs are composed of a hierarchy consisting of a core or elite leadership, a group of regular or full-time members, and additional peripheral members. Lewis Yablonsky estimated that 10 to 15 percent of youth gangs include a "hard-core" or elite group that heads the gangs and manages the day-to-day activities, with the other members serving as their subordinates.[4]

Youth Gang Violence

The overall problem of youth gangs and violent activity is of serious concern to law enforcement and often acts as an antecedent to gang-related homicidal behavior. Studies show that youth gang members are disproportionately involved in a high percentage of violent crimes as well as related property and drug offenses.[5] The Program of Research on the Causes and Correlates of Delinquency noted that 30 percent of a sample of youth gang members reported committing 68 percent of violent offenses.[6] Other self-report surveys have shown similar results, such as in Denver where 14 percent of the gang sample perpetrated 79 percent of the serious violent crimes;[7] another survey reported that 14 percent of gang members were responsible for 89 percent of all serious violent offenses.[8] Miller found that gang members accounted for one-third of all crimes of violence, the terrorizing of whole communities, and maintaining a state of siege in many of the urban schools.[9]

Gang norms appear to be a strong factor in the increased level of violence among youth gangs. According to S. H. Decker and B. Van Winkle: "Violence that is internal to the gang, especially during group functions such as an initiation, serves to intensify the bonds among members."[10] In an exploration of youth gangs, James Howell stated that "most gangs are governed by norms supporting the expressive use of violence to settle disputes and to achieve group goals associated with member recruitment, defense of one's identity as a gang member, turf protection and expansion, and defense of the gang's honor."[11]

Youth Gang Homicides

Youth gang homicides are defined as homicides involving youth gang members as victims, perpetrators, or both. Because of the lack of uniformity in defining a gang or gang member from state to state, figures on gang-related homicides are not always consistent. However, national data indicates that after youth gang homicides had generally been on the decline during much of the 1990s, they have begun to increase in the early 2000s, particularly in the biggest cities where youth gang involvement is most prevalent.

Between 1991 and 1996, gang-involved murders dropped by nearly 15 percent in more than 400 cities across the country, going from 1,748 homicides to 1,492 homicides.[12] Although 32 percent of the cities reported a decline in the number of gang homicides, 29 percent of cities reported an increase, while in 39 percent of cities there was no change.

Similarly, in a study analyzing data from the National Youth Gang Survey for 1996, 1997, and 1998, covering 1,216 cities with populations of more than 25,000 in which there was a problem with gangs or gang homicides, 237 cities reported gang problems and gang-related homicide statistics.[13] A drop in gang homicides over the 3 years was reported in 49 percent of the cities, while 36 percent of cities showed an increase in gang-related homicides, and 15 percent indicated no change. The highest rate of gang homicides occurred in Chicago and Los Angeles. From 1996 to 1998, gang homicides decreased more than twice as much in Los Angeles, dropping 41 percent compared with 19 percent in Chicago.[14]

According to the National Gang Center (NGC), between 2002 and 2009, gang-related murders in cities where the population is over 100,000 grew by and large from year to year (see Figure 12.1). From 2002 to 2009 the number of gang homicides rose 2 percent, while from 2005 to 2009 there was a 7 percent increase, and between 2008 and 2009 gang murders rose almost 11 percent. Gang homicides grew another 10 percent between 2009 and 2010.[15]

The NGC reported that nearly one in three large cities "experienced consistent and high gang-homicide prevalence rates from 1996 to 2009," with 40 percent of the annual murders in this "subgroup of cities" found to be gang related.[16]

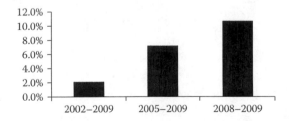

Figure 12.1 Percent change in gang-related homicides in cities of over 100,000 population, 2002–2009. (Adapted from National Gang Center, *National Youth Gang Survey Analysis: Measuring the Extent of Gang Problems*, http://www. nationalgangcenter.gov/Survey-Analysis/Measuring-the-Extent-of-Gang-Problems, April 10, 2012.)

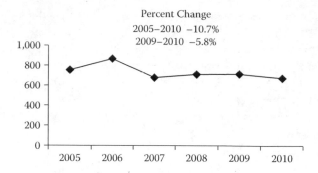

Figure 12.2 Total victims of juvenile gang killings, 2005–2010. (Derived from U.S. Department of Justice, Federal Bureau of Investigation, *Crime in the United States: Uniform Crime Reports 2010*, Expanded Homicide Data, Table 10, Murder Circumstances, by Relationship, 2005–2010, http://www.fbi.gov/about-us/cjis/ucr/crime-inthe-u.s/2010/crime-in-the-u.s.-2010/tables/10shrtbl10.xls, April 10, 2012.)

These figures notwithstanding, data from the FBI's Uniform Crime Reports show that from 2005 to 2010, the overall number of murders attributable to juvenile gang violence in the United States declined 10.7 percent (see Figure 12.2). However, the number of victims rose 2 years during the span, before dropping 5.8 percent between 2009 and 2010. The total number of murder victims from juvenile gang killings averaged 732 a year over the period.

Youth Gang versus Nongang Homicides

Studies show some major differences between gang homicides and nongang homicides with respect to demographic features, situational variables, and interrelated factors.[17] Gang-related homicides were more likely to occur in public settings such as the street and to involve strangers, multiple participants, automobiles, a fear of reprisal, and use of firearms.[18] Homicide-involved gang members tend to be younger, male, and racial and ethnic minorities more so than nongang members involved in homicides.

In particular, youth gang homicides are more likely to involve African American and Hispanic offenders and victims than nongang homicides.[19] The vast majority of gang-involved homicides are intraracial. In M. W. Klein's study of street gangs, it was found that 92 percent of Los Angeles gang homicides involved African American offenders and victims or Hispanic offenders and victims.[20] However, some studies have found increasing interracial gang homicides and other violence, relating this to territorial issues, drug trafficking, and firearms possession.[21]

Researchers have found that gangs are more likely than their nongang counterparts "to recruit adolescents who own firearms, and gang members are more than twice as likely as nongang members to own a gun for protection, more likely to have peers who own guns for protection, and more likely to carry their guns outside the home."[22] Further, adolescent males who own guns for protection as opposed to sport have been shown to be five times more likely as those not owning a gun for protection to be a member of a gang and three times as likely to perpetrate a serious or violent offense.[23]

Youth Gangs, Guns, and Homicide

A strong relationship exists between youth gangs, guns, and homicides. Most gang-related murders involve the use of a firearm.[24] Studies show that the majority of violent youth gang members either illegally own or are in possession of a gun.[25] An apparent increase in the deadly use of firearms by young members has been attributed to the greater accessibility and use of more sophisticated firearms,[26] as well as the proliferation of lethal weapons by rival gang members.[27] The possession and use of firearms by gang members is a reflection of keeping pace with competing youth gangs and maintaining power, control, and intimidation within gangs and among rival gangs.

Drive-by shootings in particular are commonly associated with street gangs, as they once were with organized criminals. These typically occur in inner cities with strong gang affiliations. Research has shown that in drive-by shootings, killing the victim or victims is only a secondary objective to raising fear and intimidating rival gangs.[28] The proportion of gang homicides that are drive-by shootings varies from city to city. For example, between 1989 and 1993, 33 percent of gang homicides in Los Angeles were the result of drive-by shootings, consisting of 590 murders.[29] In a study of Chicago gang-related homicides between 1965 and 1994, only 120 murders or around 6 percent of the total were the result of drive-by shootings.[30]

Youth Gangs and Drug-Related Homicide

There is some evidence of a link between youth gang homicides and a drug-related motive. Studies show that street gangs are becoming increasingly involved with drug offenses including drug trafficking and drug use, which in turn has been both directly and indirectly related to gang violence, migration, and firearm possession.[31]

Homicide violence by youth gangs appears to be tied to a crack cocaine epidemic in the United States. Studies have found an interrelationship between gang involvement in the sale of crack cocaine and drug trafficking, and a rise in violent criminality among youth, such as murder.[32]

However, a number of researchers have found that youth gang homicides are not strongly related to drug-offending circumstances. Only 2.2 percent of street-gang-involved homicides in Chicago from 1965 to 1994 were motivated by drug offenses, according to Carolyn Block and colleagues.[33] A similarly small proportion was found by D. M. Kennedy and associates.[34]

Other researchers contend that even an indirect relationship between youth gang homicides and drug crimes such as drug trafficking can still result in an atmosphere in which gang drug-related homicides are not only possible, but quite probable.[35]

The Dynamics of Youth Gangs

The Scope of Youth Gangs and Gang Membership

Various estimates over the years have been made on the extent of youth gangs and gang membership in the United States. In the early 1980s, Miller estimated that there were more than 2,000 gangs from nearly 300 jurisdictions, consisting of a membership of almost 100,000.[36] A 1996 estimate placed the figures at approximately 31,000 gangs in some 4,800 jurisdictions, with a membership of almost 846,000; while the NGC recently estimated that there were 28,000 gangs in the country in 2009, with gang membership at around 731,000.[37]

Youth gangs are most problematic in big cities. In a 1996 survey by the National Youth Gang Center of over 3,000 law enforcement agencies, the highest incidence of gang activity was reported in large cities.[38] Suburban counties were second most likely to have a gang problem, followed by small cities and rural counties. Nearly three-quarters of cities with a population of 25,000 or more reported having youth gangs.

Street gangs are particularly prevalent in some cities with serious gang troubles such as Los Angeles and Chicago. It is estimated that Los Angeles has the most gang members in the United States with over 58,000; while Chicago is estimated to have between 30,000 and 50,000 gang members described as hardcore.[39] The four largest and most violent Chicago gangs—including the Black Gangster Disciples Nation and the Latin Disciples—comprise around 19,000 members while accounting for two-thirds of the city's gang criminality and more than half of its gang homicides.[40]

Race, Ethnicity, and Gang Membership

Racial and ethnic minorities are overrepresented among youth gang members. Miller reported that Black youths accounted for 47.6 percent of gang members, with Hispanics representing 36.1 percent of membership.[41] In a recent law enforcement survey, 48 percent of youth gangs consisted of African Americans, 43 percent Hispanics, 5 percent Whites, and 4 percent Asians (see Figure 12.3).

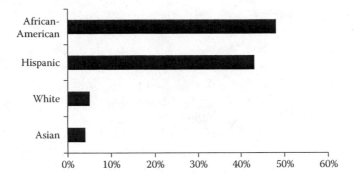

Figure 12.3 Racial and ethnic breakdown of youth gangs in the United States. (Derived from U.S. Department of Justice, *Youth Gangs: An Overview.* Washington, D.C.: Office of Juvenile Justice and Delinquency Prevention, 1998, p. 2.)

Some studies have found a higher percentage of White youths are involved in street gangs than indicated in previous research. F. Esbensen and D. W. Osgood found that 25 percent of gang membership was White, with 31 percent Black, 25 percent Asian, and 15 percent other racial and ethnic groups.[42] Miller noted seven White youth gangs in a large urban area, with many members convicted and imprisoned for serious offenses.[43]

Gender and Youth Gang Involvement

Males constitute the vast majority of youth gang members. Miller found that 90 percent of gang membership was made up of males.[44] An estimated 94 percent of street gangs were male, according to a survey of law enforcement agencies.[45] Some research reports that there may be a higher proportion of females involved in gangs than is commonly believed.[46] However, males continue to dominate gang membership and are responsible for most gang violence, including perpetrating virtually all gang-related homicides.

Age and Membership in Youth Gangs

The majority of youth gang members fall between the ages of 10 and 24, with the average gang member believed to be about 17 or 18 years of age.[47] Gang members tend to be older in cities with a long history of youth gangs, such as Chicago and Los Angeles.[48] According to Miller, in the four cities with the largest gang problem, 8 out of 10 gang members arrested were between the ages of 14 and 19.[49] Around 4 percent of members were younger than 14. Studies reveal that although younger members are becoming more prevalent in youth gangs, a greater increase has occurred in the membership of older people in gangs.[50]

Theories on Youth Gang Violence

The most influential theories on youth gang crime and violence focus on lower-class gangs. Studies indicate that lower-class or urban youth gangs are disproportionately involved in serious and violent gang offending.[51] Miller found a relationship between the greater prevalence of lower-class populations and more involvement in gangs.[52] This conclusion was generally supported by I. A. Spergal, though noting "it is not clear that either class, poverty, culture, race or ethnicity, or social change per se primarily accounts for gang problems."[53]

Reaction-Formation Theory

The reaction-formation theory was proposed by Albert Cohen.[54] The theory posited that lower-class youths resort to gang delinquency as a group response or reaction to an inability to acquire the status established by middle-class norms and values. Cohen held that although middle-class goals and values are desired by lower-class youths—including success, ambition, and talent—these youths are generally disadvantaged in institutional settings such as school, where they are subject to middle-class standards.

These blocked opportunities to attain culturally prescribed goals and conflicts with middle-class institutions, Cohen believed, caused lower-class youths to deviate in response, which he referred to as "status frustration" or "reaction-formation against a middle class organized status dilemma in which the lower class boy suffers status frustrations in competition with middle status boys."[55] This status frustration is seen as causing many such youths to "band together in juvenile gangs or a delinquent subculture, where they participate in behavior that is nonutilitarian, malicious, negativistic, and hedonistic."[56]

Cohen is credited with being among the first to explain delinquent youth group behavior. However, his theory has been criticized by many for its lack of empirical validation, limited evidence to support the notion that lower-class youths repudiate the values of the middle class, broad generalizations, and insufficient attention placed on other influences in youth antisocial behavior, such as family, race, and ethnicity.

Opportunity Theory

Opportunity theory of delinquent gangs was put forth by Richard Cloward and Lloyd Ohlin.[57] The theory advanced that an individual's access to legitimate and illegitimate means is highly influenced by the social structure. While differential opportunity is present in reaching culturally prescribed goals through legitimate means, it exists as well in using illegitimate means for achieving socially approved goals.

Opportunity theory explains gang delinquency as a discrepancy between aspirations of lower-class youths and what they have access to, with the assumption that "discrepancies between aspirations and legitimate chances of achievement increase as one descends in the class structure."[58] This inability to achieve middle-class aspirations results in deep frustration and causes lower-class youths to deviate into illegitimate means to achieve these cultural goals.

According to Cloward and Ohlin, it is the social structure within a community that determines the access youths have to "learning structures" and "performance structures." The researchers identify three main types of lower-class youth gangs, or subcultural reactions to blocked legitimate or illegitimate means for success: (1) criminal gangs, (2) conflict gangs, and (3) retreatist gangs.

- *Criminal gangs*: youth gangs who take on criminal skills and values acquired from adult and organized criminals. These gangs are motivated primarily by power, material gain, and prestige.
- *Conflict gangs*: youth gangs developed under circumstances in which both legitimate and illegitimate goals are blocked. Membership in conflict gangs enables youths to achieve status, prestige, or a reputation for toughness. The principles of these gangs typically involve fighting, violence, and intergang conflict.
- *Retreatist gangs*: youth gangs formed when youths are denied or reject legitimate or illegitimate means for success. Retreatist youths often become substance abusers and use secondary criminal activities to support habits.

Opportunity theory has been recognized for various delinquent gang subcultures in relation to differential opportunity structures. However, it has drawbacks in its focus on lower-class gang delinquency while inadequately accounting for the gang delinquency of other classes and individual delinquency; as well as failure to account for why some communities have different kinds of delinquent youth gangs.

Lower-Class Culture Theory

Lower-class culture theory was offered by Walter Miller in explaining youth gang delinquency.[59] As opposed to Cohen and Cloward and Ohlin's propositions that lower-class gang delinquency is based on a rejection of middle-class norms and values, Miller postulated that gang delinquency among the lower class is a reflection of positive attempts by youths to attain goals as established by values or focal concerns of the lower-class culture.

Miller identified six such lower-class focal concerns, or areas representing the primary concerns of lower-class youths: (1) trouble, (2) toughness, (3) smartness, (4) excitement, (5) fate, and (6) autonomy.

- *Trouble* refers to circumstances that lead to undesired involvement with the police.
- *Toughness* is concerned with masculinity, physical superiority, bravery, and daring.
- *Smartness* is the ability to outsmart, outwit, or con others, while avoiding being the victim of dupe or deception.
- *Excitement* concerns the desire for thrills, risks, and avoiding boredom.
- *Fate* refers to interests or beliefs associated with luck, fortunes, and jinxes.
- *Autonomy* is closely related to fate and a desire to be in control of one's own life or destiny.

According to lower-class culture theory, the delinquent gang serves as a social setting in which youths can achieve prestige through actions in association with lower-class focal concerns.

While Miller's theory of lower-class culture is successful in relating differential lower-class values to youth gang delinquency, it fails to explain the origins of these focal concerns or to differentiate between lower-class offenders and nonoffenders. Further, some critics reject the notion that lower-class gang members do not adhere to middle-class norms and values.

Endnotes

1. F. M. Thrasher, *The Gang* (Chicago: University of Chicago Press, 1927), p. 57.
2. W. B. Miller, *Violence by Youth Gangs and Youth Groups as a Crime Problem in Major American Cities* (Washington: Government Printing Office, 1975).
3. R. B. Flowers, *The Adolescent Criminal: An Examination of Today's Juvenile Offender* (Jefferson: McFarland, 1990), p. 99.
4. L. Yablonsky, *The Violent Gang* (Baltimore: Penguin, 1962), p. 227.
5. S. R. Battin, K. G. Hill, R. D. Abbott, R. F. Catalano, & J. D. Hawkins, The Contribution of Gang Membership to Delinquency Beyond Delinquent Friends, *Criminology* 36 (1998): 93–115; M. W. Klein, C. L. Maxson, & L. C. Cunningham, 'Crack,' Street Gangs, and Violence, *Criminology* 29 (1991): 623–50.
6. T. P. Thornberry, Membership in Youth Gangs and Involvement in Serious and Violent Offending, in R. Loeber & D. P. Farrington, Eds., *Serious and Violent Offenders: Risk Factors and Successful Interventions* (Thousand Oaks: Sage, 1998), pp. 147–66.

7. Cited in C. Maxson, Gang Homicide, in M. D. Smith & M. A. Zahn, Eds., *Studying and Preventing Homicide: Issues and Challenges* (Thousand Oaks: Sage, 1999), p. 197.
8. D. Huizinga, The Volume of Crime by Gang and Nongang Members, paper presented at the Annual Meeting of the American Society of Criminology, San Diego, 1997.
9. Miller, *Violence by Youth Gangs and Youth Groups*.
10. S. H. Decker & B. Van Winkle, *Life in the Gang: Family, Friends, and Violence* (New York: Cambridge University Press, 1996), p. 270. See also U.S. Department of Justice, *Youth Gangs: An Overview* (Washington: Office of Juvenile Justice and Delinquency Prevention, 1998), p. 9.
11. *Youth Gangs*, p. 9. See also J. F. Short, Jr. & F. L. Strodtbeck, *Group Process and Gang Delinquency* (Chicago: University of Chicago Press, 1965); R. Block and C. R. Block, *Street Gang Crime in Chicago* (Washington: National Institute of Justice, 1993).
12. U.S. Department of Justice, *Youth Gang Homicides in the 1990s* (Washington: Office of Juvenile Justice and Delinquency Prevention, 2001), pp. 1–2.
13. *Ibid.*
14. *Ibid.*
15. U.S. Department of Justice, Bureau of Justice Assistance, *NGC Newsletter* 1 (Spring 2012), p.2, www.nationalgangcenter.gov.
16. *Ibid.*
17. *Youth Gangs*, pp. 10–11; Maxson, Gang Homicide, pp. 197–206; K. Damphousse, V. E. Brewer, & C. D. Atkinson, Gangs, Race/Ethnicity and Houston Homicide in the 1990s, in U.S. Department of Justice, *Proceedings of the Homicide Research Working Group Meetings, 1997 and 1998* (Washington: National Institute of Justice, 1999), pp. 80–92.
18. Klein, Maxson, & Cunningham, 'Crack,' Street Gangs, and Violence, pp. 623–50; C. Rogers, Gang-Related Homicides in Los Angeles County, *Journal of Forensic Sciences* 38, 4 (1993): 831–34; I. Spergel, Violent Gangs in Chicago: In Search of Social Policy, *Social Science Review* 58 (1984): 199–226.
19. G. W. Bailey & N. P. Unnithan, Gang Homicides in California: A Discriminate Analysis, *Journal of Criminal Justice* 22, 3 (1994): 267–75.
20. M. W. Klein, *The American Street Gang: Its Nature, Prevalence, and Control* (New York: Oxford, 1995).
21. See, for example, I. A. Spergel, *The Youth Gang Problem: A Community Approach* (New York: Oxford, 1995).
22. *Youth Gangs*, p. 10; B. Bjerregaard & A. J. Lizotte, Gun Ownership and Gang Membership, *Journal of Criminal Law and Criminology* 86 (1995): 37–58.
23. A. J. Lizotte, J. M. Tesoriero, T. P. Thornberry, & M. D. Krohn, Patterns of Adolescent Firearms Ownership and Use, *Justice Quarterly* 11 (1994): 51–73.
24. *Youth Gangs*, pp. 10–12; Block & Block, *Street Gang Crime in Chicago*; R. B. Flowers, *Male Crime and Deviance: Exploring Its Causes, Dynamics and Nature* (Springfield: Charles C Thomas, 2003).
25. *Youth Gangs*, p. 12; J. F. Sheley & J. D. Wright, *In the Line of Fire: Youth, Guns and Violence in Urban America* (Hawthorne: Aldine De Gruyter, 1995).
26. Block and Block, *Street Gang Crime in Chicago*.
27. Decker and Van Winkle, *Life in the Gang*, p. 23.

28. H. R. Hutson, D. Anglin, & M. Eckstein, Drive-by Shootings by Violent Street Gangs in Los Angeles: A Five-Year Review From 1989 to 1993, *Academic Emergency Medicine* 3 (1996): 300–3.
29. *Ibid.*
30. C. R. Block, A. Christakos, A. Jacob, & R. Przybylski, *Street Gangs and Crime: Patterns and Trends in Chicago* (Chicago: Illinois Criminal Justice Information Authority, 1996).
31. *Youth Gangs*, pp. 11–12; C. L. Maxson & M. W. Klein, Defining Gang Homicide: An Updated Look at Member and Motive Approaches, in C. R. Huff, Ed., *Gangs in America*, 2nd ed. (Thousand Oaks: Sage, 1996), pp. 3–20.
32. J. A. Inciardi & A. E. Pottieger, Kids, Crack, and Crime, *Journal of Drug Issues* 21 (1991): 257–70.
33. Block, Christakos, Jacob, & Przybylski, *Street Gangs and Crime.*
34. D. M. Kennedy, A. A. Braga, & A. M. Piehl, The (Un)Known Universe: Mapping Gangs and Gang Violence in Boston, in D. Weisburd & T. McEwen, Eds., *Crime Mapping and Crime Prevention* (New York: Criminal Justice Press, 1997), pp. 219–62.
35. *Youth Gangs*, p. 12.
36. W. B. Miller, *Crime by Youth Gangs and Groups in the United States* (Washington: Office of Justice Programs, 1992).
37. Cited in *Youth Gangs*, p. 1; National Gang Center, *National Youth Gang Survey Analysis: Measuring the Extent of Gang Problems*, http://www.nationalgangcenter.gov/Survey-Analysis/Measuring-the-Extent-of-Gang-Problems (April 10, 2012).
38. *Ibid.*, p. 4.
39. National Youth Gang Center, *1995 National Youth Gang Survey* (Washington: Office of Juvenile Justice and Delinquency Prevention, 1997).
40. *Youth Gangs*, p. 4; Block & Block, *Street Gang Crime in Chicago.*
41. Miller, *Violence by Youth Gangs and Youth Groups*, p. 26.
42. F. Esbensen & D. W. Osgood, *National Evaluation of G.R.E.A.T.* Research in Brief (Washington: National Institute of Justice, 1997).
43. W. B. Miller, White Gangs, in J. F. Short, Jr., Ed., *Modern Criminals* (Chicago: Aldine, 1970), pp. 57, 60, 64.
44. Miller, *Violence by Youth Gangs and Youth Groups*, pp. 21–23.
45. Cited in *Youth Gangs*, p. 3.
46. Klein, *The American Street Gang*; A. Campbell, *Girl Delinquents* (New York: St. Martin's Press, 1981).
47. G. D. Curry & S. H. Decker, *Confronting Gangs: Crime and Community* (Los Angeles: Roxbury, 1998).
48. *Youth Gangs*, p. 2; Klein, *The American Street Gang.*
49. Miller, *Violence by Youth Gangs and Youth Groups*, pp. 21–23.
50. J. W. Moore, Gangs, Drugs, and Violence, in M. De La Rosa, E. Y. Lambert, & B. Gropper, Eds., *Drugs and Violence: Causes, Correlates, and Consequences* (Rockville: National Institute on Drug Abuse, 1990), pp. 160–76; J. J. Hagedorn, *People and Folks: Gangs, Crime and the Underclass in a Rustbelt City* (Chicago: Lakeview Press, 1988).
51. *Youth Gangs*, pp. 2–3; Flowers, *The Adolescent Criminal*, pp. 102–3.

52. W. B. Miller, American Youth Gangs: Past and Present, in A. Blumberg, Ed., *Current Perspectives in Criminal Behavior* (New York: Knopf, 1974), pp. 410–20.
53. Spergel, *The Youth Gang Problem*, p. 60; *Youth Gangs*, pp. 2–3.
54. A. K. Cohen, *Delinquent Boys: The Culture of the Gang* (New York: Free Press, 1951); A. K. Cohen & J. F. Short, Jr., Research on Delinquent Subcultures, *Journal of Social Issues* 14, 3 (1958): 20–37.
55. Cohen, *Delinquent Boys*, pp. 36–44.
56. Flowers, *The Adolescent Criminal*, p. 105.
57. R. A. Cloward & L. E. Ohlin, *Delinquency and Opportunity: A Theory of Delinquent Gangs* (New York: Free Press, 1960).
58. *Ibid.*, p. 80.
59. W. B. Miller, Lower-Class Culture as a Generating Milieu of Gang Delinquency, *Journal of Social Issues* 14 (1958): 5–19.

School Killings

13

In the midst of other types of homicidal violence in society, there has been a rash of fatal school shootings and other school violence in recent years. The mass murder at Columbine High School in 1999 serves as one of the worst examples and has led to increased attention on school violence and at-risk youth by policymakers, criminologists, delinquency experts, and educators. Perpetrators of deadly school violence are predominantly young, suburban males, often with deep-rooted problems that have gone unaddressed. These include pent-up frustrations, a dysfunctional family life, child abuse victimization, mental problems, and, for many, being bullied. Substance abuse is also typically a factor. A gang presence at school can further increase the potential for school shootings and violence. What appears to be the most important correlate to school killings is the availability and use of firearms. Nearly all school fatalities and serious injuries involved guns and other weapons, with both students and teachers being potential targets.

Deadly School Shootings

Although school shootings are not a new phenomenon in America, the recent number of multiple shootings at school has been alarming. Between 1993 and 2012, there have been at least 20 fatal school shootings with multiple victims across the country.[1] Some of the most deadly school shootings include the following:

- On April 2, 2012, One Goh, 43, went on a shooting spree at Oikos University in Oakland, California, killing 7 and wounding 3 others. Goh, a former nursing student at the Korean Christian University, had issues with the school administration, as well as other students, who he believed treated him poorly. He was arrested the same day at a supermarket in nearby Alameda, California.
- On February 27, 2012, 17-year-old T. J. Lane stepped inside the cafeteria at Chardon High School in Chardon, Ohio, a suburb of Cleveland, and started shooting. He killed 3 students and wounded 2 others. Lane, who was described as a social outcast and victim of bullying, was arrested.

- On April 16, 2007, 23-year-old Seung-Hui Cho, armed with two semiautomatic pistols, went on a shooting rampage at Virginia Polytechnic Institute and State University in Blacksburg, Virginia, killing 32 and wounding 25 others before taking his own life. The deadly attack was the worst case of mass murder by a lone assailant in U.S. history. Cho, a senior at Virginia Tech, had a history of mental illness and had previously been accused of stalking 2 students.
- On October 2, 2006, 32-year-old Charles Carl Roberts IV was well armed when he entered a one-room schoolhouse in Nickel Mines, Pennsylvania, and opened fire, killing 5 Amish girls and wounding 5 others. Roberts, a milk truck driver, was apparently out for revenge and then took his own life.
- On March 21, 2005, Jeffrey James Weise, a 16-year-old Native American, went berserk on an Indian reservation in Red Lake, Minnesota. He murdered his grandfather and the girlfriend of his grandfather before proceeding to Red Lake Senior High School. There, Weise, who was often bullied and suffered from depression, shot to death 7 people, including 5 students and a teacher, and wounded as many as 15 others before committing suicide.
- On April 21, 1999, Eric Harris, 18, and Dylan Klebold, 17, entered Columbine High School in Littleton, Colorado, armed with semiautomatic weapons. The pair went on a shooting spree, killing 13 and wounding 25 before taking their own lives.
- On May 21, 1998, 14-year-old Kip Kinkel was heavily armed as he entered Thurston High School in Springfield, Oregon. He opened fire, killing 2 students and wounding 25. Earlier that day, he had committed parricide in killing his mother and father.
- On March 24, 1998, Mitchell Johnson, 14, and Andrew Goldman, 12, entered a middle school in Jonesboro, Arkansas, dressed in camouflage. There they opened fire on students and teachers, killing 5 and wounding 10.
- On December 1, 1997, Michael Carneal, 14, went on a shooting spree at Heath High School in West Paducah, Kentucky, killing 3 students and injuring 5. His inspiration was the movie *The Basketball Diaries*, in which the main character had a dream about entering a classroom and shooting 5 students.
- On February 19, 1997, Evan Ramsey, 16, brought a shotgun to Bethel Regional School in Bethel, Alaska. He shot to death a fellow student and the principal and wounded 2 others.
- On February 2, 1996, Barry Loukatis, 14, walked into Frontier Junior High School in Moses Lake, Washington. Heavily armed, he shot to death 2 students and a teacher. One of the students had reportedly been verbally abusive to him.

- On January 17, 1989, Patrick Purdy, a 26-year-old drifter, entered the schoolyard of Cleveland Elementary School in Stockton, California. Armed with a semiautomatic AK-47, he opened fire, killing 5 children and wounding 29 others before killing himself.
- On March 2, 1987, Nathan Ferris, a 12-year-old overweight honor student, took his father's .45 caliber pistol to school in Missouri, where he shot to death a classmate who had teased him before killing himself.[2]

Additionally, there has been a fair share of school shootings in recent years involving a single fatality or the nonfatal injury of victims.[3] Even more disturbing is that the offenders appear to be getting younger. In a study of multiple school killings involving 15 killers, Kathleen Heide found that more than half of the perpetrators were age 14 or younger.[4] In comparison, nearly 90 percent of juveniles arrested for murder overall in this country are between 15 and 17 years of age.[5]

In spite of the tragedy of school shootings and their seemingly increasing numbers, youths are far more likely to be murder victims and offenders away from school. For instance, from 2008 to 2009, a total of 1,579 youths between the ages of 5 and 18 were homicide victims in the United States, as shown in Figure 13.1. Of these, 1,562 such deaths occurred outside a school campus. Seventeen youths were victims of school-related homicides or those that took place while the victim was on the property of an elementary or secondary school in this country, en route to, or in attendance or going to or from an official school event.

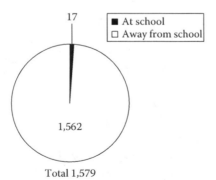

17

■ At school
□ Away from school

1,562

Total 1,579

Figure 13.1 Murders of youth ages 5–18 in school and away from school, 2008–2009. Note: "At School" includes on school property, on the way to or from school, and while attending or traveling to or from a school-sponsored event. (Derived from U.S. Department of Education, National Center for Education Statistics, *Indicators of School Crime and Safety: 2011*, Washington, D.C.: U.S. Department of Justice, 2012, p. 7.)

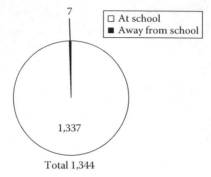

Figure 13.2 Suicides by youth ages 5–18 in school and away from school, 2008–2009. Note: "At School" includes on school property, on the way to or from school, and while attending or traveling to or from a school-sponsored event. (Derived from U.S. Department of Education, National Center for Education Statistics, *Indicators of School Crime and Safety: 2011*(Washington, D.C.: U.S. Department of Justice, 2012, p. 7.)

Similarly, student suicide or self-murder is far more likely to occur away from school than on school campuses. Between 2008 and 2009, of the 1,334 suicides committed by youths 5 to 18 years of age in the United States, only 7 were school-associated suicides (see Figure 13.2).

However, the dynamics of school shootings are similar to those of shootings elsewhere involving young people. Societal violence and its influences can often be a precursor to school shootings and other crime and violence perpetrated at school.

What are the warning signs for at-risk youth in becoming murderers at school? Experts have found the following traits to exist in many such killers:

- Depression
- Built-up hostility toward others
- History of temper tantrums
- The victim of child abuse
- A witness to family violence
- History of problems with alcohol or drugs
- Disciplinary problems
- Problems with truancy, school suspensions, or being expelled
- A strong interest in firearms or explosives
- Cruelty to animals
- Obsessed with hate or antigovernment groups
- Belonging to a gang or antisocial group
- Involvement with a satanic cult
- Fascination with violent games, books, movies, or other violent entertainment

- Suicidal
- Blaming others for problems experienced[6]

The Extent of School Violence

School shootings are representative of the greater problem of school violence occurring at high schools, middle schools, and elementary schools across the country. Various national studies attest to the seriousness of school crime and violence. In a 5-year study by the National School Boards Association, 78 percent of school districts reported student assaults against other students and 60 percent reported student assaults against teachers.[7] Sixty-one percent of districts reported school violence involving weapons; while in 82 percent of the districts school violence increased during the period.

According to the Office of Justice Program's *Crime Victimization in the United States*, there were an estimated 609,307 crimes of violence inside school buildings or on school property in the United States in 2008 (see Table 13.1). This constituted 13.3 percent of all reported crimes of violence. There were approximately 147,263 completed acts of school violence and 463,818 attempted or threatened incidents of violence at school.

Table 13.1 School Crimes of Violence, by Type of Crime, 2008

Type of Crime	Total Number of Incidents	Inside School Building/ On School Property
Crimes of violence	4,581,260	13.3
Completed violence	1,291,780	11.4
Attempted/threatened violence	3,289,490	14.1
Rape/sexual assault[b]	200,520	12.1[a]
Robbery	504,110	5.9[a]
Completed/property taken	346,240	7.1[a]
With injury	127,290	5.4[a]
Without injury	218,950	8.0[a]
Attempted to take property	157,870	3.3[a]
With injury	56,800	3.5[a]
Without injury	101,070	3.2[a]
Assault	3,876,640	14.3
Aggravated	768,770	7.3
Simple	3,107,870	16.1

[a] Estimate is based on about 10 or fewer sample cases.
[b] Includes verbal threats of rape and threats of sexual assault.
Source: Adapted from Office of Justice Programs, Bureau of Justice Statistics, *Criminal Victimization in the United States, 2008 Statistical Tables*, Table 61, Selected Personal and Property Crimes, 2008, http://bjs.ojp. usdoj.gov/index.cfm?ty=pbdetail&iid=2218 (April 16, 2012).

Table 13.2 School Crimes Against Students 12 to 18 Years Old, by Type of Crime and Student Characteristics, 2010

Student Characteristic	Total	Violent	Serious Violent[b]
At school total[a]	828,400	358,600	91,400
Sex			
Male	437,100	179,900	37,700
Female	391,300	178,700	53,600
Age			
12–14	43,400	215,300	49,600
15–18	397,900	143,300	41,800
Race/ethnicity[c]			
White	427,400	178,800	43,200
Black	167,700	78,900	28,400
Hispanic	193,900	81,700	12,600
Other	39,300	19,200	7,200
Urbanicity			
Urban	240,900	132,600	38,200
Suburban	489,000	195,900	44,200
Rural	98,500	30,100	9,000
Household income			
Less than $15,000	58,000	28,700	2,100
$15,000–29,999	135,200	64,100	27,700
$30,000–49,999	121,700	60,700	7,200
$50,000–74,999	156,600	62,300	22,400
$75,000 or more	222,400	64,100	8,200
Not reported	134,500	78,800	23,800

[a] Due to rounding, totals may not add up.
[b] Serious violent victimization is also included in violent victimization.
[c] Other includes Asians, Pacific Islanders, and American Indians, including Alaska Natives. Race categories exclude people of Hispanic ethnicity.

Source: Adapted from U.S. Department of Education, National Center for Education Statistics, *Indicators of School Crime and Safety: 2011* (Washington: U.S. Department of Justice, 2012), p. 97.

A more comprehensive portrayal of school violence is reflected in the annual National Center for Education and Statistics and Bureau of Justice Statistics' *Indicators of School Crime and Safety*, as seen in Table 13.2. The findings show that in 2010, approximately 828,400 school victimizations involving students 12 to 18 years old occurred in the United States. Some 358,600 victimizations were violent crimes. Among these, about 91,400 incidents were characterized as serious violent crimes, including rape, sexual assault, robbery, and aggravated assault.

Victims of violent school crimes were almost equally likely to be male or female, while females had a higher rate of serious violence victimization. Though White students had by far the highest number of violent victimizations, Black and Hispanic students had a higher rate of violent victimization, with Black students' rate of serious violent victimizations nearly three times that of White students and four times the rate of Hispanic students.

Violent and seriously violent victimizations occurred more often in suburban schools than urban or rural schools; violent and seriously violent crimes were most likely to be perpetrated against students with household incomes of $15,000–$29,999 and $50,000–$74,999.

The significant relationship between schools and violent crimes was further put in perspective by findings from the Centers for Disease Control and Prevention's Youth Risk Behavior Survey as follows:

- Nearly 4 in 10 high school students engaged in a physical fight within the past year.
- Almost half of male students were in a school fight in the last year.
- More than twice the number of male students as female students were likely to have been in a fight within the past year.
- Around 15 percent of high school students nationwide fought on school property within the last year.
- Racial and ethnic minority students were more likely than White students to be in school fights and to suffer injuries.
- Nearly 2 in 10 students had carried a weapon to school in the past month.
- Almost 6 percent of students had carried a firearm within the last month.
- Seven percent of high school students were threatened or injured at school with a weapon.
- More than half of the middle and high schools across the country reported at least one incident of fighting or unarmed assault during the past year.
- Around 1 in 5 middle and high schools reported at least one serious violent crime within the past year.
- Violent school crime is more than twice as likely to occur in cities as rural areas, and more than three times as likely to occur as in small towns.
- Four in 10 high school students stayed out of school at least once within the last month out of fear for their safety.[8]

School Violence Against Teachers

Teachers have also been the victims of student or other staff-perpetrated threats and nonfatal school violence. According to *Indicators of School Crime and Safety*, between 2007 and 2008, there were an estimated 154,000 physical attacks from students reported by teachers in public and private schools across the United States (see Table 13.3). Attacks tended to occur most often in suburban and city schools, and least in schools in towns and rural areas.

Female teachers were more likely to be victims of student attacks, outnumbering male teacher victims by more than 3.4 to 1. White teachers were far more likely to report crime victimization than Hispanics or other races. However, Black teachers had the highest percentage of victimization.

Table 13.3 Number of Teachers Attacked by Students, by Selected Characteristics, 2007–2008

Teacher or School Characteristic[a]	Total	City	Suburban	Town	Rural
Total[b]	154,400	52,800	53,400	20,000	28,100
Sex					
Male	34,900	14,900	12,600	3,400	3,900
Female	119,500	37,900	40,800	16,600	24,200
Race/ethnicity[c]					
White	131,000	41,200	44,900	18,400	26,600
Black	12,300	6,600	4,600	—	—
Hispanic	8,100	4,500	2,200	—	300
Other	3,000	700	—	—	400
Instructional level[d]					
Elementary	113,100	38,500	37,700	16,200	20,700
Secondary	41,300	14,400	15,700	3,900	7,400
Sector					
Public[e]	145,100	50,000	48,900	19,200	27,000
Private	9,300	2,900	4,500	800	1,100

[a] Teachers who taught only prekindergarten students are excluded.

[b] Detail may not sum to totals because of rounding. Estimates of number of reports are rounded to the nearest 100.

[c] Other includes American Indian, Alaska Native, Asian or Pacific Islander, and two or more races. Race categories exclude people of Hispanic ethnicity.

[d] Instructional level divides teachers into elementary or secondary based on a combination of the grades taught, main teaching assignment, and the structure of the teachers' class(es).

[e] The public sector includes public, public charter, and Bureau of Indian Education school teachers.

Source: Adapted from U.S. Department of Education, National Center for Education Statistics, *Indicators of School Crime and Safety: 2011* (Washington: U.S. Department of Justice, 2012), p. 107.

Elementary school and public-sector teachers were most susceptible to being physically assaulted by students across all school characteristics.

Aside from actual student physical attacks, nearly 8 percent of teachers in public and private school settings in the country during the period from 2007 to 2008 were the victims of threats of bodily harm by students. Female, White, public, and secondary school teachers were most likely to receive threats of injury by students.

Teacher threats from other teachers or school staff also occur, some of which can lead to nonfatal and fatal violence, as illustrated earlier in the chapter.

Trends in School Violence

Although school shootings and other violence continues to be a serious concern for students and teachers, the incidence of school violence in the United States has generally declined since the early 1990s.[9] As shown in Figure 13.3, violence against students 12 to 18 years of age at school went from 1,240,200 in 1992 to 358,600 in 2010, a drop of 71 percent. For serious violent crimes during the period, victimization dropped from 197,600 to 91,400, or a decline of 54 percent.

The percentage of 9th- to 12th-grade students who were threatened or injured with a weapon on school grounds within the past year actually rose slightly between 1973 and 2009, going from 7.3 percent to 7.7 percent, but fell from a peak of 9.2 percent in 2003 (see Figure 13.4). Also between 2003 and 2009, the percentage of male and female students, as well as White and minority students, reporting threats or injury with a weapon on school property one or more time during the preceding 12 months fell.

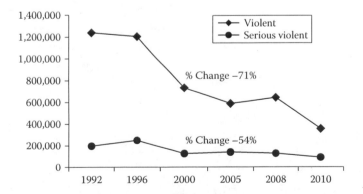

Figure 13.3 Trends in school violence victimization against students 12 to 18 years of age, 1992–2010. (From U.S. Department of Education, National Center for Education Statistics, *Indicators of School Crime and Safety: 2011*, Washington, D.C.: U.S. Department of Justice, 2012, p. 96.)

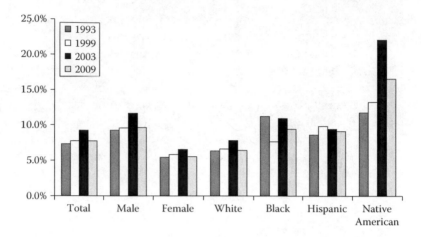

Figure 13.4 Percentage of 9th- to 12th-grade students threatened or injured at school in past year, 1993–2009. (From U.S. Department of Education, National Center for Education Statistics, *Indicators of School Crime and Safety: 2011*, Washington: U.S. Department of Justice, 2012, p. 103.)

Other trends supporting a decline in school crime and violence as reported in *Indicators of School Crime and Safety* include the following findings:

- Between 1995 and 2009, the percentage of male students who reported being victims of crime fell by half, from 10 percent to 5 percent.
- Between 1995 and 2009, the percentage of female students reporting crime victimization dropped two-thirds, from 9 percent to 3 percent.
- Public school students who reported being crime victims at school fell from 10 percent in 1995 to 4 percent in 2009.
- Private school students reporting of criminal victimization went from 7 percent in 1995 to 2 percent in 2009.
- From 1993 to 2009, the percentage of 9th and 12th graders reporting threats or injury with a weapon at school dropped from 9.4 percent to 8.7 percent, and 5.5 percent to 5.2 percent, respectively.
- The percentage of teachers threatened with harm by students fell from 12 percent in 1993 to 1994 to 7 percent in 2003 to 2004.
- Between 1993 and 2008, there was a slight drop in the percentage of teachers who reported being physically assaulted by students.[10]

Factors in School Shootings and Violence

Researchers have found a number of factors that play a significant role in school shootings and other violence at school. These include the availability and presence of firearms and other weapons; a gang presence at school; bullying; and the availability, use, and abuse of alcohol and drugs on school property.

Weapons and School Violence

The relationship between school violence and student possession of weapons has been well documented.[11] Virtually all lethal violence at school is closely associated with students carrying, using, or having easy access to guns. The Youth Risk Behavior Survey reported that 61 percent of students said they knew other students who could bring a firearm to school if they chose to.[12] One in 4 respondents indicated they could easily obtain a gun, while 1 in 5 students reported hearing rumors of another student planning to shoot someone from or at school.

A high percentage of students in the United States are likely to carry weapons, according to the research. As seen in Table 13.4, in 2009 nearly 18 percent of students in grades 9 to 12 reported carrying a weapon such as a gun, knife, or club anywhere at some point within the past 30 days alone. Comparatively, almost 6 percent of students said they had carried a weapon onto school property within the last 30 days.

Males were nearly four times as likely as females to have carried a weapon at any time and almost three times more likely than females of carrying a weapon on school property in the past month. Nearly 1 in 5 White and Hispanic students had a weapon in their possession anywhere 1 or more days within previous month.

Ninth- and 10th-grade students were the most likely to carry a weapon anywhere within the last month; however, 10th and 12th graders had the highest percentage of possessing a weapon on school property.

Youth Gangs at School

The increasing presence of youth gangs at schools in the United States has been strongly related to school shootings, violence, and illicit drug activity.[13] As shown in Table 13.5, more than 1 in 5 students 12 to 18 years of age reported that street gangs were present in their school in 2009, a decrease from 2005 and 2007, in which around one-quarter of students believed there was a gang presence in school.

Male and female students were roughly equal in their reporting of gangs at school, with about 1 in 5 believing this to be the case in 2009. In the previous years studied, a higher percentage of male students than female students reported gangs being at school.

Black and Hispanic students were far more likely than other students to report a gang presence at school in 2009. More than 3 in 10 Black and

Table 13.4   Percentage of 9th to 12th Grade Students Who Reported Carrying a Weapon During Past 30 Days, by Student Characteristics and Location, 2009

Student or School Characteristic	Anywhere	On School Property
Total	17.5	5.6
Sex		
Male	27.1	8.0
Female	7.1	2.9
Race/ethnicity[a]		
White	18.6	5.6
Black	14.4	5.3
Hispanic	17.2	5.8
Asian	8.4	3.6
American Indian/Alaska Native	20.7	4.2
Pacific Islander/Native Hawaiian	20.3	9.8
Two or more races	17.9	5.8
Grade		
9th	18.0	4.9
10th	18.4	6.1
11th	16.2	5.2
12th	16.6	6.0
Urbanicity		
Urban	—	—
Suburban	—	—
Rural	—	—

[a] Race categories exclude people of Hispanic ethnicity.

Source: Adapted from U.S. Department of Education, National Center for Education Statistics, *Indicators of School Crime and Safety: 2011* (Washington: U.S. Department of Justice, 2012), pp. 146–47.

Hispanic students believed gangs were in their schools, compared with less than 1 in 5 students in other racial groups.

Students in higher grades were more likely than those in lower grades to report the existence of gangs at school in 2009. Around one-quarter of students in grades 9 to 12 believed there were gangs at school, with the percentage descending the lower the grade.

More than 1 in 5 students in public schools reported a gang present in 2009, compared with just over 2 percent of students in private schools. Around one-third of students in urban schools believed gangs were present, well above the percentage of suburban and rural students.

Researchers have found that youth gangs are involved in a disproportionate level of violent activity at and away from school.[14] This has been greatly attributed to the availability and use of firearms and access to more sophisticated weapons.[15]

Table 13.5   Percentage of Students 12 to 18 Years of Age Reporting Presence of Gangs at School, by Student and School Characteristics, 2005–2009

Student or School Characteristic	2005	2007	2009
Total	24.2	23.2	20.4
Sex			
Male	25.3	25.1	20.9
Female	22.9	21.3	19.9
Race/ethnicity			
White	16.8	16.0	14.1
Black	37.6	37.6	31.4
Hispanic	38.9	36.1	33.0
Asian	20.2	17.4	17.2
Other	27.7	26.4	15.3
Grade			
6th	12.1	15.3	11.0
7th	17.3	17.4	14.8
8th	19.1	20.6	15.9
9th	28.3	28.0	24.9
10th	32.6	28.1	27.7
11th	28.0	25.9	22.6
12th	27.9	24.4	21.9
Sector			
Public	25.8	24.9	22.0
Private	4.2	5.2	2.3

Source: Adapted from U.S. Department of Education, National Center for Education Statistics, *Indicators of School Crime and Safety: 2011* (Washington: U.S. Department of Justice, 2012), p. 124.

School Bullying

Bullying or being bullied at school is seen by experts as a major factor in violent school behavior. This is particularly true where it concerns school shooting incidents. Research shows that of the hundreds of school-related deaths in the United States since 1992, bullying played a role in virtually every incident.[16]

What is bullying? A bully is defined as a person who "directs physical, verbal, or psychological aggression or harassment toward others with the goal of gaining power over another."[17] The act of bullying has been shown to be a persistent problem at schools and in communities across the country. An estimated 15 to 30 percent of all students are bullies or the victims of bullying.[18] According to the American Medical Association, roughly 3.7 million youths bully other youths, while more than 3.2 million people are the victims of some form of bullying in the United States each year.[19]

Boys are more likely to be bullies than girls, especially when it comes to physical bullying.[20] The victims of bullies tend to be boys more often than girls, younger students, and those who are physically or socially weak or disadvantaged. Most victims have few friends or confidants and poor social skills and academic difficulties. The rate of fighting by bullies and the victims of bullying tends to be higher than among nonbullying-involved children.[21]

Studies indicate that physical bullying tends to increase in elementary school, peaking in middle school, and decreasing in high school.[22] Verbal bullying remains steady throughout. The lack of aggressive response by schools to bullying is seen as an important part of the problem in both preventing and combating bullying behavior. More than two-thirds of students who were surveyed believed that school response to bullying has been weak at best, while about one-quarter of teachers failed to take action when told about bullying incidents.[23]

Bullying has taken on a new dimension in the modern era with what is known as cyber-bullying. It has many of the same dynamics as school bullying, only the protagonist hides behind a computer and the anonymity and relative safety from detection that exists on the Internet. In many instances, cyber-bullying is an extension of bullying at school and elsewhere.

According to the National Crime Victimization Survey's School Crime Supplement, 29 percent of students between the ages of 12 and 18 reported being the victims of bullying at school or cyber-bullying anywhere in 2009.[24] Female students are more likely to be bullied than male students, while younger students in grades 6 through 9 are more likely to be victims of bullying than older students in grades 10 through 12.

As seen in Table 13.6, in 2009, 6 percent of students 12 to 18 years of age reported being victimized by bullying anywhere within the school year. The highest percentage of cyber-bullying was from harassment through text messaging, hurtful information shared on the Internet, and harassment through instant messages.

More than 7 percent of female students reported being victims of cyber-bullying, compared with fewer than 5 percent of male students. White and Black students were more likely than those of other races and Hispanic students to be cyber bullied, while 9th and 10th graders reported the highest percentage of cyber-bullying over other grades.

Students in public and suburban schools were more likely to report being cyber bullied than private, urban, and rural schools.

The correlation between being bullied and resorting to a violent backlash can be seen in school shootings as documented earlier in the chapter and

Table 13.6 Percentage of Students 12 to 18 Years of Age Reporting Cyber-Bullying Victimization Within the School Year, by Type of Bullying and Student Characteristics, 2009

Student or School Characteristic	Total Cyber-Bullying Anywhere	Cyber-Bullying Anywhere					
		Hurtful Information on Internet	Subject of Harassing Instant Messages	Subject of Harassing Text Messages	Subject of Harassing E-Mails	Subject of Harassing While Gaming	Excluded Online
Total	6.0	2.0	1.8	3.0	1.3	0.8	0.9
Sex							
Male	4.9	1.1	1.1	2.0	0.7	1.4	0.8
Female	7.2	2.9	2.5	4.0	2.0	—	0.9
Race/ethnicity[a]							
White	6.8	2.3	2.0	3.4	1.4	0.9	1.0
Black	5.5	2.0	2.0	3.0	0.9	—	0.9
Hispanic	5.0	1.4	1.5	2.3	1.6	—	1.0
Asian	2.9	—	—	—	—	—	—
Other	4.2	—	—	—	—	—	—

Continued

Table 13.6 (*Continued*) Percentage of Students 12 to 18 Years of Age Reporting Cyber-Bullying Victimization Within the School Year, by Type of Bullying and Student Characteristics, 2009

Student or School Characteristic	Cyber-Bullying Anywhere						
	Total Cyber-Bullying Anywhere	Hurtful Information on Internet	Subject of Harassing Instant Messages	Subject of Harassing Text Messages	Subject of Harassing E-Mails	Subject of Harassing While Gaming	Excluded Online
Grade							
6th	5.0	1.8	2.1	2.1	1.6	‡	1.7
7th	4.9	1.4	2.0	2.6	1.1	0.7	1.1
8th	6.5	2.4	2.6	2.0	1.5	1.4	1.5
9th	6.7	2.4	2.2	3.3	1.6	—	1.0
10th	7.2	2.3	1.5	4.6	2.0	0.8	—
11th	5.6	2.1	1.6	2.4	0.9	0.8	—
12th	5.9	1.5	—	3.4	—	—	—
Urbanicity							
Urban	5.7	2.0	1.2	3.0	1.1	1.1	1.0
Suburban	6.3	2.1	2.0	2.8	1.5	0.7	1.0
Rural	5.7	1.6	2.0	3.6	1.3	—	—
Sector							
Public	6.2	2.0	1.9	3.1	1.4	0.8	0.9
Private	4.0	1.5	—	1.9	—	—	—

[a] Race categories do not include Hispanics. *Other* includes Native Americans and students of more than one race.

Source: U.S. Department of Education, National Center for Education Statistics, *Indicators of School Crime and Safety: 2011* (Washington: U.S. Department of Justice, 2012), p. 132.

other forms of aberrant behavior, of which the roots can often be traced back to bullying.[25]

Alcohol and Drug Use by Students

The use, abuse, and availability of alcohol and drugs by students is often cited as a factor in school shootings and teenage violence by researchers.[26] Studies show that more than half of all middle school and high school students in the United States have had at least one drink within the last year, while almost half of all high school seniors have used one or more illegal drugs in their lifetime.[27] In a 1993–1994 survey of middle and high school students undertaken by the Parent Resource Institute for Drug Education (PRIDE), a strong correlation was found between alcohol and marijuana use and such violent behavior as carrying a firearm to school and a threat of harm to another individual.[28] Other researchers' findings have supported a significant relationship between youth violence and alcohol and drug use and abuse.[29]

Male students are much more likely to have ever used alcohol or drugs than female students, as well as to have used at school.[30] In one study of student drug use, male students were found to be more than twice as likely as female students to have used marijuana while at school, and were more likely to have used alcohol on school property.[31]

The availability of illegal drugs at school has also been associated with school violence, street gangs, drug dealing, and other adolescent antisocial behavior.[32] As shown in Figure 13.5, in 1997, almost one-third of students in grades 9 through 12 nationwide reported that illicit drugs were offered, given, or sold to them on school property within the last year.

Male students were more likely than female students to report the availability of drugs at school. Nearly 4 in 10 male students said they had

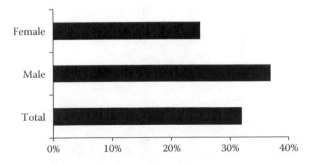

Figure 13.5 Percentage of students, grades 9–12, reporting drugs were made available to them on school property during the past 12 months, by sex, 1997. (Adapted from U.S. Department of Education and Justice, *Indicators of School Crime and Safety: 2000*, Washington, D.C.: Offices of Educational Research and Improvement and Justice Programs, 2000, p. 42.)

been offered, given, or sold illegal drugs at school, compared with 1 in 4 female students.

According to government data, in 2009 more than 2 in 10 students in 10th grade and around 1 in 4 students in 11th and 12th grade reported using marijuana on at least one occasion during the past 30 days.[33] More than twice as many male students as female students had used marijuana on school property one or more times within the past month.

Endnotes

1. R. B. Flowers & H. L. Flowers, *Murders in the United States: Crimes, Killers and Victims of the Twentieth Century* (Jefferson: McFarland, 2001), pp. 183–87; K. M. Heide, 1998 Keynote Address: School Shootings and School Violence: What's Going on and Why? in U.S. Department of Justice, *Proceedings of the Homicide Research Working Group Meetings, 1997 and 1998* (Washington: National Institute of Justice, 1997), pp. 116–30.

2. Flowers & Flowers, *Murders in the United States*, pp. 183–87; K. Dolak, Oakland Shooting Suspect Not Remorseful, Police Chief Says, *ABC News* (April 3, 2012), http://abcnews.go.com/US/oakland-shooting-suspect-remorseful-police-chief/story?id = 16059961; Suspect ID'd in Deadly Ohio School Shooting, *CBS News* (February 12, 2012), http://www.cbsnews.com/8301-201_162-57386080/suspect-idd-in-deadly-ohio-school-shooting/; 5th Girl Dies After Amish Schoolhouse Shooting, *MSNBC.com* (October 3, 2006), http://www.msnbc.msn.com/id/15105305/ns/us_news-crime_and; High School Shooting Spree Leaves 10 Dead, *FoxNews.com* (March 22, 2005), http://www.foxnews.com/story/0,2933,151085,00.html; Worst U.S. Shooting Ever Kills 33 on Va. Campus, *MSNBC.com* (April 17, 2007),. http://www.msnbc.msn.com/id/18134671/ns/us_news-crime_and_courts.

3. Flowers & Flowers, *Murders in the United States*, pp. 183–87. See also R. Barri Flowers, *Kids Who Commit Adult Crimes: A Study of Serious Juvenile Criminality and Delinquency* (Binghamton: Haworth, 2002).

4. Heide, 1998 Keynote Address, p. 117.

5. K. M. Heide, *Young Killers: The Challenge of Juvenile Homicide* (Thousand Oaks: Sage, 1999).

6. R. B. Flowers, *Male Crime and Deviance: Exploring Its Causes, Dynamics and Nature* (Springfield: Charles C Thomas, 2003).

7. Cited in R. B. Flowers, *The Victimization and Exploitation of Women and Children: A Study of Physical, Mental and Sexual Maltreatment in the United States* (Jefferson: McFarland, 1994), p. 111; Nina M. Fredland, Nurturing Hostile Environments: The Problem of School Violence, *Family & Community Health* 3, 1 (2008): S32–S41.

8. Flowers, *Kids Who Commit Adult Crimes*.

9. U.S. Department of Education and Justice, *Indicators of School Crime and Safety* (Washington: Offices of Educational Research and Imprisonment and Justice Programs, 2000), p. 4.

10. U.S. Department of Education, National Center for Education Statistics, *Indicators of School Crime and Safety: 2011* (Washington: U.S. Department of Justice, 2012), pp. 16, 22, 103.
11. Flowers, *Kids Who Commit Adult Crimes*; Flowers and Flowers, *Murders in the United States*, pp. 183–87; J. F. Sheley & J. D. Wright, *In the Line of Fire: Youth, Guns, and Violence in America* (New York: Aldine de Gruyter, Inc., 1995).
12. Youth Risk Behavior Survey, http://www.Alfred.edu/teenviolence/potential_violence.html.
13. *Indicators of School Crime and Safety*, pp. 28, 35; U.S. Department of Justice, *Youth Gangs: An Overview* (Washington: Office of Juvenile Justice and Delinquency Prevention, 1998).
14. J. C. Howell, Gangs and Youth Violence, in J. C. Howell, B. Krisberg, J. D. Hawkins, & J. J. Wilson, Eds., *A Sourcebook: Serious, Violent and Chronic Juvenile Offenders* (Thousand Oaks: Sage, 1995), pp. 261–74; T. P. Thornberry & J. H. Birch, *Gang Members and Delinquent Behavior* (Washington: Office of Justice Programs, 1997).
15. Sheley & Wright, *In the Line of Fire*; C. R. Block & R. Block, Street Gang Crime in Chicago, in M. W. Klein, C. L. Maxson, & J. Miller, Eds., *The Modern Gang Reader* (Los Angeles: Roxbury, 1995), pp. 202–11.
16. Cited in Flowers, *Male Crime and Deviance*.
17. A. Cohn & A. Carter, Bullying: What Schools and Parents Can Do, National Association of School Psychologists, http://www.guideancechannel.com/details.asp?index=508&cat=1.
18. *Ibid.*
19. Cited in *Ibid.*
20. *Ibid.*; Flowers, *Male Crime and Deviance*.
21. Cohn & Carter, Bullying: What Schools and Parents Can Do.
22. *Ibid.*
23. *Ibid.*
24. *Indicators of School Crime and Safety: 2011*, pp. 44, 130.
25. Flowers, *Kids Who Commit Adult Crimes*; T. R. Nansel, M. D. Overpeck, D. L. Haynie, W. J. Ruan, & P. C. Scheidt, Relationships Between Bullying and Violence Among U.S. Youth, *Archives of Pediatric and Adolescent Medicine* 157, 4 (2003): 348–53.
26. Heide, 1998 Keynote Address, p. 124; R. B. Flowers, *Drugs, Alcohol and Criminality in American Society* (Jefferson: McFarland, 1999), pp. 99–111.
27. Cited in Flowers, *Drugs, Alcohol and Criminality in American Society*, pp. 100, 104.
28. Cited in Heide, 1998 Keynote Address, p. 124.
29. See, for example, D. S. Elliot, D. Huizinga, & S. Menard, *Multiple Problem Youth: Delinquency, Substance Abuse, and Mental Health Problems* (New York: Springer-Verlag, 1989).
30. Flowers, *Drugs, Alcohol and Criminality in American Society*, p. 108; *Indicators of School Crime and Safety*, pp. 38–42.
31. Flowers, *Drugs, Alcohol and Criminality in American Society*, pp. 104–10.
32. *Ibid.*; R. B. Flowers, *The Adolescent Criminal: An Examination of Today's Juvenile Offender* (Jefferson: McFarland, 1990), pp. 94–97.
33. *Indicators of School Crime and Safety: 2011*, pp. 154–55.

Types of Killers   V

Sexual Killers

14

A high percentage of murderers can be termed sexual killers. These are killers whose crimes are motivated by sexual needs or gratification, sexual jealousy, sexual perversions, childhood sexual victimization, or other sex-related factors. Many who kill are driven by sexual impulses or sexually fantasize about murdering people or someone in particular. Sexual sadist killers associate sexual pleasure with violence and inflicting pain on victims. The relationship between the sexual deviant, sexual predator, or pedophile and murder is often reflected in intimate homicides, rape-murders, child murders, serial killings, and some mass murders. Sex-related killers typically abuse alcohol or drugs, come from violent and sexually abusing families, and exhibit other characteristics that may predispose them to homicidal and violent behavior.

What Is Sexual Murder?

Sexual murder reflects homicides with a sexual theme, nature, or character. The dictionary defines *sexual* as "(1) of sex, sexuality, the sexes, or the sex organs and their functions, and (2) implying or symbolizing erotic desires or activity"[1] and *homicide* as "(1) the killing of one person by another or (2) a person who kills another."[2] As such, sexual murder can be defined as "homicide in which there is a sexual element, motivation, relationship, or perversion involved such as rape, molestation, prostitution, intimacy, battering, and sexual jealousy."[3]

According to the book *Sexual Homicide: Patterns and Motives*, sexual homicide refers to the "killing of a person in the context of power, sexuality, and brutality."[4] The authors further describe sexual homicide as "murders with evidence or observations that indicate that the murder was sexual in nature."[5] Murders that are sexually motivated usually fall under the category of *lust murder*, also referred to as erotophonophilia.[6]

The *Diagnostic and Statistical Manual of the American Psychiatric Association (DSM III-R)* places sexual deviance under the term *paraphilia*, which is characterized as

arousal in response to sexual objects or situations that are not part of normative arousal activity patterns and whose essential features are intense sexual urges and sexually arousing fantasies generally involving non-human objects, the suffering or humiliation of one's self or one's partner, or children or other non-consenting persons.[7]

Paraphilic acts that are commonly involved in sexual murders include rape, incest, sadism, voyeurism, exhibitionism, fetishism, homosexuality, bestiality, coprolagnia, and urolagnia.

Studies show that sexual homicides often involve children, intimates, sex workers, and serial and ritual murders.[8] In their study of lethal violence in Chicago over a 20-year period, Carolyn Block and Antigone Christakos described sexually based homicide syndromes, or homicides based on the perpetrator's primary motive or goal when the crime of murder occurred. These included rape homicides; confrontations involving spouses, ex-spouses, romantic partners, or other intimates; and murder-suicide pacts.[9] Other research has supported a relationship between sexual factors and circumstances and homicidal behavior.[10]

The Extent of Sexual Murder

Assessing the true extent of sexual homicides can be difficult, given the often multiple and overlapping motivations and circumstances attributed to homicides, as well as limitation of official and other data. According to the FBI's Uniform Crime Reports, an estimated 12,996 murders were committed in the United States in 2010 (see Table 14.1).

Of these, 150 were identified as sex-related murders, including those involving rape, prostitution and commercialized vice, other sex offenses, and romantic triangles. Overall, males outnumbered females 4 to 1 as victims of

Table 14.1   Sex-Related Murder Circumstances, by Sex of Victim, 2010

Circumstance	Total Murder Victims	Male	Female	Unknown
Total murders	12,996	10,058	2,918	20
Felony-type total	1,923	1,601	319	3
Rape	41	0	41	0
Prostitution and commercialized vice	5	0	5	0
Other sex offenses	14	10	4	0
Other than felony-type total	6,351	4,648	1,697	6
Romantic triangle	90	72	18	0
Total sex-related	150	82	68	0

Source: Derived from U.S. Department of Justice, Federal Bureau of Investigation, *Crime in the United States: Uniform Crime Reports 2010*, Expanded Homicide Data Table 10, Murder Circumstances, by Relationship, 2010, http://www.fbi.gov/about-us/cjis/ucr/crime-in-the-u.s/2010/crime-in-the-u.s.-2010/tables/10shrtbl10.xls (April 12, 2012).

sex-related homicides. However, females were far more likely to be murdered in crimes involving rape, prostitution, or commercialized vice, for which there were no male victims during the year.

Sexual factors may often play a role in murders in which the primary circumstance was believed to be alcohol- and/or drug-related. Studies show that sexual homicides typically involved substance abuse on the part of the perpetrator, victim, or both.[11] Other types of homicide-related violent offenses and property crimes can also reflect a sexual nature, such as robbery-rape murders and burglary-rape murders.[12]

Some criminologists believe that there may be far more sex-related homicides than indicated in official data. In 2010, there were more than 4,600 murders in which the circumstances were unknown.[13] Studies suggest that a high number of these may have been sexual murders.[14]

Long-term murder trends reveal hundreds of homicides that are sexual in nature each year. According to the FBI's Supplemental Homicide Reporting program, between 1976 and 1994 an estimated 4,807 murders involved rape or other sexual offenses in the United States.[15] This represented around 2 percent of all murders committed. However, these figures do not include some types of sex-related murders.[16]

More recent years indicate that sex-related murders are generally on the decline (see Figure 14.1). Between 1994 and 2010, the number of sexual murders in the United States dropped by more than 70 percent. However, from 2008 to 2010, sex-related homicide rose nearly 4.2 percent. An even greater increase in sexual murders occurred from 2009 to 2010 at more than 17 percent.

It is important to note that although most murders are solved or cleared by law enforcement agencies, many sexual homicides are not solved. For

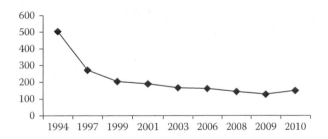

Figure 14.1 Sex-related homicides, 1994–2010; includes rape, prostitution and commercialized vice, other sex offenses, and romantic triangles. (Derived from U.S. Department of Justice, Federal Bureau of Investigation, *Crime in the United States: Uniform Crime Reports 2010*, Expanded Homicide Data, Table 12, Murder Circumstances, by Relationship, 2006–2010, http://www.fbi.gov/about-us/cjis/ucr/crime-in-the-u.s/2010/crime-in-the-u.s.-2010/tables/10shrtbl12.xls, April 15, 2012; U.S. Department of Justice, Federal Bureau of Investigation, *Crime in the United States: Uniform Crime Reports 1994–1999*, Washington, D.C.: Government Printing Office, 1995–2000.)

instance, in 2010 the clearance rate for murder in the United States was 64.8 percent. This left more than 35 percent of homicides unsolved, including those involving sexual circumstances.[17]

Characteristics of Sexual Murderers and Victims

Who are the offenders and victims of sexual homicides? What are the circumstances of sex-related murders? According to the government report *Sex Offenses and Offenders*, sexual killers are typically White, male, and between the ages of 18 and 39. As shown in Table 14.2, between 1976 and 1994, 95 percent of sexual assault killers in the United States were male, compared with nearly 87 percent of all murderers, while 58 percent of sex killers were White, compared with almost 48 percent of all killers.

Blacks were disproportionately represented as sex-offender murderers, constituting nearly 40 percent of the total. However, this was lower than the more than 50 percent of overall murderers identified as Black.

Table 14.2 Characteristics of Sexual Assault Murderers, 1976–1994

	Murders	
Offender Characteristic	All	Sexual Assault
Sex		
Male	86.6%	95.0%
Female	13.4%	5.0%
Race		
White	47.8%	58.0%
Black	50.3%	39.9%
Other	1.9%	2.1%
Age		
12 or younger	0.2%	0.1%
13–17	8.1%	9.9%
18–24	30.1%	39.1%
25–29	18.0%	22.5%
30–39	23.1%	21.1%
40–49	11.1%	5.4%
50–59	5.4%	1.5%
60 or older	3.9%	0.4%
Average age	31 years	26 years

Source: Derived from U.S. Department of Justice, Bureau of Justice Statistics, *Sex Offenses and Offenders: Executive Summary* (Washington: Government Printing Office, 1997), p. 3.

Sexual assault murderers and total killers tended to be mostly between 18 and 39 years of age. Nearly 4 in 10 murders involving a sexual assault were committed by killers between the age of 18 and 24.

In an FBI analysis of sexual killers, half were found to come from families with criminal histories, while more than half had mental illness in the family.[18] More than two-thirds of sexual murderers had families in which at least one member had a problem with alcohol, one-third had a family member with a drug problem, and half of the killers came from families in which someone had a sexual problem. Around two-thirds of sexual murderers had a childhood that was characterized by mental illness, with nearly half being the victims of physical, sexual, or emotional abuse. Most had cold, unsympathetic, uncaring parents.

Many sexual killers had violent, rape, or sadistic childhood fantasies and often displayed cruelty to other children or animals. They have been characterized by criminologists as having highly negative mental states, including anger, frustration, hostility, agitation, and excitement.[19] Sexual murderers often regard the world as "unjust [and] desire to be strong, powerful and in control, and favor autoerotic sexual activitites."[20]

The characteristics of victims of sexual assault murders between 1976 and 1994 can be seen in Table 14.3. Victims were predominantly female, White, and young. More than 8 in 10 victims of sexual assault homicides were female. This compares with all murders, in which fewer than 1 in 4 victims were female.

Whites constituted nearly 7 in 10 victims of sexual assault murders, compared with just over half of all murder victims. Almost 3 in 10 sexual assault–murder victims were Black, and fewer than 3 percent were of other races.

Most victims of sexual assault homicides were under the age of 30. Nearly 6 in 10 victims were age 29 and younger, with more than 2 in 10 victims of sexual homicides between the ages of 18 and 24. Nearly 15 percent of victims were age 12 and younger. Sexual assault–murder victims tended to be younger than total murder victims.

The majority of sexual assault homicides are intraracial in nature. Around 8 in 10 such murders involve victims and perpetrators are of the same race.[21] Sex-related homicides are twice as likely as homicides in general to involve strangers; however, they are equally likely to involve people who are acquaintances in some fashion.[22]

Types of Sexual Killers

Intimate Killers

The relationship between sexual intimacy and homicide has been strongly supported through studies and official data. According to the Bureau of

Table 14.3 Characteristics of Sexual Assault Murder Victims, 1976–1994

Victim Characteristic	Murders	
	All	Sexual Assault
Sex of victim		
Male	76.4%	18.0%
Female	23.6%	82.0%
Race of victim		
White	51.7%	68.4%
Black	46.3%	28.9%
Other	2.0%	2.7%
Age of victim		
12 or younger	10.1%	14.8%
13–17	4.6%	9.7%
18–24	21.3%	21.7%
25–29	15.7%	12.3%
30–39	22.0%	14.2%
40–49	11.7%	8.3%
50–59	6.9%	5.3%
60 or older	7.7%	13.7%
Average age	32 years	32 years

Source: Derived from U.S. Department of Justice, Bureau of Justice Statistics, *Sex Offenses and Offenders: An Analysis of Data on Rape and Sexual Assault* (Washington: Government Printing Office, 1997), p. 29.

Justice Statistics, nearly 52,000 women and men were killed by an intimate between 1976 and 1996 in the United States.[23] FBI figures show that in 2010 alone, there were 1,336 murders of wives, husbands, girlfriends, and boyfriends, with the murder tally at 1,360 in 2009.[24] Studies reveal that an estimated 3 out of every 10 women murdered in this country are victims of intimate homicides.[25] About 1 in 5 female murder victims are killed by a spouse or ex-spouse, while one-third of all intimate murders in the United States are perpetrated by the victim's boyfriend or girlfriend.[26]

The male intimate is primarily responsible for partner homicides, often motivated by sexual issues such as jealousy, desire, adultery, or separation.[27] This is especially true for spousal homicides. Women are the victims of uxoricide, or death perpetrated by a husband, more than any other type of murder.[28] Although women who murder intimates largely do so in self-defense from an abusive mate, there are cases in which women kill husbands, boyfriends, or ex-intimates out of sexual jealousy, revenge, or involvement with another man.[29]

A study of intrafamilial homicides in Detroit found that cohabiting spouses were 11 times more likely to be killed by a spouse than were family members by another relative living in the residence.[30] Other studies have found that noncohabiting spouses are also vulnerable to spouse homicide. In a comparison of uxoricide rates in several countries, including Canada and Australia, Margo Wilson and Martin Daly reported that the risk of uxoricide increased following a separation.[31]

Researchers have further found that the risk of uxoricide increased with male sexual proprietary jealousy toward young fertile wives.[32] This jealousy has been related to such issues as the wife's physical attractiveness, sexual rivals, and possible new sexual partners.

Serial Killers

Serial murders have long been associated with sexual themes. Such notable examples include the serial killer known as Jack the Ripper, who murdered streetwalking prostitutes in Victorian England; Ted Bundy, who raped and murdered as many as 40 women across the United States in the 1970s; Gerald and Charlene Gallego, who abducted, sexually assaulted, and killed 10 young women in California, Nevada, and Oregon in the late 1970s and early 1980s as part of their "sex slave" fantasies; "lust killer" Jerry Brudos who raped, mutilated, and murdered women in Oregon during the late 1980s; and Gary Ridgway, the so-called Green River Killer, who was convicted of murdering 48 females during the 1980s and 1990s, most of whom were runaways and prostitutes.[33]

According to experts, most serial killers are sexual deviants, often with a history of physical and sexual abuse. James Brown postulated that some sexual serial killers are psychotic, while some psychotic serial killers are sexually motivated in perpetrating their crimes.[34] Philip Jenkins characterized serial killers as sexual psychopaths or paranoid schizophrenic offenders.[35] David Lester wrote about lust serial murderers who experience sexual arousal and pleasure in association with their killings.[36]

The FBI found that sexually motivated serial murderers were more likely to be organized than disorganized and tended to have more victims.[37] (See Chapter 15 for further discussion on serial killers.)

Signature Killers

Another type of sexual murderer is the signature killer. This category of serial killer differs from others in that the perpetrator tends to leave a "calling card" or psychological signature behind unique to him at every crime scene. In a study of signature killers, Robert Keppel and William Birnes describe the signature serial killer as "psychologically compelled to leave [his imprint] to satisfy himself sexually."[38] The FBI Behavioral Sciences Unit's John Douglas characterized the sexual serial killer's signature as "the person's violent fantasies which are progressive in nature and contribute to thoughts of exhibiting extremely violent behavior."[39]

Signature murderers are thought to represent the greatest subtype of serial murderers, "driven by such a primal psychological motivation to act out the same crime over and over again that their patterns become obsessive. All signature murderers seek some form of sexual gratification, and their crimes are expressions of the ways they satisfy that need."[40]

Anger has been shown to be an important factor in sexual signature murders. Keppel and Birnes noted two types of anger-motivated signature killers: (1) anger-retaliation killer and (2) anger-excitation killer.[41]

The anger-retaliation killer is characterized by sexual violence and overkill, typically involving the use of more than one weapon, whereas the anger-excitation killer's signature tends to be more sadistic, characterized by "a prolonged, bizarre, ritualistic assault on the victim."[42]

The anger-driven signature killer often begins as a retaliatory murderer and evolves to an excitation killer over the course of his murders, depending on the degree of anger. The murderer's signature tends to reflect "one or more of the components of sadism, control, humiliation, progression of violence, posing, torture, overkill, necrophilia, and cannibalism."[43]

Sexually Sadistic Killers

Sadism is defined as sexual gratification through inflicting pain and suffering upon others. A high percentage of sexual killers are sadists, associating sexuality with cruelty and violence.[44] Indications of such deviant behavior often manifest themselves early in the sexual sadist's life, such as sexually violent fantasies and cruelty to animals.

Sexually sadistic killers are mostly White males who are in their 20s and 30s, and are often "intelligent, personable, sociable and seldom have criminal records. They suffer from gender-identity conflicts and a sense of purposelessness. The latter results in frequent changes in jobs, location, roles, and goals."[45] The background of this type of sex killer includes a history of substance abuse, child sexual and physical abuse, and broken homes.

Many mass and serial murderers are sexual sadists, according to researchers. Almost one in five serial killers examined by Jack Levin and James Fox based on FBI files and newspaper reports were characterized as sexual sadists.[46] In their study of sexually sadistic killers, Robert Hazelwood, Park Dietz, and Janet Warren, found that 43 percent had participated in homosexual acts during adulthood, while 20 percent had perpetrated sexual crimes such as voyeurism and exhibitionism.[47] Dietz identified one type of serial killer as a psychopathic sexual sadist, positing that every known serial killer with 10 or more victims was a male diagnosed with antisocial personality disorder and possessing sexually sadistic tendencies.[48]

Researchers have identified a number of factors that relate to the formation of sexually sadistic tendencies, including

- Genetic transmission of behavioral traits
- Abnormal hormonal levels that can negatively influence aggression and sexual behavior
- Dysfunctional child-rearing practices, such as child sexual abuse and maternal promiscuity
- Psychiatric disorders, such as antisocial personality disorder and bipolar affective disorder[49]

Endnotes

1. R. B. Flowers, *Sex Crimes, Predators, Perpetrators, Prostitutes, and Victims: An Examination of Sexual Criminality and Victimization* (Springfield: Charles C Thomas, 2001), p. 3.
2. *Ibid.*
3. *Ibid.*
4. R. K. Ressler, A. W. Burgess, & J. E. Douglas, *Sexual Homicide: Patterns and Motives* (New York: Lexington Books, 1988), p. 1.
5. *Ibid.*, p. xiii. *See also* R. K. Ressler, A. W. Burgess, C. R. Hartman, J. E. Douglas, & A. McCormack, Murderers Who Rape and Mutilate, *Journal of Interpersonal Violence 1* (1986): 273–87.
6. J. Money, Forensic Sexology, *American Journal of Psychotherapy 44* (1990): 26–36.
7. American Psychiatric Association, *Diagnostic and Statistical Manual of Mental Disorders, 3rd ed.* (Washington: American Psychiatric Association, 1987). *See also* D. Fisher, Adult Sex Offenders: Who Are They? Why and How Do They Do It? in T. Morrison, M. Erooga, & R. C. Beckett, Eds., *Sexual Offending Against Children: Assessment and Treatment of Male Abusers* (New York: Routledge, 1994), p. 7.
8. Flowers, *Sex Crimes, Predators, Perpetrators, Prostitutes, and Victims*, p. 4.
9. C. R. Block & A. Christakos, Chicago Homicide From the Sixties to the Nineties: Major Trends in Lethal Violence, in U.S. Department of Justice, *Trends, Risks, and Interventions in Lethal Violence: Proceedings of the Third Annual Spring Symposium of the Homicide Research Working Group* (Washington: National Institute of Justice, 1995), pp. 26–29.
10. See, for example, R. B. Flowers, *Domestic Crimes, Family Violence and Child Abuse: A Study of Contemporary American Society* (Jefferson: McFarland, 2000), pp. 62–64, 78–80; R. E. Dobash, R. P. Dobash, M. Wilson, & M. Daly, The Myth of Sexual Symmetry in Marital Violence, *Social Problems 39*, 1 (1992): 71–91; A. W. Burgess, C. R. Hartman, R. K. Ressler, J. E. Douglas, & A. McCormack, Sexual Homicide, *Journal of Interpersonal Violence 1* (1986): 251–72.

11. Flowers, *Sex Crimes, Predators, Perpetrators, Prostitutes, and Victims*, p. 5; Flowers, *Domestic Crimes, Family Violence and Child Abuse*, p. 61.
12. Block & Christakos, *Trends, Risks, and Interventions in Lethal Violence*, p. 28.
13. U.S. Department of Justice, Federal Bureau of Investigation, Crime in the United States: Uniform Crime Reports 2010, Expanded Homicide Data Table 10, Murder Circumstances, by Relationship, 2010, http://www.fbi.gov/about-us/cjis/ucr/crime-in-the-u.s/2010/crime-in-the-u.s.-2010/tables/10shrtbl10.xls (April 12, 2012).
14. Flowers, *Sex Crimes, Predators, Perpetrators, Prostitutes, and Victims*, pp. 5–6; B. M. Cormier & S. P. Simons, The Problem of the Dangerous Sexual Offender, *Canadian Psychiatric Association 14* (1969): 329–34.
15. U.S. Department of Justice, Bureau of Justice Statistics, *Sex Offenses and Offenders: An Analysis of Data on Rape and Sexual Assault* (Washington: Government Printing Office, 1997), p. 28.
16. The figures exclude such sexual murders as those involving prostitution and commercialized vice.
17. U.S. Department of Justice, Federal Bureau of Investigation, *Crime in the United States: Uniform Crime Reports 1999* (Washington: Government Printing Office, 2000), p. 23.
18. U.S. Department of Justice, Federal Bureau of Investigation, The Men Who Murdered, *FBI Law Enforcement Bulletin 54, 8* (1985): 2–6.
19. Ressler, Burgess, & Douglas, *Sexual Homicide*, pp. 45–56.
20. D. Lester, *Serial Killers: The Insatiable Passion* (Philadelphia: Charles Press, 1995), p. 51.
21. *Sex Offenses and Offenders*, p. 30.
22. Flowers, *Sex Crimes, Predators, Perpetrators, Prostitutes, and Victims*, p. 7. See also U.S. Department of Justice, Bureau of Justice Statistics, Rape and Sexual Assault: Reporting to Police and Medical Attention 1992–2000 (Washington: Office of Justice Programs, 2002).
23. U.S. Department of Justice, Bureau of Justice Statistics Factbook, *Violence by Intimates: Analysis of Data of Crimes by Current or Former Spouses, Boyfriends, and Girlfriends* (Washington: Government Printing Office, 1998), p. 6.
24. U.S. Department of Justice, Federal Bureau of Investigation, Crime in the United States: Uniform Crime Reports 2010, Expanded Homicide Data, Murder Circumstances, by Relationship, 2009–2010, http://www.fbi.gov/about-us/cjis/ucr/crime-in-the-u.s/2010/crime-in-the-u.s.-2010/tables/10shrtbl10.xls (April 15, 2012).
25. *Violence by Intimates*, p. v.
26. *Ibid.*, p. 6.
27. Flowers, *Domestic Crimes, Family Violence and Child Abuse*, pp. 61–64, 90–91; A. L. Kellermann & J. A. Mercy, Men, Women and Murder: Gender-Specific Differences in Rates of Fatal Violence and Victimization, *Journal of Trauma 33* (1992): 1–5.
28. Flowers, *Sex Crimes, Predators, Perpetrators, Prostitutes, and Victims*, pp. 9–10.
29. R. B. Flowers & H. L. Flowers, *Murders in the United States: Crimes, Killers and Victims of the Twentieth Century* (Jefferson: McFarland, 2001), pp. 140–41.
30. M. Daly & M. Wilson, Homicide and Kinship, *American Anthropologist 84* (1982): 372–78.

31. M. Wilson & M. Daly, Spousal Homicide Risk and Estrangement, *Violence and Victims 8* (1993): 3–15.

32. Cited in Flowers, *Sex Crimes, Predators, Perpetrators, Prostitutes, and Victims*, p. 10.

33. Flowers and Flowers, *Murders in the United States*, pp. 86–106; A. Rule, *Green River, Running Red: The Real Story of the Green River Killer—America's Deadliest Serial Murderer* (New York: Pocket Star, 2005).

34. J. S. Brown, The Historical Similarity of 20th Century Serial Sexual Homicide to Pre-20th Century Occurrences of Vampirism, *American Journal of Forensic Psychiatry 12*, 2 (1991): 11–24.

35. P. A. Jenkins, A Murder 'Wave'? *Criminal Justice Review 17*, 1 (1992): 1–19.

36. Lester, *Serial Killers*, pp. 74–77.

37. Cited in *Ibid.*, pp. 81–82.

38. R. D. Keppel & W. J. Birnes, *Signature Killers: Interpreting the Calling Cards of the Sexual Murderer* (New York: Pocket Books, 1997), p. 5.

39. *Ibid.*

40. *Ibid.*, p. 23.

41. *Ibid.*, pp. 59, 89–94.

42. *Ibid.*, p. 189.

43. *Ibid.*, p. 89.

44. Flowers, *Sex Crimes, Predators, Perpetrators, Prostitutes, and Victims*, pp. 10–11; D. T. Lunde, *Murder and Madness* (New York: Norton, 1979); R. B. Flowers, *The Sex Slave Murders: The True Story of Serial Killers Gerald and Charlene Gallego*, 2nd ed. (Honolulu: R. B. Flowers, 2011); R. Langevin, M. H. Ben-Aron, P. Wright, V. Marchese, & L. Handy, The Sex Killer, *Annals of Sex Research 1* (1988): 263–301.

45. Lester, *Serial Killers*, p. 59; R. G. Rappaport, The Serial and Mass Murderer, *American Journal of Forensic Psychiatry 9*, 1 (1988): 39–48.

46. J. Levin & J. A. Fox, *Mass Murder* (New York: Plenum, 1985).

47. R. R. Hazelwood, P. E. Dietz, & J. Warren, The Criminal Sexual Sadist, *FBI Law Enforcement Bulletin 61* (1992): 12–20.

48. P. E. Dietz, Mass, Serial and Sensational Homicides, *Bulletin of the New York Academy of Medicine 62* (1986): 477–91.

49. Lester, *Serial Killers*, pp. 90–93; Money, *Forensic Sexology*, pp. 26–36; L. B. Schlesinger & E. Revitch, Sexual Dynamics in Homicide and Assault, in L. B. Schlesinger & E. Revitch, Eds., *Sexual Dynamics of Anti-Social Behavior* (Springfield: Charles C Thomas, 1983).

Serial Killers

15

Perhaps the most frightening killer outside the family is the serial killer. Although this type of murderer constitutes only a small percentage of total killers, the multiple and often violent or sadistic killings perpetrated by the serial murderer command far more attention by criminologists, law enforcement, researchers, writers, and the media. The literature is replete with terrifying tales of infamous serial killers such as Jack the Ripper, Albert Fish, John Wayne Gacy, Ted Bundy, Henry Lucas, and Gerald Gallego. Contrary to popular belief, these killers are generally not insane but are more often than not sociopaths and sexual deviants who tend to derive sadistic pleasure from the act of killing and the attention that multiple murders generates. While most serial killers are male, females have also shown the capacity and willingness to commit serial murders, though often for different reasons, such as money and love. The serial killer will often kill until apprehended or killed, typically taunting pursuers, and seems to draw upon society's worst fears in committing heinous and violent serial murders.

What Is a Serial Killer?

The phrase *serial killer* was first introduced in the 1980s in reference to killers who kill a series of people over a course of time. This differs from a *mass murderer*, who kills a number of people at one time and place, or an individual that kills one or two people at any time and then stops or is stopped for good. The serial killer normally targets and systematically kills victims one by one until no longer able to, usually due to being captured by authorities.

Various criminologists have defined the serial killer, based on methodology, the number and type of victims, the length of time between murders, and other criteria.[1] Steven Egger defined serial murder as occurring when one or more people, predominantly male, perpetrate a second murder at a different time.[2] In general, most experts on serial murder require that a minimum of three murders be committed at different times and usually different places for a person to qualify as a serial killer.[3] Ronald Holmes and Stephen Holmes proposed that there must be at least a 30-day period between the first and last killings for the perpetrators to fit the definition of a serial killer.[4]

Law enforcement authorities tend to define the serial killer as "a nomadic, sexual sadist who operates with a strict pattern of victim selection and crime scene behavior."[5] Others have focused on motivational factors in defining the serial murderer. For instance, James Fox and Jack Levin note that the serial killer "acts as a result of some individual pathology produced by traumatic childhood experiences."[6]

Some researchers prefer to define the serial murderer by excluding or including certain types of killers and motivations. Egger's definition omits female serial killers, while requiring that the killer and victim be strangers and that the killing is not motivated by material gain.[7] Frank Browning and John Gerassi documented cases of serial killers considered professional criminals or belonging to organized crime, as well as those financially or politically motivated or for business purposes.[8] David Lester noted that different studies of serial killers excluded such multiple murderers as hospital or nursing home staff killers or landlord murderers motivated by financial gain from killing residents.[9]

The Magnitude of Serial Murder

Although much attention has been given to serial murder and its specter in society, how big is the problem? The often-unsolved cases of serial killing, unknown victims of serial killers, and differing interpretations of what constitutes a serial murderer or murder have made it difficult, if not impossible, to know the magnitude of this crime at any given time. In the 1980s, the Justice Department estimated that as many as 5,000 people are victims of serial murder every year.[10] Some criminologists have supported this figure [11]

Others have suggested that the numbers of victims of serial killers are far lower. In an examination of serial killers from 1978 to 1983, as listed in *The New York Times Index*, Egger found there to be 54 such murderers who had killed at least 4 people, or a minimum of 216 victims.[12] Eric Hickey estimated that between 1975 and 1995, there were 153 serial murders who totaled up to 1,400 victims, or fewer than 100 victims a year.[13]

Fox and Levin argued that serial killings likely accounted for less than 1 percent of the homicides in the United States.[14] In 1999, there were an estimated 15,533 people murdered nationwide.[15] One percent would amount to 155 victims of serial murder annually. In spite of the low figure, given that the number of perpetrators of such homicides is likely much smaller, the significance of serial murder is obvious and the concern of law enforcement and the public not without merit.

Infamous examples of American serial killers and their horrific crimes include the following:

- David Berkowitz, calling himself the "Son of Sam," began a 13-month reign of terror in New York City in 1976. He used a .44 caliber pistol to randomly shoot to death 6 people while wounding 7 more. He was tried and convicted of multiple murders and sentenced to 365 years in prison.
- Theodore "Ted" Bundy is believed to have sexually assaulted and murdered as many as 40 females in five states between 1974 and 1978. Thought by many criminologists to be the prototype of the modern sexual serial killer, Bundy was tried in Florida for the murders of sorority sisters, convicted, and sentenced to death. He was executed in the electric chair in 1989.
- Andrew Cunanan bludgeoned or shot to death 5 men in several states between April and July 1997, including Italian designer Gianni Versace. The 27-year-old gay hustler's murdering spree led to one of the biggest manhunts in U.S. history. Cunanan committed suicide as the police closed in on him while hiding out in a houseboat in Florida.
- Jeffrey Dahmer murdered as many as 17 young males in the early 1990s in Wisconsin and Ohio. The 31-year-old cannibal drugged, strangled, and dismembered his victims. He was brought to trial in both states and received 16 life sentences. In 1994, Dahmer was beaten to death by another inmate while serving his term in Wisconsin.
- Paul Durousseau is thought to have murdered at least 7 African American women in Florida between 1997 and 2003, sexually assaulting and strangling them. While in the army, stationed in Germany, he was also suspected of killing several German women in the early 1990s. Charged with 5 murders, in December 2007 Durousseau was given a death sentence for the killing of one of his victims.
- John Wayne Gacy sexually assaulted and murdered 33 boys between 1972 and 1978 in Illinois. The convicted sex offender and clown buried most of the victims under his house. He was arrested, tried, and convicted, receiving a death sentence. In 1994, Gacy was executed by lethal injection.
- Henry Lee Lucas claimed to have murdered at least 200 people across the country over a 17-year period during the 1970s and 1980s. Years earlier, he had stabbed to death his mother. Lucas was convicted of 11 murders and sentenced to death in Texas, before having his sentence commuted to life in prison.
- Richard Ramirez, dubbed the "Night Stalker," murdered at least 13 people in California between 1984 and 1985. The Satan worshipper also raped and mutilated his victims. He was convicted on all 13 counts of murder and sentenced to death.

- Angel Maturino Resendiz is suspected of murdering as many as 24 people between 1997 and 1999 who lived near railroad tracks in the United States and Mexico. He turned himself in to authorities in Texas in July 1999. Resendiz was found guilty of capital murder in 2000 and sentenced to death.
- Gary Ridgway, known as the "Green River Killer," is believed to have killed close to 100 females, mostly in Washington, during the 1980s and 1990s. His victims were typically runaways and prostitutes, and he often strangled them before dumping their bodies along the state's Green River. Ridgway was convicted of 48 of the murders and sentenced to life in prison without the possibility of parole.
- Arthur Shawcross murdered as many as 13 people during the 1970s and 1980s, often torturing, mutilating, and dismembering them. Two of his victims were children. Shawcross is currently serving a 250-year prison term for the murders of his last 11 female victims.
- Robert Yates is believed to have slain as many as 17 women in Washington between 1990 and 1998. Most of the victims were prostitutes and homeless women. The 48-year-old army veteran pleaded guilty to 13 of the murders and was sentenced to 408 years behind bars.
- The "Zodiac Killer" is thought to have killed anywhere from 5 to 49 people in California between 1968 and 1974. The unknown serial killer boasted of the murders, often sending letters to newspapers and signing them with the zodiac symbol. Some believe the killer is still active.[16]

Characterizing the Serial Killer

The vast majority of serial killers are White males, usually with a sexual motivation for their killings. Though few have been found to be certifiably insane, most are believed to be sociopaths, sadists, and possess some degree of mental illness or instability.[17] James Browne postulated that some sexual serial killers may also be psychotic and, conversely, some psychotic serial killers may also be sexually motivated in their murders.[18] D. T. Lunde asserted that most serial killers are schizophrenic or sadist murderers.[19] Ronald Holmes and James DeBurger characterized most serial killers as psychopathic.[20]

Richard Rappaport advanced in his study of serial killers that rather than having a sexual motivation per se, most serial homicides are "an attempt to cope with an internal conflict, a way to achieve relief from psychological pain, primarily by demonstrating power and mastery over others."[21]

Researchers have found the typical serial murderer to be a White male, 25 to 35 years old, often a loner though many are married, and intelligent and charming.[22] Victims are most often White women, though minority women and children are also at risk for victimization.

Most serial killers tend to have a history of violence, child physical and sexual abuse, substance abuse, dysfunctional families, and involvement with the criminal justice system.[23] In an FBI analysis of serial murderers and single and double sexual killers, the following characteristics emerged:

- All were male, with most White and a first or second born.
- Most grew up in homes with both parents present.
- Half came from families where members had a history of criminality.
- More than half of the killers had family members with psychiatric problems.
- Two-thirds of the murderers had childhood psychiatric problems.
- Most had dominant mothers, while half of the killers had a relationship with their mothers described as uncaring.
- The majority described disciplinary practices as hostile and abusive.
- Many were victims of sexual, physical, or psychological abuse.
- Many were cruel to animals and other children during childhood.
- Fantasies played a role in the deviant behavior of many of the killers.
- Killers became more organized with the experience of each subsequent murder.[24]

Based on a review of literature on serial killers, Donald Sears further characterized the typical serial murderer as follows:

- Raised in a home absent of nurturing and stability
- Using fantasies to escape the realities of life, turning into sexual and violent fantasies
- Not possessing a psychiatric disorder
- Self-centered and requiring attention
- Intelligent and often successful academically or professionally
- Having a fascination with police investigations
- Using alcohol or drugs before perpetrating the crime[25]

Types of Serial Killers

A number of criminologists have identified different types of serial murderers. Rappaport found there to be five kinds of serial killers:

- *Spree killers:* people who kill a series of victims during a continuous span of murders

- *Functionaries of organized criminality:* killers such as hit men for the mafia, gang members, mercenaries, and terrorists
- *Custodial killers:* people such as medical personnel or foster parents who poison or asphyxiate victims for financial gain, revenge, or altruism
- *Psychotic killers:* people who are delusional or hallucinational in their serial murders
- *Sexually sadistic killers:* murderers who derive pleasure through inflicting pain and torture on their victims[26]

A similar typology of serial killers was established by P. E. Dietz.[27]

Holmes and DeBurger suggested four types of serial murderers including visionary killers, mission-oriented killers, hedonistic killers, and control-oriented killers:

- *Visionary killers* act in response to commands to kill from voices in their head or visions.
- *Mission-oriented killers* consciously decide to murder a certain category of individuals deemed unworthy of being alive, such as prostitutes.
- *Hedonistic killers* kill for the thrill or pleasure derived from the act. This category includes lust killers.
- *Control-oriented killers* are motivated by being in control of the victim in deciding life and death, when, where, and how they will kill.[28]

Holmes later added a *predatory serial killer* type as a person who hunts for victims to kill for recreation or sport.[29]

Two types of serial murderers were identified by Philip Jenkins in his study of English serial killers between 1940 and 1985.[30] *Predictable killers* had a long and often violent history of juvenile offending. *Respectable killers* had no violent history of crime prior to reaching their 20s; they were motivated by a significant crisis in middle life, with the abuse of alcohol also a factor.

According to David Gee, there are three types of serial murderers: (1) those who secretly hide the corpses of victims and attempt to conceal the murders; (2) killers who serial murder victims but the deaths are not recognized initially as homicides; and (3) murderers who do not seek to conceal their crimes or hide the victims.[31] Jack the Ripper is a perfect example of the latter type of serial killer.

Some serial killers perpetrate their crimes as part of a team of two or more killers. This is particularly true when involving male–female multiple murderers or strong–weak killer pairs or groups.[32] A good example of the latter are the serial killer partners of Dean Corll and Elmer Henley. With

Henley, 17, acting as the 33-year-old Corll's accomplice, the two raped, tortured, and murdered 32 boys in Pasadena, Texas, in the early 1970s.[33]

Jenkins, in his study of serial killers in the United States from 1971 to 1990, found 58 serial murder cases. Twelve of these indicated involvement of multiple killers.[34] He described four types of partner or group serial killers: (1) dominant-submissive pairs, (2) equally dominant teams, (3) extended family or group of killers, and (4) organized or ceremonial social units or groups.

The Female Serial Killer

Although female serial killers are rare, they do exist, and they have a long history.[35] Most female serial murderers tend to be motivated by monetary or material gain, often through murdering successive husbands or people under their care. These serial killers are known as *black widows*. Many female serial killers act in tandem with male serial killers, usually their husbands or lovers.

Infamous examples of female serial killers include the following:

- Belle Gunness is believed to have murdered as many as 49 people between 1896 and 1908 in Illinois and Indiana. Dubbed "Lady Bluebeard," the black widow killed 2 husbands, a number of her children, and 2 suitors. She was motivated primarily by collecting insurance payments or robbery. Gunness is thought to have died in a fire at her farmhouse in 1908, though some believe she survived and continued her murderous ways well beyond that.
- Dorothea Puente murdered as many as 25 tenants living in her boarding house in Sacramento, California, in 1988. The 59-year-old ex-con killed her victims for their Social Security checks. Puente was tried and convicted for 3 of the murders and sentenced to life in prison without the possibility of parole.
- Aileen Wuornos killed at least 7 men in Florida between 1989 and 1990. The 33-year-old prostitute, who had a history of child sexual and physical abuse and alcoholism, claimed to have killed the men—all johns—in self-defense. She was tried and convicted of murdering her first victim and sentenced to death.
- Martha Beck and Raymond Fernandez murdered as many as 20 women between 1947 and 1949 in several Southeast states. The killer couple, dubbed the "Lonely Hearts Killers," lured victims through lonely hearts clubs and newspaper advertisements, stealing from them and killing them by poisoning, bludgeoning, and strangling. Beck and Fernandez were tried and convicted on multiple murder counts and sentenced to death. They were executed in Sing Sing prison's electric chair in 1951.

- Gwendolyn Graham and Catherine Wood suffocated 5 elderly nursing home patients and attempted to kill 5 others in Michigan in 1987. The lesbian serial murderers were motivated by sexual thrills. Wood pled guilty to second degree murder, and Graham was convicted on five counts of homicide and sentenced to life in prison without parole.
- Charlene Gallego and Gerald Gallego abducted, sexually assaulted, and murdered 10 people in three Western states between 1978 and 1980. The married serial killers were motivated by fulfilling "sex slave" fantasies. Charlene, who lured most of the victims to their deaths, plea bargained for a reduced sentence of 16 years and 8 months behind bars. Gerald Gallego was convicted in California and Nevada for four murders and sentenced to death in both states.[36]

In a study of female serial killers worldwide from 1580 to 1990, Kerry Segrave found that the typical killer perpetrated her initial murder at the age of 31, continuing to kill for 5 years before being caught. On average, the female serial murderer killed 17 people, with poison and arsenic the most common weapons of choice.[37] Victims were most likely to be those most vulnerable, such as children, the elderly, and ill people.

Holmes and Holmes described five types of female serial killers:

- *Visionary serial killers:* women who kill in response to directives to kill from voices in their head or visions
- *Comfort-oriented serial killers:* females who murder for financial or material benefit
- *Hedonistic serial killers:-* women who kill for sexual gratification
- *Power-seeking serial killers:* females who kill for the thrill and power gained through having full control over life and death for the victim
- *Disciple serial killers:* women who kill under the command or desire of a charismatic leader[38]

Theories on Serial Killing

Criminologists have long theorized on the causes of multicidal, sexual, and sadistic killings. Elliott Leyton held that serial homicides are a "personalized form of social protest in which killings are an act of revenge by the killer for what he perceives as his social exclusion from society."[39] Jane Caputi posited that the serial murderer reflects "an extreme in the latest expression of male supremacy which has always involved the raping and killing of women."[40]

In his review of theories of violent behavior, Sears observed that serial murderers are typically diagnosed as psychopaths—breaking down into two types: *primary psychopaths* and *secondary psychopaths*.[41] Primary psychopaths feel no anxiety, fear, or guilt for their actions; while secondary psychopaths perpetrate antisocial acts as a result of "emotional conflicts or inner distress" and often feel fear and anxiety.[42]

According to Lunde, serial killers can be described as sexual sadists and paranoid schizophrenics.[43] Fredric Wertham's notion of a *catathymic crisis* describes the repetitive nature of a serial killer's actions based upon an initial idea of perpetrating violence and the urge to follow through on the desire or fantasy, and finally the actual culmination of murder. These stages are then repeated in serial killing.[44]

The relationship between serial murder and sexual sadism has been established by a number of researchers. R. A. Prentky and colleagues noted the role of violent sexual fantasies and sexual deviance in serial homicide.[45] John Money advanced that sexual sadism was a brain disease caused by genetic factors, hormonal abnormalities, child-rearing factors, and psychiatric disorders such as antisocial personality disorder and disassociative disorders.[46]

In his research on serial killers, Joel Norris profiled such murderers as often having a history of head trauma, genetic brain abnormalities, sexual assault, sexually deviant behavior, suicidal ideation, ritualistic behavior, compulsivity, substance abuse, physical and emotional abuse, and feeling inadequate and powerless.[47]

Endnotes

1. J. A. Fox & J. Levin, Serial Murder: Myths and Realities, in M. D. Smith & M. A. Zahn, Eds., *Studying and Preventing Homicide: Issues and Challenges* (Thousand Oaks: Sage, 1999), pp. 79–96; D. Lester, *Serial Killers: The Insatiable Passion* (Philadelphia: Charles Press, 1995), pp. 10–17.
2. S. A. Egger, A Working Definition of Serial Murder and the Reduction of Linkage Blindness, *Journal of Police Science and Administration* 12 (1984): 348–57.
3. Lester, *Serial Killers*, pp. 10–13.
4. R. M. Holmes & S. T. Holmes, *Murder in America* (Thousand Oaks: Sage, 1994).
5. Fox & Levin, Serial Murder, p. 80.
6. *Ibid.*
7. Egger, A Working Definition of Serial Murder; S. A. Egger, Serial Murder, in S. A. Egger, Ed., *Serial Murder* (New York: Praeger, 1990).
8. F. Browning & J. Gerassi, *The American Way of Crime* (New York: Putnam, 1980).
9. Lester, *Serial Killers*, p. 14.
10. Fox & Levin, Serial Murder, p. 81.
11. *Ibid.*; Egger, A Working Definition of Serial Murder; R. M. Holmes & J. E. DeBurger, *Serial Murder* (Thousand Oaks: Sage, 1988).
12. Egger, A Working Definition of Serial Murder.
13. E. W. Hickey, *Serial Murderers and Their Victims*, 2nd ed. (Belmont: Wadsworth, 1997).

14. Fox & Levin, Serial Murder, p. 82.
15. U.S. Department of Justice, Federal Bureau of Investigation, *Crime in the United States: Uniform Crime Reports 1999* (Washington: Government Printing Office, 2000), p. 14.
16. R. B. Flowers & H. L. Flowers, *Murders in the United States: Crimes, Killers, and Victims of the Twentieth Century* (Jefferson: McFarland, 2001), pp. 86–105.
17. *Ibid.*; Fox & Levin, "Serial Murder," pp. 83–85; R. M. Holmes & J. E. DeBurger, Profiles in Terror, *Federal Probation* 49, 3 (1985): 53–61.
18. J. S. Browne, The Historical Similarity of 20th Century Serial Sexual Homicide to Pre-20th Century Occurrences of Vampirism, *American Journal of Forensic Psychiatry* 12, 2 (1991): 11–24.
19. D. T. Lunde, *Murder and Madness* (New York: Norton, 1979).
20. Holmes & DeBurger, Profiles in Terror.
21. Lester, *Serial Killers*, p. 59. See also R. G. Rappaport, The Serial and Mass Murderer, *American Journal of Forensic Psychiatry* 9, 1 (1988): 39–48.
22. Holmes & DeBurger, Profiles in Terror; F. H. Leibman, Serial Murderers, *Federal Probation* 53, 4 (1989): 41–45; R. R. Hazelwood, P. E. Dietz, & J. Warren, The Criminal Sexual Sadist, *FBI Law Enforcement Bulletin* 61, 2 (1992): 12–20.
23. Lester, *Serial Killers*, pp. 48–60; Hazelwood, Dietz, & Warren, The Criminal Sexual Sadist, pp. 12–20; R. K. Ressler, A. W. Burgess, & J. E. Douglas, *Sexual Homicide: Patterns and Motives* (New York: Lexington Books, 1988).
24. U.S. Department of Justice, Federal Bureau of Investigation, The Men Who Murdered, *FBI Law Enforcement Bulletin* 54, 8 (1985): 2–6.
25. D. J. Sears, *To Kill Again* (Wilmington: Scholarly Resources, 1991).
26. Rappaport, The Serial and Mass Murderer, pp. 39–48.
27. P. E. Dietz, Mass, Serial and Sensational Homicides, *Bulletin of the New York Academy of Medicine* 62 (1986): 477–91.
28. Holmes & DeBurger, *Serial Murder*.
29. R. M. Holmes, Human Hunters, *Knightbeat* 9, 1 (1990): 43–47.
30. P. A. Jenkins, Serial Murder in England, 1940–1985, *Journal of Criminal Justice* 16 (1988): 1–15.
31. D. J. Gee, A Pathologist's View of Multiple Murder, *Forensic Science International* 38 (1988): 53–65.
32. Flowers & Flowers, *Murders in the United States*.
33. *Ibid.*, p. 164.
34. P. A. Jenkins, Sharing Murder, *Journal of Crime and Justice* 12 (1990): 125–48.
35. Flowers & Flowers, *Murders in the United States*, pp. 109–16, 143–45; R. Barri Flowers, *The Sex Slave Murders: The True Story of Serial Killers Gerald and Charlene Gallego*, 2nd ed. (Honolulu: R. Barri Flowers, 2011).
36. *Ibid.*
37. K. Segrave, *Women Serial and Mass Murderers* (Jefferson: McFarland, 1992).
38. Holmes & Holmes, *Murder in America*.
39. Lester, *Serial Killers*, pp. 85–86. See also E. Leyton, *Hunting Humans* (London: Penguin, 1989); E. Leyton, *Compulsive Killers* (New York: New York University Press, 1986).
40. Lester, *Serial Killers*, p. 85. See also J. Caputi, *The Age of Sex Crime* (Bowling Green: Bowling Green State University Press, 1987).
41. Sears, *To Kill Again*.

42. *Ibid.*
43. Lunde, *Murder and Madness.*
44. F. Wertham, The Catathymic Crisis, *Archives of Neurology and Psychiatry* 37 (1937): 974–78.
45. R. A. Prentky, A. W. Burgess, F. Rokous, A. Lee, C. R. Hartman, R. K. Ressler, & J. E. Douglas, "The Presumptive Role of Fantasy in Serial Sexual Homicide," *American Journal of Psychiatry* 146 (1989): 887–91.
46. J. Money, Forensic Sexology, *American Journal of Psychotherapy* 44 (1990): 26–36.
47. J. Norris, *Serial Killers* (New York: Anchor, 1989).

Mass Murderers

16

Recent years have seen a rash of mass murders in the United States, including school shootings, workplace murders, and terrorist attacks—resulting in thousands of lost lives, all told. Although mass murder is not a new phenomenon, more individuals with various motivations and hostilities seem to be driven toward committing this type of homicide these days, often with devastating results. Understanding the rational or irrational behavior of the mass murderer and the warning signs may make it easier to identify such people and prevent their crimes.

What Is Mass Murder?

The term *mass murder* generally refers to a number of murders committed at the same time in the same location by one or more killers. Researchers differ on how many murders should constitute mass murder. Some criminologists such as Ronald Holmes and James DeBurger,[1] and Eric Hickey,[2] and Thomas Petee and colleagues[3] contend that a minimum of three murders need to be committed in a single crime of homicide for it to be considered a mass murder. Others such as Robert Hazelwood and John Douglas believe there must be at least four victims to qualify as a mass murder crime.[4] Park Dietz maintained that mass murder should include the wounding of five persons and the death of no less than three.[5]

As it is, most mass murderers that come to our attention commit many more murders than three or four. Consequently, the mass murderer tends to be synonymous with a massive slaughter of innocents. One of the most glaring examples is the bombing of the Alfred P. Murrah Federal Building in Oklahoma City, Oklahoma, in 1995. Orchestrated by Timothy McVeigh and Terry Nichols, it was a mass murder that took 168 lives and injured hundreds.[6]

Not all mass murders occur at the same time and location, or necessarily involve the same perpetrators. For instance, in the worst case of terrorist mass murder to ever hit the United States, in September 2001, 19 killers were involved in the hijacking of four airliners, resulting in the mass murder of more than 6,000 people in different locations at different times, though clearly one coordinated effort (see Chapter 10).

Mass murder is at once a crime of violence and typically an act of hatred and vengeance—designed to get maximum results from the homicidal aggression.

The Nature of Mass Murder

In spite of the multiple killings perpetrated by mass murderers that often make the headlines and perhaps have the most profound effect on the public, the fact is that mass murder accounts for only a relatively small number of murders or homicides in the United States. This notwithstanding, the sheer number of potential victims of mass murderers, as illustrated above, ensures that it will always be of special interest to criminologists and lawmakers.

Mass murderers are predominantly male, often White, and tend to direct their multicidal behavior against those they are connected to in some way, such as intimates, family members, or co-workers. The motivation is usually related to anger, revenge, and a desire to commit suicide. Most mass murders involve the use of weapons of mass destruction such as high-powered fire-arms or bombs.

Notable recent episodes of mass murder in the United States can be seen as follows:

- On November 5, 2009, 39-year-old Nidal Malik Hasan, a U.S. Army Major and psychiatrist, armed with an FN Five-seven semi-automatic pistol, entered the Soldier Readiness Processing Center at Fort Hood, Texas, and opened fire. Thirteen people were killed and 29 injured in the worst mass shooting to be perpetrated on a U.S. military base. Hasan, an American Muslim, was shot and paralyzed. He faces charges of 13 counts of premeditated murder and another 32 counts of attempted murder with his court-martial set for October 2012.
- On April 3, 2009, Jiverly Antares Wong, a 41-year-old naturalized immigrant, armed with two semi-automatic pistols, went on a shoot-ing spree at the American Civic Association immigration center in Binghamton, New York, killing 13 and wounding 4. Wong then committed suicide.
- On March 10, 2009, 28-year-old Michael McLendon went berserk in Alabama, murdering 10 people in the towns of Kinston, Geneva, and Samson, including his mother, grandmother, and other family members. McLendon, who left behind a hit list, then shot himself fatally in the head.
- On September 15, 1999, Larry Ashbrook, a 47-year-old unemployed loner, burst into a Baptist church in Fort Worth, Texas, and shot to death 8 people, wounding several others, before killing himself. It was called the worst mass murder in the city's history.

- On July 18, 1994, James Huberty, a heavily armed 41-year-old unemployed security guard, entered a McDonald's restaurant in San Ysidro, California. He opened fire and killed 20 before being shot to death by a police sniper. It was believed at the time to be the worst single-day mass murder in U.S. history.
- On October 16, 1991, George Hennard, a 35-year-old loner, drove his pickup truck through the window of a cafeteria in Killeen, Texas. He then opened fire, killing 22 people and an injuring 20 others before committing suicide. At the time, the crime was considered the worst mass murder in the nation's history.
- On December 7, 1987, David Burke, a vengeful-minded ex-airline employee, boarded a Pacific Southwest Airlines plane and forced it to crash into a California hillside, killing all 43 people on board. The murder-suicide resulted in new federal rules for security procedures involving airline personnel.
- On May 20, 1984, Michael Silka, a 25-year-old drifter, went on a deadly shooting spree in Manley Hot Springs, Alaska, killing 8 people and tossing their bodies in to the Tanana River. He was shot to death by police but not before adding a state trooper as his 9th mass murder victim.[7]

Although few mass killers have been female, some women have perpetrated this type of crime. Most cases of female mass murder have involved the killing of family members. Examples of recent mass murders committed by females include the following:

- On February 12, 2010, 44-year-old Amy Bishop, a biology professor, went on a shooting barrage with a 9 mm handgun at the University of Alabama in Huntsville in Huntsville, Alabama, killing 3 faculty members and wounding 3 others. Nearly a year earlier, the university had denied Bishop tenure. Bishop was charged with capital murder and three counts of attempted murder in the university shootings.
- On September 3, 1998, Khoua Her strangled to death her 6 children in their St. Paul, Minnesota, apartment. The 25-year-old immigrant from Laos plea bargained for a sentence of 50 years in prison.
- On March 23, 1998, Megan Hogg, a 27-year-old suffering from depression, suffocated her 3 young daughters in their home in Redwood City, California. After failing at a suicide attempt, she was charged with three counts of murder, pleading no contest, and sentenced to 25 years to life in prison.
- On October 26, 1997, Susan Eubanks, a 35-year-old divorced former nursing assistant with a history of substance abuse, shot to death her

4 young sons in their home in San Marcos, California. She was convicted on all murder counts and sentenced to death.

- On October 30, 1985, Sylvia Seegrist, a 25-year-old with a history of mental problems, entered a shopping mall in Delaware County, Pennsylvania, wearing camouflage pants and combat boots. Armed with a semiautomatic rifle, she shot to death 3 people and wounded 7 others. She was found guilty of first degree murder and given three life sentences in prison.[8]

Where and How Mass Murders Occur

Where do most mass murders take place and under what circumstances? Contrary to the recent spate of school mass murders and terrorist attack mass killings directed toward government buildings or the government itself, most multiple murders involving three or more victims occur at restaurants.

According to a study of factors in public mass murders committed between 1965 and 1998 in the United States, nearly 17 percent took place at a restaurant, just over 14 percent in a retail or grocery store, and almost 13 percent in a government office or other facility. Less than 9 percent of mass murders occurred at a school or college.[9] Around one in four mass murders took place at other locations.

The place where a mass murder occurs appears to be less related to the location itself than the perpetrators and the particular motivations for the mass killings or significance of the setting. For instance, intimate or family-related mass murder is likely to take place at a residence or other location most accessible or appropriate to the offender. A mass killer in the workplace will likely choose the location in relation to his present or previous employment and grievances to that effect.

The weapon of choice for most mass murderers is a handgun. In more than one out of four mass killings occurring between 1965 and 1998, a handgun was used by the perpetrator(s). In nearly 9 in 10 cases of mass murder, some form of firearm was used, and often more than one type.[10] Studies show that in most mass murders, the offenders used weapons that were legally purchased, as opposed to banned firearms such as assault weapons.[11]

Although recent murder-suicide mass killings have received much media attention, more often than not mass murderers do not commit suicide as part of the crime. From 1965 to 1998, nearly 60 percent of mass murder episodes ended with the killer or killers fleeing the scene of the crime.[12] Just over 15 percent of the mass killers committed suicide, while just under 15 percent were arrested after the incident.

Types of Mass Killers

Researchers have identified various character traits and motivational characteristics of the mass murderer. According to Ronald Holmes and Stephen Holmes, there are five types of mass killers:

- *Disciples* mass murder after being ordered to kill by a persuasive, dominating leader such as a Charles Manson type.
- *Family annihilators* mass murder most or all of their family. They are often the family patriarch or oldest son with a history of depression and substance abuse.
- *Pseudocommandos* are usually a single assailant who stockpiles weapons of mass murder and then targets a particular place to carry out the crime.
- *Disgruntled employees* tend to target a current or former place of work and commit mass murder against a supervisor and other employees they may hold a grudge against, while also killing others randomly.
- *Set-and-run* mass killers use something such as a bomb or poison to inflict maximum casualties, while watching the events take place out of harm's way.[13]

Psychiatrist Paul Miller puts mass murderers into two distinct categories: (1) those whose primary motive is to commit suicide, and (2) those whose primary desire is to kill people as punishment to society or the government for not recognizing or dismissing their entitlements or talents.[14] He found that the following characteristics could be found in both types of mass killers:

- A fascination with weapons and paraphernalia dealing with militarism
- Depression
- Inability to establish intimate relationships
- Obsessive behavior
- Narcissistic inclinations
- Attraction to other mass murderers

The Causes of Mass Murder

What causes one to commit mass murder? Some experts believe that most mass murderers suffer from severe mental illness. In a study of 40 mass murderers and serial killers, D. T. Lunde concluded that virtually all of the offenders could be termed as insane.[15] David Lester contended that mass murderers tend to be characterized as having "a serious psychiatric disturbance."[16]

Criminologists generally assert that while mass killers lack "normal psychosocial and emotional responses, they typically are not mentally ill."[17] Instead, most mass murderers are aware of their actions, which are often planned in advance, and are motivated by revenge, hostility, hopelessness, and/or suicidal tendencies.

In studying mass murders in other cultures, Mullen noted in particular the murder-suicide phenomenon first addressed in the Malaysian archipelago:

> The mass murderer in this situation is typically young, male, and isolated, and usually has experienced some loss of face or humiliation. And when they decide that life is not worth living, they don't just kill themselves ... instead, they take a sword or hatchet and run down the street, killing apparently at random until they themselves are struck down and killed. In this way, causing the death of others and ending lives restores faith. This model—in which you die and vindicate yourself—becomes very attractive to other angry, suicidal and humiliated young men.[18]

In Western societies, mass murderers have similar characteristics. Generally speaking, mass killings are most likely to occur in domestic or intrafamilial circumstances, with the motives being jealousy, depression, and a desire to commit suicide. Drug or alcohol abuse is often a factor. However, many mass murderers in recent years have directed their desire to kill against random targets, making for an even more frightening prospect.

Research has shown that the media itself may play an important role in the onset of mass murder. While there has not been a dramatic shift in the use and availability of firearms in the United States or the degree of social and psychological concerns that may lend to mass killings, media coverage of mass murder events has intensified as media outlets battle to see who can deliver the most detailed, sensationalistic coverage. This type of increasingly prolonged saturation and attention given to the mass murderer often inspires copycats or others seeking such attention and infamy. A study of seven mass murders found media reporting to be a significant factor in five of the mass killings.[19]

Endnotes

1. R. M. Holmes & J. E. DeBurger, *Serial Murder* (Thousand Oaks: Sage, 1988).
2. E. Hickey, *Serial Killers and Their Victims* (Pacific Grove: Brooks/Cole, 1991).
3. T. A. Petee, K. G. Padgett, & T. S. York, Debunking the Stereotype: An Examination of Mass Murder in Public Places, *Homicide Studies 1*, 4 (1997): 317–37.
4. R. R. Hazelwood & J. E. Douglas, The Last Murder, *FBI Law Enforcement Bulletin* 49, 4 (1980): 1–8.

5. P. E. Dietz, Mass, Serial, and Sensational Homicides, *Bulletin of the New York Academy of Medicine 62* (1986): 477–91.
6. R. B. Flowers & H. L. Flowers, *Murders in the United States: Crimes, Killers and Victims of the Twentieth Century* (Jefferson: McFarland, 2001), pp. 56–57.
7. *Ibid.*, pp. 78–83; S. Dewan and A.G. Sulzberger, Officials Identify Alabama Gunman, *The New York Times* (March 11, 2009), http://www.nytimes.com/2009/03/12/us/12alabama.html?_r=1; A. K. Brown, "Fort Hood Shooting Suspect Will Face Death Penalty," *ABC News* (July 7, 2011), http://abcnews.go.com/US/wireStory?id=14015624.
8. Flowers & H. L. Flowers, *Murders in the United States*, pp. 141–43; Crime Insider Staff, Amy Bishop Enters Insanity Plea in University of Alabama Shooting, *CBS News* (September 23, 2011), http://www.cbsnews.com/8301-504083_162-20110701-504083.html.
9. T. A. Petee, Situational Factors Related to Public Mass Murder Incidents: 1965–1998, in U.S. Department of Justice, *Proceedings of the Homicide Research Working Group Meetings, 1997 and 1998* (Washington: National Institute of Justice, 1999), pp. 154–56.
10. *Ibid.*, p. 154.
11. *Ibid.*, p. 155.
12. *Ibid.*
13. R. M. Holmes & S. T. Holmes, Understanding Mass Murder, *Federal Probation* 56, 1 (1992): 53–61.
14. Cited in B. Harkness, Portraying a Mass Killer, http://www.mnash.edu.au/pubs/montage/Montage_97_02/killer.html.
15. D. T. Lunde, *Murder and Madness* (New York: Norton, 1979).
16. D. Lester, *Serial Killers: The Insatiable Passion* (Philadelphia: Charles Press, 1995), p. 65.
17. Quoted in Harkness, Portraying a Mass Killer.
18. *Ibid.*
19. B. Parsons, Mass Murder, http://www.theage.com.au/daily/98061/new/news26.html.

Self-Killers

17

Suicide, or the intentional killing of oneself, is one of the leading causes of death in the United States. More than 30,000 people die each year as a result of suicide, or approximately twice as many people as are murdered. Teenagers are especially at high risk for suicide. Suicidal ideation, or thoughts about committing suicide, is fairly common in this society among all age, social, racial, and ethnic groups. Most who contemplate suicide fail to succeed or never seriously try. However, millions of Americans have attempted to kill themselves at some point.

Many suicidal people are also homicidal, or vice versa. It is not uncommon for certain types of murderers to kill themselves as well, particularly intrafamilial or intimate killers, mass murderers, and terrorist killers. Most murder-suicides are driven by factors such as control or loss of control, anger, revenge, making a statement, or an act of desperation. In rare instances, murder-suicides may be considered mercy killing or a suicide pact between two or more people who wish to die due to serious illness or other severe problems.

Depression is the leading cause of suicide. However, other factors can play an important role in self-murder such as the presence of firearms, substance abuse, child abuse, domestic violence, unemployment, and lack of a support group or adequate resources in dealing with suicidal ideation.

What Is Suicide?

Suicide, or self-killing, is the follow-through of a decision or intention to end one's life. It has been called a "permanent solution to a temporary problem."[1] However, various definitions are attached to suicide due to its complexities, motivations, interpretations, misdiagnosis, subjectivity, and in many cases, inconclusive analysis of the dead person's intent or mindset at the time of death.

The term *suicide* originated in the 17th century from the Latin *sui* (genitive), meaning of oneself, and the English -*cide* and is defined as "the act or an instance of taking one's own life voluntarily and intentionally, especially by a person of years of discretion and of sound mind."[2] Since then, the word *suicide* has been synonymous with such terms as self-murder, self-slaughter, self-killing, and self-destruction.

215

Even before the act was termed suicide, the Greeks once described suicidal behavior as "'to break up life,' 'to grasp or seize death,' 'to do violence to oneself,' [or] 'to leave the light.'"[3] In the 19th century, Emile Durkheim defined suicide as "the termination of an individual's life resulting directly from a positive or negative act of the victim himself which he knows will produce this fatal result."[4]

More recently, the World Health Organization defined suicide as simply "a suicidal act with a fatal outcome," with such an act being defined as "self-injury with varying degrees of lethal intent."[5] A medical definition was established by the Centers for Disease Control and Prevention in certifying death as caused by suicide. Commonly used by medical examiners, coroners, scientists, and officials in public health, it defined suicide as "death from injury, poisoning, or suffocation where there is evidence (either explicit or implicit) that the injury was self-inflicted and that the decedent intended to kill himself [or] herself."[6]

According to suicide researcher Kay Jamison: "Suicide is the anchor point on a continuum of suicidal thoughts and behaviors. This continuum is one that ranges from risk-taking behaviors at one end, extends through different degrees and types of suicidal thinking, and ends with suicide attempts and suicide."[7]

The term *attempted suicide* has been somewhat ambiguous in its meaning because of varying interpretations on what constitutes *attempted*. In seeking to establish a general consensus on attempted suicide, many clinicians, scientists, and researchers over the past 2 decades have effectively replaced the term with *parasuicide*, meaning "deliberate self-harm," defining it as follows:

> An act with non-fatal outcome, in which an individual deliberately initiates a non-habitual behavior that, without intervention from others, will cause self-harm, or deliberately ingests a substance in excess of the prescribed or generally recognized therapeutic dosage, and which is aimed at realizing changes which the subject desired via the actual or expected physical consequences.[8]

The Scope of Suicide

By most accounts, suicide is a serious problem globally. The World Health Organization estimated that 1.8 percent of the 54 million deaths in 1998 worldwide were the result of suicide.[9] This means there were nearly 1 million suicides that year. In the United States alone, there are more than 30,000 suicide deaths annually, according to the American Association of Suicideology.[10] A person commits suicide in this country every 17 minutes, or 84 people a day. It is estimated that anywhere from 10 to 25 suicides are attempted for every suicide that is successful.[11]

In 2006, the rate of suicide in the United States was 12.87 per 100,000 population. Table 17.1 shows the suicide rate by age, sex, and race for each age group. Males were nearly four times as likely to commit suicide as females, while Whites were almost two and a half times more likely to commit suicide as Blacks and nearly twice as likely as people of other races to kill themselves. When considering race and sex, White males had the highest suicide rate, followed by males of other races. White males were more than twice as likely to commit suicide as Black males. Black females had the lowest overall rate of suicide, followed by females of other races. White females were nearly four times more likely than Black females to take their own lives.

Among teenagers, the suicide rate was highest for males and teens of races other than White or Black. The rate of suicide for White males age 15 to 19 was more than four times that of White females, and almost 10 times higher than that of Black females. Male teens other than Blacks had the highest overall suicide rate, while Black male teens were more likely to commit suicide than White or Black female teens.

The suicide rate tended to be highest for people age 45 to 54 and 75 to 84, which may reflect midlife and elderly crises. However, the rate of suicide among Blacks and Black males peaked in the 20 to 39 age range.

In general, the rate of suicide has been on the decline in the United States. As seen in Figure 17.1, between 1986 and 2006, the suicide rate in this country went from 15.06 down to 12.87 per 100,000 population. However, there was a slight increase in the rate of suicide between 2001 and 2006.

The rate of suicide for those under the age of 20 has varied during recent decades. According to the U.S. Department of Health and Human Services, between 1980 and 2005, the suicide rate for 10- to 14-year-olds went from 0.76 to 1.35, peaking in 1995 at 1.72. For those age 15 to 19, the rate of suicide during the span went from 8.53 in 1980 to 7.67 in 2005, reaching a peak of 11.14 in 1990 (see Figure 17.2). Teenagers are especially at high risk to attempt or commit suicide. According to one study, teen suicide in North America had risen by more than 300 percent over a 30-year stretch.[12]

Parasuicide rates in the United States are inconsistently reported due to privacy issues. However, in a comprehensive government survey of parasuicide rates between 1980 and 1985, around 3 percent of respondents had ever attempted suicide.[13] Nearly 6 in 10 who had tried to kill themselves at some point were women, while the rate of prevalence for attempts was significantly higher among individuals 25 to 44 years of age than those over the age of 44.

Other data on suicide and suicidal persons show the following:

- Suicide occurs more often than homicide.
- Suicide is the second leading cause of death for females and fourth for males worldwide.
- There is an attempted suicide in the United States every 42 seconds.

Table 17.1   Suicide Rate,ᵃ by Age, Sex, and Race, United States, 2006

Age	Total	Sex		Race			Race and Sex					
							White		Black		Other	
		Male	Female	White	Black	Other	Male	Female	Male	Female	Male	Female
Total	12.87	20.77	5.30	14.31	5.92	7.96	22.90	5.97	10.72	1.63	11.83	4.32
10–14	1.05	1.43	0.65	1.03	1.09	1.23	1.40	0.63	1.73	0.42	0.96	1.50
15–19	7.31	11.57	2.83	7.81	4.17	9.43	12.35	3.01	6.98	1.28	13.83	4.80
20–24	12.55	20.90	3.62	13.22	8.53	13.83	22.03	3.72	14.60	2.29	21.61	5.69
25–29	12.44	19.86	4.70	13.48	8.64	8.65	21.14	5.31	15.74	1.91	13.32	4.00
30–34	12.37	19.81	4.74	13.55	8.16	8.00	21.30	5.39	15.28	1.71	12.14	3.98
35–39	14.75	22.79	6.63	16.51	8.20	7.24	25.03	7.69	14.95	2.18	10.86	3.75
40–44	15.49	23.67	7.37	17.48	6.52	8.42	26.36	8.47	11.43	2.19	12.27	4.74
45–49	17.10	26.02	8.39	19.35	6.14	8.37	29.07	9.65	10.91	1.99	11.80	5.24
50–54	17.27	26.45	8.46	19.50	5.78	7.63	29.50	9.69	9.95	2.26	11.67	4.06
55–59	15.34	23.94	7.22	17.16	4.98	6.68	26.39	8.26	9.30	1.42	10.65	3.22
60–64	13.42	21.15	6.35	14.77	4.65	6.78	23.06	7.05	8.31	1.79	10.14	3.85
65–69	12.58	21.98	4.36	13.77	4.08	8.27	23.83	4.81	8.67	0.69	12.90	4.25
70–74	12.64	23.62	3.72	13.83	4.26	7.06	25.85	3.85	8.92	1.06	6.83	7.25
75–79	15.58	31.61	3.85	16.89	4.52	8.70	34.01	4.10	11.62	0.27	12.26	6.18
80–84	16.30	35.67	4.18	17.59	4.26	8.18	38.61	4.32	11.65	0.36	5.39	10.07
85+	15.89	43.37	3.08	16.97	5.72	7.96	46.30	3.24	17.04	1.10	16.24	3.15

ᵃ Per 100,000 population in each age group.

Source: Adapted from U.S. Department of Justice, Bureau of Justice Statistics, *Sourcebook of Criminal Justice Statistics,* Table 3.137, *http://www.albany.edu/sourcebook/pdf/t31372006.pdf* (March 12, 2012).

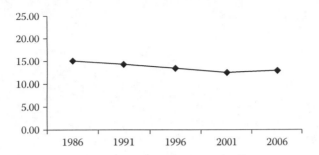

Figure 17.1 Trends in suicide rate per 100,000 population, United States, 1986–2006. (Derived from U.S. Department of Justice, Bureau of Justice Statistics, *Sourcebook of Criminal Justice Statistics*, Table 3.136, http://www.albany.edu/sourcebook/pdf/t31372006.pdf, March 13, 2012.)

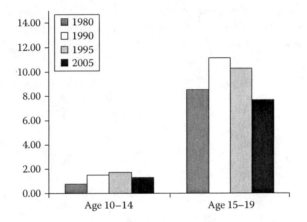

Figure 17.2 Trends in suicide rate per 100,000 population for ages 10–19, 1980–2005. (Derived from U.S. Department of Justice, Bureau of Justice Statistics, *Sourcebook of Criminal Justice Statistics*, Table 3.136,http://www.albany.edu/sourcebook/pdf/t31372006.pdf, March 12, 2012.)

- Women survive attempted suicides more often than men.
- A teenager commits suicide every 100 minutes.
- Daily, four people between the ages of 15 and 24 kill themselves.
- Female teenagers are twice as likely to attempt suicide as male teenagers.
- The rate of suicide is highest for people age 70 and over.
- Fifteen percent of people with depression take their own lives.
- Sixty percent of suicides are committed at home.
- Two-thirds of completed suicides occur after a previous suicide attempt.
- Forty percent of people who kill themselves leave a suicide note.[14]

Suicidal Ideation

How often do people seriously contemplate committing suicide or attempt to kill themselves? Estimates on suicidal thoughts have ranged from a low of 3.5 percent of the population with respect to recent thoughts, to around 19 percent when questioned about suicidal thoughts over the past 12 months, to a high of 53 percent of people who had ever considered the possibility of committing suicide.[15] The latter suggests that more than half the population has at least contemplated the notion of taking their own lives at one time or another, with about one in five considering the notion within the last year.

In one of the largest studies ever conducted on suicide, the National Institute of Mental Health reported that 11 percent of the 18,500 respondents had thought about killing themselves at some stage in their lives, while 3 percent had tried to commit suicide on at least one occasion.[16] Other surveys of adults in the general population found that between 5 and 15 percent had ever contemplated suicide.[17]

Although men are four times more likely than women to kill themselves, women attempt to commit suicide two to three times more often than men.[18] Women have been found to suffer from depression twice as much as men, which is believed to manifest itself in more suicidal ideation and suicide attempts.[19] Battered women are especially at risk for suicidal ideation and attempted suicide. Studies by Mildred Pagelow[20] and John Gayford[21] found that half of the battered women in their samples had thought about committing suicide; Evan Stark and Anne Flitcraft reported that 1 in 10 of their sample group of abused women had attempted suicide, with half of these battered women seeking to kill themselves on more than one occasion.[22] In the latter study, it was found that more than 1 in 4 attempted suicides by females (that hospitals were aware of) involved intimate partner violence.

Research on college and high school students has yielded rates on suicidal ideation among young adults. In a comprehensive nationwide study of undergraduate college students undertaken by the 1995 National College Health Risk Behavior Survey, researchers found that 10 percent of the students had thought about committing suicide on a serious level, with 7 percent having developed a plan to kill themselves.[23] Studies in the United States, Europe, and Africa have shown that mild to serious suicidal thoughts occur in anywhere from 20 to 65 percent of all students in college.[24]

Suicidal ideation among high school students may be even more common. According to the 2007 Youth Risk Behavior Surveillance Survey, which questioned students in grades 9 to 12, nearly 15 percent had seriously contemplated attempting to take their own lives in the last year, with more than 11 percent having created a plan to that effect.[25] In surveys of high school students in New York and Oregon, rates of suicidal ideation were more than 50 percent and 20 percent, respectively.[26] Other North American and European studies have yielded similar findings on thoughts of suicide among boys and girls.[27]

Teenagers and Suicide

Suicide by teenagers is a major source of concern by mental health professionals and experts on youth. Suicide is the third leading cause of death among people between the ages of 15 and 25 and the sixth leading cause for those between the ages of 5 and 14.[28] More teenagers and young adults die as the result of suicide than from such means as heart disease, stroke, cancer, AIDS, birth defects, influenza, and pneumonia put together.

An estimated 500,000 teenagers attempt suicide every year, with around 5,000 successful in killing themselves.[29] Nearly twice as many youth die as a result of suicide than from natural causes.

According to studies, male teenagers age 17 to 19 who drink alcohol are at the greatest risk to commit suicide.[30] More than 1 in 2 teen victims of suicide abused drugs or alcohol.[31]

Teenage runaways and prostitutes face a particularly high risk for attempting or committing suicide. In a study of runaways in youth shelters, Carol Canton and David Shaffer found that 50 percent had seriously considered or attempted suicide.[32] Nearly 7 out of 10 girl prostitutes and almost 4 in 10 boy prostitutes have attempted suicide.[33]

Gay teenagers are also at high risk for suicide. Some studies have reported that around one-third of all teenage suicide victims in the United States every year are homosexual males or females.[34] Gay and lesbian youth are two to three times as likely to complete attempted suicide as other youth.

Most teens that kill themselves do so out of depression, loneliness, hopelessness, or isolation, with substance abuse often a factor. Warning signs for teen or adult suicide include

- Talking about committing suicide
- Difficulty with eating or sleeping
- Drastic behavioral changes
- Withdrawing from friends or social activities
- Loss of interest in school, hobbies, or work
- The recent breakup of a relationship or death in the family
- Having attempted suicide previously
- Abuse of alcohol or drugs
- A preoccupation with death or dying

Murder-Suicide

Murder-suicide tends to occur most often in an intimate or intrafamilial setting. It is unclear just how many murder-suicides take place each year in the United States, as some are misidentified, unknown, or unclassified as such in homicide statistics. In a study of homicide followed by suicide occurring in Kentucky between 1985 and 1990, Sherry Currens and colleagues found that homicide-suicides represented 6 percent of the total homicides over the span.[35]

A male intimate is typically the perpetrator in murder-suicides. In Stuart Palmer and John Humphrey's study of offender-victim relationships in criminal homicide-suicides in North Carolina from 1972 to 1977, 94 percent were perpetrated by males.[36] Similarly, Marvin Wolfgang's analysis of 24 homicide-suicides in Philadelphia found that 92 percent were committed by men.[37] Most victims of murder-suicide are female. In the Currens and associates study, 73 percent of the homicide victims were women.[38]

Spouse battering is often a precursor to domestic partner murder-suicide, in conjunction with offender jealousy, anger, depression, psychological factors, and substance abuse.[39] In his examination of homicide followed by suicide, Steven Stack found that the risk of suicide after a homicide was significantly higher if the victim was intimately involved with the offender or was an ex-intimate or a child of the offender.[40]

Murder-suicide is also common in suicide pacts where one person kills another and then him- or herself as part of a jointly agreed-upon ending of life. Mercy killing-suicide can occur when perpetrators, usually elderly, take an ill spouse's life, and then out of guilt, loneliness, depression, and/or fear of consequences, commit suicide.[41]

Intrafamilial homicide-suicide may sometimes result in the murder of one's entire family before the killer, usually an adult male, takes his own life. Other interpersonal murder-suicides include those perpetrated in the workplace by disgruntled current or ex-employees.

Mass murders typically involve murder-suicide in which the killer or killers wish to make a violent statement, express rage, or achieve martyrdom while escaping apprehension through the act of suicide. A good example is the Columbine High School massacre in 1999, in which Eric Harris and Dylan Klebold killed 13 people and wounded 25 others and then turned their guns on themselves before authorities could close in. Mass murder-suicide is also typically perpetrated by terrorists who kill themselves because it is often the only way to ensure completing the crime with maximum effectiveness. This was painfully illustrated with the September 2001 terrorist attack on the United States, in which 19 men hijacked four airliners and crashed them, killing thousands, including themselves (see Chapter 10).

Suicide Methods

Self-killers take their own lives through a variety of means, depending upon the suicidal individual's frame of mind, accessibility to the desired method of suicide, state of health, knowledge, intent, fears, morals, and other considerations. However, use of firearms is by far the most common method of committing suicide in the United States (see Figure 17.3). Firearms account for around 60 percent of all suicides, while about 25 percent are committed by strangulation and drug or poison overdoses, with the other 15 percent of suicides committed by inhaling gases or vapors, cutting, falling, and drowning.

Figure 17.4 breaks down suicide methods by gender. Sixty-four percent of males take their own lives by use of handguns or other firearms; 14 percent commit suicide by strangulation, suffocation, or hanging; and 10 percent by

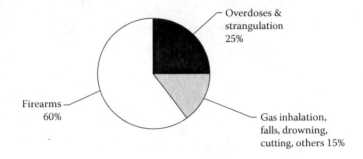

Figure 17.3 Suicide methods in the United States. (Data derived from Kay R. Jamison, *Night Falls Fast: Understanding Suicide*, New York: Vintage, 1999, p. 138.)

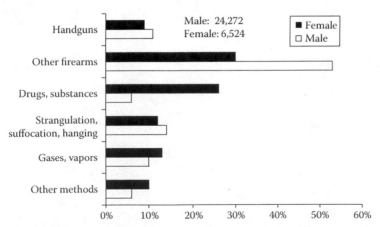

Figure 17.4 Suicide methods, by gender. (From National Center for Health Statistics, Division of Vital Statistics.)

inhalation of gases or vapors. Around 12 percent of males commit suicide by drug overdose or other methods.

Females are much less likely than males to commit suicide with firearms. However, firearms are the most common method of suicide for females, constituting about 39 percent of suicides. Twenty-six percent of females end their lives by overdosing on drugs or other substances, with 13 percent choosing to die by inhaling gases or vapors, and 12 percent committing suicide by strangulation, suffocation, or hanging. Around 10 percent of females take their lives through other means.

Age can also be an important factor in the method chosen to commit suicide, especially among young suicidal persons. According to research:

- Sixty-four percent of young men kill themselves with firearms.
- Twenty percent of young women take their own lives with firearms.
- Eighteen percent of young men end their lives by hanging.
- Fifty-three percent of young women commit suicide by drug overdose or poison.[42]

Suicide by firearms is on the decline. As shown in Figure 17.5, between 1986 and 2006, the rate of firearm-related suicides per 100,000 persons in the United States, dropped from 8.85 to 6.53. Attempted suicides involving firearms have also decreased over time. According to a recent study on firearm-related fatal and nonfatal injuries, the rate of attempted suicide fell 48 percent over a five-year period. In comparison, the rate of nonfatal assaults involving firearms dropped 49 percent during the span.[43]

In discussing various factors that may be involved in the method chosen to commit suicide, Jamison noted the importance of "the type and degree of psychopathology.... Severely mentally ill patients are more likely than others to immolate themselves, leap in front of trains, or choose particularly bizarre

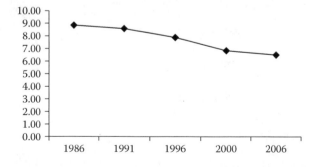

Figure 17.5 Firearm-related suicide rate per 100,000 population, 1986–2006. (Derived from U.S. Department of Justice, Bureau of Justice Statistics, *Sourcebook of Criminal Justice Statistics*, Table 3.139, http://www.albany.edu/sourcebook/pdf/t31392006.pdf, March 14, 2012.)

and self-mutilation ways to die."[44] She also contended that revenge, anger, symbolism, and suggestion could all play roles in the suicide method and circumstances thereof.

Substance Abuse and Suicide

A strong correlation exists between suicidal people and substance abuse. Studies show that a high percentage of individuals who commit suicide have a history of alcohol or drug abuse and are often under the influence of substances at the time of death. More than half of teenage suicide victims had problems with drugs or alcohol, while over one-third of all young people who took their lives were diagnosed with substance abuse problems.[45] According to research, mood disorders combined with drug and alcohol abuse are most commonly related to suicide, as are psychiatric disorders and possession of firearms.[46]

In his study on suicide, Mark Williams found that

alcohol and substance abuse represent major risk factors for suicide right across the life-span.... The number of years somebody who completes suicide has typically been abusing alcohol is between twenty and twenty-five, possibly because as alcoholism progresses, it destroys those factors known to protect against suicide.... Alcohol and substance abuse raises the risk of suicide as soon as the abuse starts.[47]

Aside from the illicit drug abuse, prescription drug dependency has also been shown to increase the risk of suicide. Persons dependent on prescription drugs are twenty times more likely to commit suicide as the population at large.[48] While those addicted to prescription drugs have a higher suicide rate than alcoholics, people who are alcohol dependent account for far more cases of suicide.[49]

Drug and alcohol abuse are often a reflection of mental illness or coping with it. "Independently or together they can precipitate acute episodes of psychosis.... Substance abuse loads the cylinder with more bullets. By acting to disinhibit behavior, drugs and alcohol increase risk taking, violence, and impulsivity. For those who are suicidal or potentially so, this may be lethal."[50]

Depression and Suicide

The relationship between depression and suicide is well documented.[51] Depression is defined as a "condition of feeling sad or despondent" and characterized by "an inability to concentrate, insomnia, and feelings of dejection and hopelessness."[52] Untreated, depression is seen by experts as the number one cause of suicide. The National Institute of Mental Health reports that 15 percent of people who suffer from a major depressive disorder such as depression, manic-depression, and schizophrenia kill themselves if their affliction goes untreated or they are unresponsive to treatment.[53] This represents a rate of suicide 35 times greater rate than that in the general population.

According to the *Diagnostic and Statistical Manual of Mental Disorders* (*DSM-IV*), "The most serious consequence of a major depressive disorder is attempted or completed suicide. Motivations for suicide may include a desire to give up in the face of perceived insurmountable obstacles or an intense wish to end an excruciatingly painful emotional state that is perceived to be without end."[54] Studies show that the severity of the depressive state is directly correlated to risk of suicide. Severe depression is far more likely to result in suicide than milder forms of depression.[55]

When depression is combined with substance abuse, the risk of attempted or completed suicide is even higher.[56] Alcohol and/or drugs can both facilitate ending one's life and act as an antecedent in dependency that may foster conditions that lead to suicide. The accessibility of alcohol and legal and illegal drugs, along with guns, and untreated depressive disorders are seen as highly contributory to the suicide rate.

High-risk groups for depression-related suicide ideation, attempts, and actual suicide include females, pregnant women, teenagers, and the elderly.[57] Suicide tends to be more common as well among talented writers and artists, as well as people successful in business or the scientific community. In most cases, depression, manic-depression, and substance abuse have been shown to be highly instrumental in such suicides.[58]

Doctor-Assisted Suicide

Interest is growing among the public in doctor-assisted suicide, or a doctor prescribing lethal medications to help a person—usually terminally ill—to end their life. According to a 2008 Gallup poll, 62 percent of the national sample believed that doctor-assisted suicide should be legal for terminally ill patients or those in severe pain, whereas 34 percent felt that it should not be legally sanctioned.[59] In a 2007 Associated Press poll, around half the respondents felt that doctor-assisted suicide should be legal; however, nearly 7 in 10 respondents believed that patients should be able to end their lives under certain circumstances.[60]

Currently in the United States, physician-assisted suicide is legal only in Oregon, Montana, and Washington.[61] Oregon's Death with Dignity Act was the first such state law after voters passed Measure 16 in 1994. According to the law, a patient "must be of sound mind when request[ing] a prescription for a lethal dose of medication. Two doctors must confirm a diagnosis of terminal illness with no more than six months to live. Two witnesses, one non-doctor unrelated to the patient, must confirm the patient's request, and the patient must make a second request after fifteen days."[62]

From the time the act went into effect in 1997 through the end of 2010, there were 525 doctor-assisted suicides in the state of Oregon, including a record number of 65 in 2010.[63]

The federal government sought to undermine Oregon's doctor-assisted suicide law by arguing before the Supreme Court that the law violates the Controlled Substances Act, regulating the manufacture, distribution, and dispensation of certain drugs. In the 2006 decision, *Gonzales v. Oregon*, the court ruled that the United States Attorney General "could not enforce the federal Controlled Substances Act against physicians who prescribed drugs in compliance with Oregon state law for the assisted suicide of the terminally ill."[64]

In some cases physicians have been circumventing the law in assisting patients to commit suicide. Perhaps the best known example is Doctor Jack Kevorkian. The retired Michigan pathologist known as "Dr. Death" was believed to have assisted in the suicides of more than 130 terminally ill people.[65] In 1999, Kevorkian was convicted of second degree murder and delivery of a control substance in the death of a man suffering from Lou Gehrig's disease. He was sentenced to 10 to 25 years in prison. Kevorkian was imprisoned for 8 years before being paroled in 2007. As a condition of his parole, he promised not to assist in any more suicides. He died in 2011 at the age of 83.

Endnotes

1. How to Cope with Suicidal Thoughts and Feelings—In Yourself and Others, http://www.healingfromdepression.com/suicidal.htm.
2. YourDictionary.com, http://yourdictionary.com/cgi-bin/mw.cgi.
3. K. R. Jamison, *Night Falls Fast: Understanding Suicide* (New York: Vintage, 1999), p. 26.
4. Quoted in M. Williams, *Cry of Pain: Understanding Suicide and Self-Harm* (New York: Penguin, 1997), p. 19. See also E. Durkheim, *Le Suicide* (Paris: Alcain, 1897).
5. Quoted in Jamison, *Night Falls Fast*, p. 27.
6. *Ibid.*
7. *Ibid.*, p. 34.
8. Williams, *Cry of Pain*, p. 69.
9. Cited in Jamison, *Night Falls Fast*, p. 48.
10. Cited in A. Tompkins, A Thoughtful Look at Suicide (July 17, 2000), http://www.flepioa.org/suicide.htm.
11. *Ibid.*; Jamison, *Night Falls Fast*, p. 46.
12. Suicide, http://www.travestyproductions.com/deadend/suicide_notes/stats.html##how.

The Dynamics of Murder: Kill or Be Killed

13. Williams, *Cry of Pain*, pp. 75–76.
14. Suicide; Jamison, *Night Falls Fast*, pp. 48–49.
15. Williams, *Cry of Pain*, pp. 77–78; R. D. Goldney, Suicidal Ideation in a Young Adult Population, *Acta Psychiatrica Scandinavica* 79 (1989): 481–9.
16. Cited in Jamison, *Night Falls Fast*, pp. 35–36.
17. *Ibid.*
18. *Ibid.*, pp. 46–47; Williams, *Cry of Pain*, p. 77.
19. Jamison, *Night Falls Fast*, pp. 46–47, 109.
20. M. D. Pagelow, *Family Violence* (New York: Praeger, 1984).
21. J. J. Gayford, Wife Battering: A Preliminary Survey of 100 Cases, *British Medical Journal* 1 (1975): 194–97.
22. E. Stark & A. Flitcraft, Violence Among Intimates: An Epidemiological Review, in V. B. Van Hasselt, R. L. Morrison, A. S. Bellack, & M. Hersen, Eds., *Handbook of Family Violence* (New York: Plenum, 1988), pp. 293–317.
23. Cited in Jamison, *Night Falls Fast*, p. 36.
24. *Ibid.*
25. Centers for Disease Control and Prevention, Youth Risk Behavior Surveillance Survey—United States, 2007, http://www.cdc.gov/mmwr/preview/mmwrhtml/ss5704a1.htm#tab22 (March 14, 2012).
26. Cited in Jamison, *Night Falls Fast*, p. 37.
27. Cited in *Ibid.*
28. Suicide is a Teenage Epidemic, http://www.jaredstory.com/teen_epidemic.html.
29. *Ibid.*
30. Suicide.
31. *Ibid.*
32. Cited in R. B. Flowers, *The Prostitution of Women and Girls* (Jefferson: McFarland, 1998), p. 93.
33. *Ibid.*, p. 87; C. Tattersall, *Drugs, Runaways, and Teen Prostitution* (New York: Rosen, 1999), p. 31.
34. Tattersall, *Drugs, Runaways, and Teen Prostitution*, p. 31; Williams, *Cry of Pain*, p. 33; J. Harry, Sexual Identity Issues, in *Report of the Secretary's Task Force Report on Youth Suicide*, Vol. 2 (Washington: Department of Health and Human Services, 1989), pp. 131–42.
35. Cited in N. Websdale, *Understanding Domestic Homicide* (Boston: Northeastern University Press, 1999), pp. 16–17.
36. S. Palmer & J. A. Humphrey, Offender-Victim Relationships in Criminal Homicide Followed by Offender's Suicide, North Carolina, 1972–1977, *Suicide and Life-Threatening Behavior* 10, 2 (1980): 106–18.
37. M. E. Wolfgang, An Analysis of Homicide-Suicide, *Journal of Clinical and Experimental Psychopathology and Quarterly Review of Psychiatry and Neurology* 19, 3 (1958): 208–18.
38. Websdale, *Understanding Domestic Homicide*, pp. 16–17.
39. *Ibid.*, p. 17; R. B. Flowers, *Domestic Crimes, Family Violence and Child Abuse: A Study of Contemporary American Society* (Jefferson: McFarland, 2000), pp. 61–67, 71–78; M. Rosenbaum, The Role of Depression in Couples Involved in Murder-Suicide and Homicide, *American Journal of Psychiatry* 147, 8 (1990): 1036–39.

40. Steven Stack, Homicide Followed by Suicide: An Analysis of Chicago Data, *Criminology* 35, 3 (1997): 435–53.
41. Peter M. Marzuk, Kenneth Tardiff, & Charles S. Hirsh, The Epidemiology of Murder-Suicide, *Journal of the American Medical Association* 267, 23 (1992): 3179–83; Patricia W. Easteal, *Killing the Beloved: Homicide Between Adult Sexual Intimates* (Canberra: Australian Institute of Criminology, 1993).
42. Suicide, http://www.travestyproductions.com/deadend/suicide_notes/stats. html##how.
43. Centers for Disease Control and Prevention, *Morbidity and Mortality Weekly Report Surveillance Summaries*, http://www.cdc.gov/mmwr/preview/ mmwrhtml/ss5002a1.htm#fig11 (March 14, 2012).
44. Jamison, *Night Falls Fast*, pp. 141–42.
45. *Ibid.*, pp. 50, 102, 126–27; Williams, *Cry of Pain*, pp. 40–41, 231; Flowers, *The Prostitution of Women and Girls*, pp. 87, 93; Suicide; Jamison, *Night Falls Fast*, p. 50.
46. Jamison, *Night Falls Fast*, pp. 47, 103–04.
47. Williams, *Cry of Pain*, pp. 40–41.
48. Jamison, *Night Falls Fast*, p. 102.
49. *Ibid.*
50. *Ibid.*, p. 127.
51. *Ibid.*, pp. 126–28, 180, 190; Williams, *Cry of Pain*, pp. 126–29.
52. *The American Heritage Dictionary* (New York: Dell, 1994), p. 232.
53. How to Cope with Suicidal Thoughts.
54. *Ibid.* See also American Psychiatric Association, *Diagnostic and Statistical Manual of Mental Disorders*, 4th ed. (Washington: American Psychiatric Association, 1994).
55. Jamison, *Night Falls Fast*, pp. 110–14.
56. *Ibid.*, pp. 110–11, 123–28.
57. *Ibid.*, pp. 46–47, 50, 103.
58. *Ibid.*, pp. 180–81.
59. Gallup, Inc., *The Gallup Poll*, http://www.gallup.com/home.aspx (May 11, 2012).
60. Americans Still Split on Doctor-Assisted Suicide, *MSNBC.com* (May 29, 2007), http://www.msnbc.msn.com/id/18923323/ns/health-health_care/t/ americans-still-split-doctor-assisted-suicide/.
61. Cited in A. S. Green, State Wins Time to Defend Suicide Law, http://www. oregonlive.com/news/oregonian/index.ssf?/xml/story.ssf/html; Wikipedia, the Free Encyclopedia, Assisted Suicide in the United States, http://en.wikipedia. org/wiki/Assisted_suicide_in_the_United_States (May 10, 2012).
62. *Ibid.*
63. T. Strode, Oregon Sets Record for Assisted Suicides, *Ethics and Religious Liberty Commission* (February 2, 2011), http://erlc.com/article/ oregon-sets-record-for-assisted-suicides/.
64. Assisted Suicide in the United States; *Gonzales v. Oregon*, 546 U.S. 243 (2006).
65. R. B. Flowers & H. L. Flowers, *Murders in the United States: Crimes, Killers and Victims of the Twentieth Century* (Jefferson: McFarland, 2001), pp. 107–08, 204.

Case Studies of Murder

VI

Gerald and Charlene Gallego

18

Gerald Gallego and Charlene Gallego were perhaps the country's first husband-and-wife serial killers, leaving their mark as a sexually motivated pair of murderers. Twice wed to each other, the Gallegos forged a once-unbreakable attachment as they kidnapped, sexually assaulted, tortured, and murdered 11 people, including an unborn child, over a 26-month stretch during the late 1970s and early 1980s.[1] The serial killer duo's killing spree was powered by perverse sex slave fantasies, substance abuse, domestic violence, and opportunistic occasions to abduct and kill those they targeted.

As with most other serial killer couples, Charlene acted mainly as the lure in leading unsuspecting, mostly female victims to the gun-wielding Gerald, who then used them as sex slaves before murdering them. Only luck and a timely intervention prevented the Gallegos from likely murdering more people. Law enforcement officials were unable to connect the killers to their many crimes until they were finally apprehended and both started talking. Only then were the two killers forced to break their attachment and go against one another in the courtroom, where the stakes were high and with little room for error. Given the nature and viciousness of their criminal acts, Gerald and Charlene Gallego undoubtedly rank as one of the most frightening serial killer pairs in U.S. history.

***

Gerald Armond Gallego was born in Sacramento, California, on July 17, 1946. The product of a broken home, his father, Gerald Albert Gallego, was convicted of killing two lawmen and became the first person executed in Mississippi State Penitentiary's gas chamber in 1955. His mother traded sex for money as a prostitute during the 1950s. Physically abused during childhood, Gerald began committing crimes early in life, including sex crimes and property offenses, which landed him in California Youth Authority's Fred C. Nelles School for Boys and eventually the Preston School of Industry in Ione, California, following an armed robbery he committed with his half brother, David Hunt.

School also proved to be difficult for Gerald, who often had poor grades and was a habitual truant. At one point, a probation officer's report contended: "His social traits were all listed as failures. He currently typifies a

233

hard-shelled young man who evidenced little motivation for improvement, remorsefulness, or insight."[2]

Gerald continued brushing with the law and criminality into adulthood, committing burglaries and robberies, among other things, causing him to spend time in state prison. This included a stint at the California Medical Facility at Vacaville, where he was treated for depression. By the time he met Charlene Williams, Gerald Gallego had been arrested at least 23 times.

He had also built a track record of failed marriages, having been married five times and abusing all of his wives. He fathered at least one child out of his marriages with his first wife, a daughter whom Gerald started molesting at 6 years of age.

With a sometimes-charming personality, street smarts, and survival instincts, Gerald was able to work through or circumvent the problems he had while outsmarting the system. This included his parole agent, who had badly missed the signs of Gerald's predilection for sexual deviance and homicidal behavior when he said prior to Gerald being released on parole in December 1975: "It is the feeling of this agent that he [Gallego] could be discharged from further parole supervision without a significant risk to the community."[3]

This decision would have rippling effects on Gerald's life and, sadly, on many others in the coming years.

***

Charlene Adell Williams was born on October 19, 1956, in Stockton, California. As an only child, she had a privileged upbringing. Growing up shy and aloof, she had a high IQ and was a gifted violin player, leading Charlene and her parents to believe she might one day be able to attend the Juilliard School of Music.

However, such hopes faded as Charlene became rebellious, promiscuous, and restless and began to use alcohol and drugs. She married twice in early adulthood, with both marriages ending badly. Charlene was alleged to have attempted suicide once by ingesting Pine-Sol disinfectant, but she survived the scare.

When Charlene Williams met Gerald Gallego at a Sacramento poker club in September 1977, the almost 21-year-old Charlene had grown bored with the confines of suburbia and was looking for an escape from an otherwise pampered, comfortable life. She found it in Gerald, a bulky man who played up the bad boy in him, impressing Charlene. There was an almost instant connection between Gerald and Charlene. Gerald found the perfect partner in the petite, blonde, younger Charlene. She in turn was looking for someone who was older and more mature, whom she could be herself with, and who would take care of her.

Within weeks, the career criminal and susceptible Charlene were living together in a duplex that she was renting, doing drugs, and finding it difficult to make ends meet. They were also beginning to have problems in the bedroom with Gerald's sexual inadequacies putting a strain on the relationship. It was around this time that Gallego started to talk about "sex slave fantasies," in which he would kidnap young girls and make them his sexual slaves. Charlene, who had found herself in competition with his fantasy girl, seemed intent on doing whatever Gerald wanted in order to be his "number one girl with heart."

In December 1977, under Gerald's orders, Charlene purchased a .25 caliber FIE automatic pistol at a Del Paso Heights, California, sporting goods store. It was an omen of things to come.

***

In the spring of 1978, Gerald Gallego moved out of Charlene's duplex and into an apartment on Watts Avenue with his 14-year-old daughter, Krista, whom he was sexually abusing along with a 14-year-old female friend who was visiting her. Charlene was present during some of the molestation and chose to either ignore it or resign herself to it. Either way, she made no attempt to stop the sexual abuse or report it. Her sexual experimentation led to a lesbian encounter, which enraged Gerald, causing him to physically lash out at Charlene, a pattern that was to continue throughout their relationship.

In July 1978, Charlene was pregnant, much to Gerald's disappointment. The following month, his daughter went back to live with Gerald's mother in Chico, California. Without his daughter to molest and with Charlene experiencing morning sickness, Gerald's sex slave fantasy took a deadly turn.

***

On September 11, 1978, while armed with the .25 caliber pistol Charlene had purchased for him, Gerald and Charlene searched for victims in a van she had recently bought with the help of her father. They spotted the perfect girls at the Country Club Plaza shopping center in central Sacramento. Charlene was to act sweet and lure the targeted girls outside, where Gerald would then take over in this sinister plan of action.

Rhonda Scheffler, 17, and Kippi Vaught, 16, were spending time at the mall as many teenagers routinely do to just hang out and have fun. When the girls were approached by the petite and harmless-looking Charlene and invited to smoke dope, the girls readily accepted the offer, unaware of the deadly trap they were walking into.

When Rhonda and Kippi reached the van, Gerald was waiting inside with a gun pointed at them. He forced them into the back of the van and quickly tied their hands and feet with adhesive tape. He then forced Charlene to watch the kidnapped girls as he drove them onto Interstate 80, headed toward the Sierra Nevada mountains.

He pulled off in the small town of Baxter, where Gerald ordered Charlene to remain in the van while he took the girls out into the trees and brutalized them. When he returned without the victims, Charlene was then told to take the van back to Sacramento and come back in the Oldsmobile she also owned with her father.

Upon her return, Charlene watched as Gerald and the unkempt girls got in the back seat. She then drove them, per Gerald's instructions, to Sloughhouse, a farming community on the other side of Sacramento County.

Again, Charlene waited in the car while Gerald, armed with his gun, disappeared with the frightened and violated girls. This time he returned alone and made it clear that Rhonda Scheffler and Kippi Vaught were dead.

These were the first two victims in the establishment of the serial killer tandem of Gerald and his willing accomplice Charlene.

***

Two days after they went missing, Kippi Vaught's and Rhonda Martin Scheffler's remains were discovered by migrant farm workers in a meadow near Sloughhouse. According to the coroner's report, the teenagers had been raped, beaten, and shot to death. At this point, authorities did not know who had murdered the girls, and their investigation initially focused on Rhonda's husband, Gregory Scheffler, and other possible suspects who may have known the victims.

Meanwhile, the actual killers concentrated on getting rid of the evidence of their violent crimes, including their clothing, the handbags of the victims, and the .25 caliber gun used to murder the girls. The clothes were thrown into a dumpster, and then Gerald and Charlene drove to an area near the Sacramento River where they put the gun and some rocks in one of the victim's purses and flung it into the water. Afterward, Gerald removed the tire iron from the trunk that had been used to beat Kippi Vaught and Rhonda Scheffler and hurled it as far as he could into the river.

The two killers had gotten away with a double homicide and were already on the lookout for their next sex slave victims.

***

In September 1978, Charlene Williams terminated her pregnancy at Gerald Gallego's insistence. While this took care of one of his concerns, another was in the making. On September 27, Gerald's daughter Krista reported being molested by him to Detective Sergeant Dan Young of the Butte County Sheriff's Office. The molestation, which had gone on for 8 years, included charges of incest, sodomy, oral copulation, and unlawful intercourse.

When Gerald learned that he was wanted for questioning in Butte County for child molestation, he opted to circumvent the law along with his girlfriend and accomplice to kidnap and murder.

On September 30, 1978, Gerald Armond Gallego and Charlene Adell Williams were married in Reno, Nevada. It was yet another means by Gerald to tighten their bond and keep the dark secrets they carried. Gerald also began going by the name Stephen Robert Feil, hoping to throw off Butte County authorities as they searched for him.

An arrest warrant was issued for Gerald Gallego on October 9, 1978, for several felonies, including incest, sodomy, and oral copulation. His bail was set at $50,000. But the Gallegos had fled to Houston, Texas, where Gerald got a job as a bartender while a fugitive and murderer.

The Gallegos' stay in Houston was short-lived; they relocated to Reno by the end of the year, hastened when Gerald got into a fight at the Houston club where he worked. According to the club's bookkeeper, "He beat the all fired hell out of this bartender."[4] It was indicative of the hot temper that had characterized Gerald Gallego for much of his life, often resulting in a violent reaction.

**

On Father's Day, June 24, 1978, the Washoe County Fair was in full swing, attracting locals and tourists alike. Gerald regarded this as an ideal place to search for new sex slaves, with Charlene once again present as the yielding lure. She carried a .38 caliber revolver in her purse in case she needed it to force the girls to come with her. Charlene spotted two girls who fit the bill exactly for what Gerald wanted.

Brenda Lynne Judd, 14, and Sandra Kay Colley, 13, were ready to leave the fair after having a good time. The plan was to get a ride home with a friend. But their plans took a deadly turn.

When Charlene approached the teenagers with an offer to make money passing out handbills, they found the opportunity too tempting to pass up. Since their ride hadn't shown up yet, Brenda and Sandra swallowed the bait, and Charlene led them to a van.

Unbeknownst to the girls, Gerald had trailed them, confronting the girls at the van with a .44 caliber over-and-under derringer pistol. Abducting the frightened teenagers, he forced them to lie facedown on a mattress in the back of the van while he tied their hands and feet. Charlene sat in the back with the abducted girls while Gerald drove out of the fairgrounds with no one the wiser as to the crime that had taken place, or other crimes to follow.

After stopping at a hardware store to purchase a shovel and hammer, Gerald drove east on Interstate 80. Soon he and Charlene traded places, and he proceeded to rape and abuse his terrified captives. Charlene was then ordered to stop the van in the high Nevada desert. Gerald left Charlene in the van while he took the girls out into the wilderness, one at a time, and murdered them.

As the serial killers moved on, authorities searching for Brenda Judd and Sandra Colley had few leads to go on. Neither girl had a history of running away, but there was no evidence of foul play or any witnesses to indicate their possible whereabouts. The investigation continued with no sign of the miss-ing teenagers. By now, investigators feared the worst without realizing that a ruthless serial killer couple was at large.

***

In September 1979, Gerald and Charlene Gallego quit their jobs and returned to Sacramento, no doubt feeling self-assured that the authorities were not on to them as the serial killers they were. However, Gerald was still concerned about the child molestation charges in Butte County. In October 1979, he and Charlene moved into an apartment on Woodhollow Way as Mr. and Mrs. Stephen Feil. During this time, Gerald began to accumulate a collection of weapons, including a .357 magnum Colt Python, a .38 revolver, an AR-15 rifle, and his over-and-under derringer.

Just before Christmas in 1979, Gerald Gallego got a job bartending at the Bob-Les Club on Del Paso Boulevard using his alias Stephen Feil. Though he and Charlene continued to struggle in their personal relationship, they were unable or unwilling to sever ties, given the kidnappings and murders they had perpetrated together.

On March 28, 1980, Gerald added a second .25-caliber Beretta automatic pistol to his arsenal that Charlene purchased for him at a sporting goods store.

***

Less than a month later, on April 24, Gerald's perverse desire for sex slaves resumed. He and his more-than-willing collaborator in crime, Charlene, again went on the hunt for victims. They wound up at the Sunrise Mall in Citrus Heights, California, a suburb of Sacramento, where Charlene was once again called upon to lure unsuspecting victims to their brutal deaths at the hands of Gallego.

Karen Chipman Twiggs and Stacy Ann Redican, both 17, had recently gotten jobs at a fast food restaurant in the mall. Having just received their first paychecks, they had hoped to do some shopping, when Charlene Gallego approached them and asked if they wanted to get high on marijuana.

The girls, feeling she was harmless and wanting to have a good time, agreed to the seemingly kind offer and accompanied Charlene as Gerald fol-lowed inconspicuously.

At the van, Karen and Stacy were met by Gerald, who was armed with a .357 magnum. As he climbed in the back with the kidnapped teenagers, Charlene drove east on Interstate 80, per Gerald's instructions, while he vio-lated his latest victims of sexual slavery.

Charlene had driven well into the Sierras when Gerald ordered her to pull off the interstate and stop at a supermarket. He tied his victims up and left, returning shortly thereafter with a new hammer. While Gerald resumed sexually assaulting the girls, Charlene continued driving, passing Sparks, Nevada, before approaching Lovelock, a town some 90 miles from Reno.

Charlene drove the van drove through the darkness to Limerick Canyon, where Gerald, with the hammer and a fold-up shovel he had recently purchased, took one girl out into the desert. Charlene was left in the van to dutifully guard the other girl at gunpoint until Gerald returned for her. Like his previous victims, Gerald Gallego murdered both teenagers as the deadly culmination of his sex slave fantasies.

***

After Karen Twiggs and Stacy Redican failed to return home from the mall, Karen's mother, Carol Twiggs, went to the Sacramento Police Department to report the girls missing. Though Stacy apparently had a history of running away, that was not the case with Karen, causing real concern for the girls' safety.

It would take more than 3 months before the horrible truth of their disappearance was confirmed. On July 27, 1980, picnickers discovered the teenagers' coyote-ravaged remains in two shallow graves located some 20 miles outside of Lovelock, Nevada.

Dental charts positively identified the dead girls as Stacy Ann Redican and Karen Chipman Twiggs. According to the pathologist who performed the autopsy, Stacy and Karen had been raped and suffered massive and fatal head injuries by a "hammer or hammer-like instrument." One of the victims had her hands bound behind her back; the other victim's hands were missing altogether, likely the result of decomposition or ravenous prairie wolves.

The vicious slaying of Karen and Stacy put the local authorities on notice that at least one killer was on the loose. Sheriff James Kay McIntosh and District Attorney Richard Wagner of Pershing County, Nevada, were eager to track down whoever was responsible for the sexual murders. With clues minimal at best, Nevada Bureau of Investigation agents Tom Moots and John Compston were recruited by McIntosh and Wagner to assist in the investigation and add to the bureau's financial resources in attempting to crack the case.

In the meantime, the serial killers remained at large and had little reason to stop their murderous onslaught.

***

Charlene Gallego realized she was pregnant a few days after Gerald had murdered his latest victims. She was determined to keep the child this time, and Gerald agreed, if only to placate her for the time being as the one person who knew their deadly secrets. But not content with that alone, Gerald sought even more leverage to keep his wife in check.

On June 1, 1980, the Gallegos got married again, this time as Mr. and Mrs. Stephen Robert Feil in the Heart of Reno Wedding Chapel in Nevada.

A few days later, on June 7, the second-time newlyweds drove to Gold Beach on Oregon's coast, between Brookings and Coos Bay. It was there that they spotted their next victim.

Twenty-one-year-old Linda Aguilar was 4 months pregnant with her second child. After picking up some items from a local store, she was headed home on foot when the van pulled up alongside her with the Gallegos inside. They offered her a ride.

Perhaps feeling a bit weary, it seemed to Linda like a better way to get where she was going. And so she accepted the lift from the unassuming strangers, unaware of their devious intentions.

After they crossed the Rogue River bridge, Gerald handed Charlene the wheel and climbed into the back of the van with Linda, surprising her when he stuck a pistol in her face. She was trapped and helpless under the circumstances. Gerald sexually assaulted Linda as Charlene drove, and the assault continued after she parked the van in a grassy, secluded area.

When Gerald had finished his violent attack, Charlene handed the naked, bruised, and debased victim her clothing. Then Gerald tied her hands and drove them to a sandy, isolated spot. At gunpoint, he led the disheveled captive past a rock formation where he bludgeoned her and left her to die.

***

Two days after Linda Aguilar's disappearance, her live-in boyfriend, Rick, reported her missing to the Sheriff's Department in Port Orford, Oregon. The pregnant mother of his 2-year-old son apparently had developed a habit of wandering off on her own, sometimes for "days at a time," according to the boyfriend.

The Curry County Sheriff's Department made a few inquiries about the missing woman. Witnesses in nearby Gold Beach (the county seat) and Wedderburn reported seeing the pregnant woman but had no indication she was in any imminent danger.

Unfortunately, nothing could have been further from the truth.

On the evening of June 22, 1980, German tourists and their dog discovered the badly decomposed remains of Linda Aguilar in Gold Beach.

The autopsy report illustrated the horrible nature of Linda's final hours, indicating that her hands and feet were bound and that she had been clubbed repeatedly on the head, cracking her skull, before being strangled. Sand was discovered in the victim's mouth, throat, and lungs, leading the medical examiner to conclude that the pregnant woman had been buried alive and suffocated in her sandy grave.

In spite of this harsh reality, authorities were no closer to putting the pieces together that would lead them to the serial killers responsible for the death of Linda Aguilar and her unborn child and the murder of six other females.

***

The Gallegos, undoubtedly feeling safe after their latest kill, returned to Sacramento, where, on the night of July 16, 1980, they spent a few hours on the Sacramento River drinking and fishing. Afterward, they went to the Sail Inn in West Sacramento for more drinking and frolic.

It was there that Gerald Gallego noticed the bartender, Virginia Mochel, and immediately targeted her as his next sex slave victim.

Virginia was a 34-year-old mother of two young children. She likely regarded the Gallegos as merely another friendly young couple out for drinks and fun, but certainly not a threat. After closing down the tavern, the bartender headed outside just after 2:00 a.m.

She had barely entered her car when Gerald Gallego—who had been waiting with Charlene in their van for Virginia to emerge from the bar—knocked on the window, pointed a .357 magnum revolver directly at her, and ordered her out of the car.

Gerald abducted Virginia Mochel on his 34th birthday, forcing her to get into the back of the van, where he bound her hands and feet before driving to the apartment on Woodhollow Way. While Charlene went inside at Gerald's insistence, he brutally raped his captive in the van. Then he tied her up again and went inside to get Charlene. She drove and, as directed, turned the music up loud while Gerald killed his latest victim.

After driving to an area near a levee road outside Clarksburg, Gerald dragged Virginia's body from the van, disposing of yet another victim of his macabre sex slave fantasies.

***

The disappearance of the well-liked and usually dependable bartender Virginia Mochel got the attention of the local community as well as the Yolo County Sheriff's Department, who feared foul play was involved. As the investigation went on, search parties were organized, combing "the barren area bordering South River Park, which was near the Sail Inn [and expanding] the search to the banks of the Sacramento River Delta, the waters around the river levees, and the Port of Sacramento area."[5] But there was still no sign of Virginia.

In the meantime, Yolo County investigators were interviewing regular patrons of the Sail Inn and came up with the names of Stephen and his companion Charlene, who were at the bar the night Virginia Mochel disappeared and had driven an early 1970s Dodge recreational van there. Stephen was reported to have bragged about being a bartender at the Argonaut Club in Del Paso Heights.

Two days later, Yolo County Sheriff Detective David Trujillo learned there was, in fact, a new employee at the Argonaut Club named Stephen

Robert Feil, who had a girlfriend named Charlene. Trujillo phoned "Feil" (Gerald Gallego) and Charlene, who unbeknownst to the detective was Gallego's twice-wed wife. Both denied having any knowledge of Virginia Mochel's disappearance or whereabouts, with Charlene revealing that they had been fishing in southeastern Yolo County that night and probably had way too much to drink.

At the time, Detective Trujillo had little reason to believe the pair was guilty of cold-blooded murder and, as such, didn't pursue this path further. Before the pieces of the deadly puzzle would be put together, the killers would strike again.

***

On October 3, 1980, the worst-case scenario was realized. Virginia Mochel's nude, decomposed remains were discovered by fishermen in thick brush near Clarksburg in southeastern Yolo County. The bartender's hands were tied behind her back with fishing line. The poor condition of her body made it difficult to determine the exact cause of death or if she had been sexually assaulted. Only later would the authorities learn the true nature of Virginia's abduction and horrific murder.

Detective Trujillo did recall that Charlene Gallego had mentioned that she and her boyfriend Stephen Feil had gone fishing the day Virginia Mochel vanished. The fact that fishing line had been used to tie up the victim suggested to the detective that he might have a possible lead into her killer.

Trujillo paid Charlene, who had since moved back in with her parents, a visit. She maintained her earlier story. "I'm really sorry, Detective Trujillo, to hear about the lady bartender," she told him in a believable and soft-spoken voice. "She was nice to me and Stephen when we were at the bar. I hope you find whoever did this to her!"[6]

In fact, the detective had unknowingly identified Virginia Mochel's killers, but wouldn't come to terms with it for another month.

***

Shortly after the murder of Virginia Mochel, the Gallegos sold their van to a couple in Orangevale, California. Since it had been used to abduct and kill eight women, they knew it was too hot to keep.

In early August 1980, the strain in the Gallegos' volatile relationship erupted when Charlene's mother, Mercedes Williams, was visiting the couple at the Woodhollow Way apartment, where they were once again living together. An argument resulted in Gerald Gallego choking the much smaller Charlene. Only when Mercedes came to her daughter's rescue by beating Gallego repeatedly on the side of the head with one of his own guns did he release his powerful grip around Charlene's neck. The following month, Charlene again went to live with her parents.

As the two killers drifted apart briefly, Gerald went to Oregon accompanied by his new and pregnant girlfriend. By fall 1980, he had returned to Sacramento and, on October 7, rented an apartment on Bluebird Lane.

By November 1, 1980, Gerald and Charlene had gotten back together. That evening, they picked up their Oldsmobile Cutlass from Charlene's parents' house and went in search for new victims to satisfy Gerald's sex slave fantasies. In his possession was the .25 caliber Beretta Charlene had purchased for him earlier that year.

Gerald ordered Charlene to pull the car into the Arden Fair shopping center parking lot, as his eyes landed on a young couple to target.

***

Craig Miller and his fiancée, Mary Elizabeth Sowers, both 21, had just departed the Sigma Phi Epsilon Founder's Day dinner–dance at the Carousel Restaurant in Arden Fair and were walking toward Mary Beth's Honda, when they were approached by Gerald Gallego. At gunpoint, he forced them to get into the back seat of the Cutlass.

A fraternity brother of Craig's witnessed the abduction and tried to intervene, only to be rebuffed by the Gallegos, who sped from the scene. However, the fraternity brother was able to take down the license plate number of the car that was taking his friends to some place unknown.

***

Whatever thoughts may have gone through their heads at the outset of the kidnapping at gunpoint, Mary Beth Sowers and Craig Miller must have begun to fear the worst while Charlene Gallego drove, as directed, east on U.S. 50 and Gerald Gallego aimed the weapon at the young couple.

Charlene pulled off at the Bass Lake Road exit, driving till Gerald ordered her to stop. They were in the middle of a gravel road near Bass Lake in El Dorado County. Gerald forced Craig to get out of the car and told him to start walking before he shot him point-blank in the back of the head. The killer stepped closer to his fallen victim and shot him two more times in the head, leaving Craig's dead body there as Gerald got back into the car.

Charlene then drove to Gerald's apartment, where he brutalized and sexually assaulted Mary Beth for several hours till he forced her again at gunpoint into the car. Charlene, his loyal accomplice to kidnapping and murder, drove onto Interstate 80 toward Reno, per Gerald's instructions. She exited near Sierra College in Placer County, bringing the vehicle to a stop at the end of a remote road and remained inside while Gerald took his victim into a pasture, before shooting her to death.

The Gallegos left the murder scene, which had becoming chillingly habitual, believing that they had once more committed the perfect crime. Unbeknownst to them, their run of good fortune was about to come to a halt.

***

On Sunday morning, November 2, 1980, a group of Mary Beth Sowers and Craig Miller's friends, which included the fraternity brother who witnessed the kidnapping, reported the college sweethearts as missing to the police.

Sacramento Police Department Detective Lee Taylor of the missing persons squad ran a trace with the Department of Motor Vehicles on the license number the fraternity brother had taken down from the Oldsmobile. Listed as the legal owner of the 1977 Oldsmobile Cutlass in which Craig Miller and Mary Beth Sowers were last seen alive was Charles Williams, with his daughter, Charlene A. Williams, the registered owner.

Taylor and fellow detective Larry Burchett paid a visit to the Williams house that morning and spoke with the pregnant Charlene, as Gerald Gallego quietly went out the back door. She smoothly denied any knowledge of the missing coeds, insisting that she and Gallego had gone to see a movie the previous night and drank quite a lot. Charlene told the detectives she wasn't feeling well that morning.

The detectives searched her Oldsmobile and took down information on a red Triumph parked on the street that Charlene told them belonged to Gerald Gallego.

The detectives did not arrest Charlene at that point but promised to return later, if necessary. Back at the police station, Taylor and Burchett ran a check on the Triumph's license number and found it was registered to Stephen Robert Feil. After getting a copy of Feil's driver's license, the detectives showed it to Craig Miller's fraternity brother. He identified the person in the photograph as the man who had been in the front seat of the Oldsmobile Cutlass while a terrified Craig and Mary Beth sat in the back as captives.

The detectives went to Stephen Feil's (aka Gerald Gallego) apartment, but could not locate the suspect. A return visit to the Williams house to see Charlene also came up short, as she and Gerald had fled, quickly becoming fugitives from justice.

***

On the afternoon of November 2, 1980, Craig Miller's body was discovered next to a gravel road near Bass Lake in El Dorado County, California, 20 miles from Placerville. He had been shot three times at close range. An autopsy performed the following day showed that Craig had been shot once above the right ear, once in the back of the neck, and once in the right cheekbone—all apparently at the scene.

Mary Beth Sowers was still missing and presumed dead.

***

The now-wanted Gallegos drove the Oldsmobile east down Highway 50—toward the Sierras again as they had so often done during their 26-month reign of abduction, rape, and death—on their way to Reno, Nevada, by way of Lake Tahoe and Carson City.

In Reno, they abandoned the vehicle in the Circus Circus Casino hotel parking lot. Under Gerald's orders, Charlene phoned her parents from the casino and told them where the car could be found in hopes of throwing the authorities off their trail.

The Gallegos then took a Greyhound bus to Salt Lake City, Utah, where Charlene's parents wired them $500 to a Western Union office. The fugitive couple used the money to stay afloat, as they fled to Denver, Colorado, before heading to Omaha, Nebraska.

Once again, Charlene turned to her parents for more money, and they agreed to send another $500 to the Western Union office in Omaha.

***

Charles and Mercedes Williams were unaware that they had been under constant surveillance by the FBI and Sacramento Police Department. Using unmarked cars, agents followed the Williamses as they left their home on Saturday, November 15, and drove to Sparks, Nevada.

On November 16, the two were observed entering a Sparks Western Union office. When confronted by FBI agents, Charles and Mercedes Williams confessed to sending $500 to their daughter in Omaha. This information was quickly relayed to the FBI's Omaha field office.

On Monday, November 17, 1980, just before noon, the FBI confronted Charlene Gallego inside the Western Union office. Agent Harlan Phillips told her, "You are under arrest on an unlawful flight to avoid prosecution on a murder charge!"[7]

An order to "take Gallego" was then radioed to agents who were following Gerald Gallego closely. Though he had once claimed he would never be taken alive, Gerald was arrested without incident by FBI agents, who were armed with shotguns.

***

On November 22, 1980, the remains of Mary Elizabeth Sowers were discovered in a Placer County pasture in a shallow trench. The 21-year-old college senior was still wearing the purplish-blue silk evening gown she had worn to the Sigma Phi Epsilon Founder's Day dinner–dance nearly 3 weeks earlier. Her hands were bound and she had been shot execution-style three times in the head.

According to a Placer County Sheriff's detective, "The mood was very solemn, very serious. When you get a homicide of this nature, it stirs some real feelings within the law enforcement community."[8]

In an autopsy conducted the following day, Mary Beth Sowers was positively identified by Dr. James Nordstrom of Auburn, California, an expert in forensic dentistry, upon studying her dental charts.

Mary Beth was buried alongside her fiancé, Craig Miller. The couple's violent death would not be in vain, for it led to the capture of serial killer couple Gerald and Charlene Gallego. They would now have to answer for their lethal crimes.

***

Two hours after their arrest, Gerald Gallego and his 7-months-pregnant wife, Charlene, appeared before U.S. Magistrate Richard Peck in Omaha. Assistant U.S. Attorney Thomas Thalken argued that bail should be set at $500,000 for each defendant, noting the particularly brutal nature of the crime believed to have been perpetrated by the pair. In spite of this, Peck set bail at $100,000 for each defendant.

The Gallegos waived extradition proceedings and agreed to return to California, where they were to be charged with the kidnap and murder of Craig Miller and Mary Elizabeth Sowers. Officers from El Dorado County and Sacramento were sent to Nebraska to escort the murder suspects back to California.

"We're not animals!" Gerald Gallego yelled in the Placerville, California, courtroom where he and Charlene appeared for a bail and arraignment hearing.[9] Gerald and Charlene entered not-guilty pleas to the charges against each of one count of kidnapping and one count of first degree murder.

The judge ordered them held without bail, pending a preliminary hearing, and remanded the Gallegos back to the El Dorado County jail.

The case against Gerald and Charlene Gallego had become a jurisdictional quagmire with three Northern California jurisdictions involved in the kidnap-murder of Craig Miller and Mary Beth Sowers. The district attorneys from each wanted to put Gerald and Charlene Gallego on trial.

On November 25, 1980, it was agreed by all parties that the Sacramento County District Attorney's office would prosecute the kidnap-murder case against Gerald and Charlene Gallego due to its size, resources, and assistance of the California Department of Justice, along with Sacramento County Crime Laboratory.

At this stage, the authorities were unaware that they had serial killers in custody.

***

On January 17, 1981, Charlene Gallego, now 24, gave birth to Gerald Armond Gallego, Jr., in a hospital prison ward. Through her attorney, Charlene tried to get bail on the grounds that a refusal "violated the rights of her unborn child."

Sacramento Municipal Court Judge Peter Mering denied the motion, arguing that bail for Charlene Gallego would only be considered if the defense could provide "evidence or affidavits" that contradicted the prosecutors' case against her.

Other attempts by Gerald and Charlene to have the case against them tossed also failed.

By February 1982, Charlene Gallego had two new attorneys, Hamilton Hintz, Jr., and Fern Laethem, to help her try to find a way out of the deep hole she had dug for herself as Gerald Gallego's collaborator in serial homicides. She offered to disclose the depths of their criminality in murdering 11 people, including an unborn child, and to assist in the conviction of Gerald Gallego in exchange for a reduced sentence.

The local authorities and public were stunned by Charlene's confession to a string of murders. "The scale of the murders appalled West Coast residents," noted a law enforcement official involved with the case. "It wasn't until the public fully understood how many different homicides Gerald Gallego had committed that the full impact of what had taken place over a period of time ... There was a great deal of shock to the local community."[10]

On November 10, 1982, after prolonged negotiations with the district attorneys of California, Nevada, and Oregon, a deal was reached. Charlene Adell Gallego pleaded guilty to two counts of first degree murder in the deaths of Craig Miller and Mary Elizabeth Sowers. In exchange for her testimony against Gerald Gallego, Charlene was given a "guaranteed" sentence of 16 years and 8 months to be served with no chance for early release on parole. As part of the plea bargain, Charlene also pleaded guilty in Nevada to second degree murder in the deaths of Stacy Redican and Karen Twiggs, with the same sentence to be served concurrently while placing the onus of the murders on Gerald Gallego and testifying to this extent.

Aware of the controversy surrounding such a sweet deal for the confessed serial killer, prosecutor James Morris tried to justify the plea bargain. "By [Charlene] disclosing her involvement in several additional murders, she has created a compelling argument that she deserves no leniency for herself. The focus, however, cannot just be limited to her alone. All 10 victims and both defendants must be considered together for the purposes of obtaining at least substantial justice."[11]

***

In November 1982, Judge Norman Spellberg presided over Gerald Gallego's trial. According to Morris in his opening statement, "Gerald A. Gallego admitted killing a young Sacramento college couple," indicating that the "confession" occurred during "lawfully monitored" jailhouse conversations with his mother-in-law, Mercedes Williams, and a former girlfriend.[12]

Gerald Gallego, who represented himself, had tried to block Charlene's testimony on the grounds of spousal privilege. But since he had failed to legally divorce his second wife, both marriages to Charlene and her three predecessors were declared illegal and invalid. In January 1983, the California Supreme Court ruled without comment to Gerald's petition to this effect, legally clearing the way for Charlene to testify against the man she believed had been her legal husband. Charlene had since returned to using her maiden name of Williams.

The State called 30 witnesses who offered damaging testimony against Gerald Gallego. Charlene Williams was their star witness. She told the jury that on November 1, 1980, Gerald announced, "he was getting that feeling," indicating that he wanted her to find a girl for him.

Morris asked the witness if she had ever said no or otherwise refused to go along with Gerald's orders. "No," she responded concisely, glaring at the suspect. "You don't say no to Gerry."[13]

Adding to the State's strong case was a ballistics match of the .25 caliber bullets that entered and killed Craig Miller and bullets that were fired into the ceiling of a tavern by Gerald Gallego. Circumstantial evidence "pointed towards the .25 caliber Beretta automatic, which gun registration records indicated had been purchased by Charlene Gallego in March of 1980. It was consistent with the weapon used to kill Miller and Sowers, which had a barrel with a right-hand twist."[14] Furthermore, there was a match of the ejection and firing pin marks on the shell casings found near both Craig and Mary Beth's bodies, supporting the argument that both were shot with the same gun.

Gerald's often awkward, ill-prepared, and occasionally heated cross-examination was unable to break Charlene. Once, she testified, "I'd been under your control even after being arrested, up until the time when you said, 'Stay in love and you'll stay alive.'"[15]

A desperate Gerald Gallego ultimately took the stand himself, completing the debacle of his own doing and sealing the outcome.

On June 21, 1983, after less than 2 hours of jury deliberation, Gerald Armond Gallego was sentenced to death in California for the November 2, 1980, kidnapping-murders of Craig Miller and Mary Beth Sowers.

***

On May 23, 1984, Gerald Gallego went on trial in Nevada for the kidnapping and murders of Karen Chipman Twiggs and Stacy Ann Redican. Pershing County District Attorney Richard Wagner presented a strong case against the accused, including evidence that macramé rope found in the defendant's car matched the rope used to bind the hands of Karen and Stacy.

Charlene, once again the State's key witness, would testify that, under Gerald's orders, she had cut the rope and he used it to tie the victims' hands before killing them. She also talked about Gerald Gallego's "sex slave fantasies," of "having girls that would be there whenever he wanted them and do whatever he wanted them for, [who were] ripe for picking."[16]

Wagner further used Charlene's damaging testimony to establish a "common scheme" in Gerald's killing spree, in the defendant's murder of his first two victims, Kippi Vaught and Rhonda Scheffler. As was the case previously,

Charlene withstood tough opening statements and cross-examination by Gerald Gallego's public defenders Gary Marr and Tom Perkins, who tried hard to undermine her credibility.

In his opening statements, Marr argued, "Charlene Gallego made a plea bargain in this case. She testifies against Gerald Gallego—she lies and escapes the death penalty." He went on to portray her as a "confessed murderess" who has "told different stories at different times ..."[17]

Later, under cross-examination, Perkins followed the same pattern, accusing Charlene of lying to protect herself. It appeared to make little difference in the outcome of the case.

***

It took the six-man, six-woman jury only two and a half hours of deliberation before condemning Gerald Gallego to death for a second time by lethal injection for the murders of Karen Chipman Twiggs and Stacy Ann Redican. He was also convicted of two counts of kidnapping and sentenced to consecutive life terms in state prison without the possibility of parole.

On June 25, 1984, at a formal sentencing, the twice-convicted multiple murderer and death-row inmate lambasted those who convicted him, calling the entire proceeding a travesty based on the testimony of one witness—Charlene Williams—whom Gerald argued had fabricated her story to save her own life.

"What you people done to me is wrong!" Gallego spat defiantly to the court, media, and anyone else in the courtroom that he believed was against him. "You sentenced me to death with no damned evidence at all. I didn't kill those girls and you don't have a damned thing that says I did!"[18]

Wagner begged to differ, insisting that Gallego had been tried and found guilty "by a fair jury of the people" and, moreover, that the verdicts were strictly "in line with the evidence." The prosecutor would go on to say, "I guess the worst part of it all is that everyone keeps hoping that maybe there's a little bit of humanity ... just a little bit of something worth saving. But it hasn't been shown. Not even today. That great macho image hasn't been man enough to acknowledge it."[19]

Gerald Gallego was formally sentenced by District Judge Llewellyn A. Young to death by lethal injection.

***

In July 1997, after serving almost 17 years behind bars, Charlene Adell Williams was released from the Department of Prisons Women's Center in Carson City, Nevada.

In November 1999, the skeletal remains of teenage murder victims Brenda Judd and Sandra Colley were unearthed by a tractor operator near U.S. Highway 395 just north of Reno.

For nearly 2 decades, Gerald Gallego sat on death row in the Nevada State Penitentiary in Carson City and Ely State Prison in White Pine County, Nevada, as he fought his execution through the protracted appeals process. On July 18, 2002, before his death sentence could be carried out, Gallego died of rectal cancer at 56 years of age while being treated at the state prison system's regional medical center.

Neither Gerald Gallego nor Charlene Williams would ever face justice, per se, for the abductions and sex-motivated murders of Rhonda Martin Scheffler, Kippi Vaught, Brenda Judd, Sandra Colley, Virginia Mochel, or Linda Aguilar and her unborn child who met their grisly fate in Oregon, which had no death penalty at the time and deferred prosecution of the suspects to the death-penalty states of California and Nevada. Nevertheless, Charlene's testimony and that of other witnesses, along with ample evidence presented at Gerald Gallego's two trials clearly connected the former couple to their murders.

The Bad Seed Theory

The homicidal similarities between Gerald Armond Gallego and his father, Gerald Albert Gallego, have not gone unnoticed by criminologists, sociologists, and biologists. The notion of a genetic predisposition to commit murder has long been explored. Indeed, the classic 1956 movie *The Bad Seed* presented the theory of passing homicidal tendencies from generation to generation in fictional form, but it was also clearly meant to spur debate.[20]

Most modern-day experts on violent criminal behavior generally dismiss the transmission of deviance through heredity in favor of an environmentally based explanation for violence. This includes learning to become violent through the socialization process, criminal behavior in the family, among social contacts, and the social setting, in association with substance abuse, and other environmental factors.[21]

However, there has been some evidence to show a correlation between biological-based hypotheses and violent and deviant behavior. This is especially true where it concerns twin, adoption, and fosterling studies. Most such approaches tend to take a multidisciplinary view in explaining violence as a reflection of environment, family, society, social class, education, drug use, mental illness, and genetic elements (see Chapter 23).

The Female Partner in Serial Murder

Charlene Williams's role as the lure, or partner, in serial kidnapping and murder is a typical example of the weaker part of a dominant-submissive killer team, as examined in Chapter 15. Being easily susceptible to a strong and violent male partner, Charlene willingly followed Gerald Gallego's lead in perpetrating crimes of violence in hopes of winning his approval as well as out of fear of not measuring up to his ideal woman with the strong attachment she had to him. Substance abuse and domestic violence were also important factors in understanding Charlene's role in the serial murders, as these were other means employed effectively by Gerald Gallego in keeping her tied to him and the sex slave fantasies that would forever bond them.

Cable Television and the Sex Slave Murders

The disturbing tale of Gerald and Charlene Gallego and their sex slave fantasy murders has recently been the subject of cable television crime investigation series exploring serial killers and team killers.

The Biography Channel's *Crime Stories* included an episode called "The Love Slave Murders," based on the bestselling true-crime book *The Sex Slave Murders: The True Story of Serial Killers Gerald and Charlene Gallego*. It was first broadcast on February 1, 2008.[22]

Investigation Discovery's *Wicked Attraction* series episode "Twisted Twosome" debuted on September 11, 2008.[23] The show's airing corresponded with the day in which the Gallegos abducted and murdered their first victims, Rhonda Scheffler and Kippi Vaught, in 1978.

Endotes

1. R. B. Flowers & H. L. Flowers, *Murders in the United States: Crimes, Killers and Victims of the Twentieth Century* (Jefferson: McFarland, 2004), pp. 45–46.
2. R. B. Flowers, *The Sex Slave Murders: The True Story of Serial Killers Gerald and Charlene Gallego*, 2nd ed. (Honolulu: R. Barri Flowers, 2011).
3. *Ibid.*, p. 16.
4. *Ibid.*, p. 32.
5. R. B. Flowers, *Serial Killer Couples: Bonded by Sexual Depravity, Abduction, and Murder* (Honolulu: R. Barri Flowers, 2012).
6. Flowers, *The Sex Slave Murders*.
7. *Ibid.*, p. 182.
8. Biography Channel, *Crime Stories, The Love Slave Murders* (February 1, 2008), http://www.youtube.com/watch?v = J_H20I-9K6E.
9. Flowers, *Serial Killer Couples*.
10. *Crime Stories*.
11. Flowers, *The Sex Slave Murders*.
12. *Ibid.*, p. 184.
13. Flowers, *Serial Killer Couples*.
14. *Ibid.*

15. Flowers, *The Sex Slave Murders*.
16. *Ibid.*, p. 217.
17. *Ibid.*, p. 216.
18. Flowers, *Serial Killer Couples*.
19. *Ibid.*
20. Warner Brothers, *The Bad Seed* (September 12, 1956), http://www.imdb.com/title/tt0048977/.
21. R. B. Flowers, *Male Crime and Deviance: Exploring Its Cause, Dynamics, and Nature* (Springfield: Charles C Thomas, 2003).
22. *Crime Stories*.
23. Investigation Discovery, *Wicked Attraction: Twisted Twosome* (September 11, 2008), http://www.imdb.com/title/tt1277357/.

Sahel Kazemi 19

Sahel Kazemi was a 20-year-old waitress who went from obscurity to the subject of national attention and curiosity when she shot her boyfriend, former NFL star quarterback Steve McNair, multiple times with a 9 mm semi-automatic pistol, fatally wounding him in a condominium in downtown Nashville, Tennessee, on July 4, 2009. Reportedly distraught over money issues and the belief that the married McNair was seeing someone else, Kazemi then turned the gun on herself, completing a murder-suicide. This type of tragedy typically involves a love triangle, jealousy, despair, hopelessness, and desperation. In this case, Kazemi set a course in motion designed to end her life and that of the man she loved and could not bear to see with anyone else.

***

Sahel Kazemi was born in Iran on May 29, 1989. Growing up in Tehran as one of five children, tragedy struck the family when she was 9 years old, when Sahel's mother, Ghodsyeh, was murdered during a home invasion robbery. This had a lasting effect on Sahel. After living in Turkey for 2 years, she relocated to the United States as an Iranian refugee on August 29, 2002.

The 13-year-old spoke no English when she moved to Jacksonville, Florida, to live with her sister Soheyla, who was now her guardian. According to those who knew her, Sahel adjusted with little problem to the American culture and teen lifestyle. She quickly learned to speak English, along with Turkish and Farsi.

However, she had difficulty getting along with other students at school, some of whom bullied her, and moved from one high school to another. After meeting Keith Norfleet, Sahel dropped out of school at age 16 and moved to Nashville, Tennessee, to live with him. The relationship lasted 4 years.

Sahel, known as "Jenni," was working as a waitress at Dave & Buster's restaurant when she met the big-spending, retired quarterback Steve McNair there in December 2008. The two apparently hit it off right away and started to date.

***

Steve McNair was born in Mount Olive, Mississippi, on February 14, 1973. After excelling in multiple sports at Mount Olive High School, particularly football, he went to Alcorn State University—a historically Black

253

university—where he became a star quarterback. As a senior, he finished third in the voting for the Heisman Trophy.

McNair was drafted in 1995 by the Houston Oilers, who had the third pick in the draft. He went on to have a successful career as a quarterback with the team, which eventually became the Tennessee Oilers/Titans. McNair led the team to Super Bowl XXXIV before finishing his career with the Baltimore Ravens in 2008.

He was married to Mechelle McNair and had four children. The 35-year-old McNair was dividing his time between Nashville and a farm he owned in Mississippi when he met the attractive 20-year-old Sahel Kazemi. He quickly became smitten with her.

***

Soon Sahel was living in a downtown Nashville condominium on Second Avenue that she co-rented with McNair. He also put a down payment on a Cadillac Escalade for her to drive, but Sahel reportedly found herself "swallowed up in the massive payments."[1] Yet she was apparently spending less time at work and more time with McNair, with him footing the bill.

In June 2009, Sahel's seeds of jealousy were planted when she caught another female coming out of the condominium. Sahel reportedly followed the woman after she left the condo, convinced that McNair was cheating on her. According to her sister Azadeh, who lived in Australia, Sahel complained that the Britney Spears song "Womanizer" made her think of McNair because that was how she viewed him.[2]

Though she supposedly reciprocated this unfaithfulness by having affairs with other men, Sahel's heart apparently still belonged with Steve McNair. And she was having trouble letting go.

***

Two days before the fatal encounter, Sahel Kazemi was pulled over by police in Nashville while driving the 2007 Cadillac Escalade that was registered in both her and McNair's names. McNair was in the passenger seat and a chef who worked at McNair's restaurant was in the back. Sahel was charged with driving under the influence of alcohol.

McNair, who was not arrested, bailed Sahel out of jail. According to police, it was after her release that she purchased a 9 mm gun for $100 from Adrian Gilliam, Jr., a 33-year-old convicted killer. Sahel fully intended to use the weapon.

***

On July 4, 2009, Wayne Neely and Robert Gaddy, friends of Steve McNair, found the ex-football star and his girlfriend Sahel Kazemi shot dead in their downtown condominium and called 911.

According to the Nashville Police Chief Ronal Serpas, "McNair was seated on the sofa and likely was asleep, and we believe that Kazemi shot him in the right temple, then shot him twice in the chest, and then shot him a final time in the left temple."[3] He went on to say, "Kazemi then positioned herself next to McNair on the sofa and shot herself once in the right temple and expired ... We do believe she tried to stage it so that when she killed herself, she would fall in his lap."[4]

A 9 mm pistol, thought to be the murder-suicide weapon, was found under Sahel's body. Tests would show a trace of gunshot residue was present on her left hand.

From their investigation, authorities reported that Sahel "had become very distraught and on two occasions told friends and associates that her life was all messed up and that she was going to end it all."[5] The evidence indicated "she was spinning out of control" when she decided to take her life and Steve McNair's.

The police conclusion of murder-suicide was supported by the assistant medical examiner working the case, Dr. Feng Li, who reported that all the evidence backed up the belief that Sahel Kazemi "killed Mr. McNair and killed herself ... It's almost an assured thing. We have to be convinced otherwise."[6]

***

Some have questioned the Nashville Police Department's account of the deaths of Steve McNair and Sahel Kazemi. For instance, according to a CBS News investigation, video from the jail upon Sahel's arrest appeared to indicate that she was "in good spirits."[7] Also, a copy obtained of her bank statement on the day she died revealed that Sahel had more than $2,500 in a checking account, which appears to debunk the belief that she was over her head in debt.[8]

"There are a bunch of inconsistencies that would cause me to go back and investigate it further," argued former police detective Wayne Black.[9]

However, the police released text messages between Sahel and McNair the day before the murder-suicide that illustrated her deteriorating mental state and financial struggles. For example, a text message sent from Sahel on Friday, July 3, at 10:05 a.m., read: "Baby I might have a break down im so stressed"; then there was the suggestion that she may have to pay "the cell phone bills in the hospital."[10]

At one point, Sahel asked McNair to transfer $2,000 to her account. A little later she talked about money owed by her, complaining that she "can hardly breath," along with "I just want this pain in my chest to go away."[11] By 4:04 p.m. that day, Sahel, in an apparent desperate attempt to draw McNair to her, texted him, "Baby I have to be w u 2nite. I dnt care where."[12]

"The totality of the evidence clearly points to a murder-suicide," concluded Police Chief Serpas, noting that no evidence was uncovered at the condominium to indicate that anyone else was present at the time the deaths occurred sometime after 1:00 a.m. on Saturday, July 4.[13]

In December 2009, the case was officially closed by the Metropolitan Nashville Police Department as a murder-suicide.[14]

On December 18, 2009, Adrian Gilliam, Jr., was sentenced to two-and-a-half years behind bars after pleading guilty to selling to Sahel Kazemi the gun used to kill Steve McNair and herself.[15]

Murder-Suicide in the United States

How often does murder-suicide occur in the United States? Although there are no national statistics on murder-suicides (where an individual murders one or more people before killing oneself), it is estimated that between 1,000 and 2,000 such combination deaths take place in this country annually.[16] The majority of murder-suicide deaths tend to involve spouses, significant others, or past romantic partners.[17] (See also Chapter 4.)

Males are far more likely to be the perpetrators of domestic murder-suicides than females.[18] In more than 9 out of 10 such incidents, a firearm is used to perpetrate the murder and suicide.[19]

Motivating factors on murder-suicides include depression, which is often severe, financial problems, jealousy, revenge, relationship breakup, illness, hopelessness, and other issues in which the despondent killer plots and carries out this crime of passion and murder (see also Chapter 17).

Endnotes

1. E. Merrill, The Woman Forever Tied to Steve McNair, *ESPN.com* (July 4, 2010), http://sports.espn.go.com/espn/otl/news/story?id = 5347315.
2. *Ibid.*
3. Quoted in W. Drash, Police Call McNair Killing a Murder-Suicide, *CNN Justice* (July 8, 2009), http://articles.cnn.com/2009-07-08/justice/mcnair.shooting_1_steve-mcnair-sahel-kazemi-police-chief-ronal-serpas?_s = PM:CRIME.
4. *Ibid.*
5. *Ibid.*
6. *Ibid.*
7. S. R. Saltzman, Exclusive: Was Steve McNair Murder Investigation Flawed? Was Lover Really Suicidal? *CBS News* (October 19, 2009), http://www.cbsnews.com/8301-504083_162-5390156-504083.html?tag=contentMain%3bcontentBody.
8. *Ibid.*
9. Quoted in *Ibid.*

10. S. R. Saltzman, Sahel Kazemi and Steve McNair Final Texts Show Worries of Love and Money, *CBS News* (October 20, 2009), http://www.cbsnews.com/8301-504083_162-5400986-504083.html?tag=contentMain%3bcontentBody.
11. *Ibid.*
12. *Ibid.*
13. Drash, Police Call McNair Killing a Murder-Suicide.
14. Police Close McNair Case After Nearly Six Mos., WKRN-TV Nashville (December 18, 2009), http://www.wkrn.com/global/story.asp?s=11700859.
15. Felon Sentenced to 2 1/2 Years in McNair Gun Case, WKRN-TV Nashville (December 18, 2009), http://www.wkrn.com/global/Story.asp?s=11699594.
16. Violence Policy Center, *American Roulette: The Untold Story of Murder-Suicide in the United States*, www.vpc.org/studies/amroul2006.pdf (May 2, 2012).
17. Wikipedia, the Free Encyclopedia, Murder-Suicide, http://en.wikipedia.org/wiki/Murder-suicide#cite_note-3 (May 2, 2012); R. B. Flowers, *Domestic Crimes, Family Violence and Child Abuse: A Study of Contemporary American Society* (Jefferson: McFarland, 2000).
18. *Ibid.*; Murder-Suicide; R. B. Flowers, *Male Crime and Deviance: Exploring Its Causes, Dynamics and Nature* (Springfield: Charles C Thomas, 2003); K. van Wormer & A. R. Roberts, *Death by Domestic Violence: Preventing the Murders and Murder-Suicides* (Westport: Praeger, 2009).
19. Murder-Suicide.

Byran Koji Uyesugi

20

Byran Koji Uyesugi had been employed by Xerox for 15 years when he suddenly went on a shooting rampage in Honolulu, Hawaii, on November 2, 1999. Entering the Xerox Corporation building a little after 8:00 a.m., armed with a 9mm Glock semi-automatic pistol, the 40-year-old disgruntled Xerox copier repairman opened fire. He killed seven people, including his supervisor, attempted to kill another, and escaped briefly before he was taken into custody.[1] It was the worst case of mass murder in Hawaii's history, shattering the façade of paradise on the islands. The shooting is also indicative of the threat that is posed in the workplace by dissatisfied employees and/or customers who have access to firearms and the willingness to use them to act upon their grievances in a dramatic and lethal way (see also Chapters 8 and 16).

***

Byran Koji Uyesugi was born in Honolulu, Hawaii. He grew up in the Nuuanu section of the city and attended President Theodore Roosevelt High School. Uyesugi was a member of the school's Army Junior Reserve Officers' Training Corps and had a fascination with guns. He also joined the rifle team at school.

By most accounts, Uyesugi was a quiet, aloof individual who stayed out of trouble. In 1977, while driving his father's car home from a high school graduation party, he was in a car accident and hit his head on the windshield. His brother Dennis stated that Byran was a different person from that point on.

Byran Uyesugi started working as a technician for Xerox in 1984. His hobbies included "raising and breeding goldfish and koi, which he would sell to local pet stores," along with amassing firearms.[2] He eventually would own dozens of guns, most of which were registered in his name.

According to his father, Hiro Uyesugi, Byran had anger management issues. In 1988, Byran Uyesugi told people that "he had a poking sensation in his head."[3] Troubles on the job appeared to start when he was transferred to a different work group and "began making unfounded accusations of harassment and product tampering against fellow repairmen, who had great difficulty placating his anger."[4] This led some co-workers on his team to reportedly ostracize him, causing Uyesugi to feel "isolated and withdrawn."[5]

Uyesugi's hot temper was said to have led to his threatening the lives of some co-workers. In 1993, he was arrested for damaging an elevator door and charged with third degree criminal property damage. He was ordered to submit to a psychiatric evaluation and take classes in anger management.

According to co-workers, a few years before the shooting spree, Uyesugi spoke brazenly about retaliating through mass murder should he ever be terminated.

***

During the latter part of 1999, management personnel at the Xerox Engineering Systems office planned to phase out the type of photocopier that Uyesugi worked on. He reportedly was reluctant to learn how to service the new copier for fear of being unable to handle its technical aspects. But on November 1, 1999, his manager ordered him to begin training on the photocopier the following day.

On November 2, Byran Uyesugi showed up at work with a 9 mm handgun, along with ammunition. After going up to the second floor, he opened fire, killing two fellow employees. Moving to a conference room where a meeting was in progress, Uyesugi continued his deadly assault, taking several more lives.

The dead were identified as Christopher "Jason" Balatico, 33; Ford Kanehira, 41; Ronald Kataoka, 50; Ronald Kawamae, 54; Melvin Lee, 58; Peter Mark, 46; and John Sakamoto, 36.[6]

According to witnesses, the shooter was smiling and "waved goodbye" as he fatally wounded his co-workers before he fled and drove off in a green company van.[7]

***

Now the hunted rather than the hunter, Byran Uyesugi was able to evade the police for a couple of hours following the mass killing before a jogger came upon him inside the van in the posh Makiki Heights neighborhood of Honolulu and called the police.

The area was quickly cordoned off, and authorities moved in on a killer who was obviously armed and very dangerous.

After a police standoff with the suspect for several hours and the pleas of Uyesugi's brother Dennis to give up peacefully, Uyesugi finally surrendered to authorities at around 3:00 p.m. with no further loss of life.

***

On May 15, 2000, Byran Uyesugi went on trial for first degree murder in the deaths of seven people. He pleaded not guilty by reason of insanity, asserting that he was treated like an outcast by his fellow employees and believed they were trying to get him fired. Forensic psychiatrists Dr. Park Dietz and

Dr. Daryl Matthews testified as defense witnesses that Uyesugi was insane, referring to him as delusional regarding "how others were tampering with his fish."[8]

Testifying for the prosecution, Dr. Michael Welner said that while he believed the defendant was schizophrenic, Uyesugi perpetrated the mass murder due to anger in believing he "would be fired for insubordination, and that his own account of concealment before the crime demonstrated that he knew what he had done was wrong."[9]

On June 13, 2000, Byran Uyesugi was judged to be sane and found guilty in the murders of seven of his colleagues, along with one attempted murder. He was sentenced to life in prison with no possibility of parole and ordered to pay the families of his murdered victims $70,000 in restitution.

Uyesugi appealed his conviction and it was upheld by the State of Hawaii Supreme Court in 2002.

In 2005, a lawsuit was settled by the hospital that had examined Uyesugi and Xerox Corporation. The lawsuit had been filed by the family members of the victims of Uyesugi's onslaught, as they believed both the hospital and company had ignored warning signs that indicated the mass killer's mental instability.[10]

***

The shooting rampage by Byran Uyesugi led to a new Hawaii law requiring doctors to disclose information concerning the mental state of those seeking to purchase guns.[11]

Following the mass shooting, Xerox Corporation moved out of the facility on 1200 North Nimitz Highway. It remained empty until 2004, when it was used by the producers of the hit televisions series *Lost* as a sound stage to shoot indoor scenes.[12]

Mass Murder in the Workplace

Workplace killings and mass murder, such as perpetrated by Byran Uyesugi, have become all too common in society, with many of the same dynamics from crime scene tragedy to killer motivation to victimization (see also Chapter 8). These types of mass shootings are often perpetrated by disgruntled current or former employees bent on retaliation. The victims, however, are in many cases randomly targeted by the angry, unbalanced killer on a mission to take as many lives as he or she can to gain some warped sense of fulfillment.

According to psychiatrist Paul Miller, most mass murders fall into two categories: killers motivated primarily by committing suicide and those who wish to punish others for perceived wrongs against them.[13] In a study of mass murders occurring in the United States between 1900 and 1999, 47 percent of the killers took their own lives. This compares to fewer than 5 percent of murderers on the whole.[14]

Revenge is perhaps the most common motivating factor in workplace mass killings. According to criminologist Jack Levin, apart from revenge aimed at members of a mass killer's family, which accounts for around one-third of all mass murders, "the next most likely target is the workplace, where an ex-worker who was fired or laid off comes back shooting, killing the boss and coworkers."[15]

Other common characteristics of mass murderers include being a loner with limited social interaction and placing the blame on other people for his or her troubles. Mass killers are also more likely than other killers to suffer from mental illness than other killers, particularly paranoid schizophrenia.[16]

Most mass killers plan their deadly assaults carefully and may take anywhere from days to months to prepare and carry out the mass killing.[17]

In virtually every instance of mass murder in the workplace, the offenders are heavily armed in order to have the most lethal means for a successful mass attack. Handguns are often the weapon of choice for mass killers, but many killers come equipped with powerful firearms to perpetrate their crimes.[18] Studies reveal that for most cases of mass murder, the weapons used by the killers were legally purchased rather than banned firearms such as assault weapons.[19]

Whether suicidal or not, mass murderers can often be unpredictable in their actions and the outcome as it pertains to fleeing, surrendering, or committing suicide. This is often dependent upon the particular situation and response to their mass killing. "Most of these guys don't plan an exit strategy," noted Eric Hickey, director of forensic studies at San Diego–based Alliant International University and expert on mass murder. "If they get caught, it's not by design—it's more that they've vented and they're just out of ammo, and so they sit down and say come and get me."[20]

Endnotes

1. R. B. Flowers & H. L. Flowers, *Murders in the United States: Crimes, Killers and Victims of the Twentieth Century* (Jefferson: McFarland, 2004), p. 83.
2. Wikipedia, the Free Encyclopedia, Xerox Murders, http://en.wikipedia.org/wiki/Byran_Uyesugi (May 4, 2012).
3. *Ibid.*
4. *Ibid.*
5. *Ibid.*
6. Flowers & Flowers, *Murders in the United States*; J. K. Song, 7 Dead in Nimitz Hwy. Xerox Shooting, StarBulletin.com (November 2, 1999), http://archives.starbulletin.com/1999/11/02/news/story1.html.

7. R. Bell, "The Xerox Murders," TruTV Crime Library, http://www.trutv.com/library/crime/notorious_murders/mass/work_homicide/5.html (May 4, 2012).

8. "Xerox Murders."

9. *Ibid.* See also S. Tswei, Judge's Leave to Delay Trial for One Week, StarBulletin.com (June 2, 2000), http://archives.starbulletin.com/2000/06/02/news/story2.html.

10. "Xerox Murders."

11. *Ibid.*

12. *Ibid.*

13. Cited in B. Harkness, "Portraying a Mass Killer," http://www.mnash.edu.au/pubs/montage/Montage_97_02/killer.html.

14. M. Roth, Experts Track the Patterns of Mass Murders, *Pittsburgh Post-Gazette* (March 15, 2012), http://www.post-gazette.com/stories/local/neighborhoods-city/experts-track-the-patterns-of-mass-murders-337604/.

15. *Ibid.*

16. *Ibid.*

17. *Ibid.*

18. T. A. Petee, Situational Factors Related to Public Mass Murder Incidents: 1965–1998, in U.S. Department of Justice, *Proceedings of the Homicide Research Working Group Meetings*, 1997 and 1998 (Washington: National Institute of Justice, 1999), p. 154.

19. *Ibid.*, p. 155.

20. Roth, Experts Track the Patterns of Mass Murders.

Charles Stuart 21

Charles Stuart did the unthinkable on October 23, 1989, when he fatally shot his pregnant 30-year-old wife, Carol Stuart, in the head while the couple sat in their car in the Mission Hill district of Boston, Massachusetts.[1] The 30-year-old Stuart then shot himself in the abdomen and used his car phone to call 911, falsely reporting that he and his wife, who was 7 months pregnant, had just been the victims of a carjacking with the perpetrator described as a "raspy-voiced" African American man wearing a jogging suit. Stuart and his wife were both White, so the accusation caused a nationwide manhunt for the suspect that divided the country along racial lines.

Once the truth was uncovered, authorities closed in on the real killer, Charles Stuart. He was apparently involved with another woman and concerned about starting a family, as well as motivated by an insurance payout. However, he committed suicide before he could be arrested, by jumping off the Tobin Bridge and into the Mystic River in Massachusetts. His child, Christopher, who was born 2 months premature shortly after the death of Stuart's wife, died earlier from complications related to the shooting of Carol Stuart. Charles Stuart's brother Matthew Stuart was sent to prison for helping him to cover up the crime.

The case is a sad example of how playing the race card can easily ignite racial tensions, while leading the authorities awry as the killer sought, but failed, to commit the perfect crime.

***

Charles "Chuck" Stuart, Jr., was born in Boston, Massachusetts, on December 18, 1959. On October 23, 1989, he was making $100,000 a year as the general manager for Edward F. Kakas & Sons' furs on Newbury Street. His wife, Carol DiMaiti Stuart, was born on March 26, 1959, in Boston. She was a tax attorney and 7 months pregnant with the young couple's first child.

That Monday night, the Stuarts were driving home through the Roxbury section of Boston after attending a birthing class at Brigham and Women's Hospital when they were allegedly the victims of a violent carjacking. The perpetrator, described as a raspy-voiced Black man, forced his way into the couple's car while at a stoplight and made them drive to Mission Hill, a nearby neighborhood. It was there that the alleged gunman then shot Charles Stuart in the stomach and his wife Carol in the head, before fleeing. A wounded Charles then claimed to have driven off and phoned 911 on a car phone.

***

As Carol Stuart lay gravely wounded in the hospital, her baby boy was delivered by Cesarean section 2 months prematurely and was named Christopher. Shortly thereafter, at around 3:00 a.m., Carol died from her injuries. Her son, who was baptized in the neonatal intensive care unit at Brigham and Women's Hospital, died 17 days later after suffering trauma and oxygen deprivation as a result of Carol's shooting.

On Saturday, October 28, 1989, while Charles Stuart remained hospitalized recuperating from his injuries, funeral services were held for his wife, drawing hundreds of mourners to the church, including Governor Michael Dukakis, Boston's Mayor Raymond Flynn, the Police Commissioner Francis Roache, and Cardinal Bernard F. Law.

A message from Charles was read aloud: "Good night sweet wife, my love. God has called you to his hands. Not to take you away from me, but to bring you away from the cruelty and the violence that fills this world."[2]

On November 20, 1989, the family held a private funeral service for Christopher Stuart.

The senseless shooting that destroyed a family left the city on edge and touched nerves as race relations weakened and racial stereotypes floated to the surface.

***

As the investigation proceeded into the murder mystery, authorities briefly considered the possibility that the injuries suffered by Charles Stuart may have been self-inflicted. This angle was more or less dismissed. The general consensus was that the severity of Stuart's wounds were such that it was highly improbable he would have shot himself to try to make it look like someone else had done it.

Consequently, the police focused their efforts on trying to locate the African American mugger that Charles had described as the assailant, interviewing thousands of possible suspects. Their search focused mainly on the predominantly Black housing projects of Mission Hill. Many there accused the police of "indiscriminately harassing Black men."[3]

Though African Americans believed they were being unfairly singled out with no solid evidence to back Charles Stuart's story, it resonated with many "suburban Whites, reinforc[ing] perceptions that the inner city had become a savage and dangerous place."[4] Whereas "for Blacks and others who live in neighborhoods where crime is an everyday occurrence often ignored by the public and media, the unprecedented manhunt for the killer of an affluent woman lawyer only added to long-festering bitterness in a metropolitan area that has long been troubled by racial divisiveness."[5]

The police brought in Willie Bennett, a 39-year-old African American with a criminal record, on suspicion of being the culprit in this deadly carjacking. Bennett immediately claimed he was being framed, but few outside his family and neighborhood believed him.

When Charles Stuart picked Bennett out of a police lineup on December 28, 1989, and claimed he was the man responsible for the attack, it became more or less a foregone conclusion by many that Willie Bennett was guilty of this violent crime.

They were wrong.

***

On January 3, 1990, the case against Willie Bennett took a dramatic turn when Charles Stuart's 23-year-old brother, Matthew Stuart, fingered Charles as the actual shooter and admitted to helping him cover up the murder. According to Matthew, he had "driven to meet Stuart that night to help him commit what he'd been told was to be an insurance fraud."[6] When he arrived, Matthew claimed that "Carol had been shot, and his brother had shot himself to make it appear as a carjacking."[7]

Matthew admitted to taking "the gun and a bag of valuables, including the couple's wedding rings, and [throwing] them off the Pines River Bridge in Revere," a city in Suffolk County about 5 miles from Boston. Authorities recovered the items.[8]

Digging further into Charles Stuart's background for possible motives, the police discovered that he was unhappy that his wife was pregnant and feared that she might want to be a stay-at-home mother, causing them to lose her income. Charles was also reportedly involved in a relationship with a fellow employee of Kakas & Sons named Deborah Allen, though she denied it.

As with many cases of uxoricide, when a wife is murdered by her husband, a financial motive is often present. In this crime, authorities learned that Charles Stuart was the beneficiary of insurance policies on his wife totaling several hundred thousand dollars.[9] The couple's joint estate was valued at more than half a million dollars, including a home they owned in Reading, an affluent suburb in Middlesex County, Massachusetts.

Equipped with new information, Suffolk County District Attorney Newman Flanagan revealed to the stunned residents of Boston along with the nation, who had been riveted by the case, that the "entire drama had been an elaborate ruse on the part of Stuart."[10]

The police immediately issued an arrest warrant for Charles Stuart for the murders of Carol and Christopher Stuart.

***

On January 4, 1990, shortly after Charles Stuart confessed to his attorney about the horrible crime and before an arrest could be made, Charles took his life by jumping off the Tobin Bridge in Chelsea, Massachusetts, into the Mystic River's chilly waters some 145 feet below. His car was found abandoned on the bridge along with a driver's license and note that indicated he was distraught over the allegations about him that had surfaced.

Charles Stuart's body was recovered from Boston Harbor the following day.

Authorities discovered that the revolver used to commit the crime had been taken from an unlocked cabinet at Charles Stuart's employer, Edward F. Kakas & Sons, after he had apparently been unable to get a gun anywhere else.

Investigators would also learn that Charles had talked about wanting to murder his wife previously and that his other siblings apparently were also aware of the murder plot that had been carried out.

***

In September 1991, Matthew Stuart was indicted by a grand jury on charges of "conspiracy to obstruct justice and compounding a felony," along with insurance fraud, for participating with his brother Charles in the cover-up of Carol Stuart's murder.[11]

In November 1992, Matthew pleaded guilty to fraud, possession of a firearm, and additional charges, and was sentenced to 3 to 5 years behind bars.[12] After he was released on probation in 1997, he was rearrested for trafficking in cocaine and returned to prison for violating probation. The charges were eventually dropped for insufficient evidence.

On September 3, 2011, Matthew Stuart was found dead at a Cambridge homeless shelter, apparently the victim of a drug overdose.[13]

***

In October 1992, Carol DiMaiti Stuart's family filed a wrongful death lawsuit against Edward F. Kakas & Sons, former employer of Charles Stuart, claiming that the Back Bay furrier "carelessly stored a revolver allegedly used by Charles Stuart to kill his pregnant wife and unborn son."[14] In December 1996, a Superior Court dismissed the case.[15]

On January 25, 1990, the Carol DiMaiti Stuart Foundation was established by Carol Stuart's family, providing scholarships to residents of Mission Hill. As of 2010, nearly $1.4 million had been awarded to 230 students by the foundation. According to Marvin Gellar, the attorney for the DiMaitis, "Carol would not want to be remembered as the victim of a sensational murder, but rather as a woman who left behind a legacy of healing and compassion."[16]

The Carol Stuart Tragedy and Television Interest

The elements of uxoricide, infanticide, racism, family cover-up, and a rush to judgment made the murder of Carol Stuart and her newborn child by Charles Stuart an almost-made-for-television drama, inspiring a slew of projects for the small screen.

In the 1990 movie on CBS *Good Night Sweet Wife: A Murder in Boston,* Ken Olin played Charles Stuart;[17] the *Law & Order* franchise aired episodes called "Happily Ever After" and "Tangled" that were apparently based on the Carol Stuart murder.[18] The case also was profiled in the documentary series *City Confidential* on A&E in the episode "Boston: Betrayal in Beantown."[19]

Spouse Homicide

The murder of one's spouse is endemic of the broader issue of domestic violence in society (see Chapter 4). Spouse murders are typically fueled by anger, jealousy, infidelity, love triangles, financial problems, insurance payouts, substance abuse, and mental illness. In many instances, the perpetrator kills him- or herself and/or innocent bystanders, such as other family members or people in the community or workplace.

Men are much more likely to be the perpetrator of spouse homicide than the victim. According to the FBI, between 2005 and 2010, there were an average of 587 murders of wives compared with 128 murders of husbands in the United States.[20] Spouse homicides account for one-tenth of all murders committed in this country, as reported by the U.S. Department of Justice.[21]

Approximately 1 in 5 victims of murder are killed by an intimate, with around 50 percent of all intimate homicides committed by spouses in the United States.[22] Women are especially at risk to be murdered by an intimate compared with men. Between 1980 and 2008, about 40 percent of female victims of murder in the nation were killed by an intimate partner.[23] In 1980, around 10 percent of male murder victims were killed by an intimate. By 2008, fewer than 5 percent of total male homicide victims were murdered by intimates.[24]

Guns are used more than any other weapon in intimate homicides. According to the Bureau of Justice Statistics, from 1980 to 2008, two-thirds of wives were murdered by their husbands with a gun and three-quarters of ex-wives were killed by ex-husbands with a firearm.[25] In comparison, two-thirds of husbands and more than 8 in 10 ex-husbands were the victims of guns in intimate homicides.[26]

Similar to other types of killers, spouse murderers often have precursors to their fatal violence, such as spouse abuse, drug abuse, family dysfunction, sexual or health issues, and concerns about money that can lead to a deadly outcome when not identified or acted upon earlier.

Endnotes

1. R. B. Flowers & H. L. Flowers, *Murders in the United States: Crimes, Killers and Victims of the Twentieth Century* (Jefferson: McFarland, 2004), pp. 50–51, 76–78.
2. Boston Mourns Pregnant Woman Killed by Robber, *United Press International* (October 29, 1989), http://articles.latimes.com/1989-10-29/news/mn-501_1_boston-police.
3. K. Tumulty & D. Treadwell, Suicide of Man Whose Wife Was Slain Stuns Boston, *Los Angeles Times* (January 5, 1990), http://articles.latimes.com/1990-01-05/news/mn-204_1_charles-stuart.
4. *Ibid.*
5. *Ibid.*
6. Wikipedia, the Free Encyclopedia, Charles Stuart (Murderer), http://en.wikipedia.org/wiki/Charles_Stuart_(murderer) (May 7, 2012).
7. *Ibid.*; Flowers & Flowers, *Murders in the United States.*
8. Charles Stuart (Murderer).
9. *Ibid.*; E. Mehren, Civil Suit Is Filed in Boston Murder Case: Courts: Carol Stuart's Family Wants to Bar Her Husband's Heirs From Inheriting Any of Her Estate. They Claim 'Public Policy' Prevents Profiting From Her Death, *Los Angeles Times* (January 10, 1991), http://articles.latimes.com/1991-01-10/news/vw-11239_1_carol-stuart.
10. Tumulty & Treadwell, Suicide of Man Whose Wife Was Slain Stuns Boston.
11. "Nation in Brief: Massachusetts: Brother Charged in Stuart Slaying, *Los Angeles Times* (September 27, 1991), http://articles.latimes.com/1991-09-27/news/mn-2919_1_charles-stuart.
12. C. B. Daly, Young Stuart Pleads Guilty to Fraud; Alleged Wife Killer's Brother Gets 3 to 5, *Washington Post* (November 3, 1992), http://www.highbeam.com/doc/1P2-1033002.html.
13. Mass. Man Convicted of Aiding In-Law Killing Dies, *Seattle Times* (September 4, 2011), http://seattletimes.nwsource.com/html/nationworld/2016108848_apusstuartbrotherdeath.html.
14. D. S. Wong, Kakas Furs Is Sued Over Gun in Stuart Slaying, *Boston Globe* (October 22, 1992), http://www.highbeam.com/doc/1P2-8764877.html.
15. The Free Library, DiMaiti Family Files Appeal, http://www.thefreelibrary.com/DiMaiti+family+files+appeal.-a018949219 (May 7, 2012).
16. Charles Stuart (Murderer); Devoted Husband or Sick Psychopath, *Dark Deeds* (February 11, 2012), http://darkdeeds.susanfleet.com/blog_1.php?tag = carol+dimaiti.
17. Arnold Shapiro Productions, *Goodnight Sweet Wife: A Murder in Boston* (September 25, 1990), http://www.imdb.com/title/tt0099684/.
18. Charles Stuart (Murderer).
19. *Ibid.*

20. U.S. Department of Justice, Federal Bureau of Investigation, *Crime in the United States: Uniform Crime Reports 2010*, Expanded Homicide Data, http://www.fbi.gov/about-us/cjis/ucr/crime-in-the-u.s/2010/crime-in-the-u.s.-2010/offenses-known-to-law-enforcement/expanded/expandhomicidemain (May 7, 2012).
21. U.S. Department of Justice, Office of Justice Programs, *Homicide Trends in the United States, 1980–2010* (Washington: Bureau of Justice Statistics, 2011) p. 16.
22. *Ibid.*, pp. 18–19.
23. *Ibid.*, p. 18.
24. *Ibid.*
25. *Ibid.*, p. 20.
26. *Ibid.*

Sarah Marie Johnson

22

Sarah Marie Johnson was 16 years old when, according to police, she used a Winchester rifle to shoot to death her parents, Alan Scott Johnson and Diane Johnson, on September 2, 2003, at their home in Bellevue, Idaho. The murders came after a heated confrontation about an older man Sarah was involved with. As with similar cases of teen familicide (killing of family), parricide (killing of father or mother), patricide (killing of father), and matricide (killing of mother) across the country, this one was no less shocking for both its brutality and attempt to make sense of for those who knew the family. Alas, many such violent youth crimes make sense only to the perpetrator, whose rage and desperation at the time tend to overshadow the short- and long-term implications of her or his actions.

***

By most accounts, in the summer of 2003, Alan Johnson, 46, and his wife of 20 years, Diane, 52, had a good life together. They had two loving children Matt, 22, and Sarah Marie, 16. The Johnsons had a nice home in Bellevue, Idaho, in Blaine County's Wood River Valley, just south of the resort city of Sun Valley. Alan co-owned a landscaping business and Diane was employed by a medical clinic.

But their storybook life ended violently when Alan and Diane Johnson were shot to death in their home just after Labor Day on September 2, 2003. Diane was shot in the head while she lay sleeping in bed. Then Alan was shot in the chest above his heart while he was taking a shower.

Authorities initially turned their attention to the Johnson's 16-year-old daughter, Sarah, as a suspect in their murder after learning that she was romantically involved with 19-year-old Bruno Santos, an illegal immigrant from Mexico. Bruno was a high school dropout and lived on the poor side of town.

The relationship between Sarah and Bruno became a source of contention in the Johnson household, and even among some of Sarah's friends. According to one friend, "I felt she could do a lot better. He was a high school dropout and was selling drugs and she was from a nice family. It just didn't seem like it was right."[1]

The stress and strain over this unwelcome romance threatened to boil over on Saturday of Labor Day weekend, when Alan and Diane learned that

Sarah was staying over at Bruno's place. After going to his apartment to get her, Alan warned Bruno not to see Sarah anymore or he would have him charged with having sexual relations with a minor.

The following Tuesday morning, Alan and Diane Johnson were found murdered.

***

According to Blaine County Sheriff Walt Femling, the crime scene was the worst he could remember ever seeing, noting, "There was blood and hair on the carpet. It was on the ceiling. It was on all the walls. There was part of a skull cap in the hallway."[2]

The police went into full investigation mode, blocking off the street and searching a garbage truck that had just picked up trash from the house. In it was a treasure trove of DNA evidence on "a bloody bathrobe, a left-handed leather glove and a right-handed latex glove."[3]

Though the number one suspect at the time was Bruno Santos, it was Sarah who insisted that it was an intruder who had murdered her parents, in spite of the fact that there was no evidence to indicate someone had broken into the house.

When the forensic evidence failed to match Bruno's DNA, the focus turned toward Sarah, who had apparently changed her story repeatedly during police interrogation and appeared to those who knew her to be less than convincing in her sorrow and more interested in keeping "hair and nail appointments."[4]

Investigators got the "smoking gun" they were looking for after the state lab found Sarah's DNA inside the latex glove. Also, the leather glove had gunshot residue on it and police found the matching glove in Sarah's bedroom.

Upon failing to get a confession from her, Sarah Johnson, a junior in high school, was arrested and charged with two counts of first degree murder.

***

Sarah Johnson's trial began in November 2005. Though the lead prosecutor, Jim Thomas, was confident the forensic evidence was powerful enough to get a conviction, his concern was being able to convince the jury "that a bright, athletic high school girl suddenly became a killer."[5]

Sarah's defense attorney, Robert Pangburn, had a strategy to focus on the lack of blood on the defendant at the time of the killing. He argued, "Her mother's head literally exploded in a spherical fashion. The gun itself had blood on it. Yet there was none on her. Absolutely none."[6] The clear implication was that Sarah was not the person who fired the shots into her parents.

The trial lasted 5 weeks before going to an Ada County, Idaho, jury. On March 16, 2005, they came back with a verdict of guilty on two counts of murder in the first degree in the deaths of Diane and Alan Johnson. Sarah

Johnson received a sentence of two concurrent life terms, along with 15 years for the use of a firearm to murder her parents. She was given no possibility of parole.[7]

The conviction was upheld by the Idaho Supreme Court.[8]

As of May 2012, Sarah Johnson was seeking a new trial with the help of Idaho Innocence Project.[9]

Interest in the Sarah Marie Johnson Case

The tragedy of Alan and Diane Johnson's deaths and the conviction of their daughter as the killer has sparked public outrage and fascination, resulting in a number of crime investigation television shows and documentaries on the case. These include episodes of such popular crime series as ABC's *Primetime Crime*, Investigation Discovery's *Deadly Women* and *Solved*, Oxygen's *Snapped*, and TruTv's *Forensic Files*.[10] The tale also ranked number nine in the E! documentary *Too Young to Kill: 15 Shocking Crimes*.[11]

When Teens Kill

The relationship between youth and homicide has been well documented and has been proven to be a serious problem in American society.[12] How many murders are committed by teenagers? According to the FBI's Uniform Crime Reports, in 2010 there were 1,901 arrests of people between the ages 13 and 19 for murder and nonnegligent manslaughter in the United States.[13] In the FBI's Expanded Homicide Data, there were 2,012 murder offenders ages 13 to 19 in 2010.[14]

Male teens are much more likely to commit murder than female teens. However, in 172 murders during 2010 the perpetrator was a female between the ages of 13 and 19.[15] Though the FBI data does not break down murder circumstances by age of the offender, in 242 murders in 2010, the victim was a mother or father of the killer.[16] Undoubtedly the offender was a teenager in some of these cases, as was true in 2003 with the murder conviction of Sarah Marie Johnson.

Teens who commit murder often do so as a response to authority, pressure, romance, rejection, early introduction to violence, hyperactivity, opportunity, child physical or sexual abuse, substance abuse, mental illness, school problems, bullying, gang involvement, and accessibility of firearms.[17] Often a combination of such reasons are in play for violent youth. Moreover, for many contemporary teen killers there appears to be a disconnect from right and wrong, value of human life, and consequences for perpetrating acts of violence (see also Section IV).

Studies have indicated that a teenager's brain goes through various stages during adolescence "that may make them more susceptible to dangerous, impetuous behavior or lack of control over their violent actions."[18] This notwithstanding, most criminologists believe that such factors of homicidal behavior as premeditation, free will, use of guns, and the ability to understand right and wrong on other levels lessens the impact of violent youthful behavior due to inadequate control mechanisms.

Endnotes

1. E. R. Grodd & J. L. Diamond, Primetime Crime: Teen Charged With Parents' Gruesome Murder, *ABC Primetime* (August 13, 2008), http://abcnews.go.com/TheLaw/story?id = 3451371&page = 1.
2. *Ibid.*
3. *Ibid.*
4. *Ibid.*
5. *Ibid.*
6. *Ibid.*
7. T. Smith, Attorney Seeks to Reopen Johnson Case, *Idaho Mountain Express*, http://mtexpress.com/story_printer.php?ID = 2005141831 (May 3, 2012).
8. *Idaho v. Johnson*, Opinion 89, Idaho Supreme Court (June 26, 2008).
9. Associated Press, Woman Convicted of Parents' Murder Wants New Trial, *KTVB.com* (May 2, 2012), http://www.ktvb.com/home/Woman-convicted-of-parents-murder-wants-new-trial-149859845.html.
10. Wikipedia, the Free Encyclopedia, Murder of Diane and Alan Scott Johnson, http://en.wikipedia.org/wiki/Sarah_Marie_Johnson (May 3, 2012).
11. *Ibid.*; E! Entertainment Television, *Too Young to Kill: 15 Shocking Crimes* (January 10, 2010), http://www.imdb.com/title/tt1686119/.
12. R. B. Flowers, *Kids Who Commit Adult Crimes: A Study of Serious Juvenile Criminality and Delinquency* (Binghamton: Haworth, 2002); M. R. Chaiken, *Violent Neighborhoods, Violent Kids* (Washington: Office of Juvenile Justice and Delinquency Prevention, 2000); C. A. Davis, *Children Who Kill: Profiles of Pre-Teen and Teenage Killers* (London: Allison & Busby, 2003); K. Kelly & M. D. Totten, *When Children Kill: A Social-Psychological Study of Youth Homicide* (Toronto: University of Toronto Press, 2002).
13. U.S. Department of Justice, Federal Bureau of Investigation, *Crime in the United States: Uniform Crime Reports 2010*, Table 38, Arrests by Age, 2010, http://www.fbi.gov/about-us/cjis/ucr/crime-in-the-u.s/2010/crime-in-the-u.s.-2010/tables/10tbl38.xls (May 3, 2012).
14. *Ibid.*; Expanded Homicide Data, Table 3, Murder Offenders by Age, Sex, and Race, 2010, http://www.fbi.gov/about-us/cjis/ucr/crime-in-the-u.s/2010/crime-in-the-u.s.-2010/tables/10shrtbl03.xls (May 3, 2012).
15. *Ibid.*
16. *Ibid.*; Expanded Homicide Data, Table 10, Murder Circumstances by Relationship, 2010, http://www.fbi.gov/about-us/cjis/ucr/crime-in-the-u.s/2010/crime-in-the-u.s.-2010/tables/10shrtbl10.xls (May 3, 2012).

17. Flowers, *Kids Who Commit Adult Crimes*.

18. R. B. Flowers, Should Violent Juvenile Offenders Be Tried and Sentenced as Adults? in R. B. Flowers, ed., *Issues: Enduring Question*, ABC-CLIO Solutions Database, 2010, http://www.abc-clio.com/product.aspx?id = 2147483704.

Explanations
for Murder

VII

Criminal Homicide Theories

23

Theories on criminal homicide and other violent behavior can generally be broken down into three categories: (1) a belief in free will or the conscious and voluntary choice of behavior; (2) a deterministic view of violence, or the notion that such behavior is the result of biological, psychological, and sociological factors independent of free will; and (3) a critical approach to criminality, which is less concerned with explaining crime and violence, per se, and more with how society interprets criminal behavior.

Although there is strong individual support over the notion of free will in explaining deviant behavior, modern criminology has, for the most part, moved away from this school of thought, preferring instead to focus primarily on biological, psychological, and sociocultural determinants of homicidal and violent behavior. Critical criminology is less relied upon in terms of explaining violent criminality, though is somewhat more effective in understanding social policy and the criminal justice system in relation to crime.

Classical Theories of Criminality

The origins of the classical criminology school of thought are commonly believed to be the writings of Cesare Beccaria in the 18th century. In his 1764 essay *On Crimes and Punishment*, Beccaria advanced that "people were by nature, inherently rational (capable of logical thought), intelligent (capable of creative thought), hedonistic (motivated by pain/pleasure), and self-determining (free willed)."[1] He believed behavior to be "freely chosen based on assessments of the pain/pleasure or cost/benefits of the actions."[2]

With respect to criminal behavior, Beccaria saw this as a matter of choice. In short, the answer to the prevention or deterrence of crime was to "make the punishment fit the crime," or "increase the pain/cost of an action to the point where it overwhelms its possible pleasure/benefits."[3] Beccaria observed that such punishment for criminal actions should not only be in response to the particular offense and its severity but also be doled out swiftly and surely, "since even the severest punishment has no deterrent quality if it can be escaped."[4]

The classical perspective on criminality lost credibility in the 19th century as a preeminent means of explaining criminal behavior. This was due largely to its propositions of free will in determining one's involvement in criminal actions, along with the progression of "physical and medical science ... and [discovery of] an increasing number of ways in which human beings were not self-determining."[5]

Classical criminology theories reemerged in the 20th century with more sophisticated approaches, such as *criminological economic theories*,[6] *deterrence theories*,[7] and *rational choice theories*.[8] However, while such theories rely primarily on the individual's own free will or choice in behavior, there is also the recognition that other factors beyond the person may play a role in the perpetration of violent and other types of crimes.

Positivistic Theories of Criminality

A positivistic approach in explaining criminal behavior as an alternative to classical criminology gained strength in the 19th century. Positivistic criminology assumed that human behavior was to some extent influenced "by factors which were largely outside the control of any specific individual."[9]

Within this school of thought lies two particular types of determinism, or the belief that every act or decision made is the inevitable result of certain antecedents aside from human will: *individual determinism* and *sociocultural determinism*.

Individual determinism attributes human behavior to influences "largely located inside the individual, either in [one's] physical/biological nature or [one's] mental/psychological processes."[10] Sociocultural determinism, however, posits that crime is not a consequence of "flawed people but rather ... a flawed society."[11] Within this context, homicide offenders and other criminals "are seen as being primarily influenced by social or cultural factors, which are, again, largely outside their control."[12]

Biological Theories on Crime and Violence

The biological-positivistic school of thought in explaining criminal behavior was pioneered by Italian physician Cesare Lombroso. Highly influenced by the work of Charles Darwin, Lombroso, who was called the "father of criminology," introduced his *theory of atavism* in the 1876 book *L'Uomo Delinquente*.[13] He argued that criminals were throwbacks to earlier genetic forms and, as such, could be differentiated from noncriminals by physical stigmata. This perspective has been essentially dismissed as methodologically flawed, among other reasons. Although Lombroso would later modify some of his hypotheses, the basic tenet of his work remained.

Other early biological perspectives on criminality included *body-type theories* and *hereditary theories*. In the 1930s and 1940s, such criminologists as Ernest Hooten,[14] William Sheldon,[15] and Sheldon and Eleanor Glueck[16] postulated that certain body types were characteristic of criminals. For example, Hooten believed that tall, heavy men were more likely than other body types to be murderers; whereas Sheldon and the Gluecks advanced that certain somatotypes such as mesomorphics—characterized as aggressive, assertive, muscular, and hard—were disproportionately likely to engage in delinquent or criminal behavior.

Hereditary theories attributed criminal behavior to genetically transmitted mental or physical defectiveness or deficiencies. Such theorists as Richard Dugdale[17] and Henry Goddard[18] examined the long histories of criminality, feeblemindedness, and other aberrant behavior in some families. Like atavism theory, body-type theories and early hereditary theories have been rejected as unscientific and otherwise weak.

Twin, Adoption, and Fosterling Studies

More recent biological theories have shown greater promise in understanding criminal behavior. *Twin studies* have linked antisocial behavior to genetic traits found in identical twins, in particular. Studies by Johannes Lange[19] and Karl Christiansen[20] found that the rate of criminal *concordance*—a genetic term referring to the degree in which twins or related pairings demonstrate a specific behavior or condition—was much greater among identical than fraternal twins. In a review of twin studies, Hans Eysench asserted that heredity is "beyond any doubt ... an extremely important part in the genesis of criminal behaviour."[21]

Similarly, *adoption and fosterling studies* have explored the relationship between the criminality of adopted or foster children and the criminal behavior of their biological and adoptive or foster parents. The most significant research in this area was conducted by Bernard Hutchings and Sarnoff Mednick. In examining 1,145 male adoptees and the same number of nonadoptees, controlling such factors as age, sex, and the occupations of fathers, it was concluded that adoptees were nearly twice as likely as nonadoptees to have criminal records, and that the biological fathers of adoptees were three times more likely to be involved in criminal activity than either the adoptive fathers or fathers of the control group.[22]

In an even more comprehensive study of adoptees, Mednick, William Gabrielli, and Hutchings compared conviction records of 14,427 adoptees with the conviction records of their biological and adoptive parents. They concluded the the genetic transmission of criminal tendencies increased the probability of children becoming antisocial.[23]

In both twin and adoption and fosterling research, theorists have noted the importance of environment as well as genetics in criminal behavior.

The most current research on biologically based deviant behavior has relied upon a multidisciplinary perspective in explaining crime. "Scientists in such fields as genetics, biochemistry, endocrinology, neuroscience, immunology, and psychophysiology have been intensely studying aspects of human behavior that are relevant to the criminologist and criminal justice practitioner."[24] Among the areas being explored with respect to biology and crime is the relationship between violent criminal behavior and brain disorders such as brain tumors and epilepsy.[25]

Psychological Theories on Crime and Violence

The psychological or psychogenic school of thought on criminality is largely attributed to the work of Sigmund Freud and his *psychoanalytic theory*.[26] The Austrian physician saw criminal behavior as the conflict between the drives and unresolved instincts of the id, ego, and superego of the individual's personality. Supporters of psychoanalytic theory believe that the answer to understanding and treating antisocial behavior is psychoanalysis, an "individualistic therapy program which concentrates on delving deep into the individual's past experiences to uncover the unconscious conflicts."[27]

The major criticism against the psychoanalytic theories to criminality is that they cannot be empirically validated. Because the personality parts are neither able to be observed nor measured, psychoanalytic findings are essentially just the "analyst's interpretation of a patient's interpretation of what is occurring in the subconscious."[28]

However, the psychological-positivistic approach to explaining crime has remained influential in criminological theory. Richard Bootzin and Joan Acocella divided psychological theories on violent behavior into three categories:

- *Psychodynamic perspective.* Unconscious conflicts during childhood causes criminal behavior.
- *Behavioral perspective.* Improper conditioning leads to criminal behavior.
- *Humanistic-existential perspective.* Antisocial behavior is the result of failure on a personal level.[29]

Two key subtypes of psychological theories to receive their share of support in explaining criminal behavior are *personality-disorder theories* and *mental dysfunction theories*.

Personality-Disorder Theories

The psychopathic personality theory is perhaps the most visible personality-disorder theory today. The psychopath has been defined as "a person with an antisocial personality disorder, especially one manifested in aggressive, perverted, or criminal behavior."[30] Others view the psychopathic individual as one who is "mentally unstable, antisocial, amoral, hostile, egocentric, insensitive, callous, and fearless."[31] According to Warren Wille, murderers can be classified as depressives, psychotics, psychopaths, passive-aggressives, and hysterical personalities.[32]

Some of the most extensive study on the psychopath has been done by William McCord and Joan McCord, who postulated that the two traits that set the psychopath apart from others are guiltlessness and lovelessness.[33] They attribute the psychopathic personality to brain damage, physical trauma, and severe emotional deprivation during childhood.

Another type of personality-disorder theory is the *criminal personality theory*.[34] Developed by Samuel Yochelson and Stanton Samenow after years of studying violent criminal patients, the theory held that violent offenders sought out excitement through criminal activity, in response to the boredom of normal family life. The researchers rejected explanations for criminal behavior outside the individual.

Both psychopathic personality theory and criminal personality theory have been criticized for their lack of scientific validation. Furthermore, psychopathic adults are believed to account for less than one-quarter of all criminals, with the number of juvenile psychopaths proportionately much smaller.[35]

Mental Dysfunction Theories

Mental deficiency theories or *intelligence quotient (IQ) theories* have argued that criminal behavior is a reflection of low intelligence. While there was empirical support for early IQ research that found low intelligence to be a major cause of antisocial conduct,[36] more recent studies have, for the most part, found little difference between offenders and nonoffenders with respect to IQ.[37] However, research by Travis Hirschi and Michael Hindelang does suggest that a relationship exists between juvenile delinquency and intelligence.[38] IQ was shown to affect school performance, causing failure and incompetency, leading to antisocial behavior.

Mental illness theories have long purported criminal behavior, particularly violent criminality, to be caused by mental illness of some type. Manfred Guttmacher identified a number of types of killers including schizophrenics acting in response to delusions and hallucinations, sociopaths, sadists, and persons with no major psychopathology.[39] However, most mental health experts contend that mental illness accounts for only a relatively small proportion of serious and violent criminals.[40] Environmental and situational variables are seen as more causal of criminal behavior.

Sociological-Cultural Theories on Crime and Violence

The sociological-cultural determinism approach to criminality tends to explain criminal behavior as a normal response to the social structure, social life, and cultural factors. Such prominent criminologists as Marvin Wolfgang and Franco Ferracuti have taken a sociological-cultural approach in their study of criminal homicides and a subculture of violence in society.[41] There are three primary perspectives within this thought: *social control theories*, *strain theories*, and *cultural transmission theories*.

Social Control Theories

Social control theories assume that all people have the potential to commit criminal acts, but fear and social constraints prevents such. Criminality is explained as the result of external social control and internalized social values for some, creating the freedom to commit crimes. Control theorists are less concerned with what motivates one to violate the law than the social institutions that produce conditions favorable to committing crimes or refraining from such.

Prominent social control theories include *social disorganization theory*, *social bonding theory*, and *containment theory*. The concept of social disorganization was developed by the University of Chicago's sociology department, which became known as the Chicago School. This was used to describe "the breakdown in social conventional structure within a community ... and the incapability of organizations, groups, and individuals [in] that community to effectively solve its problems."[42] Social disorganization theorists such as Clifford Shaw and Henry McKay contended that these ineffective social controls in certain areas directly correlated with the high crime rate.[43]

Social bonding theory was established by Travis Hirschi.[44] He advanced that a social bond consisting of attachment, commitment, involvement, and belief tied youths to the social order. The weaker these bonds, the more likely one was to become involved in criminal activity.

A similar theory of containment was put forth by Walter Reckless, who believed that youths are restrained from becoming involved in antisocial behavior by a combination of inner and outer containments that act as buffers against the influences of criminal behavior.[45]

Social control theories have generally received empirical support for their basic principles. However, they have been criticized for failure to account for the role of internalized norms and values or the sociostructural causes of criminality.

Strain Theories

Strain theories also evolved from the Chicago School, explaining crime as a response to a lack of socially approved opportunities. Two of the more influential strain theories are *theory of anomie* and *subcultural theory*.

The concept of anomie was developed by Emile Durkheim at the turn of the 20th century, in reference to a condition of relative normlessness within a group or society, whereby the social structure was unable to control deviance.[46] It was Robert Merton who applied anomie theory to society and cultural values in the United States.[47] He postulated that criminality was caused by the anomie interaction of culturally defined goals and the socially structured means of achieving them. Unequal access to approved means by some leads them to deviate from the norm, or commit crimes to achieve goals.

Although Merton's theory has been attacked for various shortcomings, such as doubt that all Americans share the same goals and expectations for success, the sophistication of his work contributed to subsequent theories on the correlation between criminal behavior and differential economic opportunity.

Subcultural theories were established in the 1950s and 1960s, primarily to study lower-class youth criminality and gang violence. Major contributors include Albert Cohen,[48] Walter Miller,[49] and James Short.[50] However, it was Richard Cloward and Lloyd Ohlin's opportunity theory that has been most influential in this school of thought.[51] The theory argued that the social structure largely influences one's access to legitimate and illegitimate means for achieving socially approved goals. It is the differential opportunity among the lower class, particularly youths and gangs, that the researchers believe results in deep frustration and involvement in criminal activities in order to achieve these goals. Critics have long argued that opportunity theory is flawed because of its concentration mainly on lower-class criminality. Most agree that the theory does succeed in recognizing the existence of differential opportunity structures.

Cultural Transmission Theories

Cultural transmission theories view crime as learned behavior, or reflecting of the norms, values, beliefs, and behavioral characteristics acquired from others. As such, cultural transmission theorists believe that criminal behavior is caused mainly "by conforming to the behavioral norms of a culture or subculture that are contrary to conventional norms and values with respect to behavior and the law."[52] Two of the more recognized cultural transmission theories are *differential association theory* and *social learning theory*.

Differential association theory was first introduced by Edwin Sutherland in his 1939 text *Principles of Criminology*.[53] The theory postulated that criminality is learned through interaction with those who frequently violate the law and express beliefs to justify their behavior. As such, crime is seen as a social rather than antisocial behavior, with the degree of involvement dependent upon the priority, frequency, intensity, and duration of one's criminal contacts and, inversely, noncrimnal contacts.

The major fault with differential association theory is that it cannot be validated through empirical testing. It has also been criticized for failing to explain how crime originated as a learned process. However, Sutherland's theory continues to receive overall support as a sociological explanation for criminal behavior.

Social learning theory is a modification of differential association theory. Developed by Ronald Burgess and Ronald Akers, the theory posited that deviant behavior is learned through social interaction with people who represent one's primary source of reinforcement.[54] These social reinforcements are seen as symbolic and verbal rewards for supporting group norms and expectations. Nonsocial reinforcements are noted but believed to be less significant in the learning process and criminal behavior.

Critics of social learning theory contend that nonsocial reinforcers may actually be more influential than social reinforcers in antisocial behavior. Questions have also been raised about the scientific reliability of the theory. However, the basic belief of social learning theory has been empirically supported.[55] Furthermore, its principles have been incorporated within such later theoretical perspectives as deterrence theories and control theories.[56]

Critical Theories of Criminality and Criminal Law

Critical or radical criminology is the most recent school of thought in theorizing on crime and violence. Its focus is more on the relationship between crime and social responses rather than an explanation for criminal behavior. In a study of homicide theories, Christine Rasche observed the perspective of the critical school of thought on homicide:

> What causes [human] behaviors to be designated as crimes ... Why are some homicides designated as criminal while others are viewed as justified, or excused, or even mandatory (as in time of war)? The homicidal act remains the same, the outcome (a death) remains the same, but our interpretation of it and social responses to it varies considerably depending on how we label it.[57]

The critical criminological approach can be broken down into two inter-related yet different perspectives: *conflict theory* and *Marxist theory*. Conflict theory was introduced in the early 20th century by Thorsten Sellin.[58] The theory basically contends that crime is in effect the product of the powers that be in terms of the labeling mechanism. "When one nation conquers another and imposes its law over the conquered land, behaviors that might not have been acceptable yesterday may become criminalized today.... [As such], it is [more] important to understand the actions of norm creators, norm inter-preters and norm enforcers than it is to understand norm breakers."[59]

Marxist theory, also known as radical theory on criminology, holds that the criminal laws themselves primarily serve the greater interests of the rul-ing class, who "use these laws to exploit, dominate and victimize the working and lower classes in order to perpetuate the economic and political system of capitalism."[60] As these laws are a function of the wealthy or capitalists, their socially harmful "crimes," including demoralization and exploitation, are generally not defined as crimes, unlike offenses that are labeled as such.[61]

Radical criminologists blame the high rate of street or lower-class crimi-nality on the economic functioning of the capitalist system, which creates unemployment and underemployment, leading to conditions that promote criminal behavior.

Critical criminology theories have been routinely criticized for their pre-dictability, disregard for objective reality, failure to account for intragroup and racial and ethnic disparities in crime rates, and overstatement of principles.

Endnotes

1. C. E. Rasche, Theorizing About Homicide: A Presentation on Theories Explaining Homicide and Other Crimes, in U.S. Department of Justice, *The Nature of Homicide: Trends and Changes—Proceedings of the 1996 Meeting of the Homicide Research Working Group* (Washington: National Institute of Justice, 1998), pp. 27–28.
2. *Ibid.*, p. 27.
3. *Ibid.* See also C. Beccaria, *On Crimes and Punishment*, trans. H. Paolucci (Indianapolis: Bobbs-Merrill, 1963). Originally published in 1764.
4. Rasche, Theorizing About Homicide, p. 28.
5. *Ibid.* See also G. Vold & T. Bernard, *Theoretical Criminology*, 3rd ed. (Oxford: Oxford University Press, 1986).
6. See, for example, J. R. Harris, On the Economics of Law and Order, *Journal of Political Economy* 78 (1970): 165–74; R. F. Sullivan, The Economics of Crime: An Introduction to the Literature, *Crime and Delinquency* 19, 2 (1973): 138–49.
7. F. E. Zimring & G. J. Hawkins, *Deterrence* (Chicago: University of Chicago Press, 1973).

8. See, for example, D. B. Cornish & R. V. Clarke, Eds., *The Reasoning Criminal: Rational Choice Perspectives on Offending* (New York: Springer, 1986).

9. Rasche, Theorizing About Homicide, p. 28.

10. *Ibid.*, p. 29.

11. *Ibid.*

12. *Ibid.*

13. C. Lombroso & W. Ferrero, *Criminal Man* (Montclair: Patterson Smith, 1972). Originally titled *L'Uomo Delinquente* in its 1876 publication. See also Charles Darwin, *Origin of Species* (New York: Bantam, 1999).

14. E. A. Hooten, *Crime and the Man* (Cambridge, Harvard University Press, 1939).

15. W. A. Sheldon, *Varieties of Temperament* (New York: Harper & Row, 1942).

16. S. Glueck & E. T. Glueck, *Physique and Delinquency* (New York: Harper & Row, 1956).

17. R. L. Dugdale, *The Jukes: A Study in Crime, Pauperism, and Heredity* (New York: Putnam, 1877).

18. H. H. Goddard, *Feeblemindedness, Its Causes and Consequences* (New York: Macmillan, 1914).

19. J. Lange, *Crime as Destiny* (London: George Allen & Unwin, 1931). Originally published as *Vebrecken als Sochicksal* in 1928.

20. K. O. Christiansen, Seriousness of Criminality and Concordance Among Danish Twins, in R. Hood, Ed., *Crime, Criminology and Public Policy* (London: Heinemann, 1977); K. O. Christiansen, A Preliminary Study of Criminality Among Twins, in S. A. Mednick & K. O. Christiansen, Eds., *Biosocial Bases of Criminal Behavior* (New York: Gardner Press, 1977).

21. H. J. Eysench, *The Inequality of Man* (San Diego: Edits Publishers, 1973), p. 167.

22. B. Hutchings & S. A. Mednick, Registered Criminality in the Adoptive and Biological Parents of Registered Male Criminal Adoptees, in R. R. Fieve, D. Rosenthal, & H. Brill, Eds., *Genetic Research in Psychiatry* (Baltimore: John Hopkins University Press, 1975).

23. S. A. Mednick, W. F. Gabrielli, & B. Hutchings, Genetic Influences in Criminal Convictions: Evidence From an Adoption Cohort, *Science* 234 (1984): 891–94.

24. D. H. Fishbein, Biological Perspectives in Criminology, in D. G. Rojek & G. F. Jensen, Eds., *Exploring Delinquency: Causes and Control* (Los Angeles: Roxbury, 1996), p. 102.

25. See, for example, V. Pollock, S. A. Mednick, & W. F. Gabrielli, Jr., Crime Causation: Biological Theories, in S. H. Kadish, Ed., *Encyclopedia of Crime and Justice*, Vol. 1 (New York: Free Press, 1983); H. D. Kletschka, Violent Behavior Associated with Brain Tumors, *Minnesota Medicine* 49 (1966): 1835–55.

26. S. Freud, *New Introductory Lectures on Psychoanalysis* (New York: W. W. Norton, 1933).

27. R. B. Flowers, *The Adolescent Criminal: An Examination of Today's Juvenile Offender* (Jefferson: McFarland, 1990), p. 119.

28. J. F. Sheley, *America's "Crime Problem": An Introduction to Criminology* (Belmont: Wadsworth, 1985), p. 202.

29. R. R. Bootzin & J. R. Acocella, *Abnormal Psychology: Current Perspectives*, 3rd ed. (New York: Random House, 1980). See also R. K. Ressler, A. W. Burgess, and J. E. Douglas, *Sexual Homicide: Patterns and Motives* (New York: Lexington Books, 1988), pp. 4–7.

30. *The American Heritage Dictionary* (New York: Dell, 1994), p. 667.
31. Flowers, *The Adolescent Criminal*, p. 120.
32. W. S. Wille, *Citizens Who Commit Murder* (St. Louis: Warren Greene, 1974).
33. W. McCord & J. McCord, *The Psychopath* (Princeton: Van Nostrand, 1964). See also L. N. Robins, *Deviant Children Grown Up* (Baltimore: Williams & Wilkins, 1966); F. Schulsinger, Psychopathy: Heredity and Environment, *International Journal of Mental Health* 1 (1972): 190–206.
34. S. Yochelson & S. E. Samenow, *The Criminal Personality*, Vol. 1 (New York: Jason Arsonson, 1976); S. E. Samenow, *Inside the Criminal Mind* (New York: Time Books, 1984).
35. H. C. Quay, Crime Causation: Psychological Theories, in S. H. Kadish, Ed., *Encyclopedia of Crime and Justice*, Vol. 1 (New York: Free Press, 1983), p. 340; H. C. Quay, Patterns of Delinquent Behavior, in H. C. Quay, Ed., *Handbook of Juvenile Delinquency* (New York: Wiley-Interscience, 1987), pp. 118–38.
36. See, for example, Goddard, *Feeblemindedness, Its Causes and Consequences*; W. Healy and A. Bronner, *Delinquency and Criminals: Their Making and Unmaking* (New York: Macmillan, 1926).
37. See, for example, S. H. Tulchin, *Intelligence and Crime* (Chicago: University of Chicago Press, 1972).
38. T. Hirschi & M. J. Hindelang, Intelligence and Delinquency: A Revisionist Review, *American Sociological Review* 42 (1977): 571–86.
39. M. Guttmacher, *The Mind of the Murderer* (New York: Arno Press, 1973).
40. Flowers, *The Adolescent Criminal*, p. 123; President's Commission on Mental Health, *Report to the President*, Vol. l (Washington: Government Printing Office, 1978).
41. M. Wolfgang, *Patterns in Criminal Homicide* (Philadelphia: University of Pennsylvania Press, 1958); M. Wolfgang & F. Ferracuti, *The Subculture of Violence: Toward an Integrated Theory in Criminology* (London: Tavistock, 1967); F. Ferracuti and M. Wolfgang, *Violence in Sardinia* (Rome: Bulzoni, 1970).
42. Flowers, *The Adolescent Criminal*, pp. 124–25. See also R. E. Park & E. W. Burgess, *The City* (Chicago: University of Chicago Press, 1925).
43. C. R. Shaw & H. D. McKay, *Juvenile Delinquency and Urban Areas* (Chicago: University of Chicago Press, 1969). See also F. M. Thrasher, *The Gang* (Chicago: University of Chicago Press, 1927).
44. T. Hirschi, *Causes of Delinquency* (Berkeley: University of California Press, 1969).
45. W. C. Reckless, *The Crime Problem*, 5th ed. (Santa Monica: Goodyear, 1973); W. C. Reckless, S. Dinitz, & E. Murray, Self-Concept as an Insulator Against Delinquency, in J. E. Teele, Ed., *Juvenile Delinquency: A Reader* (Itasca: Peacock, 1970).
46. E. Durkheim, *The Division of Labor in Society*, George Simpson, trans. (New York: Free Press, 1933).
47. R. K. Merton, Social Structure and Anomie, *American Sociological Review* 8 (1938): 672–82; R. K. Merton, *Social Theory and Social Structure* (New York: Free Press, 1957).
48. A. K. Cohen, *Delinquent Boys* (New York: Free Press, 1955); A. K. Cohen and J. F. Short, Jr., Research on Delinquent Subcultures, *Journal of Social Issues* 14, 3 (1958): 20–37.

49. W. B. Miller, *Violence by Youth Gangs and Youth Groups as a Crime Problem in Major American Cities* (Washington: Law Enforcement Administration, 1975); W. B. Miller, Lower-Class Culture as a Generating Milieu of Gang Delinquency, *Journal of Social Issues* 14 (1958): 5–19.

50. J. F. Short, Jr., Gang Delinquency and Anomie, in M. B. Clinard, Ed., *Anomie and Deviant Behavior* (New York: Free Press, 1964), pp. 98–127.

51. R. A. Cloward & L. F. Ohlin, *Delinquency and Opportunity: A Theory of Delinquent Gangs* (New York: Free Press, 1960).

52. Flowers, *The Adolescent Criminal*, p. 129.

53. E. H. Sutherland, *Principles of Criminology* (Philadelphia: Lippincott, 1939); E. H. Sutherland & D. R. Cressey, *Criminology*, 9th ed. (Philadelphia: Lippincott, 1974).

54. R. L. Burgess & R. L. Akers, A Differential Association-Reinforcement Theory of Criminal Behavior, *Social Problems* 14 (1966): 128–47; R. L. Akers, *Deviant Behavior: A Social Learning Approach*, 3rd ed. (Belmont: Wadsworth, 1985).

55. See, for example, B. McLaughlin, *Learning and Social Behavior* (New York: Free Press, 1971); A. Staats, *Social Behaviorism* (Homewood: Dorsey Press, 1975); W. Honig, *Operant Behavior: Areas of Research and Application* (New York: Appleton-Century-Crofts, 1966).

56. See, for example, Hirschi, *Causes of Delinquency*; Akers, *Deviant Behavior*; M. P. Feldman, *Criminal Behavior: A Psychological Analysis* (London: Wiley, 1977).

57. Rasche, Theorizing About Homicide, p. 31.

58. T. Sellin, *Culture Conflict and Crime* (New York: Social Science Research Council, 1938).

59. Rasche, Theorizing About Homicide, p. 31. See also T. Bernard, The Distinction Between Conflict and Radical Criminology, *Journal of Criminal Law and Criminology* 72 (1981): 366–70.

60. Flowers, *The Adolescent Criminal*, p. 132; R. B. Flowers, *Minorities and Criminality* (Westport: Greenwood, 1988), pp. 71–72.

61. G. M. Sykes, The Rise and Fall of Critical Criminology, *Journal of Criminal Law and Criminology* 65 (1974): 206–13.

Bibliography

ABCNews.com. (April 5, 2010) Pair Sentenced in Brooklyn Hate Crime Murder. http://abclocal.go.com/wabc/story?section=news/local&id=7594314.

ABC News Videos. (August 15, 2010) Alleged Craigslist Killer Commits Suicide. http://abcnews.go.com/WNT/video/alleged-craigslist-killer-commits-suicide -11407124.

Akers, R. L. (1985) *Deviant Behavior: A Social Learning Approach*, 3rd ed. Belmont: Wadsworth.

Alba, R. D., J. R. Logan, & P. Bellair. (1994) Living With Crime: The Implications of Racial/Ethnic Differences in Suburban Location. *Social Forces* 73: 395–434.

Alexander, Y., & M. S. Swetman. (2001) *Usama bin Laden's al-Quada: Profile of a Terrorist Network.* Ardsley: Transnational Publishers.

American Psychiatric Association. (1987) *Diagnostic and Statistical Manual of Mental Disorders,* 3rd ed. Washington: American Psychiatric Association.

American Psychiatric Association. (1994) *Diagnostic and Statistical Manual of Mental Disorders*, 4th ed. Washington: American Psychiatric Association.

Arbetter, S. (1995) Family Violence: When We Hurt the Ones We Love. *Current Health* 22, 3: 6.

Arnold Shapiro Productions. (September 25, 1990) *Goodnight Sweet Wife: A Murder in Boston.* http://www.imdb.com/title/tt0099684/.

Associated Press. (May 2, 2012) Woman Convicted of Parents' Murder Wants New Trial. *KTVB.com.* http://www.ktvb.com/home/Woman-convicted-of-parents-murder-wants-new-trial-149859845.html.

Auerhahn, K., & R. N. Parker. (1999) Drugs, Alcohol, and Homicide." In M. D. Smith & M. A. Zahn, Eds., *Studying and Preventing Homicide: Issues and Challenges.* Thousand Oaks: Sage, 1999.

Avila, J., G. Martz, and J. Napolitano. (August 27, 2011) Online Love Triangle, Deception, End in Murder. *ABC 20/20.* http://abcnews.go.com/US/online-love-triangle-deception-end-murder/story?id=14371076.

Bachman, R. (1992) *Death and Violence on the Reservation: Homicide, Family Violence, and Suicide in American Indian Populations.* Westport: Auburn House.

Bailey, G. W., & N. P. Unnithan. (1994) Gang Homicides in California: A Discriminate Analysis. *Journal of Criminal Justice* 22, 3: 267–75.

Barnard, G. W., H. Vera, M. Vera, & G. Newman. (1982) 'Till Death Do Us Part?' A Study of Spouse Murder. *Bulletin of the American Academy of Psychiatry and Law* 10: 271–80.

Battin, S. R., K. G. Hill, R. D. Abbott, R. F. Catalano, & J. D. Hawkins. (1998) The Contribution of Gang Membership to Delinquency Beyond Delinquent Friends. *Criminology* 36: 93–115.

Beaman, V., J. L. Annest, J. A. Mercy, M. Kresnow, & D. A. Pollock. (2000) Lethality of Firearm-Related Injuries in the United States Population. *Annals of Emergency Medicine* 35: 258–66.

Bean, F., & M. Tienda. (1987) *The Hispanic Population of the United States.* New York: Russell Sage.

Beasley, R. W., & G. Antunes. (1974) The Etiology of Urban Crime: An Ecological Analysis. *Criminology* 22: 531–50.

Beccaria, C. (1963) *On Crimes and Punishment.* Indianapolis: Bobbs-Merrill.

Bell, C. A. (1991) Female Homicides in United States Workplaces, 1980–1985. *American Journal of Public Health* 81: 729–32.

Bell, R. (April 25, 2012) Internet Assisted Suicide: The Story of Sharon Lopatka. *TruTV.* http://www.trutv.com/library/crime/notorious_murders/classics/sharon_lopatka/1.html.

Bell, R. (May 4, 2012) The Xerox Murders. *TruTV Crime Library.* http://www.trutv.com/library/crime/notorious_murders/mass/work_homicide/5.html.

Bender, L., & F. J. Curran. (1940) Children and Adolescents Who Kill. *Journal of Criminal Psychopathology* 1, 4: 297.

Benedek, E. P. (1982) Women and Homicide. In B. L. Danto, J. Bruhns, & A. H. Kutscher, Eds., *The Human Side of Homicide.* New York: Columbia University Press.

Bergen, P. L. (2001) *Holy War, Inc.: Inside the Secret World of Osama Bin Laden.* New York: Free Press.

Berkowitz, L. (1986) Some Varieties of Human Aggression: Criminal Violence as Coercion, Rule-Following, Impression Management and Impulsive Behavior. In A. Campbell & J. J. Gibbs, Eds., *Violent Transactions: The Limits of Personality.* Oxford: Basil Blackwell.

Berman, A. L. (1979) Dyadic Death: Murder-Suicide. *Suicidal and Life-Threatening Behavior* 9: 15.

Bernard, T. (1981) The Distinction Between Conflict and Radical Criminology. *Journal of Criminal Law and Criminology* 72: 366–70.

Berry-Dee, C., & S. Morris. (2006) *Killers on the Web: True Stories of Internet Cannibals, Murderers and Sex Criminals.* London: John Blake.

Bettin, R. (March 31, 1992) Young Women's Resource Center. Testimony at Iowa House of Representatives Public Hearing on Dating Violence.

Biography Channel. (February 1, 2008) *Crime Stories: The Love Slave Murders.* http://www.youtube.com/watch?v=J_H20I-9K6E.

Bjerregaard, B., & A. J. Lizotte. (1995) Gun Ownership and Gang Membership. *Journal of Criminal Law and Criminology* 86: 37–58.

Block, C. R. (1985) Race/Ethnicity and Patterns of Chicago Homicide, 1965–1981. *Crime and Delinquency* 31: 104–16.

Block, C. R., & A. Christakos. (1995) Chicago Homicide From the Sixties to the Nineties: Major Trends in Lethal Violence. In U.S. Department of Justice, *Trends, Risks, and Interventions in Lethal Violence: Proceedings of the Third Annual Spring Symposium of the Homicide Research Working Group.* Washington: National Institute of Justice.

Block, C. R., A. Christakos, A. Jacob, & R. Przybylski. (1996) *Street Gangs and Crime: Patterns and Trends in Chicago.* Chicago: Illinois Criminal Justice Information Authority.

Block, C. R., and R. Block. (1995) Street Gang Crime in Chicago. In M. W. Klein, C. L. Maxson, & J. Miller, Eds., *The Modern Gang Reader*. Los Angeles: Roxbury.

Block, H. A., & G. Geis. (1962) *Man, Crime, and Society*. New York: Random House.

Block, R., & C. R. Block. (1993) *Street Gang Crime in Chicago*. Washington: National Institute of Justice.

Blount, W. R., I. J. Silverman, C. S. Sellers, & R. A. Seese. (1994) Alcohol and Drug Use Among Abused Women Who Kill, Abused Women Who Don't, and Their Abusers. *Journal of Drug Issues* 24: 165–77.

Blumstein, A. (1995) Youth Violence, Guns, and the Illicit-Drug Industry. *Journal of Criminal Law and Criminology* 86: 10–36.

Bonger, W. (1943) *Race and Crime*. New York: Columbia University Press.

Bootzin, R. R., & J. R. Acocella. (1980) *Abnormal Psychology: Current Perspectives*, 3rd ed. New York: Random House.

BostonGlobe.com. (March 12, 2012) Trial Delayed for Professor in Ala. Shooting Spree. http://www.boston.com/news/local/massachusetts/articles/2012/03/12/trial_delayed_for_professor_in_ala_shooting_spree/.

Brown, J. S. (1991) The Historical Similarity of 20th Century Serial Sexual Homicide to Pre 20th Century Occurrences of Vampirism. *American Journal of Forensic Psychiatry 12*, 2: 11–24.

Browne, A. (1987) *When Battered Women Kill*. New York: Free Press.

Browne, A. (July 7, 2011) Fort Hood Shooting Suspect Will Face Death Penalty. *ABC News*. http://abcnews.go.com/US/wireStory?id=14015624.

Browne, A., & K. R. Williams. (1989) Exploring the Effect of Resource Availability and the Likelihood of Female-Perpetrated Homicides. *Law and Society Review* 23: 75–94.

Browne, A., K. R. Williams, & D. G. Dutton. (1999) Homicide Between Intimate Partners. In M. D. Smith & M. A. Zahn, Eds., *Studying and Preventing Homicide: Issues and Challenges*. Thousand Oaks, Sage.

Browning, F., & J. Gerassi. (1980) *The American Way of Crime*. New York: Putnam.

Brownstein, H. H., H. Baxi, P. Goldstein, & P. Ryan. (1992) The Relationship of Drugs, Drug Trafficking, and Drug Traffickers to Homicide. *Journal of Crime and Justice* 15: 25–44.

Brumm, H. J., & D. O. Cloninger. (1995) The Drug War and the Homicide Rate: A Direct Correlation? *Cato Journal* 14: 509–17.

Burgess, A. W., C. R. Hartman, R. K. Ressler, J. E. Douglas, & A. McCormack. (1986) Sexual Homicide. *Journal of Interpersonal Violence 1*: 251–72.

Burgess, R. L., & R. L. Akers. (1966) A Differential Association-Reinforcement Theory of Criminal Behavior. *Social Problems* 14: 128–47.

Buteau, J., A. Lesage, & M. Kiely. (1993) Homicide Followed by Suicide: A Quebec Case Series, 1988–1990. *Canadian Journal of Psychiatry* 38: 552–56.

Campbell, A. (1981) *Girl Delinquents*. New York: St. Martin's Press.

Campbell, J. (1992) "If I Can't Have You, No One Can": Power and Control in Homicide of Female Partners. In J. Radford & D. E. Russell, Eds., *Femicide: The Politics of Woman Killing*. New York: Twayne.

Campbell, J. (1995) *Assessing Dangerousness: Violence by Sexual Offenders, Batterers, and Child Abusers*. Thousand Oaks: Sage.

Campbell, J. (1995) Prediction of Homicide of and by Battered Women. In J. Campbell & J. Milner, Eds., *Assessing Dangerousness: Potential for Further Violence of Sexual Offenders, Batterers, and Child Abusers.* Thousand Oaks: Sage.

Campion, J. F., J. M. Cravens, & F. Covan. (1988) A Study of Filicidal Men. *American Journal of Psychiatry* 145: 1141.

Caputi, J. (1987) *The Age of Sex Crime.* Bowling Green: Bowling Green State University Press.

Carlson, B. E. (1977) Battered Women and Their Assailants. *Social Work* 22, 6: 456.

Castillo, D. N. (1995) Nonfatal Violence in the Work Place: Directions for Future Research. In U.S. Department of Justice, *Trends Risks; and Interventions in Lethal Violence: Proceedings of the Third Annual Spring Symposium of the Homicide Research Working Group.* Washington: National Institute of Justice.

Castillo, D. N., & E. L. Jenkins. (1994) Industries and Occupations at High Risk for Work-Related Homicide. *Journal of Occupational Medicine* 36: 125–32.

CBS News. (December 21, 2011) NY Mom Sends Husband on Errand, Then Kills Family. http://www.cbsnews.com/8301-501363_162-57346734/ny-mom-sends.

CBS News. (February 12, 2012) Suspect ID'd in Deadly Ohio School Shooting. http://www.cbsnews.com/8301-201_162-57386080/suspect-idd-in-deadly-ohio-school-shooting/.

Celona, L., & K. Conley. (February 10, 2011) Man Brings Flowers to Ex, Then Shoots Her in the Face. *New York Post.* http://www.nypost.com/p/news/local/queens/man_kills_ex_wife_in_astoria_pharmacy_wPcii5rwVNJAC0pbv6v8TO.

Chaiken, M. R. (2000) *Violent Neighborhoods, Violent Kids.* Washington: Office of Juvenile Justice and Delinquency Prevention.

Chamberlain, T. J. (1986) The Dynamics of Parricide. *American Journal of Forensic Psychiatry* 7: 11–23.

Chapman, S. G. (1986) *Cops, Killers and Staying Alive: The Murder of Police Officers in America.* Springfield: Charles C Thomas.

Christiansen, K. O. (1977) A Preliminary Study of Criminality Among Twins. In S. A. Mednick & K. O. Christiansen, Eds., *Biosocial Bases of Criminal Behavior.* New York: Gardner Press.

Christiansen, K. O. (1977) Seriousness of Criminality and Concordance Among Danish Twins. In R. Hood, ed., *Crime, Criminology and Public Policy.* London: Heinemann.

Cloward, R. A., & L. E. Ohlin. (1960) *Delinquency and Opportunity: A Theory of Delinquent Gangs.* New York: Free Press.

CNN Justice. (September 15, 2011) Grand Jury Indicts Teen Accused of Killing Parents, Having Party. http://www.cnn.com/2011/CRIME/09/15/florida.parents.killed/index.html?iref=allsearch.

Cohen, A. K. (1951) *Delinquent Boys: The Culture of the Gang.* New York: Free Press.

Cohen, A. K., & J. F. Short, Jr. (1958) Research on Delinquent Subcultures. *Journal of Social Issues* 14, 3: 20–37.

Cohen, D. A. (1995) Homicidal Compulsion and the Conditions of Freedom: The Social and Psychological Origins of Familicide in America's Early Republic. *Journal of Social History.* Summer: 725–64.

The Commonwealth Fund. (July 14, 1993) First Comprehensive National Health Survey of American Women Finds Them at Significant Risk. News release. New York.

Cook, P. J. (1981) The Effect of Gun Availability on Violent Crime Patterns. *Annals of the American Academy of Political and Social Sciences* 455: 63–79.

Cook, P. J., & J. Ludwig. (1996) *Guns in America: Results of a Comprehensive National Survey on Firearms Ownership and Use.* Washington: Police Foundation.

Cook, P. J., & M. H. Moore. (1999) Guns, Gun Control, and Homicide. In M. D. Smith & M. A. Zahn, Eds., *Studying and Preventing Homicide: Issues and Challenges.* Thousand Oaks: Sage.

Cooper, H. A. (1982) Terroristic Fads and Fashions. In B. L. Danto & A. H. Kutscher, Eds., *The Human Side of Homicide.* New York: Columbia University Press.

Cormier, B. M., & S. P. Simons. (1969) The Problem of the Dangerous Sexual Offender. *Canadian Psychiatric Association* 14: 329–34.

Cornish, D. B., & R. V. Clarke, Eds. (1986) *The Reasoning Criminal: Rational Choice Perspectives on Offending.* New York: Springer.

Cox, J. W. (March 7, 2012) John Kalisz Sentenced to Death for the Murder of Two Hernando County Women. *Tampa Bay Times.* http://www.tampabay.com/news/courts/criminal/john-kalisz-sentenced-to-death-for-murder-of-two-hernando-county-women/1218566.

Crime Insider Staff. (September 23, 2011) Amy Bishop Enters Insanity Plea in University of Alabama Shooting. *CBS News.* http://www.cbsnews.com/8301-504083_162-20110701-504083.html.

Crow, W. J., & R. Erickson. (1989) *The Store Safety Issue: Facts for the Future.* Alexandria: National Association of Convenience Stores.

Curry, G. D., & S. H. Decker. (1998) *Confronting Gangs: Crime and Community.* Los Angeles: Roxbury.

Daily Mail Reporter. (December 23, 2010) Sentenced to Death: The Father and Son Who Bombed Oregon Bank … Then Blamed Each Other. *Mail Online.* http://www.dailymail.co.uk/news/article-1341030/Oregon-bank-bombers-Bruce-Joshua-Turnidge-sentenced-death.html.

Daly, C. B. (November 3, 1992) Young Stuart Pleads Guilty To Fraud; Alleged Wife Killer's Brother Gets 3 to 5. *Washington Post.* http://www.highbeam.com/doc/1P2-1033002.html.

Daly, M., & M. Wilson. (1982) Homicide and Kinship. *American Anthropologist* 84: 372–78.

Damphousse, K., Vi. E. Brewer, & C. D. Atkinson. (1999) Gangs, Race/Ethnicity and Houston Homicide in the 1990s. In U.S. Department of Justice. *Proceedings of the Homicide Research Working Group Meetings, 1997 and 1998.* Washington: National Institute of Justice.

Dark Deeds. (February 11, 2012) Devoted Husband or Sick Psychopath. http://dark-deeds.susanfleet.com/blog_1.php?tag=carol+dimaiti.

Darwin, C. (1999) *Origin of Species.* New York: Bantam.

Davis, C. A. (2003) *Children Who Kill: Profiles of Pre-Teen and Teenage Killers.* London: Allison & Busby.

Davis, H. P., A. Honchar, & L. Suarez. (1987) Fatal Occupational Injuries of Women, Texas 1975–1984. *American Journal of Public Health* 77: 1524–27.

Decker, S. H., & B. Van Winkle. (1996) *Life in the Gang: Family, Friends, and Violence.* New York: Cambridge University Press.

Decker, S. H., S. Pennell, & A. Caldwell. (1997) *Illegal Firearms: Access and Use by Arrestees.* Washington: National Institute of Justice.

Dewan, S., & A. G. Sulzberger. (March 11, 2009) Officials Identify Alabama Gunman. *New York Times.* http://www.nytimes.com/2009/03/12/us/12alabama.html?_r=1.

Dewan, S., S. Saul, & K. Zezima. (February 20, 2010) For Professor, Fury Just Beneath the Surface. *New York Times.* http://www.nytimes.com/2010/02/21/us/21bishop.html?pagewanted=1&_r=1.

Dietz, P. E. (1986) Mass, Serial and Sensational Homicides. *Bulletin of the New York Academy of Medicine* 62: 477–91.

Dillon, J. S. (August 11, 2009) Judge Routson: No Early Release for Kimberlee Snyder. *TheCourier.com.* http://www.thecourier.com/Issues/2009/Aug/11/ar_news_081109_story2.asp?d=081109_story2,2009,Aug,11&c=n.

Dobash, R. E., R. P. Dobash, M. Wilson, & M. Daly. (1992) The Myth of Sexual Symmetry in Marital Violence. *Social Problems 39,* 1: 71–91.

Dolak, K. (April 3, 2012) Oakland Shooting Suspect Not Remorseful, Police Chief Says. *ABC News.* http://abcnews.go.com/US/oakland-shooting-suspect-remorseful-police-chief/story?id=16059961.

Drash, W. (July 8, 2009) Police Call McNair Killing a Murder-Suicide. *CNN Justice.* http://articles.cnn.com/2009-07-08/justice/mcnair.shooting_1_steve-mcnair-sahel-kazemi-police-chief-ronal-serpas?_s=PM:CRIME.

Dugdale, R. L. (1877) *The Jukes: A Study in Crime, Pauperism, and Heredity.* New York: Putnam.

Durkheim, E. (1897) *Le Suicide.* Paris: Alcain.

Durkheim, E. (1933) *The Division of Labor in Society.* New York: Free Press.

E! Entertainment Television. (January 10, 2010) *Too Young to Kill: 15 Shocking Crimes.* http://www.imdb.com/title/tt1686119/.

Easteal, P. W. (1993) *Killing the Beloved: Homicide Between Adult Sexual Intimates.* Canberra: Australian Institute of Criminology.

Egger, S. A. (1984) A Working Definition of Serial Murder and the Reduction of Linkage Blindness. *Journal of Police Science and Administration* 12: 348–57.

Egger, S. A. (1990) Serial Murder. In S. A. Egger, Ed., *Serial Murder.* New York: Praeger.

Elliot, D. S., D. Huizinga, & S. Menard. (1989) *Multiple Problem Youth: Delinquency, Substance Abuse, and Mental Health Problems.* New York: Springer-Verlag.

Erickson, R. (1991) Convenience Store Homicide and Rape. In U.S. Department of Justice., *Convenience Store Security: Report and Recommendations.* Alexandria: U.S. Department of Justice.

Esbensen, F., & D. W. Osgood. (1997) *National Evaluation of G.R.E.A.T.* Research in Brief. Washington: National Institute of Justice.

Ewing, C. P. (1997) *Fatal Families: The Dynamics of Intrafamilial Homicide.* Thousand Oaks: Sage.

Eysench, H. J. (1973) *The Inequality of Man.* San Diego: Edits Publishers.

Fagan, J. (1989) The Social Organization of Drug Use and Drug Dealing Among Urban Gangs. *Criminology* 27: 633–69.

Fagan, J. (1990) Intoxication and Aggression. In M. Tonry & J. Q. Wilson, Eds., *Drugs and Crime.* Chicago: University of Chicago Press.

Fagan, J. (1993) *Set and Setting Revisited: Influences of Alcohol and Illicit Drugs on the Social Context of Violent Events.* Rockville: National Institution on Alcohol Abuse and Alcoholism Research.

Fagan, J., D. Stewart, & K. Hanson. (1983) Violent Men or Violent Husbands: Background Factors and Situational Correlates of Domestic and Extra-Domestic Violence. In D. Finkelhor, R. Gelles, G. Hotaling, & M. Straus, Eds., *The Dark Side of Families*. Thousand Oaks: Sage.

Feldman, M. P. (1977) *Criminal Behavior: A Psychological Analysis*. London: Wiley.

Fendrich, M., M. E. Mackesy-Amiti, P. Goldstein, B. Spunt, & H. Brownstein. (1995) Substance Involvement Among Juvenile Murderers: Comparisons With Older Offenders Based on Interviews With Prison Inmates. *International Journal of the Addictions* 30: 1363–82.

Ferracuti, F., & M. Wolfgang. (1970) *Violence in Sardinia*. Rome: Bulzoni.

Fingerhut, L. A., & J. C. Kleinman. (1990) International and Interstate Comparisons of Homicide Among Young Males. *Journal of the American Medical Association* 263: 292–95.

Fishbein, D. H. (1996) Biological Perspectives in Criminology. In D. G. Rojek & G. F. Jensen, Eds., *Exploring Delinquency: Causes and Control*. Los Angeles: Roxbury.

Fisher, D. (1994) Adult Sex Offenders: Who Are They? Why and How Do They Do It? In T. Morrison, M. Erooga, & R. C. Beckett, Eds., *Sexual Offending Against Children: Assessment and Treatment of Male Abusers*. New York: Routledge.

Flowers, R. B. (1986) *Children and Criminality: The Child as Victim and Perpetrator*. Westport: Greenwood.

Flowers, R. B. (1988) *Minorities and Criminality*. Westport: Greenwood.

Flowers, R. B. (1989) *Demographics and Criminality: The Characteristics of Crime in America*. Westport: Greenwood.

Flowers, R. B. (1990) *The Adolescent Criminal: An Examination of Today's Juvenile Offender*. Jefferson: McFarland.

Flowers, R. B. (1994) *The Victimization and Exploitation of Women and Children: A Study of Physical, Mental and Sexual Maltreatment in the United States*. Jefferson: McFarland.

Flowers, R. B. (1995) *Female Crime, Criminals and Cellmates: An Exploration of Female Criminality and Delinquency*. Jefferson: McFarland.

Flowers, R. B. (1998) *The Prostitution of Women and Girls*. Jefferson: McFarland.

Flowers, R. B. (1999) *Drugs, Alcohol and Criminality in American Society*. Jefferson: McFarland.

Flowers, R. B. (2000) *Domestic Crimes, Family Violence and Child Abuse: A Study of Contemporary American Society*. Jefferson: McFarland.

Flowers, R. B. (2001) *Sex Crimes, Predators, Perpetrators, Prostitutes, and Victims: An Examination of Sexual Criminality and Victimization*. Springfield: Charles C Thomas.

Flowers, R. B. (2002) *Kids Who Commit Adult Crimes: A Study of Serious Juvenile Criminality and Delinquency*. Binghamton: Haworth.

Flowers, R. B. (2003) *Male Crime and Deviance: Exploring Its Causes, Dynamics and Nature*. Springfield: Charles C Thomas.

Flowers, R. B. (2010) Should Violent Juvenile Offenders Be Tried and Sentenced as Adults? In R. B Flowers, Ed., *Issues: Enduring Question*. ABC-CLIO Solutions Database. http://www.abc-clio.com/product.aspx?id=2147483704.

Flowers, R. B. (2011) *The Sex Slave Murders: The True Story of Serial Killers Gerald and Charlene Gallego*, 2nd Ed. Honolulu: R. B Flowers.

Flowers, R. B. (2012) *Serial Killer Couples: Bonded by Sexual Depravity, Abduction, and Murder*. Honolulu: R. B Flowers.

Flowers, R. B, & H. L Flowers. (2001) *Murders in the United States: Crimes, Killers and Victims of the Twentieth Century*. Jefferson: McFarland.

Fontana, Vincent J. (1973) *Somewhere a Child Is Crying*. New York: Macmillan.

48 Hours Mystery. (August 20, 2010) The Craigslist Killer: Seven Days of Rage. http://www.cbsnews.com/2100-18559_162-6791591.html.

Fox, J A., & J Levin. (1999) Serial Murder: Myths and Realities. In M. D Smith and M A. Zahn, Eds., *Studying and Preventing Homicide: Issues and Challenges*. Thousand Oaks: Sage.

FoxNews.com. (March 22, 2005) High School Shooting Spree Leaves 10 Dead. http://www.foxnews.com/story/0,2933,151085,00.html.

FoxNews.com. (April 7, 2006) Woman Tried for Severing Baby's Arms Found Not Guilty by Insanity. http://www.foxnews.com/story/0%2C2933%2C190955%2C00.html.

FoxNews.com. (January 21, 2007) 22-Year-Old New York Man Murdered After Being Drawn Into Internet Love Triangle. http://www.foxnews.com/story/0,2933,245222,00.html.

Fredland, N. M. (2008) Nurturing Hostile Environments: The Problem of School Violence. *Family & Community Health* 3, 1: S32–S41.

The Free Library. (April 25, 2012) Internet Lures Sexual Predators, Experts Say. http://www.thefreelibrary.com/ INTERNET+LURES+SEXUAL+PREDATORS%2c+EXPERTS+SAY.-a084001234.

The Free Library. (May 7, 2012) DiMaiti Family Files Appeal. http://www.thefreelibrary.com/DiMaiti+family+files+appeal.-a018949219.

Freeman, M. A. (1979) *Violence in the Home*. Farnborough: Saxon House.

Freud, S. (1933) *New Introductory Lectures on Psychoanalysis*. New York: W. W. Norton.

Gallup, G., Jr., & A. Gallup. (1999) *The Gallup Poll Monthly*, No. 401. Princeton: The Gallup Poll.

Gallup, Inc. (May 11, 2012) *The Gallup Poll*. http://www.gallup.com/home.aspx.

Gayford, J. J. (1975) Wife Battering: A Preliminary Survey of 100 Cases. *British Medical Journal* 1: 194–97.

Gee, D. J. (1988) A Pathologist's View of Multiple Murder. *Forensic Science International* 38: 53–65.

Gelles, R. J. (1972) *The Violent Home: A Study of Physical Aggression Between Husbands and Wives*. Thousand Oaks: Sage.

Gelles, R. J. (October 1979) The Myth of Battered Husbands. *Ms*, 65–66, 71–72.

Gelles, R. J., & M. A. Straus. (1979) Violence in the American Family. *Journal of Social Issues* 35, 2: 15–39.

Glueck, S., & E. T. Glueck. (1956) *Physique and Delinquency*. New York: Harper & Row.

Goddard, H. H. (1914) *Feeblemindedness, Its Causes and Consequences*. New York: Macmillan.

Goldney, R. D. (1989) Suicidal Ideation in a Young Adult Population. *Acta Psychiatrica Scandinavica* 79: 481–89.

Goldstein, P. J., H. H. Brownstein, P. J. Ryan, & P. A. Bellucci. (1989) Crack and Homicide in New York City, 1988: A Conceptually Based Event Analysis. *Contemporary Drug Problems* 16: 651–87.

Goldstein, P. J., P. A. Bellucci, B. J. Spunt, & T. Miller. (1989) *Frequency of Cocaine Use and Violence: A Comparison Between Women and Men*. New York: Narcotic and Drug Research.

Gonzales v. Oregon. (2006) 546 U.S. 243.

Goudreau, J. (September 10, 2010) Female Employee Yvonne Hiller Kills Two in Kraft Shooting. *Forbes*. http://www.forbes.com/sites/jennagoudreau/2010/09/10/female-shooter-yvonne-hiller-kills-two-at-kraft-shooting.

Graves, R. (1962) *Greek Myths*. New York: Penguin.

Green, A. (December 13, 2008) Two Officers Confirmed Dead in Woodburn Bank Bombing. *OregonLive.com*. http://www.oregonlive.com/news/index.ssf/2008/12/police_identify_colleagues_kil.html.

Green, A. S. State Wins Time to Defend Suicide Law. http://www.oregonlive.com/news/oregonian/index.ssf?/xml/story.ssf/html.

Green, E. (1970) Race, Social Status, and Criminal Arrest. *American Sociological Review* 35: 476–90.

Grodd, E. R., & J. L. Diamond. (August 13, 2008) Primetime Crime: Teen Charged With Parents' Gruesome Murder. *ABC Primetime*. http://abcnews.go.com/TheLaw/story?id=3451371&page=1.

Guttmacher, M. (1973) *The Mind of the Murderer*. New York: Arno Press.

Hagedorn, J. J. (1988) *People and Folks: Gangs, Crime and the Underclass in a Rustbelt City*. Chicago: Lakeview Press.

Hales, T., P. Seligman, C. Newman, & C. L. Timbrook. (1988) Occupational Injuries Due to Violence. *Journal of Occupational Medicine* 30: 483–87.

Harries, K. (1990) *Serious Violence: Patterns of Homicide and Assault in America*. Springfield: Charles C Thomas.

Harris, J. R. (1970) On the Economics of Law and Order. *Journal of Political Economy* 78: 165–74.

Harris, M. B. (1996) Aggression, Gender, and Ethnicity. *Aggression and Violent Behavior* 1, 2: 123–46.

Harrison, M., & S. Gilbert. (1996) *The Murder Reference: Everything You Never Wanted to Know About Murder in America*. San Diego: Excellent Books.

Harry, J. (1989) Sexual Identity Issues. In *Report of the Secretary's Task Force Report on Youth Suicide*, Vol. 2. Washington: Department of Health and Human Services.

Havens, C., & J. Walsh. (October 8, 2007) Online Nanny Ad Ends in Slaying. *Star Tribune*. http://www.startribune.com/local/south/11545261.html?page=1&c=y.

Hawkins, D. F. (1990) Explaining the Black Homicide Rate. *Journal of Interpersonal Violence* 5: 151–63.

Hawkins, D. F. (1999) African Americans and Homicide. In M. D. Smith and M. A. Zahn, Eds., *Studying and Preventing Homicide: Issues and Challenges*. Thousand Oaks: Sage.

Hazelwood, R. R., & J. E. Douglas. (1980) The Last Murder. *FBI Law Enforcement Bulletin* 49: 1–8.

Hazelwood, R. R., P. E. Dietz, & J. Warren. (1992) The Criminal Sexual Sadist. *FBI Law Enforcement Bulletin* 61: 12–20.

Healy, W., & A. Bronner (1926) *Delinquency and Criminals: Their Making and Unmaking*. New York: Macmillan.

Heide, K. M. (1993) Parents Who Get Killed and the Children Who Kill Them. *Journal of Interpersonal Violence* 8, 4: 531–44.

Heide, K. M. (1995) *Why Kids Kill Parents: Child Abuse and Adolescent Homicide.* Thousand Oaks: Sage.

Heide, K. M. (1996) Why Kids Keep Killing: The Correlates, Causes, and Challenges of Juvenile Homicide. *Stanford Law and Policy Review* 71: 43–49.

Heide, K. M. (1997) 1998 Keynote Address: School Shootings and School Violence: What's Going On and Why? In U.S. Department of Justice. *Proceedings of the Homicide Research Working Group Meetings, 1997 and 1998.* Washington: National Institute of Justice.

Heide, K. M. (1997) Dangerously Antisocial Kids Who Kill Their Parents: Toward a Better Understanding of the Phenomenon. In U.S. Department of Justice, *The Nature of Homicide: Trends and Changes—Proceedings of the 1996 Meeting of the Homicide Research Working Group.* Washington: National Institute of Justice.

Heide, K. M. (1999) Youth Homicide. In M. D. Smith & M. A. Zahn, Eds., *Studying and Preventing Homicide: Issues and Challenges.* Thousand Oaks: Sage.

Heide, K. M. (1999) *Young Killers: The Challenge of Juvenile Homicide.* Thousand Oaks: Sage.

Hickey, E. (1991) *Serial Killers and Their Victims.* Pacific Grove: Brooks/Cole.

Hickey, E. (1997) *Serial Murderers and Their Victims.* 2nd ed. Belmont: Wadsworth.

Hirschi, T. (1969) *Causes of Delinquency.* Berkeley: University of California Press.

Hirschi, T., & M. J. Hindelang. (1977) Intelligence and Delinquency: A Revisionist Review. *American Sociological Review* 42: 571–86.

Holmes, R. M. (1990) Human Hunters. *Knightbeat* 9, 1: 43–47.

Holmes, R. M., & J. E. DeBurger. (1985) Profiles in Terror. *Federal Probation* 49, 3: 53–61.

Holmes, R. M., & J. E. DeBurger. (1988) *Serial Murder.* Thousand Oaks: Sage.

Holmes, R. M., & S. T. Holmes. (1992) Understanding Mass Murder. *Federal Probation* 56, 1: 53–61.

Holmes, R. M., & S. T. Holmes. (1994) *Murder in America.* Thousand Oaks: Sage.

Honig, W. (1966) *Operant Behavior: Areas of Research and Application.* New York: Appleton-Century-Crofts.

Hooten, E. A. (1939) *Crime and the Man.* Cambridge, Harvard University Press.

Horney, J. (1978) Menstrual Cycles and Criminal Responsibility. *Law and Human Behavior* 2, 1: 25–36.

Houts, M. (1970) *They Asked for Death.* New York: Cowles.

Howell, J. C. (1995) Gangs and Youth Violence. In J. C. Howell, B. Krisberg, J. D. Hawkins, & J. J. Wilson, Eds., *A Sourcebook: Serious, Violent and Chronic Juvenile Offenders.* Thousand Oaks: Sage.

Huizinga, D. R. (1997) The Volume of Crime by Gang and Nongang Members, paper presented at the Annual Meeting of the American Society of Criminology. San Diego.

Huizinga, D. R., R. Loeber, & T. P. Thornberry. (1994) *Urban Delinquency and Substance Abuse.* Washington: Office of Justice Programs.

Hutchings, B., & S. A. Mednick. (1975) Registered Criminality in the Adoptive and Biological Parents of Registered Male Criminal Adoptees. In R. R. Fieve, D. Rosenthal, and H. Brill, Eds., *Genetic Research in Psychiatry.* Baltimore: John Hopkins University Press.

Hutson, H. R., D. Anglin, & M. Eckstein. (1996) Drive-by Shootings by Violent Street Gangs in Los Angeles: A Five-Year Review From 1989 to 1993. *Academic Emergency Medicine* 3: 300–03.

Idaho v. Johnson. (June 26, 2008) Opinion 89. Idaho Supreme Court.

Inciardi, J. A., & A. E. Pottieger. (1991) Kids, Crack, and Crime. *Journal of Drug Issues* 21: 257–70.

Investigation Discovery. (September 11, 2008) *Wicked Attraction: Twisted Twosome.* http://www.imdb.com/title/tt1277357/.

Jamison, K. R. (1999) *Night Falls Fast: Understanding Suicide.* New York: Vintage.

Jenkins, P. (1988) Serial Murder in England, 1940–1985. *Journal of Criminal Justice* 16: 1–15.

Jenkins, P. (1990) Sharing Murder. *Journal of Crime and Justice* 12: 125–48.

Jenkins, P. (1992) A Murder 'Wave'? *Criminal Justice Review 17,* 1: 1–19.

Jung, R. S., & L. A. Jason. (1988) Firearm Violence and the Effects of Gun Control Legislation. *American Journal of Community Psychology* 16: 515–24.

Jurik, N. C., & R. Winn. (1990) Gender and Homicide: A Comparison of Men and Women Who Kill. *Violence and Victims* 5, 4: 227–42.

Kalmuss, D. S. (1984) The Intergenerational Transmission of Marital Aggression. *Journal of Marriage and the Family* 46: 16–19.

Kantor, G. K., & J. L. Jasinski. (1998) Dynamics and Risk Factors in Partner Violence. In J. L. Jasinski & L. M. Williams, Eds., *Partner Violence: A Comprehensive Review of 20 Years of Research.* Thousand Oaks: Sage.

Kantor, G. K., & M. A. Straus. (1989) Substance Abuse as a Precipitant of Wife Abuse Victimization. *American Journal of Drug and Alcohol Abuse* 15: 173–89.

Kasarda, J. (1993) Inner-City Concentrated Poverty and Neighborhood Distress: 1970–1990. *Housing Policy Debate* 4, 3: 253–302.

Kellermann, A. L., & J. A. Mercy. (1992) Men, Women, and Murder: Gender-Specific Differences in Rates of Fatal Violence and Victimization. *Journal of Trauma* 33: 1–5.

Kellermann, A. L., F. P. Rivara, N. B. Rushforth, J. G. Banton, D. T. Reay, J. T. Francisco, A. B. Locci, J. P. Prodzinski, B. B. Hackman, & G. Somes. (1993) Gun Ownership as a Risk Factor for Homicide in the Home. *New England Journal of Medicine* 329: 1084–91.

Kelly, K., & M. D. Totten. (2002) *When Children Kill: A Social-Psychological Study of Youth Homicide.* Toronto: University of Toronto Press.

Kemp, D. (June 9, 2011) Father Sentenced to Life Without Parole in Quadruple Slaying. *WLKY.com.* http://www.wlky.com/news/28182980/detail.html.

Kennedy, D. M., A. A. Braga, & A. M. Piehl. (1997) The (Un)Known Universe: Mapping Gangs and Gang Violence in Boston. In D. Weisburd & T. McEwen, Eds., *Crime Mapping and Crime Prevention.* New York: Criminal Justice Press.

Keppel, R. D., & W. J. Birnes. (1997) *Signature Killers: Interpreting the Calling Cards of the Sexual Murderer.* New York: Pocket Books.

King, L. (October 12, 2011) Bucks Woman Who Clubbed, Burned Mother Gets Life. *The Inquirer.* http://articles.philly.com/2011-10-12/news/30271297_1_murder-conviction-first degree-murder-life-sentence.

Kleck, G. (1991) *Point Blank: Guns and Violence in America.* New York: Aldine de Gruyter.

Kleiman, D. (1988) *A Deadly Silence*. New York: Atlantic Monthly Press.

Klein, M. W. (1995) *The American Street Gang: Its Nature, Prevalence, and Control*. New York: Oxford.

Klein, M. W., C. L. Maxson, & L. C. Cunningham. (1991) "Crack," Street Gangs, and Violence. *Criminology* 29: 623–50.

Kletschka, H. D. (1966) Violent Behavior Associated with Brain Tumors. *Minnesota Medicine* 49: 1835–55.

Kraus, J. F. (1987) Homicides While at Work: Persons, Industries, and Occupations at High Risk. *American Journal of Public Health* 77, 10: 1285–89.

Krugman, R. D. (1983–1985) Fatal Child Abuse: An Analysis of 20 Cases. *Pediatrics* 12: 68–72.

Kuehl, S. (1998) Legal Remedies for Teen Dating Violence. In B. Levy, Ed., *Dating Violence: Young Women in Danger*. Seattle: Seal Press.

LaFree, G. (1995) Race and Crime Trends in the United States, 1946–1990. In D. F. Hawkins, Ed., *Ethnicity, Race and Crime: Perspectives Across Time and Place*. Albany: State University of New York Press.

Lange, J. (1931) *Crime as Destiny*. London: George Allen & Unwin.

Langevin, R., M. H. Ben-Aron, P. Wright, V. Marchese, & L. Handy. (1988) The Sex Killer. *Annals of Sex Research* 1: 263–301.

Langley, R., & R. C. Levy. (1977) *Wife Beating: The Silent Crisis*. New York: Dutton.

Laquer, W. (1987) *The Age of Terrorism*. New York: Little, Brown.

Largo, M. (2006) *Final Exits: The Illustrated Encyclopedia of How We Die*. New York: William Morrow.

Leibman, F. H. (1989) Serial Murderers. *Federal Probation* 53, 4: 41–45.

Leibowitz, B. (December 8, 2010) Bruce and Joshua Turnidge, Father-Son Bank Bombers, Convicted of Murdering Two Ore. Cops in '08. *CBS News*. http://www.cbsnews.com/8301-504083_162-20025053-504083.html?tag=contentMain;contentBody.

Lerner, R. M. (1994) *America's Youth in Crisis*. Thousand Oaks: Sage.

Lester, D. (1995) *Serial Killers: The Insatiable Passion*. Philadelphia: Charles Press.

Leventhal, J M. (1999) The Challenges of Recognizing Child Abuse: Seeing Is Believing. *Journal of the American Medical Association* 281, 7: 657.

Levin, J., & J. A. Fox. (1985) *Mass Murder*. New York: Plenum.

Levine, M., J. Freeman, & C. Compaan. (1994) Maltreatment-Related Fatalities: Issues of Policy and Prevention. *Law and Policy* 16, 449: 458.

Leyton, E. (1986) *Compulsive Killers*. New York: New York University Press.

Leyton, E. (1989) *Hunting Humans*. London: Penguin.

Lichtblau, E. (February 3, 1989) A Long Road for Massip: Postpartum Psychosis: Recovery Is Torturous. *Los Angeles Times*, p. 1.

Lin, W. (1997) Perpetrators of Hate. *Yale Political Quarterly* 19, 2: 12.

Lindquist, P. (1991) Homicides Committed by Abusers of Alcohol and Illicit Drugs. *British Journal of Addiction* 86: 321–26.

Liscomb, J. A., & C. C. Love. (1992) Violence Toward Health Care Workers: An Emerging Occupational Hazard. *American Association of Occupational Health Nurses Journal* 40: 219–28.

Liss, G. M., & C. A. Craig. (1990) Homicide in the Workplace in Ontario: Occupations at Risk and Limitations of Existing Data Sources. *Canadian Journal of Public Health* 81: 10–15.

Lizotte, A. J., J. M. Tesoriero, T. P. Thornberry, & M. D. Krohn. (1994) Patterns of Adolescent Firearms Ownership and Use. *Justice Quarterly* 11: 51–73.

Lombroso, C., & W. Ferrero. (1972) *Criminal Man.* Montclair: Patterson Smith.

Los Angeles Times. (September 27, 1991) Nation in Brief: Massachusetts: Brother Charged in Stuart Slaying. http://articles.latimes.com/1991-09-27/news/mn-2919_1_charles-stuart.

Lunde, D. T. (1975) Hot Blood's Record Month: Our Murder Boom, *Psychology Today* 9: 35–42.

Lunde, D. T. (1979) *Murder and Madness.* New York: Norton.

Lyshak, M. (November 29, 2011) Police Suspect Murder Victims Found on Long Island's Gilgo Beach Were Murdered by Single Serial Killer. *NYDailyNews. com.* http://www.nydailynews.com/new-york/police-suspect-murder-victims-found-long-island-gilgo-beach-murdered-single-serial-killer-article-1.984318.

Maloney, M. (1994) Children Who Kill Their Parents. *Prosecutor's Brief: California District Attorney's Association Journal* 20: 20–22.

Martinez, R. (1996) Latinos and Lethal Violence: The Impact of Poverty and Inequality. *Social Problems* 43: 131–46.

Martinez, Ramiro. (1997) Homicide Among Miami's Ethnic Groups: Anglos, Blacks, and Latinos in the 1990s. *Homicide Studies* 1: 17–34.

Martinez, R, & M T. Lee. (1999) Latinos and Homicide. In M. D Smith & M A. Zahn, Eds., *Studying and Preventing Homicide: Issues and Challenges.* Thousand Oaks: Sage.

Marzuk, P. M., K. Tardiff, & C. S. Hirsh. (1992) The Epidemiology of Murder-Suicide. *Journal of the American Medical Association* 267, 23: 3179–83.

Maxson, C. (1999) Gang Homicide. In M. D. Smith & M. A. Zahn, Eds., *Studying and Preventing Homicide: Issues and Challenges.* Thousand Oaks: Sage.

Maxson, C., & M. W. Klein. (1996) Defining Gang Homicide: An Updated Look at Member and Motive Approaches. In C. R. Huff, Ed., *Gangs in America*, 2nd ed. Thousand Oaks: Sage.

Mayhall, P. D., & K. Norgard. (1983) *Child Abuse and Neglect: Sharing Responsibility.* Toronto: John Wiley & Sons.

McCord, W., & J. McCord. (1964) *The Psychopath.* Princeton: Van Nostrand.

McDowall, D., C. Loftin, & B. Wiersema. (1995) Easing Concealed Firearms Laws: Effects on Homicide in Three States. *Journal of Criminal Law and Criminology* 86: 193–206.

McLaughlin, B. (1971) *Learning and Social Behavior.* New York: Free Press.

Mears, B. (April 4, 2008) Woman Gets Death Sentence in Fetus-Snatching Murder. *CNN Justice.* http://articles.cnn.com/2008-04-04/justice/pregnant.slaying_1_lisa-montgomery-bobbie-jo-stinnett-death-sentence?_s=PM:CRIME.

Mednick, S. A., W. F. Gabrielli, & B. Hutchings. (1984) Genetic Influences in Criminal Convictions: Evidence From an Adoption Cohort. *Science* 234: 891–94.

Meehan, P. J., & P. W. O'Carroll. (1992) Gangs, Drugs, and Homicide in Los Angeles. *American Journal of Disease Control* 146: 683–87.

Mehren, E. (January 10, 1991) Civil Suit Is Filed in Boston Murder Case: Courts: Carol Stuart's Family Wants to Bar Her Husband's Heirs From Inheriting Any of Her Estate. They Claim "Public Policy" Prevents Profiting From Her Death. *Los Angeles Times.* http://articles.latimes.com/1991-01-10/news/vw-11239_1_carol-stuart.

Meloy, J. R. (1992) *Violent Attachments*. Northvale: Aronson.

Merrill, E. (July 4, 2010) The Woman Forever Tied to Steve McNair. *ESPN.com*. http://sports.espn.go.com/espn/otl/news/story?id=5347315.

Merton, R. K. (1938) Social Structure and Anomie. *American Sociological Review* 8: 672–82.

Merton, R. K. (1957) *Social Theory and Social Structure*. New York: Free Press.

Michels, S. (April 1, 2009) Craigslist Killer Lured Victim With Baby Sitter Ad. *ABC News*. http://abcnews.go.com/Technology/story?id=7227285&page=1.

Miller, W. B. (1958) Lower-Class Culture as a Generating Milieu of Gang Delinquency. *Journal of Social Issues* 14: 5–19.

Miller, W. B. (1970) White Gangs. In J. F. Short, Jr., Ed., *Modern Criminals*. Chicago: Aldine.

Miller, W. B. (1974) American Youth Gangs: Past and Present. In A. Blumberg, Ed., *Current Perspectives in Criminal Behavior*. New York: Knopf.

Miller, W. B. (1975) *Violence by Youth Gangs and Youth Groups as a Crime Problem in Major American Cities*. Washington: Government Printing Office.

Miller, W. B. (1992) *Crime by Youth Gangs and Groups in the United States*. Washington: Office of Justice Programs.

Mones, P. A. (1991) *When a Child Kills: Abused Children Who Kill Their Parents*. New York: Pocket Books.

Money, J. (1990) Forensic Sexology. *American Journal of Psychotherapy* 44: 26–36.

Moore, J. W. (1978) *Homeboys: Gangs, Drugs and Prison in the Barrios of Los Angeles*. Philadelphia: Temple University Press.

Moore, J. W. (1990) Gangs, Drugs, and Violence. In M. De La Rosa, E. Y. Lambert, & B. Gropper, Eds., *Drugs and Violence: Causes, Correlates, and Consequences*. Rockville: National Institute on Drug Abuse.

Morales, A. (1998) Seeking a Cure for Child Abuse, *USA Today 127*, 2640: 34.

Morris, C. (1967) *The Tudors*. London: Fontana.

MSNBC.com. (October 3, 2006) 5th Girl Dies After Amish Schoolhouse Shooting. http://www.msnbc.msn.com/id/15105305/ns/us_news-crime_and.

MSNBC.com. (April 17, 2007) Worst U.S. Shooting Ever Kills 33 on Va. Campus. http://www.msnbc.msn.com/id/18134671/ns/us_news-crime_and_courts.

MSNBC.com. (May 29, 2007) Americans Still Split on Doctor-Assisted Suicide. http://www.msnbc.msn.com/id/18923323/ns/health-health_care/t/americans-still-split-doctor-assisted-suicide/.

MSNBC.com Crime & Courts. (November 23, 2004) "Mother Confesses to Severing Baby's Arms." http://www.msnbc.msn.com/id/6561617.

Murderpedia.org. (April 26, 2012) James D. Pritchert. http://www.murderpedia.org/male.P/p/pritchert-james.htm.

Nansel, T. R., M. D. Overpeck, D. L. Haynie, W. J. Ruan, & P. C. Scheidt. (2003) Relationships Between Bullying and Violence Among U.S. Youth. *Archives of Pediatric and Adolescent Medicine* 157, 4: 348–53.

National Commission on Terrorist Attacks. (2004) *The 9/11 Commission Report: Final Report of the National Commission on Terrorist Attacks Upon the United States*. New York: W.W. Norton.

National Gang Center. (April 10, 2012) *National Youth Gang Survey Analysis: Measuring the Extent of Gang Problems*. http://www.nationalgangcenter.gov/Survey-Analysis/Measuring-the-Extent-of-Gang-Problems.

National Youth Gang Center. (1997) *1995 National Youth Gang Survey.* Washington: Office of Juvenile Justice and Delinquency Prevention.

Newhill, C. E. (1991) Parricide. *Journal of Family Violence 64*: 375–94.

Norris, J. (1989) *Serial Killers.* New York: Anchor.

Northwest National Life. (1993) *Fear and Violence in the Workplace: A Survey Documenting the Experience of American Workers.* Minneapolis: Northwest National Life.

NY1.com. (November 15, 2011) Teen Convicted of Fatally Stabbing Brooklyn Radio Reporter. http://brooklyn.ny1.com/content/top_stories/150835/teen-convicted-of-fatally-stabbing-brooklyn-radio-reporter/.

NYDailyNews.com. (April 3, 2009) Craigslist killer Michael John Anderson gets life in murder of Katherine Olson. http://www.nydailynews.com/news/world/craigslist-killer-michael-john-anderson-life-murder-katherine-olson-article-1.361506.

O'Brien, S. (1980) *Child Abuse: Commission and Omission.* Provo: Brigham Young University Press.

Oliver, J. E. (1978) The Epidemiology of Child Abuse. In S. M. Smith, Ed., *The Maltreatment of Children.* Baltimore: University Park Press.

Osgood, D. W. (1995) *Drugs, Alcohol, and Violence.* Boulder: University of Colorado, Institute of Behavioral Science.

Ovalle, D. (October 15, 2009) Miami Teen Who Raped, Killed Sister, to Use Insanity Defense. *Palm Beach Post News.* http://www.wsvn.com/news/articles/local/MI134548.

Pagelow, M. D. (1984) *Family Violence.* New York: Praeger.

Palmer, S., & J. A. Humphrey. (1980) Offender–Victim Relationships in Criminal Homicide Followed by Offender's Suicide, North Carolina, 1972–1977. *Suicide and Life-Threatening Behavior* 10, 2: 106–18.

Park, R. E., & E. W. Burgess. (1925) *The City.* Chicago: University of Chicago Press.

Parker, R. N. (1989) Poverty, Subculture of Violence, and Type of Homicide. *Social Forces* 67: 983–1007.

Parker, R. N., & L. Rebhun. (1995) *Alcohol and Homicide: A Deadly Combination of Two American Traditions.* Albany: State University of New York Press.

Pelisek, C. (April 17, 2011) Terror on Long Island, *The Daily Beast.* http://www.thedailybeast.com/newsweek/2011/04/17/terror-on-long-island.html.

Petee, T. A. (1999) Situational Factors Related to Public Mass Murder Incidents: 1965–1998. In U.S. Department of Justice, *Proceedings of the Homicide Research Working Group Meetings, 1997 and 1998.* Washington: National Institute of Justice.

Petee, T. A., K. G. Padgett, & T. S. York. (1997) Debunking the Stereotype: An Examination of Mass Murder in Public Places. *Homicide Studies 1*, 4: 317–37.

Pettus, M. (April 29, 2011) Mom Gets 55 Years in Prison for Killing Daughter. *WUSA9.com.* http://www.wusa9.com/news/article/148815/373/Mom-Gets-55-Years-In-Prison-For-Killing-Daughter.

Piers, M. W. (1978) *Infanticide.* New York: W. W. Norton.

Pitt, S. E., & E. M. Bale. (1995) Neonaticide, Infanticide, and Filicide: A Review of the Literature. *Bulletin of the American Academy of Psychiatry and Law 23*: 379.

Polk, K., & D. Ransom. (1991) The Role of Gender in Intimate Homicide. *Australian and New Zealand Journal of Criminology* 24: 20.

Pollock, V., S. A. Mednick, & W. F. Gabrielli, Jr. (1983) Crime Causation: Biological Theories. In S. H. Kadish, Ed., *Encyclopedia of Crime and Justice*, Vol. 1. New York: Free Press.

Prentky, R. A., A. W. Burgess, F. Rokous, A. Lee, C. R. Hartman, R. K. Ressler, & J. E. Douglas. (1989) The Presumptive Role of Fantasy in Serial Sexual Homicide. *American Journal of Psychiatry* 146: 887–91.

President's Commission on Mental Health. (1978) *Report to the President*, Vol. 1. Washington: Government Printing Office.

Quay, H. C. (1983) Crime Causation: Psychological Theories. In S. H. Kadish, Ed., *Encyclopedia of Crime and Justice*, Vol. 1. New York: Free Press.

Quay, H. C. (1987) Patterns of Delinquent Behavior. In H. C. Quay, Ed., *Handbook of Juvenile Delinquency*. New York: Wiley-Interscience.

Rappaport, R. G. (1988) The Serial and Mass Murderer. *American Journal of Forensic Psychiatry 9*, 1: 39–48.

Rasche, C. E. (1998) Theorizing About Homicide: A Presentation on Theories Explaining Homicide and Other Crimes. In U.S. Department of Justice, *The Nature of Homicide: Trends and Changes—Proceedings of the 1996 Meeting of the Homicide Research Working Group*. Washington: National Institute of Justice.

Reckless, W. C. (1973) *The Crime Problem*, 5th ed. Santa Monica: Goodyear.

Reckless, W. C., S. Dinitz, & E. Murray. (1970) Self-Concept as an Insulator Against Delinquency. In J. E. Teele, Ed., *Juvenile Delinquency: A Reader*. Itasca: Peacock.

Resnick, P. J. (1969) Child Murder by Parents: A Psychiatric Review of Filicide. *American Journal of Psychiatry 126*, 3: 325–34.

Ressler, R. K., A. W. Burgess, & J. E. Douglas. (1988) *Sexual Homicide: Patterns and Motives*. New York: Lexington Books.

Ressler, R. K., A. W. Burgess, C. R. Hartman, J. E. Douglas, & A. McCormack. (1986) Murderers Who Rape and Mutilate. *Journal of Interpersonal Violence* 1: 273–87.

Robins, L. N. (1966) *Deviant Children Grown Up*. Baltimore: Williams & Wilkins.

Roche, T. (March 18, 2002) Andrea Yates: More to the Story. *Time U.S.* http://www.time.com/time/nation/article/0,8599,218445,00.html

Rogers, C. (1993) Gang-Related Homicides in Los Angeles County. *Journal of Forensic Sciences* 38, 4: 831–34.

Romero, L. M., & L. G. Stelzner. (1985) Hispanics and the Criminal Justice System. In P. Cafferty & W. C. McCready, Eds., *Hispanics in the United States: A New Social Agenda*. New Brunswick: Transaction Books.

Rose, H. M., & P. D. McClain. (1990) *Race, Place, and Risk: Black Homicide in Urban America*. Albany: State University of New York Press.

Rosenbaum, M. (1990) The Role of Depression in Couples Involved in Murder-Suicide and Homicide." *American Journal of Psychiatry* 147, 8: 1036–39.

Roth, M. (March 15, 2012) "Experts Track the Patterns of Mass Murders. *Pittsburgh Post-Gazette*. http://www.post-gazette.com/stories/local/neighborhoods-city/experts-track-the-patterns-of-mass-murders-337604/.

Rule, A. (2005) *Green River, Running Red: The Real Story of the Green River Killer—America's Deadliest Serial Murderer*. New York: Pocket Star.

Russell, D. E. (1982) *Rape in Marriage*. New York: Macmillan.

Russell, D. E. (1984) A Study of Juvenile Murderers of Family Members. *International Journal of Offender Therapy and Comparative Criminology* 28: 177–92.

Saltzman, L., & J. Mercy. (1993) Assaults Between Intimates: The Range of Relationships Involved. In A. Wilson, Ed., *Homicide: The Victim/Offender Connection*. Cincinnati: Anderson.

Saltzman, S. R. (October 19, 2009) Exclusive: Was Steve McNair Murder Investigation Flawed? Was Lover Really Suicidal? *CBS News*. http://www.cbsnews.com/8301-504083_162-5390156-504083.html?tag=contentMain%3bcontentBody.

Saltzman, S. R. (October 20, 2009) Sahel Kazemi and Steve McNair Final Texts Show Worries of Love and Money. *CBS News*. http://www.cbsnews.com/8301-504083_162-5400986-504083.html?tag=contentMain%3bcontentBody.

Samenow, S. E. (1984) *Inside the Criminal Mind*. New York: Time Books.

Sargeant, D. (1971) Children Who Kill: A Family Conspiracy? In J. Howells, Ed., *Theory and Practice of Family Psychiatry*. New York: Brunner-Mazel.

Schaefer, R. T. (1993) *Racial and Ethnic Groups*, 5th ed. New York: Harper Collins.

Schlesinger, L. B., & E. Revitch. (1983) Sexual Dynamics in Homicide and Assault. In L. B. Schlesinger & E. Revitch, Eds., *Sexual Dynamics of Anti-Social Behavior*. Springfield: Charles C Thomas.

Schloesser, P., J. Pierpont, & J. Poertner. (1992) Active Surveillance of Child Abuse Fatalities. *Child Abuse and Neglect 16*: 3–10.

Schulsinger, F. (1972) Psychopathy: Heredity and Environment. *International Journal of Mental Health* 1: 190–206.

Schultz, L. (1968) The Victim-Offender Relationship. *Crime and Delinquency* 14, 2: 135–41.

Sears, D. J. (1991) *To Kill Again*. Wilmington: Scholarly Resources.

Seattle Times. (September 4, 2011) Mass. Man Convicted of Aiding In-Law Killing Dies. http://seattletimes.nwsource.com/html/nationworld/2016108848_apusstuartbrotherdeath.html.

Segrave, K. (1992) *Women Serial and Mass Murderers*. Jefferson: McFarland.

Sellin, T. (1938) *Culture Conflict and Crime*. New York: Social Science Research Council.

Severson, K. (March 22, 2012) Three Plead Guilty to Hate Crimes in Killing of Black Man in Mississippi. *New York Times*. http://www.nytimes.com/2012/03/23/us/three-plead-guilty-to-hate-crimes-in-killing-of-black-man-in-mississippi.html?scp=1&sq three%20plead%20guilty%20to%20hate%20crime&st=cse.

Shaefer, R. T. (1993) *Racial and Ethnic Groups*, 5th ed. New York: Harper Collins.

Shah, S., & L. Roth. (1974) Biological and Psychological Factors in Criminality. In D. Glaser, Ed., *Handbook of Criminology*. Chicago: Rand McNally.

Shaw, C. R., & H. D. McKay. (1969) *Juvenile Delinquency and Urban Areas*. Chicago: University of Chicago Press.

Sheldon, W. A. (1942) *Varieties of Temperament*. New York: Harper & Row.

Sheley, J. F. (1985) *America's "Crime Problem": An Introduction to Criminology*. Belmont: Wadsworth.

Sheley, J. F., & J. D. Wright. (1995) *In the Line of Fire: Youth, Guns, and Violence in America*. New York: Aldine de Gruyter, Inc.

Shin, Y., D. Jedlicka, & E. S. Lee. (1977) Homicide Among Blacks. *Phylon* 39: 399–406.

Shireman, C. H., & F. G. Reamer (1986) *Rehabilitating Juvenile Justice*. New York: Columbia University Press.

Short, J. F., Jr. (1964) Gang Delinquency and Anomie. In M. B. Clinard, Ed., *Anomie and Deviant Behavior*. New York: Free Press.

Short, J. F., Jr., & F. L. Strodtbeck. (1965) *Group Process and Gang Delinquency.* Chicago: University of Chicago Press.

Shortopedia.com. (April 25, 2012) American Murderers. http://www.shortopedia. com/A/M/American_murderers__page4.

Smart, C. (1977) *Women, Crime and Criminology: A Feminist Critique.* Boston: Routledge and Kegan Paul.

Smith, E. E. (October 6, 2010) Korena Roberts Pleads Guilty; Sentenced to Life in Prison. *OregonLive.com.* http://www.oregonlive.com/washingtoncounty/index. ssf/2010/10/korena_roberts_pleads.html

Smith, M. D. (1996) Sources of Firearm Acquisition Among a Sample of Inner City Youths: Research Results and Policy Implications. *Journal of Criminal Justice* 24: 361–67.

Smith, T. (May 3, 2012) Attorney Seeks to Reopen Johnson Case. *Idaho Mountain Express.* http://mtexpress.com/story_printer.php?ID=2005141831.

Solomon, T. (1973) History and Demography of Child Abuse. *Pediatrics 51,* 4: 773–76.

Song, J. K. (November 2, 1999) 7 Dead in Nimitz Hwy. Xerox Shooting. *StarBulletin. com.* http://archives.starbulletin.com/1999/11/02/news/story1.html.

Spergel, I. A. (1984) Violent Gangs in Chicago: In Search of Social Policy. *Social Science Review* 58: 199–226.

Spergel, I. A. (1995) *The Youth Gang Problem: A Community Approach.* New York: Oxford.

Spunt, B., H. Brownstein, P. Goldstein, M. Fendrich, & H. J. Liberty. (1995) Drug Use by Homicide Offenders. *Journal of Psychoactive Drugs* 27: 125–34.

Staats, A. (1975) *Social Behaviorism.* Homewood: Dorsey Press.

Stack, S. (1997) Homicide Followed by Suicide: An Analysis of Chicago Data. *Criminology* 35, 3: 435–53.

Stark, E., & A. Flitcraft. (1988) Violence Among Intimates: An Epidemiological Review. In V. B. Van Hasselt, R. L. Morrison, A. S. Bellack, & M. Hersen, Eds., *Handbook of Family Violence.* New York: Plenum.

Steinmetz, S. K. (1978) The Battered Husband Syndrome. *Victimology* 2: 507.

Straus, M. A. (1976) Domestic Violence and Homicide Antecedents. *Bulletin of the New York Academy of Medicine 62*: 446–65.

Straus, M. A., R. J. Gelles, & S. K. Steinmetz. (1980) *Behind Closed Doors: Violence in the American Family.* Garden City: Doubleday/Anchor.

Strode, T. (February 2, 2011) Oregon Sets Record for Assisted Suicides. *Ethics and Religious Liberty Commission.* http://erlc.com/article/oregon-sets-record-for-assisted-suicides/.

Sullivan, R. F. (1973) The Economics of Crime: An Introduction to the Literature. *Crime and Delinquency* 19, 2: 138–49.

Sutherland, E. H. (1939) *Principles of Criminology.* Philadelphia: Lippincott.

Sutherland, E. H., & D. R. Cressey. (1974) *Criminology,* 9th ed. Philadelphia: J. B. Lippincott.

Sutherland, E. H., & D. R. Cressey. (1978) *Criminology,* 10th ed. Philadelphia: J. B. Lippincott.

Sykes, G. M. (1974) The Rise and Fall of Critical Criminology. *Journal of Criminal Law and Criminology* 65: 206–13.

Tattersall, C. (1999) *Drugs, Runaways, and Teen Prostitution.* New York: Rosen.

Terrace, T. (April 14, 1991) A Gift Abandoned, *St. Petersburg Times,* p. 5.

Thomas, J. L. (1992) Occupational Violent Crime: Research on an Emerging Issue. *Journal of Safety Research* 23: 55–62.

Thornberry, T. P. (1998) Membership in Youth Gangs and Involvement in Serious and Violent Offending. In R. Loeber & D. P. Farrington, Eds., *Serious and Violent Offenders: Risk Factors and Successful Interventions*. Thousand Oaks: Sage.

Thornberry, T. P., & J. H. Birch. (1997) *Gang Members and Delinquent Behavior.* Washington: Office of Justice Programs.

Thrasher, F. M. (1927) *The Gang.* Chicago: University of Chicago Press.

Totman, J. (1978) *The Murderesses: A Psychosocial Study of Criminal Homicide.* San Francisco: R & E Associates.

Toufexis, A. (June 20, 1998) Why Mothers Kill Their Babies. *Time,* p. 81.

Tsakas, D. (April 25, 2012) John Katehis, 18, Given Maximum Sentence for Brutal Slaying. *National Herald.* http://www.thenationalherald.com/article/52974.

Tswei, S. (June 2, 2000) Judge's Leave to Delay Trial for One Week. *Star-Bulletin.com.* http://archives.starbulletin.com/2000/06/02/news/story2.html.

Tucker, L. S., & T. P. Cornwall. (1977) Mother-Son Folie a Duex: A Case of Attempted Parricide. *American Journal of Psychiatry 134,* 10: 1146–47.

Tulchin, S. H. (1972) *Intelligence and Crime.* Chicago: University of Chicago Press.

Tumulty, K., & D. Treadwell. (January 5, 1990) Suicide of Man Whose Wife Was Slain Stuns Boston. *Los Angeles Times.* http://articles.latimes.com/1990-01-05/news/mn-204_1_charles-stuart.

United Press International. (October 29, 1989) Boston Mourns Pregnant Woman Killed by Robber. http://articles.latimes.com/1989-10-29/news/mn-501_1_boston-police.

U.S. Department of Education. (2012) National Center for Education Statistics. *Indicators of School Crime and Safety: 2011.* Washington: U.S. Department of Justice.

U.S. Department of Education and Justice. (2000) *Indicators of School Crime and Safety.* Washington: Offices of Educational Research and Imprisonment and Justice Programs.

U.S. Department of Health and Human Services. (1999) *Child Maltreatment 1997: Reports from the States to the National Child Abuse and Neglect Data System.* Washington: Government Printing Office.

U.S. Department of Health and Human Services. (March 31, 2012) Administration of Children and Families. Children's Bureau. *Child Maltreatment 2010.* http://www.acf.hhs.gov/programs/cb/pubs/cm10/index.htm.

U.S. Department of Justice. (1994) *Murder in Families.* Washington: Bureau of Justice Statistics.

U.S. Department of Justice. (1998) *Youth Gangs: An Overview.* Washington: Office of Juvenile Justice and Delinquency Prevention.

U.S. Department of Justice. (1999) *Juvenile Offenders and Victims: 1999 National Report.* Washington: Office of Juvenile Justice and Delinquency Prevention.

U.S. Department of Justice. (2001) *Youth Gang Homicides in the 1990s.* Washington: Office of Juvenile Justice and Delinquency Prevention.

U.S. Department of Justice. (April 26, 2012) "Computer Crime and Intellectual Property Section." http://www.justice.gov/criminal/cybercrime/.

U.S. Department of Justice. Bureau of Justice Assistance. (Spring 2012) *NGC Newsletter* 1. www.nationalgangcenter.gov.

U.S. Department of Justice. Bureau of Justice Statistics. (1991) *Female Victims of Violent Crime.* Washington: Office of Justice Programs.

U.S. Department of Justice. Bureau of Justice Statistics. (1992) *Drugs, Crime, and the Justice System.* Washington: Government Printing Office.

U.S. Department of Justice. Bureau of Justice Statistics. (1993) *Murder in Large Urban Counties, 1988.* Washington: Government Printing Office.

U.S. Department of Justice. Bureau of Justice Statistics. (1993) *Survey of State Prison Inmates, 1991.* Washington: Government Printing Office.

U.S. Department of Justice. Bureau of Justice Statistics. (1994) *Criminal Victimization in the United States 1992: A National Crime Victimization Survey Report.* Washington: Government Printing Office.

U.S. Department of Justice. Bureau of Justice Statistics. (1997) *Criminal Victimization in the United States 1994: A National Crime Victimization Survey.* Washington: Government Printing Office.

U.S. Department of Justice. Bureau of Justice Statistics. (1997) *Sex Offenses and Offenders: An Analysis of Data on Rape and Sexual Assault.* Washington: Government Printing Office.

U.S. Department of Justice. Bureau of Justice Statistics. (1999) *Prior Abuse Reported by Inmates and Probationers.* Washington: Office of Justice Programs.

U.S. Department of Justice. Bureau of Justice Statistics. (2000) *Correctional Populations in the United States, 1997.* Washington: Department of Justice.

U.S. Department of Justice. Bureau of Justice Statistics. (2002) *Rape and Sexual Assault: Reporting to Police and Medical Attention 1992–2000.* Washington: Office of Justice Programs.

U.S. Department of Justice. Bureau of Justice Statistics. (March 26, 2012) *Sourcebook of Criminal Justice Statistics 2012.* http://www.albany.edu/sourcebook/index. html.

U.S. Department of Justice. Bureau of Justice Statistics. (April 2, 2012) *Criminal Victimization in the United States: Statistical Tables Index.* Victim-Offender Relationship. http://www.bjs.gov/content/pub/html/cvus/victim_offender_ relationship.cfm.

U.S. Department of Justice. Bureau of Justice Statistics Bulletin. (2000) *Capital Punishment 1999.* Washington: Office of Justice Programs.

U.S. Department of Justice. Bureau of Justice Statistics Bulletin. (2000) *Prisoners in 1999.* Washington: Office of Justice Programs.

U.S. Department of Justice. Bureau of Justice Statistics Crime Data Brief. (2000) *Homicide Trends in the United States: 1998 Update.* Washington: Office of Justice Programs.

U.S. Department of Justice. Bureau of Justice Statistics Factbook. (1998) *Violence by Intimates: Analysis of Data of Crimes by Current or Former Spouses, Boyfriends, and Girlfriends.* Washington: Government Printing Office.

U.S. Department of Justice. Bureau of Justice Statistics Selected Findings. (2000) *Firearm Injury and Death From Crime, 1993–97.* Washington: Office of Justice Programs.

U.S. Department of Justice. Bureau of Justice Statistics Special Report. (1998) *Workplace Violence, 1992–96.* Washington: Office of Justice Programs.

U.S. Department of Justice. Bureau of Justice Statistics Special Report. (2000) *Effects of NIBRS on Crime Statistics*. Washington: Office of Justice Programs.

U.S. Department of Justice. Bureau of Justice Statistics Special Report. (2000) *Intimate Partner Violence*. Washington: Office of Justice Programs.

U.S. Department of Justice. Bureau of Justice Statistics Special Report. (2011) *Workplace Violence, 1993–2009*. Washington: Office of Justice Programs.

U.S. Department of Justice. Federal Bureau of Investigation. (1985) "The Men Who Murdered." *FBI Law Enforcement Bulletin* 54, 8: 2–6.

U.S. Department of Justice. Federal Bureau of Investigation. (2000) *Crime in the United States: Uniform Crime Reports 1999*. Washington: Government Printing Office.

U.S. Department of Justice. Federal Bureau of Investigation. (April 3, 2012) *Crime in the United States: Uniform Crime Reports 2010*. http://www.fbi.gov/about-us/cjis/ucr/crime-in-the-u.s/2010/crime-in-the-u.s.-2010.

U.S. Department of Justice. Federal Bureau of Investigation. (April 25, 2012) "FBI Cyber Action Teams: Traveling the World to Catch Cyber Criminals." http://www.fbi.gov/news/stories/2006/march/cats030606.

U.S. Department of Justice. Federal Bureau of Investigation. (April 25, 2012) "National Cyber Investigative Joint Task Force." http://www.fbi.gov/about-us/investigate/cyber/ncijtf.

U.S. Department of Justice. Federal Bureau of Investigation. (April 25, 2012) "Netting Cyber Criminals: Inside the Connecticut Computer Crimes Task Force." http://www.fbi.gov/news/stories/2006/january/ccctf012506.

U.S. Department of Justice. National Crime Victimization Survey. (2011) *Criminal Victimization, 2010*. Washington: Office of Justice Programs. http://bjs.ojp.usdoj.gov/content/pub/pdf/cv10.pdf.

U.S. Department of Justice. Office of Justice Programs. (2011) *Homicide Trends in the United States, 1980–2010*. Washington: Bureau of Justice Statistics.

Valdez, A. (1993) Persistent Poverty, Crime, and Drugs: U.S.–Mexican Border Region. In J. Moore & R. Pinderhughes, Eds., *In the Barrios: Latinos and the Underclass Debate*. New York: Russell Sage.

van Wormer, K., & A. R. Roberts. (2009) *Death by Domestic Violence: Preventing the Murders and Murder-Suicides*. Westport: Praeger.

Violence Policy Center. (May 2, 2012) *American Roulette: The Untold Story of Murder-Suicide in the United States*. www.vpc.org/studies/amroul2006.pdf.

Vold, G., & T. Bernard. (1986) *Theoretical Criminology*, 3rd ed. Oxford: Oxford University Press.

Voss, H. L., & J. R. Hepburn. (1968) Patterns in Criminal Homicide in Chicago. *Journal of Criminal Law, Criminology, and Political Science* 59: 499–508.

Walker, L. E. (1984) *The Battered Woman Syndrome*. New York: Springer.

Walker, L. E. (1989) *Sudden Fury*. New York: St. Martin's Press.

Warner Brothers. (September 12, 1956) *The Bad Seed*. http://www.imdb.com/title/tt0048977/.

Websdale, N. (1999) *Understanding Domestic Homicide*. Boston: Northeastern University Press.

Weimann, G., & C. Winn. (1994) *The Theater of Terror: Mass Media and International Terrorists*. New York: Longman.

Weisman, A. M., & K. K. Skarma. (1997) Parricide and Attempted Parricide. In U.S. Department of Justice, *The Nature of Homicide: Trends and Changes— Proceedings of the 1996 Meeting of the Homicide Research Working Group*. Washington: National Institute of Justice.

Welte, J. W., & E. L. Abel. (1989) Homicide: Drinking by the Victim. *Journal of Studies on Alcohol* 50: 197–201.

Wertham, F. (1937) The Catathymic Crisis. *Archives of Neurology and Psychiatry* 37: 974–78.

Wieczorek, W., J. Welte, & E. Abel. (1990) "Alcohol, Drugs, and Murder: A Study of Convicted Homicide Offenders." *Journal of Criminal Justice* 18: 217–27.

Wikipedia, the Free Encyclopedia. (March 28, 2012) Andrea Yates. http://en.wikipedia.org/wiki/Andrea_Yates.

Wikipedia, the Free Encyclopedia. (April 8, 2012) September 11 Attacks. http://en.wikipedia.org/wiki/September_11_attacks.

Wikipedia, the Free Encyclopedia. (April 24, 2012) John Edward Robinson. http://en.wikipedia.org/wiki/John_Edward_Robinson_(serial_killer).

Wikipedia, the Free Encyclopedia. (April 25, 2012) Internet Homicide. http://en.wikipedia.org/wiki/Internet_homicide.

Wikipedia, the Free Encyclopedia. (April 25, 2012) Lisa M. Montgomery. http://en.wikipedia.org/wiki/Lisa_M._Montgomery.

Wikipedia, the Free Encyclopedia. (April 25, 2012) Long Island Serial Killer. http://en.wikipedia.org/wiki/Long_island_killer.

Wikipedia, the Free Encyclopedia. (May 2, 2012) Murder-Suicide. http://en.wikipedia.org/wiki/Murder-suicide#cite_note-3.

Wikipedia, the Free Encyclopedia. (May 3, 2012) Murder of Diane and Alan Scott Johnson. http://en.wikipedia.org/wiki/Sarah_Marie_Johnson.

Wikipedia, the Free Encyclopedia. (May 4, 2012) Xerox Murders. http://en.wikipedia.org/wiki/Byran_Uyesugi.

Wikipedia, the Free Encyclopedia. (May 7, 2012) Charles Stuart (Murderer). http://en.wikipedia.org/wiki/Charles_Stuart_(murderer).

Wikipedia, the Free Encyclopedia. (May 10, 2012) Assisted Suicide in the United States. http://en.wikipedia.org/wiki/Assisted_suicide_in_the_United_States.

Wille, W. S. (1974) *Citizens Who Commit Murder*. St. Louis: Warren Greene.

Williams, M. (1997) *Cry of Pain: Understanding Suicide and Self-Harm*. New York: Penguin.

Wilson, M., & M. Daly. (1993) Spousal Homicide Risk and Estrangement. *Violence and Victims* 8, 1: 3–16.

Wissow, L. S. (1998) Infanticide. *New England Journal of Medicine 339*, 17: 1239.

WKRN-TV Nashville. (December 18, 2009) Felon Sentenced to 2 1/2 Years in McNair Gun Case. http://www.wkrn.com/global/Story.asp?s=11699594.

WKRN-TV Nashville. (December 18, 2009) Police Close McNair Case After Nearly Six Mos. http://www.wkrn.com/global/story.asp?s=11700859.

Wolfgang, M. E. (1958) An Analysis of Homicide-Suicide. *Journal of Clinical and Experimental Psychopathology and Quarterly Review of Psychiatry and Neurology* 19, 3: 208–18.

Wolfgang, M. E. (1958) *Patterns in Criminal Homicide*. Philadelphia: University of Pennsylvania Press.

Wolfgang, M. E. (1969) Who Kills Whom. *Psychology Today* 3, 5: 54–56.

Wolfgang, M. E., & F. Ferracuti. (1967) *The Subculture of Violence: Toward an Integrated Theory in Criminology.* London: Tavistock.

Wolfgang, M. E., & R. B. Strohm. (1956) The Relationship Between Alcohol and Criminal Homicide. *Quarterly Journal of Studies on Alcoholism* 17: 411–26.

Wolman, B. B. (1999) *Antisocial Behavior: Personality Disorders From Hostility to Homicide.* Amherst: Prometheus Books.

Wong, D. S. (October 22, 1992) Kakas Furs Is Sued Over Gun in Stuart Slaying. *Boston Globe.* http://www.highbeam.com/doc/1P2-8764877.html.

Wright, J. D., J. F. Sheley, & M. D. Smith (1992) Kids, Guns, and Killing Fields. *Society* 30, 1: 84–89.

Yablonsky, L. (1962) *The Violent Gang.* Baltimore: Penguin.

Yen, M. (August 23, 1988) High-Risk Mothers; Postpartum Depression, in Rare Cases, May Cause an Infant's Death. *Washington Post,* p. 18.

Yllo, K., & M. A. Straus. (1978) Interpersonal Violence Among Married and Cohabitating Couples. Paper presented at the annual meeting of the National Council on Family Relationships. Philadelphia.

Yochelson, S., & S. E. Samenow. (1976) *The Criminal Personality,* Vol. 1. New York: Jason Arsonson.

Young, T. J. (1993) Parricide Rates and Criminal Street Violence in the United States: Is There a Correlation? *Adolescence 28,* 109: 171–72.

Zahn, M. A. (1989) Homicide in the Twentieth Century: Trends, Types and Causes. In T. R. Gurr, Ed., *Violence in America; Vol. 1. The History of Violence.* Thousand Oaks: Sage.

Zimring, F. E., & G. J. Hawkins. (1973) *Deterrence.* Chicago: University of Chicago Press.

Zimring, F. E., & G. J. Hawkins. (1997) *Crime Is Not the Problem: Lethal Violence in America.* New York: Oxford University Press.

Index

About the Author

R. Barri Flowers is an award-winning criminologist and bestselling author of more than 60 books. His criminology titles include *Prostitution in the Digital Age: Selling Sex From the Suite to the Street*; *Street Kids: The Lives of Runaway and Thrownaway Teens*; *College Crime: A Statistical Study of Offenses on American Campuses*; *Male Crime and Deviance: Exploring Its Causes, Dynamics and Nature*; and *Female Crime, Criminals and Cellmates: An Exploration of Female Criminality and Delinquency*.

True-crime titles by the author include *The Sex Slave Murders: The True Story of Serial Killers Gerald and Charlene Gallego*; *Serial Killer Couples: Bonded by Sexual Depravity, Kidnapping, and Murder*; *Mass Murder in the Sky: The Bombing of Flight 629*; and *Murder in the United States: Crimes, Killers and Victims of the Twentieth Century*.

Mystery and thriller fiction written by R. Barri Flowers includes *Murder in Honolulu: A Skye Delaney Mystery*; *Murder in Maui: A Leila Kahana Mystery*; *Dark Streets of Whitechapel*; *Persuasive Evidence*; *State's Evidence*; *Justice Served*; *Killer in the Woods*; and *Ghost Girl in Shadow Bay*.

Follow the author and discover more about his writings and future releases on Twitter, Facebook, YouTube, LinkedIn, MySpace, Goodreads, LibraryThing, CrimeSpace, and www.rbarriflowers.com.